Greening the Red, White, and Blue

Greening the Red, White, and Blue

The Bomb, Big Business, and Consumer Resistance in Postwar America

THOMAS JUNDT

OXFORD
UNIVERSITY PRESS

OXFORD
UNIVERSITY PRESS

Oxford University Press is a department of the University of Oxford.
It furthers the University's objective of excellence in research, scholarship,
and education by publishing worldwide.

Oxford   New York
Auckland   Cape Town   Dar es Salaam   Hong Kong   Karachi
Kuala Lumpur   Madrid   Melbourne   Mexico City   Nairobi
New Delhi   Shanghai   Taipei   Toronto

With offices in
Argentina   Austria   Brazil   Chile   Czech Republic   France   Greece
Guatemala   Hungary   Italy   Japan   Poland   Portugal   Singapore
South Korea   Switzerland   Thailand   Turkey   Ukraine   Vietnam

Oxford is a registered trademark of Oxford University Press
in the UK and certain other countries.

Published in the United States of America by
Oxford University Press
198 Madison Avenue, New York, NY 10016

© Oxford University Press 2014

All rights reserved. No part of this publication may be reproduced, stored in a
retrieval system, or transmitted, in any form or by any means, without the prior
permission in writing of Oxford University Press, or as expressly permitted by law,
by license, or under terms agreed with the appropriate reproduction rights organization.
Inquiries concerning reproduction outside the scope of the above should be sent to the
Rights Department, Oxford University Press, at the address above.

You must not circulate this work in any other form
and you must impose this same condition on any acquirer.

A portion of this work appears in "Dueling Visions for The Postwar World: The UN and
UNESCO 1949 Conferences on Resources and Nature, and the Origins of Environmentalism," in
the *Journal of American History*, 101, No. 1 (June 2014).

Library of Congress Cataloging-in-Publication Data
Jundt, Thomas.
Greening the red, white, and blue : the bomb, big business, and consumer resistance in postwar America /
Thomas Jundt.
pages cm
Includes index.
ISBN 978-0-19-979120-0 (hardback)
1. Green movement—United States—History.   2. Environmentalism—United States—History.
3. Big business—United States—History.   4. Industries—Environmental aspects—United States.
5. Green products—United States—History.   6. Consumption (Economics)—Environmental
aspects—United States—History.   7. Environmental policy—United States.   I. Title.
GE197.J86 2014
363.700973—dc23
2013047260

*For my parents,
Donald T. Jundt, 1934–2008,
and Lucille B. Jundt (Peters)*

CONTENTS

Acknowledgments ix

Introduction: Shopping as if Their Lives (and the Planet's) Depended on It 1

PART ONE A NEW ERA

1. "Sons of Bitches": Sources of Postwar Anxiety 11
2. Green Consumption in a Dangerous World 48
3. Downwinders 74
4. Chemicals and Romance 101

PART TWO A NEW RESPONSE

5. "A Ground Swell of Public Indignation" 127
6. The "New" Conservation 158
7. "Striking Back at the Goddam Sons-of-Bitches" 189
8. Green Consumerism Goes Mainstream 217
Conclusion: "The Clock is Ticking" 240

Notes 249
Index 293

ACKNOWLEDGMENTS

This book was a collaborative effort. I received generous institutional support for this project from Brown University. The J. Walter Thompson Research Fellowship from the John W. Hartman Center for Sales, Advertising, and Marketing History at Duke University provided the opportunity to explore its rich archives with the aid of a kind and helpful staff. I would also like to thank the terrific staffs at the John Hay and Rockefeller libraries at Brown University, the Humanities and Social Sciences Library at McGill University, the New York Public Library, the Western History and Genealogy Archives at Denver Public Library, the Library of Congress, the Conservation Resource Library at the Bronx Zoo, the Widener Library at Harvard University, the Boston Public Library, the Paley Center for Media in New York, the Bancroft Library at the University of California, the Harry S. Truman Presidential Library, the Dwight D. Eisenhower Presidential Library, the Lyndon B. Johnson Presidential Library, the John F. Kennedy Presidential Library, and the Bennett Martin Public Library in Lincoln, Nebraska with its collection of popular magazines. I appreciate the work that all of you did to help me locate sources. Ronald Eber, Denis Hayes, Michael McCloskey, Bill Mauk, and Senator Gaylord Nelson were all very generous in sharing their memories of sixties environmental activism and Earth Day. Their recollections and insights were invaluable in helping me better understand environmentalism during that era.

For their invaluable comments on full drafts of my manuscript, I am extremely grateful to Karl Jacoby, Elliott Gorn, Mari Jo Buhle, Carmen Gardner, Douglas Watson, and anonymous readers from Oxford University Press. For their expert advice on portions of this book, I am indebted to Sheyda Jahanbani, Jonathan Hagel, David Meren, Don Nerbas, Benjamin Rader, Robert Self, and anonymous readers from the *Journal of American History*. I also benefited from feedback on portions of this work presented at annual conferences of the American Society for Environmental History. Susan Ferber helped me by showing early interest in my work, and improved my work with with her masterful, if not magical, editing. The best part of the experience of writing this book was getting to work with all of you. Beyond the intelligence of your generous insights, criticisms, and recommendations, I was touched by your kindness. Although the result surely has faults due to my own limitations, it is considerably better than it would have been without your help. Thank you.

Throughout my education I was lucky to have a number of teachers who provided not only valuable education and lessons but, just as important, encouragement. In high school, dedicated and smart teachers including Gary Largo, Joan Merrigan-Hiller, Clancy Trump, and Bruce Rolls showed me how to channel my social and political concerns into intellectual pursuits. At the University of Nebraska I was extremely fortunate to work under the guidance of Benjamin Rader who, as a mentor, friend, and one of the finest people I have ever met, taught me much about history and being a historian. Other scholars at Nebraska, including David Cahan, Timothy Mahoney, Susan Miller, Ralph Vigil, and especially David Wishart, were all instrumental in guiding me from the working class to the academic life. I remain grateful to all of you.

My good fortune continued in my graduate work at Brown University. Karl Jacoby is an exceptional scholar, historian, and writer, and I could not have asked for a better advisor. As a mentor and friend he patiently and tirelessly guided my work, challenged me when I needed it, asked just the right questions, and inspired me during moments of doubt. Mari Jo Buhle's legacy of fine historians whom she has mentored into the profession speaks for itself, and I benefited greatly from her kindness and the care that she gave to my work. Mary Gluck, whose lectures on European cultural and intellectual history remain treasured moments in my life, was generous in teaching me how to be a better historian. Carl Kaestle has been a dear friend and teacher, and during my time as his research assistant I gained invaluable insight into the successful habits and practices of a fantastic scholar. I remain very grateful to all of you. I owe a special thanks to Elliott Gorn. In addition to providing significant feedback on various drafts of this work, Elliott challenged me to have the courage to follow the story where it led. He was unwavering in his support for this project and me, and endured countless conversations as I worked to make sense of this history. Even when I was overcome with self-doubt and at my gloomiest, I could have a cup of coffee with Elliott and take comfort in the realization that I had a friend who was even gloomier. That's a true friend.

I was lucky to enter graduate school at Brown with Doug Watson, with whom I shared an appreciation for beer and a skeptical, yet stubbornly hopeful, worldview. Today he is my favorite writer, and a cherished friend, the kind who always offers to read drafts of my work. Nick Anastasakos, Jonathan Hagel, Sheyda Jahanbani, and Erica Ryan joined us later, and provided much-valued friendship, wisdom, and encouragement, with many laughs to boot. I am particularly indebted to Sheyda and Jonathan for their resolute support that aided my research and writing of this book. I was fortunate to be in graduate school with such talented people, and I am even more blessed to call them my friends.

At McGill University I was privileged to work in a wonderful department. Lynn Kozak and David Meren gave the lie to the contention in *Stand by Me* that we will never again have friends as good as the ones we had during childhood. Nick Dew reached out to help me navigate the move to Montreal, and became a valued friend. Len Moore and Jason Opal were outstanding colleagues, and I was proud to be counted with them as the department's historians of the United States; I remain proud to be counted as their friend. Brian Lewis, Lorenz Lüthi, Suzanne Morton, Seb Normandin, Jarret Rudy, and Daviken Studnicki-Gizbert all helped to make my time at McGill memorable and meaningful. And Colleen Parish and Sylvia Crawford were endlessly kind, helpful, and supportive. I miss you all.

During my years in Brown's Department of History, Academic Program Manager Mary Beth Bryson and Administrative Assistant Julissa Bautista have saved me on numerous occasions. But, more than that, their office is a place on campus where I feel at home, and where I always know that two wonderful people are looking out for me and wishing me the best. I am very grateful to both of you.

I have devoted years to teaching in secondary schools and universities, where I have had the great fortune to spend my days with thousands of interesting, intelligent, kind, caring, and funny students. I have learned from you in countless ways, and I am thankful for the time that I got to spend with you.

I am the youngest of four children, and my siblings, Sue Wehrwein, and Joe and Steve Jundt, have provided love and support throughout this project, just as they have my entire life. I am endlessly fortunate, and grateful to all of you for always having my back.

My partner, Meg Myette, has been with me since the start of this project, and despite that has never left. She has provided indefatigable support and encouragement, while reminding me to take time from the history of the lives of others to live life myself. Your love, kindness, and relentless optimism are more than I deserve, and you make me feel insanely lucky. I am privileged and honored to have Ella Myette call me dad. Watching her grow from a precocious toddler to a talented and funny young woman has been one of the greatest joys of my life. Thanks, both of you (and Nigel), for providing the most mysterious and greatest gift of all: Home. I love you.

My parents, Donald and Lucille Jundt, were two farm kids from North Dakota who worked tirelessly—dad in packinghouses and mom as a bookkeeper—to provide their children with opportunities. It has been an extraordinary gift to live life knowing that I am always loved and supported, even when choosing to do something as zany as becoming a historian. When my father told me good-bye, he added sage advice: "Keep your powder dry." Although Dad did not live to see this book published, I hope very much that it is infused with at least some of his spirit, intelligence, and grace. I know that Mom will be the first to read this book when it comes off the press. When she does she will see these words, and know that they are from my heart: This book is for you and Dad, with eternal gratitude.

Greening the Red, White, and Blue

Introduction

Shopping as if Their Lives (and the Planet's) Depended on It

> He plants a tree and his mind travels a thousand years into the future, and he sees visions of the happiness of the human race.
> —Anton Chekhov, *Uncle Vanya*, 1897

In Columbus Circle, at the southwest corner of Central Park, Whole Foods, Incorporated built a megastore in 2004. Here, where the city borders idealized nature, commerce blends with environmental concern. Descended from the tiny natural-foods shops that first surfaced in the early 1950s, and from the sixties co-ops that followed, this 59,000-square-foot chain store that places organic foods and "caring for the environment" at the center of its corporate philosophy is the largest supermarket in Manhattan.[1] Milling about its preternaturally clean aisles and sculptured displays of produce, shoppers move pastorally slowly by New York standards. To shift the metaphor, they sometimes seem almost reverential, more like patrons at an art gallery or worshippers in a cathedral than shoppers in a grocery store.

For cultural critics this joining of commerce and nature is sometimes dismissed as a sign of the failure of environmentalism at the hands of corporations. Here, surely, is an example of the self-deluding practice that historian Thomas Frank provocatively calls "commodifying dissent," in this case co-opting environmentalists' ideals and selling them back to them as artisanal cheese.[2] While this analysis is seductive, stopping the enquiry there misses a deeper significance at this busy intersection of environmentalism and consumer culture. In this Whole Foods, somewhere between the bulk bins of millet and the David Glass Ultimate Chocolate Truffle Cake, the spirit of environmentalism can still be found. There, beneath the (natural) cosmetic surface of "green" consumption, in the conduct of daily living, lies something truly significant.

This book is about the origins of the movement that we know today as "environmentalism." The growing interest in environmentalism—focused on issues of ecology, pollution, and sustainability—did not displace nineteenth-century notions of conservation, which was more concerned with preserving those natural spaces deemed aesthetically pleasing and with the efficient use of natural resources. But due to environmentalism's broader concerns that sometimes challenged the tenets of corporate capitalism, not all conservationists embraced environmentalism.

The ideas that would form the ideological foundation of environmentalism began to coalesce in the earliest days after the atomic bomb blasts at the end of the Second World War. After the unprecedented destruction of the war, the impulse for preservation was great. Once humans realized that they were capable of destroying the planet by nuclear means, other ways that they might be accomplishing that horrifying task came into focus. Just as fallout from atomic bomb testing was found to be polluting the environment and making its way into the food chain, air and water pollution from corporations producing goods was linked to serious health issues. Population growth threatened to overwhelm the planet's carrying capacity and lead to resource wars and even mass starvation. Competing for apocalyptic honors was the revolution in synthetic chemicals that increasing evidence suggested might be devastating both the earth's environment and its inhabitants. A growing chorus of voices declared that there was something inherently wrong with the way Americans were living.

Fundamental questions came to light in the blast of the bomb: Who and what would America be following the war? How would Americans define themselves as a people and a nation? Environmentalism emerged as a direct response to such queries. For some, the Bomb inspired a rare moment of American self-reflection—one that the country's corporate and political leadership quickly moved to undermine—leaving citizens who were unhappy with the trend toward America as a supercorporate superpower searching for an alternative vision. Environmentalism developed in response to the sense that corporate capitalism and the ideology of unlimited growth that buttressed it posed an ever-deepening threat to the planet, culture, and democracy.

In popular imagination, environmentalism begins in 1962 with Rachel Carson's *Silent Spring*. Historians have tied the rise of environmentalism to the postwar affluence and political activism of the 1960s and 1970s that moved increasing numbers of Americans to insist on a better quality of life: open spaces, clean air and water, beautification campaigns.[3] But these interpretations have led us to overlook the significant origins of environmentalism as a moral and intellectual broadside against the growing power of corporate capitalism, both at home and in the new liberal international order the United States was working to put in place in Western Europe and other parts of the world following World War II.[4]

Greening the Red, White, and Blue demonstrates that the origins of environmentalism are more accurately viewed as a response to anxieties and tensions over the growing power of big business that came to light in the 1940s and 1950s. More than ever, powerful corporations and a federal government bent on economic growth were seen by many Americans as threats to human health and the environment. Fallout from atomic testing, air and water pollution, the proliferation of pesticides and herbicides—all connected to the growing dominance of technology and corporate capitalism in American life—led a variety of constituencies to seek solutions in what came to be known as environmentalism. Striking at the very heart of America's postwar project, critics maintained that the only hope for securing a future for themselves, democracy, and the planet was to stop thinking of humans as living outside of nature. The environment became a site of negotiation over postwar American culture.

This book joins revisionist "long" histories of the New Left, civil rights, women's rights, and gay rights movements that have also exposed the more complicated reality of a postwar era formerly deemed a period of consensus in the history of the United States.[5] Following World War II, citizens, in proto-environmentalist fashion, began to see connections between corporate capitalism, what they were consuming, the health of the environment, and their bodies. Long before the era of ecology that is associated with the sixties, when the term *environmentalism* came into being, people were beginning to think ecologically because of threats to the environment and their health that they blamed on ever more powerful corporations and a government unwilling to regulate them.

There were many responses to this perceived crisis, but one of them involved controlling consumption. In time, green consumption seemed like one of the only available solutions. Frustrated in their efforts to attain meaningful environmental laws and regulations in a political system that was dominated by the very corporate power they hoped to contain, environmentally minded citizens turned instead to unconventional civic participation through their actions as consumers in an attempt to assert agency and protect themselves, their families, and their environment from harm. With so much that seemed beyond their control, citizens could at least decide what and what not to buy. Perhaps a country dominated by corporate capitalism could be brought, one purchase at a time, into a new epoch of environmentalism. Short of that, environmentally concerned citizens could at least have a means to live truer to their ideals in their daily lives. Environmentalists, in some respects, felt alienated from "the national mainstream" and postwar modernity. But it is a mistake to view environmentalists as necessarily antimodern. Instead, most were simply seeking a modernity different than the one dominated by corporate capitalism that characterized the postwar United States.

In addition to consumption, environmentalism constituted an alternative aesthetic of production in its embrace of small-scale methods. The growing taste for wilderness and natural goods was no mere surface fashion. When the

American Way was stretched to include an allegiance to unfettered corporate capitalism, the budding environmental impulse challenged dominant methods and mechanisms that were shaping the postwar world. It dissolved barriers carefully constructed by big business to conceal the unhealthy relationship between corporate capitalism and an abused environment, and it attempted to build a bridge to a new American Way.

Beyond challenging conventional narratives about the periodization and causation of environmentalism, this book also complicates popular notions of consumption by asserting that shopping, rather than being necessarily a passive activity of consumers led by producers, can instead be a means for the people to assert political agency when effectively shut out of the electoral political process. During the postwar era, with its anticommunist crusades, environmentalism provided a relatively safe space from which to critique government and corporate culture. In subsequent decades, as the limits of structural change became clear, green consumers opted for things like organic foods, natural-fiber clothing, clean water, alternative energy, and a wide variety of products to enhance the enjoyment of the natural environment, as well as everyday products designed to have minimal environmental impact. A whole host of new ways to develop and bring goods to market were advocated, tried and tested. Environmentally minded green consumers constructed what amounted to a separate "green economy" and a distinct subculture. Its influence was widespread, and its imprint was soon evident in the creation of a number of new environmentally sensitive businesses, changes in existing businesses, and products that sought to earn the respect and dollars of this demanding group.

This story is located at the roundabout where environmental, social, policy, cultural, capitalist, and intellectual histories converge. This book examines the myriad forces, large and small, that citizens faced in the postwar United States, forces that ultimately gave rise to the ideology of environmentalism. It argues that the environmental movement's driving force was more fundamental to the course of American life since the mid-twentieth century than has so far been acknowledged.[6] Although the environmental movement is sometimes associated with the rebellious sixties, it was well established long before the Summer of Love. Some 20 million Americans took to the streets on Earth Day, April 22, 1970, not spontaneously, but because years of thoughtful writing and campaigning had failed to halt environmental degradation. Underlying all of the anxiety for the planet was a simmering frustration with corporate capitalism and the government it often appeared to control.

It was not as if all policy initiatives were stymied in these years. Under citizen pressure, environmental legislation that began appearing during the postwar era finally gathered momentum during the sixties. But in the end, watered down by corporate influence and limited enforcement, it was always too little too late; by the latter part of the decade the environment appeared to be in worse shape than ever. Disillusioned by the seeming impossibility of genuine change through electoral politics, by the late Sixties growing numbers tapped into the environmentalism and green consumption that had been growing since World War II as a personal solution to a wide variety of cultural and political ills. As the movement gained momentum, some feared that withdrawing from mainstream culture into the counterculture was not a sufficient response and that it remained necessary to seek political means to affect fundamental societal change. They sought to harness the energy of countercultural environmentalism and bring the movement up from the underground into the mainstream of American politics and life.

This book ends with the most significant of those efforts and the place where some popular accounts of the movement begin: Earth Day, 1970.[7] Frustrated in his efforts to get environmental legislation through Congress, longtime conservationist and US Senator Gaylord Nelson hoped a national environmental teach-in might generate sufficient interest and publicity to pressure Washington into more comprehensive and stricter environmental regulations and laws. Indeed, politicians did take notice, and Earth Day ushered in the most significant environmental legislation in the nation's history, even if corporate influence meant it was not always adequately enforced.

Beyond its political influence, Earth Day spawned something even more significant and lasting. The rush of the 20 million people who turned out for the event was a force great enough to pull into mainstream currents the green consumerism that had been trickling for years at the margins of American life. Consumption, for many critics of American society long a source of great anxiety, was instead, in this view, the stuff of romantic dreams of a better world. Environmentalism affirmed consumer culture even as it critiqued it. For most, the problem was not so much consuming as it was the system of taint that consuming supported. Advertisers and producers recognized possibilities in the numbers drawn to Earth Day from the start and set about to woo them with products to appeal to their growing environmental sensibilities.

Standing in the middle of the midtown Whole Foods Market, I am struck by just how far green consumption and environmentalism have progressed in the years since World War II. Green consumerism has so influenced American society it now occupies a privileged position in American culture. But it is that realization of privilege, the sort of thing that leads some to only half-jokingly refer to Whole Foods as "Whole Paycheck," that makes many uneasy and leads to questions of what, exactly, green consumption is all about.

Like much of green consumption, the market is decidedly upscale. The produce is arranged in artful displays, fish and meat are laid out with precise care, the holistic health products look to contain the wisdom of the ages, an organic mantra hums quietly but insistently, and no gaudy sales promotions spoil the impression of great seriousness. People behind the counters are eager to help, and their smiles seem warmer than the smiles you get from your own family and friends. It all recalls the corner grocer of days past who knew your name and cared about your community. Even if things never really were that way, in our hearts and memories they were. It is a market vision that combines nostalgia and the romantic-aesthetic yearnings of the old-line conservationists with the ideals of the counterculture, and it is all given a stamp of approval by alternative health advocates. They all come together somewhere around the Hip Whip tofu non-dairy dessert topping from the Now & Zen company. It is consumption made safe, if not noble. But it is not cheap.

Although environmentalists have begun to address issues like environmental justice to help assure that race, ethnicity, and wealth do not unfairly determine one's exposure to environmental pollutants, the question "Whose environmentalism?" remains. Back at the Whole Foods Market it is evident. The upscale nature of the store places its benefits out of the reach of many. Even as organic products have made inroads into mainstream supermarkets, they are often segregated in a section separate from the rest of the store. Without continual efforts to democratize the benefits of the environmental movement, environmentalism becomes yet another feature of modern American life that permits elites to elude the dangers and discomforts of modern living while others suffer the costs.[8] Although environmentalists have come a long way since 1971, when Standard Oil Company could gain approval by boasting about leaving pollutants overseas when shipping fuels to the United States—"We take sulfur out of oil in Venezuela to keep it out of the air at home"—sticky issues of globalization and the global environment remain.[9] Is green consumption, which has now spread into nearly every aspect of material living, from architecture and engineering to one's choice of toilet paper, still a means for citizens to assert some authority while feeling abandoned by corporations and government, or has it simply become a way for those who possess the means to shelter themselves and their families from the negative effects of a system from which they benefit most?

This book is divided into two parts, with chapters organized around themes that move forward in time from the Bomb through Earth Day. In the first four chapters, which make up "Part I: A New Era," the focus is on the dramatic changes ushered in by the Bomb and World War II, along with the ideas and early actions that developed in response as citizens struggled to make sense of their altered world. There it becomes clear that the origins of environmentalism, usually thought to reside in the 1960s, can instead be found in the 1940s. For that reason, although the term itself did not come into use until the sixties, I refer to those putting forth environmental ideas and actions as "environmentalists" throughout the text, reflecting the fact that decades before the term came into popular use thinkers were constructing the ideology of environmentalism, and citizens were acting as environmentalists.[10]

In the next four chapters, which together make up "Part II: A New Response," the focus shifts to the mainstreaming of actions that flowed out of those new ideas. Some of those actions were political and policy-based. Although a demanding public pushed the government into environmental action, when government finally acted, its efforts regularly were thwarted by the growing power of corporations. In response, the ranks of green consumers grew as citizens sought some means to effect change and wrest control in a polity where they had been effectively shut out of power when their demands posed a threat to corporate hegemony.

Because environmentalism and green consumerism are such pervasive parts of our contemporary culture, it is frequently surprising to find that these notions were being voiced almost 70 years ago. These citizens who, fraught with anxieties unleashed by the power of the Bomb and corporations but sensing no real solution in electoral politics, turned to the control they could exert through their actions as consumers to effect desired changes. It was an imperfect solution to an intractable problem, born of limited options. The real importance of environmentalism is found not only in its effect on public policy and regulations, but also in the way it has changed people's thinking and habits of everyday living and challenged power and polity in American culture.

PART ONE

A NEW ERA

The bomb that fell on Hiroshima punctuated history.
—Harry Stack Sullivan, "The Cultural Revolution to End War," 1946

1

"Sons of Bitches"

Sources of Postwar Anxiety

In 1947 the *Bulletin of the Atomic Scientists*, a publication founded two years earlier by scientists who had worked on the Manhattan Project to create the atomic bomb, first featured its monthly "doomsday clock" on the cover. The editors, activists now working to prevent the atomic bomb from ever being used again, set the metaphoric clock at seven minutes to midnight, with midnight unmistakably symbolizing nuclear apocalypse—the cataclysmic end of the world; the end of time. It became an icon of the Cold War and has remained on the *Bulletin*'s cover, each month moving closer to or further from midnight in response to the likelihood of nuclear annihilation.[1] Time, once the measure of the seasons and life's passing, and more recently the gauge of efficiency in the industrialized world, was suddenly a calculation of the planet's uncertain future—and it appeared the end was drawing near. When people knew the world could end at any moment—when they really knew it and could insert images of mushroom clouds into nervous visions of exactly how it would happen—the end became considerably more palpable than it had been when it was largely confined to religious faith. Envisioning the nuclear apocalypse required no leap of faith.

Frighteningly vincible, the 20 million who gathered for the first Earth Day on April 22, 1970, were the first modern generation to inhabit a planet that appeared disconcertingly vulnerable. After the atomic bomb was dropped on Hiroshima on August 6, 1945—what *Life* magazine called "the biggest event since the birth of Christ"—it felt as if the world might end at any moment.[2] The ultimate fate of the world, a determination previously made by the gods, was now thrust into the hands of humans. The enormity of that responsibility, and doubts that humanity was ready for the challenge, unleashed nervous fallout that permeated America's culture and consciousness and set it on a path to Earth Day 25 years later.

To be sure, following the bombings of the Japanese cities of Hiroshima and Nagasaki, most Americans were enormously relieved that the war was finally over and enamored with the confidence that they alone possessed the most fearsome and powerful weapon in the world. The majority were happy to accept the official government explanation that the Bomb "saved American lives" by hastening the war's end and, after years of economic depression and war, settle back into comforting routines of daily living.[3]

But, from the start, there were also concerns about the larger meaning of the power unleashed by the splitting of the atom, and even many of those who supported its use in the war conceded that history would now be divided between the time before the atomic bomb and the new atomic age. "A new era was born," stated *Time* magazine, "the age of atomic force."[4] As with those who founded the *Bulletin of the Atomic Scientists*, many of the earliest concerns came from those who had worked on the Bomb and felt a responsibility, if not guilt, to warn others about its true nature. Witnessing the Trinity test of the first atomic bomb at the White Sands Proving Ground in southern New Mexico, on July 16, 1945, J. Robert Oppenheimer, the scientific director of the Manhattan Project who once studied Sanskrit to read Hindu scriptures in their original form, recalled lines from the *Bhagavad-Gita* to summarize the meaning of the event:

> If the radiance of a thousand suns
> were to burst into the sky,
> that would be like the splendor of the Mighty One—
> I am become Death,
> the destroyer of worlds.[5]

Kenneth Bainbridge, the director of Trinity, turned to Oppenheimer after the blast and stated more bluntly, though no less poetically, "Now we are all sons of bitches."[6] In a January 1946 *Collier's* article on the Bomb, Nobel Prize chemist Harold C. Urey began by saying, "I write this to frighten you. I'm a frightened man, myself. All the scientists I know are frightened—frightened for their lives—and frightened for *your* life."[7]

These anxieties soon radiated out from the scientific community, triggering incremental symptoms that plagued the public. Already, in September 1945, when a nationwide poll asked Americans, "If there is another world war, about how much danger do you think there'll be of most city people on earth being killed by atomic bombs," 83 percent polled believed there was a "very real danger."[8] The celebrated middle-class affluence of postwar sprawling suburbs, backyard barbecues, electric appliances, and gigantic cars decked out in shiny chrome was accompanied by an underlying awareness that it might all end in an instant.

With the advent of the Bomb it seemed dreadfully clear to many that human technology had dangerously outpaced humanity. Although such fears had accompanied industrialization for some time—sociologist William F. Ogburn coined the phrase "cultural lag" in 1922 to describe his theory that technology always advances at a pace greater than the ability of people to adjust their values, ideals, and beliefs to those changes—after the Bomb many wondered whether the planet would survive long enough for humanity to catch up.[9] The *St. Louis Dispatch* reported on August 7, the day after the first bomb dropped on Hiroshima, that science may have "signed the mammalian world's death warrant, and deeded an earth in ruins to the ants." The *Philadelphia Inquirer* headlined: "Atomic Energy for War: New Beast of Apocalypse."[10]

As the larger implications of the Bomb gradually became known, an awareness of its power to devastate both humans and the environment continued to grow. In March 1946, a US mission sent to Japan to study the atomic bomb's effects made some of its findings public for the first time. Captain Shields Warren, chief medical officer of the Naval Technical Mission to Japan, delivered a report to the American Association for Cancer Research revealing that more Japanese died of the effects of radiation poisoning than from the initial flash of the bombs, and that further long-term effects would not be known for many years.[11] Similar truths were revealed more compellingly in John Hersey's bestselling *Hiroshima*, which first appeared in *The New Yorker* in August 1946. The magazine devoted an entire issue to the story, focusing on the harrowing experiences of six Japanese civilians and the Bomb. They recalled seeing skin falling off bodies in sheets and empty eye sockets whose melted eyeballs could be seen running down the faces of victims.[12]

In his popular memoir *No Place to Hide* (1948), David Bradley was among the first to alert the public to the Bomb's potential for environmental apocalypse. In his factual account of the effects of the Bomb on land and humans based on his observations of the United States's surface and underwater Bikini Atoll bomb tests in the Pacific during July 1946, Bradley cautioned: "The devastating influence of the Bomb and its unborn relatives may affect the land and its wealth—and therefore its people—for centuries through the persistence of radioactivity." The book was condensed in *Reader's Digest*, spent 10 weeks on the *New York Times* bestseller list, and sold 250,000 copies by the end of 1949.[13]

James B. Conant, one of the leaders of the Manhattan Project and president of Harvard University, met with a Harvard librarian to sketch out a plan to save civilization in the event of a nuclear war. "We are living in a very different world since the explosion of the A-bomb," Conant told the startled librarian. "We have no way of knowing what the results will be, but there is the danger that much of our present civilization will come to an end." He then detailed his plan to microfilm enough printed material to adequately preserve the present civilization, then bury 10 copies in different places throughout the United States to serve as a guide for a post-apocalyptic civilization. Although the plan was never carried out (the librarian later reported that it would require some 2.5 billion pages), the fear that all might soon be lost was palpable in the postwar era.[14]

Apocalyptic visions were hardly new in American life, but the sense of the end drawing near had never approached the level of concreteness, nor was it ever before felt so widely or so palpably, as it was during the Cold War era. Although previously a cause of some distress, belief that the world was going to end usually had been confined to relatively small groups, most often based on religious beliefs or superstitions.[15] Even the specific apocalyptic dread of earth-shattering projectiles and their fallout was not unprecedented. As recently as 1910 there was fear that the approaching Halley's Comet was going to destroy the earth, or if the impact of the comet itself did not do it, the deadly cyanogen gas that some scientists warned was in its tail would do the job. But such fears were not terribly widespread. Newspaper accounts at the time were careful to attribute such panic mostly to the poor and uneducated.[16] With the Bomb, the situation was in many ways reversed. The more you knew, the more frightened you were likely to be. When the Soviet Union exploded its first atomic bomb in 1949, triggering the arms race and moving the doomsday clock forward to three minutes to midnight, for many people it felt like it was only a matter of time until there was no time.

Imagining a World Without a Planet

It is not that concern about environmental issues did not exist prior to World War II. The greatest environmental disaster in the nation's history—the Dust Bowl—had devastated the Southern Plains and its inhabitants only a decade earlier. Since the mid-nineteenth century polluted water from industrial mills and sewage had been a growing source of anxiety, when it was linked to waterborne diseases like cholera, dysentery, and typhoid. Nineteenth-century farmers, fishermen, and sportsmen sought to protect forests, fisheries, and wildlife from commercial threats, and by the second half of the century they began to understand that the health of each was dependent on the health of the other: depleted forests resulted in greater flooding; runoff and silt polluted the waters; and mill dams built by factory owners obstructed spawning and dumped pollutants, all resulting in fewer fish, and fewer fish put pressure on animals whose diets depended on them. Air pollution, long derided as an irritating nuisance, began drawing concern from doctors as a threat to health early in the century, and by the late 1930s women in St. Louis and Pittsburgh marched with mops and brooms in hand to demand cleaner air.[17]

But not until fused by the intense heat of the atomic bomb blasts at the end of the Second World War did these isolated environmental issues combine to form what some recognized as a planetary threat. The Bomb's tremendous metaphoric power provoked a coherent alternative ideology that resonated with a nervous public. Two days after the first bomb fell, journalist Anne O'Hare McCormick wrote that it caused "an explosion in men's minds as shattering as the obliteration of Hiroshima."[18] That psychic fracture, and the global conflagration that had produced it, moved an influential group of thinkers to ponder whether there were other ways that humanity might be hastening its end. Their focus turned to the relationship between humans and their natural environment. As Fairfield Osborn, director of the New York Zoological Society, would state in an address delivered to the annual convention of the National Association of Biology Teachers: "There are two major threats in the world today, either one of which would cause incalculable loss of human life, if not the breakdown of the entire structure of our civilization. The first is the misuse of atomic energy.... The other is the continuing destruction of the natural living resources of this earth.... Human beings, wildlife, forests, soils, water sources, are all in the same basket. Let's not kid ourselves."[19]

The Bomb triggered public awareness that there might be other ways humanity was threatening its own existence. A full-page advertisement urging readers to subscribe to *Time* magazine in 1946 featured a large picture of an atomic mushroom cloud with Albert Einstein's famous equation, "$E=mc^2$," etched across its detritus, and an accompanying headline that asked, "Is mankind dying of curiosity?" The ad presented a four-question quiz to readers who, it was expected, would have known the answers had they subscribed to *Time*. Among the questions were: "Which is increasing least rapidly? (1) The speed of planes (2) The divorce rate (3) The range of projectiles (4) Life expectancy (5) The destructive power of explosives." The correct answer was "Life expectancy," implying, along with the divorce rate (and mushroom cloud), that technology was, at best, having mixed results for humanity. That point was made still clearer with another of the questions: "When DDT was tried out as a mosquito killer in fishponds, what happened? (1) It started the water boiling. (2) It killed the fish. (3) It dried up the ponds. (4) It developed a race of fish-eating mosquitos [sic]. (5) Nothing happened." The correct answer was, as Rachel Carson would emphasize 16 years later in *Silent Spring*, "It killed the fish."[20] The bomb signified unprecedented human power, but it also revealed a fragile planet.

In addition, it unearthed questions about the nature of the United States. Following the war, *Life* magazine questioned the United States's moral standing in the world. Its editorial on August 20, 1945, in an issue with a full-page photograph of the bombing of Nagasaki that first introduced most Americans to the iconic image of the atomic mushroom cloud, stated: "It is bootless to argue at what stage of modern warfare, or by whom, the old Hague rules of war were violated. The point is that Americans, no less than Germans, have emerged from the tunnel with radically different practices and standards of permissible behavior toward others."[21] The Federal Council of the Churches of Christ, representing

21 major Protestant denominations, later condemned the "irresponsible" bombings of Hiroshima and Nagasaki.[22] The question of exactly how the United States would define itself as it "emerged from the tunnel" preoccupied some Americans. Environmentalism quickly took shape as a means to establish an identity deemed appropriate for the nuclear era—a means to recreate and redefine the nation as it confronted both its own image in the mirror and the nervous gaze of the world.

Long before the advent of the Bomb awakened fears of environmental apocalypse there had already been a growing dread of cultural apocalypse in nations where old ways of life were being rapidly displaced by corporate capitalism. Time and space, to the growing dismay of critics, were corporatized. By the postwar era, when those institutions and conventions that dominated modern life since the late-nineteenth century had grown exponentially more powerful and influential, they created an ever-greater sense of cultural doom. A succession of best-selling books, including *The Organization Man, The Man in the Grey Flannel Suit, White Collar, The Hidden Persuaders, The Status Seekers,* and *The Lonely Crowd*, expressed anxiety that the conformist institutions and material consumption that governed modern commercial life were distorting American culture, all the while sucking the spontaneity, joy, and meaning from the fundamental act of living.[23] But added now to these long-simmering fears of cultural apocalypse was the dread of planetary doom.

A New Beginning?

The realization that humans possessed the ability to destroy all life forced a radical transformation in the way some Americans viewed their world and their relationship to the earth. The triumphalism of the immediate postwar era in the United States was challenged by feelings of anxiety and doubt, often the product of an apocalyptic sensibility that grew to characterize the Cold War era. "Our world faces a crisis as yet unperceived by those possessing the power to make great decisions for good or evil," Albert Einstein observed in 1946. "The unleashed power of the atom has changed everything save our modes of thinking, and thus we drift toward unparalleled catastrophe."[24]

From the start, some hoped that the Bomb's blast would prove powerful enough to shake the United States out of its complacency and set it on a saner course—a new mode of thinking—that might permit it to live more intelligently, and harmoniously, on the planet. As writer and conservationist Howard Zahniser, charter member of the Wilderness Society in 1936, stated in *Nature Magazine* shortly after the bombs dropped on Japan: "We who have learned how to shatter an atom stand in open-mouthed wonder at what we have done, and may do, with the energy we have learned how to release. Remembering the ancient observation that 'the fear of the Lord is the beginning of wisdom,' we can hope that this new human awe at human possibilities may indeed be a beginning of wisdom."[25]

Zahniser's dissenting view of the Bomb was echoed in one of the most memorable works from the postwar artistic Beat movement on the topic, Gregory Corso's poem "Bomb," which drew attention not only because the verse was arranged in the shape of a mushroom cloud, but also because Corso spoke of the Bomb in loving terms for its potential to elevate human consciousness: "Toy of universe Grandest of all snatched sky I cannot hate you."[26] Like Einstein and Zahniser, Corso hoped the power of the Bomb might do more than keep people frightened, that it would instead awaken humanity to a new and deeper appreciation of life and the world.

By the end of the 1940s the activism displayed by scientists trying to protect the planet from peril had been mostly quieted and discredited amid charges of disloyalty and communism.[27] But it was nevertheless sustained and built upon by environmentalists who emerged during the postwar era carrying the hopes and dreams that life, on earth, might somehow be salvaged and maintained. There was no way to make sense of the unprecedented levels of destruction that characterized World War II. Fascism, genocide, and the sheer brutality of the war forever altered humanity's notion of itself. Technology, and the human willingness to use it without restraint, made possible levels of devastation—with not only atomic bombs but the infamous fire bombings of Dresden and Tokyo that each killed tens of thousands and destroyed large portions of those cities—in many ways so horrifying that they remained impossible to truly comprehend. Architectural historian Siegfried Giedion observed in 1948 that "after the Second World War, it may well be that there are no people left, however remote, who have not lost their faith in progress."[28] In the aftermath, was there any other response, any other way to honor the war's unavoidable lesson of the viciousness of humankind, than to act to protect an innocent planet from humanity's destructive impulses? After the fall a preserved planet would constitute a living war memorial, a monument that in some measure might make comprehensible the incomprehensible violence and destruction of the war through its suggestion that humanity had, at the end of it all, at least been shaken into changing its ways.

An Environmental Response

A genre of postwar environmental books proved appealing to citizens struggling to come to terms with the precariousness of their new world. These texts broke from earlier literary traditions that embraced Cartesian dualism and placed nature "out there" somewhere, remote from humans. By emphasizing ecology they sought to integrate humans back into the natural environment in their psyches and everyday lives after they were further severed from nature when they made the fateful decision to eat from the forbidden tree of knowledge in order to create the Bomb. It was the beginning of what would be a long-term effort, as evidenced by Joni Mitchell's lyrics 22 years later in the song "Woodstock," released during the same month as Earth Day: "We are stardust / Billion-year-old carbon / We are golden / Caught in the devil's bargain / And we've got to get ourselves / Back to the garden."[29]

The term *ecology* was dubbed by German biologist Ernst Haeckel in 1866, but it did not enter into popular use among American scientists until the last decade of the nineteenth century. The related term *ecosystem* did not appear until 1935, in an article in *Ecology* by Arthur George Tansley. After World War II, though, concepts like ecology and ecosystem resonated with survivors made acutely aware of the interdependence and vulnerability of their planet, and the terms moved from scientific journals into the popular lexicon. By 1949 Fairfield Osborn could observe that "the science of ecology [is] now a basic element in conservation thinking."[30] Industrialists regarded natural resources as discrete entities that should be mined for production and profits, while proto-environmentalists insisted they were interconnected and should be maintained for a healthy planet. The needs of the environment were paramount, more important than profits. Ironically, professional ecologists were largely absent from popular discourse during the 1940s and 1950s, when they responded to market forces by reducing ecology to "bioeconomics" and withdrawing into their academic ranks in a concerted effort to enhance their scientific and professional credibility, and gain research dollars, by distancing themselves from ethics and nature-loving romantics.[31] Further, during the 1950s many professional ecologists began to believe that the holistic notion of highly organized, interdependent communities was simply a construct of the human imagination, that in reality various species were not interdependent with all other species but instead, like Americans, were individualistic.[32] Nevertheless, the earlier notion of ecology continued to spread through the words of environmentalists concerned about the fate of the planet and resonate with a public that believed holistic ecology held forth the promise of healing both the damaged environment and the fragmented culture within it.

The word *environment*, which formerly denoted "social influences" that might impact individual behavior, began taking on the definition of an all-encompassing system of which humans are just one part. As historian Donald Worster has written, "An environmentalist, consequently, became anyone who was concerned with the preservation of those biophysical surroundings from pollution, depletion, or degradation."[33] Although that term did not come into popular use until the 1960s, a number of thinkers began pioneering elements of a powerful new ideology that would come to be known as *environmentalism*.

One of these proto-environmentalists was ornithologist, ecologist, and chief of the conservation section of the Pan American Union, William Vogt, whose 1948 international bestseller *Road to Survival* described how, led by the United States's relentless demand for productive resources, humans the world over were destroying the environment and the conditions that make life possible through postwar industrialization, mindless materialism, and a rapidly expanding human population. After the Dust Bowl of the 1930s, Vogt emphasized the problem of erosion—a problem that was exacerbated, he argued, by government subsidizing big business. It was the government's massive land giveaways to the railroad companies that, for example, resulted in environmental disaster when the railroads sold that land to settlers who, along with their children and grandchildren, cleared the land and cleared the way for the Dust Bowl.[34] Ultimately, Vogt feared, the profit-driven nature of business clouded its vision, rendering it blind to the severe environmental toll that sometimes resulted from its technologies and spelling planetary doom if it could not somehow be curbed. "The nineteenth century's enthusiasm for railroads paid little heed to what these were doing to the land," he warned. "The Dust Bowl was one of their contributions to modern living and the destruction of forests was, in part, another. We must avoid repeating such mistakes now that the twentieth century is indulging its own enthusiasms for roads, airfields, and dams."[35]

Vogt believed that environmental problems could not be solved without confronting the destructive power of big business that was the source of so many environmentally harmful technologies and practices. "One of the most ruinous limiting factors is the capitalistic system," he emphasized. "Free enterprise—divorced from biophysical understanding and social responsibility...must bear a large share of the responsibility for devastated forests, vanishing wildlife, crippled ranges, a gullied continent, and roaring flood crests."[36] The ideology of corporate capitalism that took hold in the late nineteenth century and dominated the twentieth had created massive wealth, Vogt recognized, but did so at the expense of the environment. "In other words," he concluded sharply, "land is managed on the basis of so-called economic laws and in very general disregard of the physical and biological laws to which it is subject. Man assumes that what has been good for industry must necessarily be good for the land. This may prove to be one of the most expensive mistakes in history."[37]

When Vogt detailed the expanding environmental issues resulting from the attitudes of corporate capitalism toward "land," he meant it in the economic sense of the word: all natural resources. Much of the concern focused on the scale of the enterprises. "Commercial fishermen, assuming the pirate's prerogative to take whatever he can get," Vogt protested, "have reduced the population of several important fishes to a point where it is no longer economically possible to take them." The whale had likewise been "practically exterminated from most of its arctic range."[38] Careless corporate practices were also threatening the supply of clean water. "Industry has been allowed to treat our underground water supplies as if they were inexhaustible," Vogt complained, "and...our cities have been jeopardized through waste of waters." In addition, "Business has been turned loose to poison thousands of streams and rivers with industrial wastes; and hundreds of cities are spending millions of dollars so that they may safely drink the waste dumped into the rivers upstream." As Vogt explained, identifying early on the imbalance of power and cost shifting that meant that businesses could often pollute with relative impunity while citizens would be left to pay the price with their health and lives, not to mention tax dollars for cleanup efforts: "The manufacturer cashes in—and the American citizen pays the cost of increased environmental resistance."[39]

In the end, careless resource use would destroy ecological balance and cause enormous human suffering, Vogt cautioned, or result in fighting over resources that would lead to nuclear annihilation. "Indeed, if we continue to ignore these relationships there is little probability that man can long escape the searing downpour of war's death from the skies," he warned. "A...search for economic and political solutions that ignores the ecological is as helpless as a bird with one wing." Vogt's own solution emphasized population control or, as he put it, "outwitting the libido."[40]

Population was a source of considerable anxiety. For some critics, it appeared that Thomas Malthus's dire warnings were coming true. Already, in 1935, one agricultural expert warned that Germany had "crossed the Malthusian threshold" and predicted that the country could not "long delay insuring the future of her crowded population, or avoid resorting to force to win and keep a larger place in the economic sun...the inevitable conflict may well be precipitated at the first favorable opportunity."[41] He cautioned that Japan was in similar dire resource straits and in desperate need of Chinese resources: "When we cross over to Japan we shall find a population problem with every element of Malthusianism present and acting.... It is inevitable that they will try to shut the [Chinese] Open Door in the face of populations like the British, the Russians, and the Americans whose real needs... are not half as great."[42] Not surprisingly, then, during the Second World War overpopulation was sometimes identified as the underlying source of German, Italian, and Japanese aggression, with reports citing a population expert who calculated that Germany's birth rate jumped almost 40 percent in the six years after the Nazis came to power.[43] Afterward the *Los Angeles Times* reported that "war-bent Germany and Italy freely admitted that they had more people than they could prosperously support on their own resources...and Japan took the same position."[44]

Vogt and others feared that if population growth was not curtailed misery resulting from inadequate resources was sure to follow, if not renewed aggression and war that, with the advent of the Bomb, placed the entire planet in peril.[45] Before having children then, the new thinking went, potential parents should check their passions and pause to consider the environmental ramifications of their actions. "Where human populations are so large that available land cannot decently feed, clothe, and shelter them, man's destructive methods of exploitation mushroom like the atomic cloud over Hiroshima," Vogt warned.[46] Paul Ehrlich, whose *The Population Bomb* drew upon the metaphor of the Bomb to arouse tremendous popular anxiety toward population growth during the 1960s, was first drawn to the subject when he read Vogt's book in 1949.[47] *Road to Survival* was translated into nine languages. Vogt later served as the national director of Planned Parenthood and secretary of the Conservation Foundation.[48]

Fairfield Osborn, a former Wall Street banker, was imbued with a love of nature and concern for the well-being of the environment at an early age. Sierra Club founder John Muir was a close family friend. Osborn's father, Henry, was a leading paleontologist (and eugenicist) who, in 1904, likened the endangerment of animals like the bison to the rapid decline of sequoia trees and called for immediate legislation to preserve them.[49] Muir began visiting the Osborns at their estate in Garrison, New York, as early as 1893. In 1910 he gave the Osborn family a tour of Yosemite "for a few days," and the Osborns joined Muir in the unsuccessful fight to stop the Hetch Hetchy dam that flooded part of the park.[50]

In *Our Plundered Planet* (1948), Osborn echoed Muir's observation that, "When we try to pick out anything by itself, we find it hitched to everything in the universe."[51] As Osborn emphasized, "All the component parts in the machinery of nature are dependent one upon the other. Remove any essential part and the machine breaks down. This is a primary fact and there is no other comparable to it in importance."[52] In the aftermath of the war, Osborn moved beyond Muir's emphasis on preserving spaces of natural aesthetic beauty and warned that exploitation of the environment was threatening ecology and human survival. "The impulse to write this book came towards the end of the Second World War," he explained. "It seemed to me, during those days, that mankind was involved in *two* major conflicts—not only the one that was in every headline," he recalled. "The other war, the silent war, eventually the most deadly war... is bringing more widespread distress to the human race than any that has resulted from armed conflict. It contains potentialities of ultimate disaster greater even than would follow the misuse of atomic power. This other war is man's conflict with nature." Osborn joined Vogt in expressing apocalyptic concerns over increasing population and urging Americans to view the postwar world through an ecological lens. Both books devoted considerable space to a survey of relative environmental health around the world, and both placed considerable blame on big business for environmental ills.[53]

Like historian Bernard DeVoto, who began railing against the trend in his *Harper's* magazine column a year earlier, Osborn showed particular contempt for the trend of allowing private, commercial use of public lands in the West for livestock grazing and timber: "The powerful minority groups of livestock men, skillfully supported by their representatives in Congress having taken over virtual control of the Federal Grazing Service," he warned, "now are attempting similarly to control the Forest Service." He concluded bitterly, "The powerful attacks now being made by small minority groups upon the public lands of the West have one primary motivation and one consuming objective—to exploit the grazing lands and these last forest reserves for every dollar profit that can be wrung from them." As Osborn saw it, then, the exploitation of public lands by private business interests with the consent of government was undemocratic. When he talked about "their" representatives in government in reference to powerful livestock and timber interests, he meant just that—those representatives were no longer representing the interests of "'We' the People" but were instead working for big business. "The raids of the herdsmen of earlier times find their twentieth-century counterpart in the work of political pressure groups representing powerful livestock owners in the halls of Congress," Osborn complained.[54]

His observations were later confirmed, and elaborated upon, by political scientist Phillip O. Foss's examination of livestock grazing on public lands under the New Deal's 1934 Taylor Grazing Act. Foss revealed that the livestock industry, a powerful big business lobby, unduly influenced the provisions of the act—which permitted private industry to use millions of acres of public lands, and even allowed "improvements" on those lands, including fences, wells, and reservoirs. In a further display of big business's power, the administration of the act was carried out not by disinterested officials but instead by members of the very industry that it was supposed to be regulating.[55]

This inherent imbalance of power between the public interest and the private sector was widespread. "Representatives of the lumber industry are there [in the halls of Congress] too," Osborn emphasized, "striving to effect arrangements so that the profits of their corporations may be assured and, if possible, increased.... For the moment, it is the American way of doing business."[56] The theme struck a chord with reviewers. "Both are barking up the right tree," said the *New Republic* of Vogt's and Osborn's books. "They have put their finger on the soil and water robber. This robber is an economic and business system which makes it profitable to destroy the elements that give us our food, our clothes, our houses, and our gadgets—and, of course, ultimately ourselves."[57] Speaking of writers like Osborn and Vogt, Malvina Lindsay of the *Washington Post* concluded, "One has a strange fatalistic sense of being back among the Biblical Israelites listening carelessly and unheedingly to impassioned prophets warning of impending doom.... We sit indifferently while Congress pinches pennies over conservation (only 1 percent of the Federal budget is spent on it) and financial descendants of the robber barons seek to open remaining public lands and resources to exploitation."[58]

That same undue influence of corporate capitalism on American culture and politics was clear in many of the environmental threats that Osborn addressed, including a chemical called DDT which was made public shortly after the war. Vogt's book had also sounded a warning about the pesticide, but Osborn was even more emphatic.[59] "Some of the initial experiments with this insect killer have been withering to bird life as a result of birds eating the insects that have been impregnated with the chemical," he warned. "The careless use of D.D.T. can also result in destroying fishes, frogs and toads, all of which live on insects. The new chemical is deadly on many kinds of insects—no doubt about that. But what of the ultimate and net result to the life scheme of earth?"[60] Osborn, then, brought an ecological perspective to his subject, bringing his readers around to recognize that their own lives, and their families', were implicated in the overall health of the planet—that they were only as healthy as the health of the larger environment of which they were a part. "There would seem to be no real hope for the future," he cautioned, "unless we are prepared to accept the concept that man, like all other living things, is a part of one great biological scheme."[61]

Although arsenic and other chemical pesticides had been in use in the United States since shortly after the Civil War, and health concerns involving chemical residues on food dated back as far as an 1891 grape scare, earlier critics could not imagine the toxic power and pervasiveness of the new crop of synthetic chemicals first used during World War II and later sold for agriculture.[62] During the war, the government pushed entomologists to drop other research interests and train their focus on the issues of secure food production and insect-borne diseases. The power of chemicals, combined with their lower cost and easier application, overrode concerns about their effects on humans and the environment. The war effort had a significant effect on the shift toward chemical insect control. From 1937 to 1947 articles in the *Journal of Economic Entomology* exploring biological controls dropped from 33 percent to 17 percent, while those discussing chemical controls increased from 58 percent to 76 percent.[63]

DDT was first synthesized by a German chemist in 1874 before being developed by the Swiss chemical giant J. R. Geigy in the 1930s, but it received little attention in the United States until the army became desperate for a new delousing product. Because it is synthetic, DDT could be manufactured in mass quantities to control lice and the spread of typhus, a scourge that had killed more soldiers throughout European history than all battles combined, as well as malaria-carrying mosquitoes in the South Pacific. The military demanded such huge quantities that the government eventually pushed Geigy to give the rights to 11 different companies to manufacture the pesticide. Although a federal entomologist who had 127 square miles of forest sprayed aerially with DDT in 1944–1945 was encouraged by its effectiveness, and its cost of $1.45 per acre compared to the $15 to $25 per acre formerly spent to ground-spray older insecticides made it especially attractive, some scientists began issuing warnings about the potential dangers of DDT early on when research indicated it could be harmful to crops, animals, and humans, as well as beneficial insects like bees.[64]

Acting on such evidence, the army and the US Public Health Service, the two agencies that at the time controlled DDT, restricted its use for domestic spraying. "Much still must be learned about the effect of DDT on the balance of nature important to agriculture and wild life before general outdoor application of DDT can be safely employed in this country," they stated in a press release, noting that risks that might be taken in wartime abroad could not be justified for peaceful uses at home.[65] From the start, then, those who worked most closely with DDT warned of the threat it posed to food and the planet's ecosystem.

Despite myriad warnings, many of the companies producing DDT during the war hoped to maintain their production and profits afterward, and so fought to get it approved for routine domestic use. The War Production Board that oversaw the production of war materials required producers to sell all war goods to the government as long as the quantity it demanded was equal to or greater than the quantity supplied. In July, only three months after the army and Public Health Service had restricted the domestic use of DDT, the War Production Board announced that it believed there would be a surplus of DDT by the fourth quarter of 1945. Under the policy of the board, a surplus would free it for sale to civilians for use in homes and agriculture. Thus the declaration of surplus was a victory for manufacturers that, given the membership of the board, surely came as no surprise. As historian Edmund Russell has succinctly described the process: "The board (made up of industry representatives temporarily working for the government) usually followed the advice of its chemicals division (made up of chemical company managers temporarily working for the government), which usually accepted the advice of its DDT Producers Industry Advisory Committee (made up of representatives of companies that made DDT and its precursors)." The entire oversight of the controversial chemical was therefore in the hands of representatives from chemical companies who stood to profit from its use. As soon as the board released DDT for civilian use it was no longer under the exclusive control of the military, effectively negating the authority of the army and Health Service to restrict its domestic use. Thereafter the vagaries of the market governed DDT.[66]

In the harsh light of the Bomb, anxieties rapidly became apocalyptic threats. Demonstrating yet again the atomic bomb's power to create apocalyptic metaphors, in 1945, only months after it was released to the consumer market, one writer compared DDT to the Bomb, a metaphor Rachel Carson would use to powerful effect seventeen years later. In his article entitled "DDT: The Atomic Bomb of the Insect World," C. H. Curran, curator of insects and spiders at the American Museum of Natural History, cautioned that DDT should be used only indoors, where it could be contained, and asked, "Are we going to use it indiscriminately and possibly damage the life of our planet quite seriously?... If improperly used, it might actually prove more devastating to man's economy than the atomic bomb."[67] A research study that same year revealed that DDT collected in the body fat of mammals, and also concentrated in mother's milk.[68]

Our Plundered Planet was reprinted eight times during its first year and was soon translated into 13 languages.[69] Along with Vogt's *Road to Survival*, it was one of 10 books nominated for the Gutenberg Award for the book that "most progressively influenced American thought in the year 1948."[70] Clearly the message of these books reflected a genuine concern among the public at large. "I imagine that what you and I are both most earnestly striving for is to arouse consciousness that these [ecological] interactions are of the essence," Osborn wrote to his friend Vogt when thanking him for reading and commenting on his manuscript. "I think we really are making progress, although of course it will never be enough."[71]

In 1948 Osborn also cofounded the Conservation Foundation to address ecology and postwar environmental issues, like population, chemicals, and pollution, which had yet to garner much attention from established conservation groups like the Wilderness Society and Sierra Club. When he announced the creation of the Conservation Foundation, Osborn echoed one of the apocalyptic themes of his book and a concern that would, explicitly and implicitly, consciously and unconsciously, come to occupy a central place in environmental thought in the United States. That concern centered on the challenge that the increasing power of corporations posed to American democracy. Clear in Osborn's assessment of the threat that powerful commercial interests posed to the environment was the recognition that, although they were a "minority," they had come to possess unparalleled power that, coupled with their influence over government, was upsetting the balance of the American polity by marginalizing the role of citizens. If corporate and commercial interests could not be reined in, Osborn warned, they would make the planet uninhabitable. "The conservation movement is at the core of the fight for democracy," he emphasized. He and others warned that if corporations refused to operate for the general good and protect the environment, a new form of totalitarianism would necessarily arise to rein them in.[72] "Big business has got to become an active partner with Government in the Conservation movement if this country is to survive as a great nation," Osborn told a meeting of the New York Chamber of Commerce in 1947. "Time is running out."[73] To preserve the country and democracy, Osborn urged Americans to view the postwar world through an ecological lens: "We are compelled to recognize that animal life in all its forms, forest and other plant life, water sources and finally fertile soil are four elements all related to one another," he said. "We are destroying all of these natural resources at a faster rate than they are being replaced."[74]

The nascent ideology of environmentalism also spread through other mediums. In September 1948 Osborn was heard in "millions of American homes" when he was one of four scientists with the American Association for the Advancement of Science on the popular ABC radio program, *America's Town Meeting of the Air*, for an episode called "What Hope for Man?" All of the panelists agreed that the United States and the world were at a crucial juncture, one that required new modes of thinking and living if civilization was to survive. As the program's host summed it up: "We're in one of those critical periods of history when it matters terribly, it just matters very much indeed, what each and every one of us think and do individually or through our governments."[75] In June 1949 Osborn appeared on the CBS television series *People's Platform*, for a show titled "Is Destruction of the Earth's Resources Threatening Man's Survival?"[76] Six months later he was a guest on NBC radio's broadcast of *Living in 1950*, in an episode called "Man and His Environment."[77]

Much as Sigmund Freud had earlier led many to see that complicated components underlie the surface of human existence and must be maintained in a stable balance to assure a healthy individual, the postwar generation learned that intricate forces underlie the surface of nature and must be maintained in a stable balance to assure a healthy planet. Environmentalists played the role of therapist, revealing the dark secrets that lay hidden behind the innocent facade of big business. Even as it warned of impending peril if humans did not correct their course, the ecology put forward by environmentalists nevertheless suggested a path to physical and psychological security that might right the wrongs of postwar corporate capitalism.

Roll Over, Washington, Tell Jefferson the News

If the Bomb made clear that humans must reconnect with nature, then big business appeared to pose the biggest obstacle to achieving that goal. More than anything else, it was the threat of cultural and environmental doom at the hands of corporations that inspired environmentalism during the postwar era. For some Americans the corporate culture that dominated the twentieth century was the antithesis of the culture of environmentalism that they deemed essential for human and planetary survival.

Those concerned about the power wielded by corporate capitalism had earlier sensed some reason for hope. The stock market crash in 1929, and the ensuing Depression, tarnished the image of big business and called into question its ability to provide for the needs of the nation. The hopelessness and chaos of that era lent fresh legitimacy to arguments going back decades to the Populist and Progressive eras that the structure of capitalism itself was flawed, and it was government's job to locate and repair its defects so that it might better function for the benefit of all citizens. Widespread labor strikes and protests during the Depression amplified that view, and New Deal welfare-state programs followed in response.[78]

That restructuring spirit proved short-lived. During the war American big business moved aggressively to bolster its position and win the hearts and minds of the American public. Corporate capitalism's massive structures of organization and control, designed with a singular obsession for profits, emerged in the final decades of the nineteenth century when, aided by new technology, supportive new laws, government subsidies, and a tradition of American distrust of strong central government that meant there was relatively little resistance or regulation from the top to get in the way, it quickly grew to dominate American life.[79] Nevertheless, corporate leaders feared that business's loss of stature in the wake of the Depression, which shattered its aura of infallibility, might convince the public that government, and not business, was best equipped to care for the public's well-being. Corporations waged major public relations offensives aimed at diminishing the role and status of government, while persuading the public that without the industrial might of corporate capitalism the United States could not win the war. This campaign also implied that business would make the nation great again in the war's aftermath.[80] For example, a 1943 advertisement by the International Minerals and Chemicals Corporation declared: "Conceived by chemical research for the grim purpose of war, new processes and new materials are blue-printing today the pattern of things to come in a world of peace." Corporations promised to convert technologies of destruction into methods of abundance: "*Fertilizers* of greater crop producing power to increase the abundance and quality of our farm yields. *Feeds* to expand our production of poultry, cattle and swine...."[81] They extolled the virtues of free enterprise and wide-ranging consumer abundance and ascribed it all to the American Way of Life.[82]

Besides supplying the war effort, corporations also gained from the victor's spoils in the aftermath. The government established the Office of Technical Services to search the files and records of enemy labs and obtain scientific and technical secrets that might benefit American businesses. Among those uncovered were German chemical giant I. G. Farben's secrets of powerful organophosphate nerve gases and insecticides (e.g., parathion and malathion) that could now be had for free by any American company wishing to manufacture them.[83]

Consequently, it was not only apprehensions about technology that were greatly intensified by World War II. For those citizens leery of the prevailing corporate trend, fear of big business was also escalating. The nature of capitalism itself was changing. Large corporations, which had already fared much better than small companies during the Depression, gained even greater dominance during the war thanks to government largesse and cost-plus contracts.[84] Senate investigations revealed that during the war more than two-thirds of the $175 billion in prime government contracts issued to supply the effort went to only 100 large companies. The same held true for government contracts for scientific research, where the top 100 corporations received more than 70 percent of the $750 million awarded. Companies with over 10,000 workers that employed 13 percent of industrial labor in 1939 expanded their share to 30 percent only five years later, while those employing 500 or fewer decreased from 52 to 38 percent during the same period. Corporations with 500 or more employees, though only 2 percent of the number of firms in the United States, employed a remarkable 62 percent of workers by 1944. The 250 largest companies held two-thirds of the nation's manufacturing facilities, with the 31 largest corporations controlling nearly half of that total. Financial power was even more concentrated. Furthering a trend that began in the late nineteenth century, eight groups of bankers controlled 106 of the 250 largest companies in 1946, exerting tremendous influence not only on the economy but also on government policy.[85]

The expanded industrial capacity financed by the government during the war required increased consumption afterward to sustain the massive systems of production. The government, in partnership with corporations and financial institutions, did its part to assure sufficient levels of consumption by doggedly pursuing easy credit and economic growth, in a Keynesian policy effort so pronounced that it was soon dubbed "growthmanship."[86] And if consumer demand proved insufficient, military spending would help to assure adequate aggregate demand for corporate capitalism's production. Consumer desires, pent up since the Depression, were met by a flood of new products. Personal consumption increased 20 percent during 1946 from just a year earlier—and was a whopping 70 percent higher than it had been in 1941.[87] But the processes that provided the flood of new consumer goods, as automation amplified Fordism and was accompanied by yet a further intensification of the commercialization of American culture, wrought changes that some believed neither individuals nor society—nor nature—could assimilate. After the nearly generation-long deprivations of the Depression and the war, to those concerned about the demoralizing potential of consumption the postwar explosion of consumer culture was particularly glaring and troubling. All of this consumption carried considerable costs, both cultural and environmental.

To many, the giant corporations that were providing for so many consumer desires following the war seemed like a necessary evil. But some believed their massive power was too great to contain and posed an apocalyptic threat to the earth and its inhabitants, not to mention America's experiment in democracy. Senator James E. Murray, Democrat from Montana, who chaired the Special Senate Committee to Study Small Business Problems, which issued one of the reports on how big business was growing bigger during the war, concluded that "in nearly every industry in our country, we find four or five large organizations in control." He warned: "Strenuous efforts will be made by big business to gain control of the next Congress.... [N]ot only small business will be in danger, but our entire American Democratic system."[88]

The corporation possessed power so all-encompassing that it appeared it might ultimately overwhelm the individual self. For some Americans, the massive scale of corporations after the war suggested the potential for a new form of totalitarianism. A former Assistant Secretary of State and professor of corporate law at Columbia University, Adolf A. Berle, Jr., testified to a House Judiciary subcommittee that the economy was controlled by large corporations that had become "a fifth estate—a small group of self-perpetuating oligarchies which probably control the industrial future of America."[89] There was some movement in Congress to do something to counter the trend of the corporate behemoths, especially since one of the Senate reports on the growth of corporations characterized the response of executive department agencies to the trend as ineffective and "weak-kneed." Maverick Republican Senator Wayne Morse from Oregon introduced jointly sponsored legislation in 1947 to both strengthen government authority over corporations and provide greater support for small businesses. But it was widely understood that such legislation would never make it through the gauntlet of corporate lobbyists who would align to greet it. As one *New York Times* writer stated, "Despite the evidence of renewed interest in the monopoly problem, it is entirely possible that the various recommendations... are destined for the same pigeonhole to which similar efforts in the past have usually been consigned."[90] Former Vice President and Secretary of Commerce Henry A. Wallace summed up the situation in 1947, fourteen years before President Dwight Eisenhower popularized the phrase "military-industrial complex," when he stated that the policies of both the Truman Administration and Congress were controlled by "the military and Wall Street."[91]

That control was gained not only through economic and lobbying might but concerted efforts by corporations to manufacture the national discourse. The major public relations campaigns waged by big business to curry favor with the public during the war continued to escalate even as the fighting ended. Organizations like the American Heritage Foundation, the Foundation for Economic Education, and the Advertising Council were founded shortly after the war to promote corporate capitalism. They joined existing business associations such as the Chamber of Commerce, American Liberty League, and National Association of Manufacturers (NAM) in waging multimillion-dollar public relations campaigns to undermine faith in New Deal government and promote business interests in order to convince citizens that those interests were synonymous with their own. In 1947 NAM alone sent free promotional materials to 7,500 newspapers and 2,500 journals and distributed over two million pamphlets. It purchased ads in 265 daily newspapers, 1,876 small-town papers, and many magazines. NAM's speakers' bureau organized speeches across the country and a trained full-time staff of "radio debaters" to appear on popular talk shows; it sponsored a radio show called *Your Business Reporter* that could be heard in some three million homes. By 1950 the Advertising Council had carpet-bombed Americans with 13 million lines of newspaper advertising, over 600 magazine ads, 8,000 billboards, 3.5 million pamphlets, and some 300,000 ads placed on subways, buses, and taxis. Typical ads stressed that the solution to economic woes was not structural changes (which could lead to communism) but instead increased productivity and mechanization.[92] The corporation was not only a form of business organization; it spawned an ideology of "corporate capitalism" in the late nineteenth century that grew to dominate American life during the postwar era.

Corporate capitalism might persuade public opinion with waves of public relations campaigns and well-placed beneficence, but to acquire the authority necessary to sway public policy and ensure long-term success it sought the credibility that could only be gained from the intellectual gravitas bestowed by an academic imprimatur. None of these efforts was more pronounced than the formalization of the long-term project of neoliberalism—an international effort whose epicenter in the United States was the University of Chicago. Neoliberals believed that free markets were the only guarantor of freedom, and that the job of the state was to take all necessary steps to insure a stable market society.[93] Austrian economist Friedrich A. Hayek took up residence at Chicago in 1950 and began working in concert with corporate backers to reshape the Western world's conception of freedom and democracy. Hayek rose to fame championing free markets as the antidote to totalitarianism in his popular 1944 book *The Road to Serfdom*. After the war, when the focus turned from totalitarianism to an obsession with socialism's threat to free markets, he was brought to Chicago by a Kansas City businessman who, recognizing the power that academic backing could lend to the free market cause, used his family's philanthropic fund to pay Hayek's University of Chicago salary for 10 years.[94] Hayek and other leading free market fundamentalists at the university were soon known as "the Chicago School." Milton Friedman became the group's most famous and influential economist. By the 1950s, as he moved from theory to policy, his belief in an extremely limited regulatory role for government in the economy exceeded the neoliberalism of Hayek. Friedman insisted that the Food and Drug Administration should be abolished, for example, along with all national parks. Giant corporations, monopolies, and concentrations of power no longer needed to be regulated because competition would always return and prevail in the end.[95]

Free markets, in what became the wildly influential vision of the Chicago School and conservative business activists, trump political and social concerns and provide the ethical system that should guide human behavior. As Friedman later stated, "there is one and only one social responsibility of business—to use its resources and engage in activities designed to increase its profits so long as it stays within the rules of the game, which is to say, engages in open and free competition, without deception or fraud."[96] It was a moral philosophy that readily accommodated the unfettered growth of corporate power—and environmental degradation. It would be wrong for a corporate leader "to make expenditures on reducing pollution beyond the amount that is in the best interests of the corporation or that is required by law in order to contribute to the social objective of improving the environment," Friedman concluded shortly after Earth Day in 1970.[97] Shareholders enjoyed the profits gained by corporations; the environmental damage done to get those profits was borne by citizens as well as the ecosystem. As economists Philip Mirowski and Rob Van Horn have summed up the Chicago School's particular take on the American concept of freedom, "In promoting 'freedom,' they were primarily intent on guaranteeing the freedom of corporations to conduct their affairs as they wished."[98] In this view corporations claimed they deserved all the rights afforded to a person by the US Constitution but insisted they should not be encumbered by the responsibilities typically associated with citizenship. Thus the environment could be sacrificed at the altar of neoliberal economic orthodoxy.

Corporate capitalism was increasingly embedded with the state. Although neoliberalism did not grow to dominate policy until the late 1970s, in the immediate postwar era the corporate capitalist state was keenly illustrated by the oil industry. In the midst of exploding demand and an energy crisis during 1947–48, American oil companies, with the support of the US government, gained control of Middle East oil fields, a source of cheap energy. In 1945 there were 26 million automobiles operating in the United States; only five years later 40 million cars filled the nation's roads, and gasoline sales had increased by 42 percent. By the end of 1948 four US companies had secured the rights to Saudi Arabia's production, and Gulf Oil shared Kuwait's output with Dutch giant Shell. That year the nation's crude oil imports exceeded exports for the first time.[99] "For the immediate future the rapid development of Middle Eastern reserves should ease the tight world petroleum situation," observed Paul Nitze, Deputy to the Assistant Secretary for Economic Affairs in the State Department, in 1948. "In the long run the problem would not be so great in the energy field if water, solar, atomic, or wind sources could be harnessed in adequate volume."[100] However, the illusion of cheap energy provided by Middle Eastern oil fields, and the enormous political power amassed by the corporations that profited from it, would help to assure that alternative energy sources would not be adequately developed.

Not all economic thinkers supported the policies shaping the postwar United States. Political economist Karl Polanyi, for instance, argued that in classical economics land and labor were rendered commodities—items for sale in the marketplace—when neither should be reduced to such. In his 1944 book, *The Great Transformation*, Polanyi warned: "To allow the market mechanism to be sole director of the fate of human beings and their natural environment...would result in the demolition of society." Without protection from the ravages of free market forces, "Nature would be reduced to its elements, neighborhoods and landscapes defiled, rivers polluted...the power to produce food and natural resources destroyed." Some regulations were put into place to provide a measure of protection, which Polanyi referred to as a "double movement." As markets spread during the nineteenth century they were met with policies designed to check their power in order to safeguard both labor and the environment.[101]

But such protective measures were, warned economist K. William Kapp, inadequate because they did not fully account for what he termed "social costs," "all those harmful consequences and damages which third persons or the community sustain as a result of the productive process, and for which private entrepreneurs are not easily held accountable."[102] Other economists termed these "negative externalities," but for Kapp that euphemism hid their true meaning and made them sound like infrequent occurrences when, in reality, social costs were "a characteristic phenomenon of the market economy."[103] The "value theory" of neoclassical economics insists that expenditures by businesses and their private returns "constitute a theoretically adequate measure of the costs and benefits of productive activities," Kapp summarized, but in reality they have "shifted" many of the costs "which cannot be [easily] expressed in dollars and cents" to other persons, the community, and the environment, in effect redistributing income from those who suffer the costs to the businesses that shift the costs.[104] In *The Social Costs of Private Enterprise* (1950), Kapp detailed how this distorted market results in air and water pollution, extinction or near extinction of fish and wildlife, wasted energy resources, soil erosion, and deforestation. These are the modern plagues of advanced industrialized economies. "The harmful effects of air and water pollution are important social costs which may be said to have taken the place of the contagious diseases and epidemics still prevalent in the underdeveloped parts of the world," Kapp warned.[105] Too often, "the ecological balance" was ignored "in the interest of maximizing current returns or minimizing current costs."[106] What was needed to protect the environment, he concluded, was "a new science of economics...to include those omitted aspects of reality which many economists have been inclined to dismiss or neglect as 'noneconomic,'" one that incorporated the best insights of the social sciences.[107]

Attuned as they were to the limits of the advanced market economy, its tendency to harm third parties and the environment, and the need for creative solutions to make it sustainable, Polanyi and Kapp, unlike Hayek and Friedman, did not become the darlings of business people and politicians. Elite societies did not form to develop and promote their ideas, nor did business people and politicians push to translate their ideas into policy. Other economists largely ignored them. Instead, business and economics continued to bask in the market mentality of eighteenth-century economists who could not have anticipated the marketplace's power to threaten all of creation.[108]

However, at the same time that US policy was dominated by military Keynesianism and neoliberalism was being formalized at the University of Chicago, an alternative vision for the postwar world was also taking shape. For some, big business's benefits masked long-standing concerns about its structure. Even as its leaders positioned corporate capitalism for the long haul, critics feared it was too often blinded by a shortsighted focus on profits above all else. For those citizens who added the death of the planet to existing fears of big business, unfettered corporate capitalism could not stand the test of time. As Fairfield Osborn stated in a speech to the annual meeting of the US Chamber of Commerce in 1949, "The future of our country's wellbeing depends upon our getting on a sustained-yield basis."[109] Environmentalism emerged as an alternative vision to challenge the orthodoxy of the postwar corporate capitalist state.[110]

But getting business to take honest, meaningful environmental action would prove difficult. Osborn was outraged when, after agreeing to speak at the Chamber of Commerce gathering, he discovered that the organization had grossly misrepresented his beliefs in its weekly newsletter, claiming that he had stated: "There is no question whatever that our soils, our forests, and our water supplies can be maintained and restored. We are able today through science and technology to increase the productivity of good lands to a point even far in advance of their original production as virgin soils." Osborn fired off a memo to the Chamber of Commerce: "Frankly [I] am quite shocked by a quote you make of my remarks which were never made at all. I wonder if you can explain how this happened? Unfortunately, it puts me into the position that all is well with the conservation of renewable resources picture, and this is far from the case." Perhaps the Chamber had not anticipated that Osborn's assistant would write to ask for copies of the newsletter. It offered its sincere apology and noted the error in a later edition.[111]

To model the environmentalism that he hoped might save the world from careless corporate capitalism, Osborn's Conservation Foundation opened a 12-acre conservation exhibit in the Bronx Zoo in 1949. The exhibit championed the vision of conservation as ecological interdependence being promoted by Osborn and other proto-environmentalists, a vision that reached well beyond the efficient use of natural resources and preservation of aesthetically pleasing landscapes. Containing a variety of wildlife, birds, trees, and fish, the exhibit was expected to teach some 500,000 visitors each year about reforestation, soil reclamation, erosion control, and, especially, ecology. "Here in one small area," enthused Osborn, "we have magnificent facilities for showing their relationship, how these resources are depleted and how they can be restored."[112]

The Bomb, then, not only forced humans to ponder other ways that they might be destroying the planet; it also provided a means for environmental thinkers to frame the issue in a way that would gain greater attention for their cause. Linking environmental concerns to atomic and national security anxieties during the Cold War created a sense of urgency that helped ensure that the issues were noticed and taken seriously. Previously, dark forces within nature, such as Halley's Comet, were feared as a threat to humanity. But with the Bomb, humans turned the tables. Now, dark forces within humanity, expressed through atomic weapons, were feared as a threat to nature. Efforts to prevent the use of atomic force were fused to efforts to protect the planet from the threat of corporate capitalism, triggering a powerful ideological movement.

Dueling Visions for the Postwar World

The postwar era's growing environmental consciousness was evidenced by major conferences on the subject in the late 1940s. In 1946, at the behest of US President Harry Truman, the United Nations announced that it would hold a conference to "consider the conservation and effective utilization of natural resources." The impetus was the belief that among the primary causes of the Second World War was Germany and Japan's desperation to secure scarce materials, and a growing fear after the war that other industrialized nations—including the United States—would soon find themselves in similar straits. "The real or exaggerated fear of resource shortages and declining standards of living has in the past involved nations in warfare," said Truman in his letter to the United Nation's US representative to the Economic and Social Council calling for the conference. "Conservation can become a major basis of peace."[113] After three years in the making, the United Nations Scientific Conference on the Conservation and Utilization of Resources (UNSCCUR) was held in 1949 at the UN's temporary headquarters in Lake Success, New York.

UNSCCUR was challenged, however, when one of its own agencies, the United Nations Educational, Scientific and Cultural Organization (UNESCO) decided to hold its own conference at Lake Success at the same time as UNSCCUR. The title of its conference made obvious how it defined itself in contrast to the UN conference: "The International Technical Conference on the Protection of Nature" (ITCPN). In the wake of the war, UNESCO found the UN's economic focus based on traditional conservation inadequate, and urged a more comprehensive and robust ideology to protect the planet, one that embodied the expanded environmental consciousness beginning to take hold during the postwar era.

It may be tempting to view the dual conferences as yet another example of the split between progressive utilitarian conservationists, who focused on the efficient wise use of resources, and preservationists who sought to protect aesthetically pleasing spaces. But limiting the analysis to that historical dichotomy misses the significant origins of environmentalism as a critique of the growing power of corporate capitalism. The United States was not only placing tremendous strain on the planet with its system of corporate capitalism, critics argued, it modeled its plans for international development on its own postwar affluence. Even if much of the world did not actually achieve American levels of production and consumption, the broad cultural, political, and environmental implications of its designs for a liberal international order unleashed waves of anxiety both at home and around the globe.[114] The conferences reveal starkly contrasting, competing visions—the dueling visions of corporate capitalism and environmentalism for the postwar world that persist to this day.

The United Nations Scientific Conference on the Conservation and Utilization of Resources

The three-week UNSCCUR meeting, held from August 17 to September 6, 1949, provided a forum on the "wise use" of the materials of the earth. Almost half a century earlier Gifford Pinchot defined conservation as "the greatest good to the greatest number for the longest time," and his utilitarian conservationist approach was the animating spirit of the meetings.[115] As Secretary of the Interior Julius A. Krug stated in one of the conference's opening addresses, "I think it's high time that we start a new era in conservation, an era consecrated to the development and wise use of what is available to the people of the world. There is not the slightest question in my mind that scientists and engineers can find and develop food, fuels, and material to meet the demands of the world's increasing population with a greatly improved standard of living."[116] There were 706 participants on hand from 52 countries. The Soviet Union and its satellites were conspicuously absent, but scientists from Poland and Czechoslovakia submitted papers. "Almost without exception," reported the *New York Times*, "documents which will serve as starting points for conference discussions are practical blueprints for economic progress."[117]

The United States dominated the proceedings with 440 participants and had a heavy hand in establishing the conference agenda. Truman attached a "preliminary and condensed programme outline prepared by the resource agencies of this Government" to his letter requesting the conference.[118] While most countries sent scientists and engineers, along with representatives from various governmental agencies and an occasional representative from private industry, the US contingent contained an unusual number of participants from business, including representatives from the Carbide and Carbon Chemicals Corporation, General Electric, Standard Oil, Crown Zellerbach (paper), the Union Pacific Coal Company, Johnstown Coal and Coke Company, Homestake Mining Company, Bell Telephone, the US Chamber of Commerce, IBM, Simpson Logging Company, Champion Paper, American Association of Oil Well Drilling Contractors, American Gas and Electric, Kennecott Copper, and Gulf Oil.[119]

Sessions on soil, water, fuel and energy, forests, minerals, and fish and wildlife reflected the broad resource anxieties of the era.[120] Although it is difficult to adequately summarize 550 papers, some common themes clearly emerged. That the war was an enormous waste of resources was a common refrain. Future wars must be assiduously avoided, proclaimed the participants.[121] The world population was growing exponentially, and as that growing number of people sought to emulate the United States's standard of living, some natural resources would quickly be exhausted.[122] The goal, then, was to better exploit known reserves, seek out additional ones, and, if all else failed, find alternative resources that might substitute for those in short supply.

Proposals put forth at UNSCCUR typically reflected its stated goal of "utilization" of resources, with little concern for ecology or the health of the larger environment. The spirit of the proceedings can be gleaned from the titles of the papers presented, which included "Oil from Oil Shale"; "Control and Utilization of Polluted Waters"; "Treatment of Trees with Toxic Chemicals to Facilitate Removal of Bark to Reduce Weight"; "Gypsy Moth Control by Means of Spraying from Aircraft"; and "Log Transportation in Tropical Forest Exploitation." A series of papers discussed new methods for discovering minerals in India, Sardinia, Liberia, Bolivia, Brazil, and Yugoslavia.[123] Among the more extreme examples were multiple sessions on the availability and use of chemical fertilizers. "During the past ten years," enthused Robert M. Salter of the US Department of Agriculture in a paper titled "Techniques for Increasing

Agricultural Production," "farmers in the United States have doubled their use of chemical fertilizers, and they are now applying them in granular, liquid, and gaseous forms."[124] A presentation on "Petroleum Production from Continental Shelves" reported that, since 1945, fully 50 wells adjacent to Louisiana and Texas had been or were about to be drilled.[125] Yet another paper breathlessly described the fishing boat *Pacific Explorer* as the most advanced of its kind, "an 8,800 ton, 410 ft., steel vessel built during the First World War," re-outfitted by the federal government and now leased to the Pacific Exploration Company, Inc. Designed to operate in the Bering Sea with a crew of as many as 240, the hybrid fishing boat/factory was capable of freezing 260,000 pounds of fish, canning 600 cases of crab, and producing 50,000 pounds of fillets in an eight-to-ten-hour day.[126]

For every problem, it seemed, the scientists and engineers at the conference believed there was a solution. The issue of declining ocean fish stocks could be solved by harvesting the "underfished" waters of the tropics, combined with an expansion of fish farming.[127] Various other shortages would be eased by new developments in aerial reconnaissance, geophysical surveys, and ocean sonar to reveal long-hidden minerals, petroleum, timber, and other resources. Secretary of the Interior Krug dismissed the era's nascent environmental perspective: "I do not side with those who 'view with alarm' the increasing world population and the decreasing reserves of some things which now appear to be essential to our way of living," he emphasized. The majority of those at the conference appeared to agree with him.[128]

UNSCCUR's promotion of corporate capitalism extended beyond the meeting itself. Attendees were urged to participate in a six-day field trip, conducted and financed by the Department of State, immediately following the conference. One hundred and thirty-seven people from 39 countries boarded a special train for a carefully planned journey. In Pittsburgh, Pennsylvania they toured U.S. Steel, the Metals Research Laboratory at the Carnegie Institute of Technology, an H. J. Heinz Company plant, and the Bureau of Mines Central Experiment Station and Experimental Coal Mine at nearby Bruceton, Pennsylvania. The Pittsburgh Chamber of Commerce treated them to a reception and dinner. At Columbus, Ohio they inspected a mining machinery factory and the US Forest Service offices, where they learned about forestry measures for strip-mined land. They next visited dams and other projects of the Tennessee Valley Authority, often promoted as the model for how the United States planned to develop the Global South. In a stop at Washington, DC, the tour included a visit to the Bureau of Mines in College Park, Maryland, as well as a 12,000-acre US Department of Agriculture research center and a tour of the Timber Engineering Company for a demonstration of the latest developments in wood processing.[129] It was an intensive State Department education in the American Way.

UNESCO Moves to Hold a Separate Conference

UNESCO feared that the UN conference was bent upon maintaining and amplifying the unsustainable status quo and determined that its conference would instead reflect the growing interest in what would come to be called "environmentalism." Originally, UNESCO was invited by the organizing UN Economic and Social Council to merely help the UN plan and conduct its United Nations Scientific Conference on the Conservation and Utilization of Resources.[130] Some members of UNESCO, however, including its Director-General, the evolutionary biologist Julian Huxley, were unhappy with UNSCCUR's "wise use" emphasis. They grew increasingly concerned that UNESCO's budding environmental voice would be overwhelmed by UNSCCUR's emphasis on economics and concluded that the only way for it to receive an adequate hearing was to hold a separate conference. The State Department opposed a separate meeting and pushed UNESCO to lend its support to Truman's UN conference.[131] Nevertheless, Huxley succeeded in gaining UNESCO's authorization to hold a separate International Technical Conference on the Protection of Nature (ITCPN).[132]

In December 1947, Huxley, along with William Vogt and six other Americans—three officials from the Department of the Interior, one from the Department of Agriculture, and another from the National Research Council—made plans for the conference. They worried that UNSCCUR's preoccupation with "industrial aspects of conservation" would result in talk of subjects like hydroelectric power crowding out discussion about things like wildlife conservation that offered little opportunity for profit.[133]

ITCPN was intended to ensure that the triumphant vision of ever more efficient use of resources through ever-improving science and technology was tempered by newer thinking grounded in the holistic vision of ecology that was capturing the imagination of forward thinkers like Osborn and Vogt. "Protection of nature," Huxley observed, "was steadily changing over from the aesthetic and sentimental to the social and economic plane."[134] It enlisted the Swiss-based International Union for the Protection of Nature (IUPN), founded less than a year earlier with UNESCO's aid, to cosponsor the event. "To day [sic], the balance has been upset," declared UNESCO in explaining its rationale for a separate conference. Clearly, power had tilted too heavily toward corporations and their allies in government; the enormous scale of both meant that a single decision by either one carried the potential for enormous environmental harm: "Technical power has become disquieting. Demands are increasing. An unruffled decision made at a gathering of members of a Board or by a group of officials is enough to determine the felling of a large forest thousands of miles away, or the killing of the wild fauna of a whole area on the pretext of a campaign against the tsetse fly."[135] The power of business and government made it improbable that they would be held responsible for ruinous actions, while their size made it unlikely that individuals within them could be held accountable.

A more capacious concept of conservation was needed to counter the growing power of massive organizations. "The time is over when the focus of conservation ideas can be directed towards merely making regulations or establishing nature reserves and national parks to safeguard biotopes and species for aesthetic or scientific purposes only," stated the preamble to the IUPN's constitution. "Protection of Nature may be defined as the preservation of the entire world biotic community."[136] The goal, added Fraser Darling of the United Kingdom, was to "appeal to public opinion while there was still time to check the destructive economic methods which were driving our planet to an inevitable catastrophe."[137]

With the world so recently made smaller by two world wars, an international depression, and new technologies, the interconnectedness of nature, the environment, and the planet was easier than ever to imagine. Ironically, the complex bureaucratic systems that evolved to oversee both massive corporations and an ever-expanding government also made the myriad ways that they were damaging a complex, interconnected earth system more readily grasped. Minds conditioned to the familiar flow charts mapping extensive bureaucratic networks did not have to struggle to visualize the webs of life that were central to ecology.

Thus, while UNSCCUR's official aim was to promote technology and the "wise use" of resources, UNESCO sought to convey to participants and the public a vision that challenged the traditional progressive notion of conservation as the efficient use of natural resources for corporate capitalism. The UNESCO conference questioned the underlying assumptions of UNSCCUR and urged a radically new relationship between humans and the planet. As Belgium's Jean-Paul Harroy, Secretary General of the cosponsoring IUPN characterized it, the conference included men and women from five continents "whose parity of interests brought them together to synchronize their love of Nature, their uneasiness about the abuses of modern economy, and also their courageous hope for the future."[138]

The International Technical Conference on the Protection of Nature

Participants from some 32 nations attended UNESCO's International Technical Conference on the Protection of Nature at Lake Success. This was a smaller group that gathered for eight days during UNSCCUR's three-week meeting to discuss 100 papers in 11 sessions. Unlike UNSCCUR, where nearly all of the participants were men, 10 percent of ITCPN's attendees were women.[139] Although held concurrently, ITCPN meetings were scheduled to begin each day after the UNSCCUR proceedings ended in order to attract as many participants from that conference as possible. Ecology, education, and research proposals dominated the ITCPN agenda.[140] Conservationist thought was not hermetically sealed from the new environmental ideas, but at ITCPN the latter predominated. The fact that the Soviet Union exploded its first atomic bomb on August 29, while the conferences were in session, surely added to the sense of urgency.

UNESCO's ITCPN conference had an overarching goal aimed at accomplishing Einstein's plea for a "new mode of thinking." John P. Shea of the US Department of Agriculture's Soil Conservation Service argued, "People are creatures of custom rather than reason" and spoke of the need to use the best thinking of social scientists and psychologists to instill ecological habits of thought.[141] Fairfield Osborn delivered an opening address at the ITCPN that emphasized ecology. He pushed attendees to abandon older, narrower concepts of nature, to instead view it as "the sum total of conditions and principles which influence, indeed govern, the existence of all living things—man included." "Above all," he implored, "we must hope that the final half of this century may witness a reawakening in the minds of people of the inestimable values that nature is capable of providing for us."[142]

Endangered flora and fauna received considerable attention at the ITCPN. The UK's Harry Lillie lamented that whalers, having decimated the population of blue whales in the Antarctic, were turning their attention to the already protected humpback whale in order to fill their quotas.[143] Conference experts constructed lists—understood to be woefully incomplete—of the world's most threatened birds, mammals, and plants to urge their protection. Among the greatest threats to flora and fauna cited were "intensive harvesting to meet pressing economic demands" and "fuel oil refuse discharged on the water, pollution of rivers by factories, etc."[144]

Plans by the United States to implement TVA-style developments throughout the Global South also drew concern at the ITCPN. "Because the Tennessee Valley Authority, of and in Tennessee Valley, succeeded in some ways, do we have to run around jamming in Tennessee Valley Authorities everywhere in the world?" asked Dartmouth naturalist Douglas Wade.[145] Experts lamented that a lack of ecological data gathering meant that no clear picture of the environmental impact of such massive projects was available. But there was evidence of considerable harm. They recommended that an independent board of review be established to assess the ecological impact of plans for such projects and modify them to protect the environment. In order to protect other nations, they urged "that the U.S.A. refrain from 'selling' its plans to other places before the operations of this Board of Review have been experimented with and perfected."[146]

William Vogt, who as the chief of the conservation section of the Pan American Union had traveled in 10 Latin American countries and studied others, earlier warned that only those who worked with abstract science and economic theories could propose massive dam projects as the solution for what ailed the Global South. The underlying issue, as Vogt and others saw it, was that such plans were generated from habits of economic thinking that could no longer be accommodated. "Nineteenth-century man, with his small, rural population and vast store of untapped natural resources, built a neuro-linguistic and neuro-semantic barrier between himself and the process level of his physical environment," Vogt reasoned. "Elementalistic, imprisoned by 'allness,' unconscious of functional relationships, he pinned the label 'development' on the destruction of five continents, built his notion of 'expanding economy' on unrecognized, high-order abstractions, sought for all the world a 'high' standard of living unrelated to the soil, waters, forests, and grasslands that make it possible, and arrived at inferential short-circuits that in the twentieth century are profoundly distorting both national and international policy." Rather than the United States forcing TVA-styled developments on other countries, what was needed, Vogt stressed, was an embrace of environmentalism: "Emphasis must be on cooperation with nature, not on trying to force nature into a strait-jacket, and reorganization of use of the land, not on trying to ignore the land and, hundreds of miles away from the seat of trouble, trying to cope with the end results." Rather than the "development" of river resources, Vogt concluded, the goal should be "restoration" of watersheds.[147]

Not the Traditional American Way

Constructing plans for further educating the public about these issues, using every means and medium imaginable, was a central mission of UNESCO and the conference. At the same time that the United States and UNSCCUR were working to assure access to resources and development worldwide, UNESCO's ITCPN countered by seeking to spread environmental education as a means for global defense. Vogt chaired sessions on education that went straight to the heart of the budding ideology of environmentalism. "Conservation is a way of life," said Ollie Fink of Friends of the Land, "but it is not the traditional American way."[148] With the postwar American Way defined by corporate capitalism and hyperconsumption, Fink joined other proto-environmentalists seeking an alternative way, what he called "a new culture," and "an ecological conscience." The goal was a new approach to all aspects of living and a deep understanding of the interrelationship of humans with other life forms. As a result, Fink hoped, "the citizen will develop a willingness to act intelligently upon the basis of the best evidence about the natural environment and a sense of social responsibility."[149]

Fink's emphasis on citizens was significant. For many proto-environmentalists, the new paradigm held the promise of liberating and empowering citizens in the face of corporations and their political allies. "A good citizen embraces the principles of democracy," said the supervisor of conservation education for Zanesville, Ohio's public schools. "He will not stand by and see his fellow citizens or his community resources exploited for the selfish gain of a few, *if* such exploitation is to the detriment of the many."[150]

Summing up the conference, Jean-Paul Harroy emphasized that the ITCPN made a bold decision to focus on deliberately altering the discourse and practice of conservation, noting that many speakers stressed that scientists and naturalists who might intervene in nature "must be imbued with the idea that all phenomena is [sic] actually one phenomenon and that an abrupt change in any of the factors in play can only have profound repercussions on the complex whole even if [they have] not been able to anticipate the repercussions in [their] imagination." He continued, "Repeatedly throughout the discussion at the Conference meetings this truth was emphasized and reiterated, whether the disruptive factor in the natural equilibrium was the introduction of an exotic species, the extermination of big game herds, or the unwise use of powerful modern insecticides." The emphasis on ecology and education, he concluded, "gave a new orientation to the idea of Nature Protection."[151]

During the postwar era, then, the threat of cultural apocalypse was joined with intense fears of environmental apocalypse. Life, as it had been known, might now be ending not only figuratively, but literally. The most immediate threat of environmental apocalypse came from the Bomb, but additional hazards were becoming apparent. "More toxic compounds are being discovered daily," said the president of the American Academy of Nutrition, Dr. Granville Night, "and may prove as ruinous to health as an atomic bomb working very slowly."[152] Those who were fearful for the future of the planet turned their gaze toward big business, seen now as the driving force behind cultural, political, and environmental ruin.

Ecologist Aldo Leopold recognized that even if government could be convinced to establish regulations to protect the environment they would be fought by business at every turn: "Industrial landowners and users, especially lumbermen and stockmen, are inclined to wail long and loudly about the extension of government ownership and regulation to land," he wrote. Yet, without government interventions, Leopold recognized, business would not take necessary actions to protect the environment: "(with notable exceptions) they show little disposition to develop the only visible alternative: the voluntary practice of conservation on their own lands."[153] Although government regulation was essential, Leopold worried that it could never be completely effective because it would continually struggle to catch up to rapidly emerging technologies, not yet fully understood, that could be damaging the environment anywhere at any time. "It tends to relegate to government many functions eventually too large, too complex, or too widely dispersed to be performed by government," he said of conservation.[154] Leopold believed something more fundamental that would guide all business actions and be elemental to where humans operated from in every decision and action was needed. Environmentalism emerged in the postwar era in the hope that it might both mediate and moderate the American Way, and thereby offer an alternative to the corporate capitalism that dominated postwar modernity.

The Emerging Land Ethic

Leopold's *A Sand County Almanac,* published posthumously shortly before the conference—a year after its author died fighting a grass fire near his Wisconsin farm—sounded these very themes: "We abuse the land because we regard it as a commodity that belongs to us," he observed. But he sensed a new mindset emerging. "The extension of ethics to...[the] environment is, if I read the evidence correctly, an evolutionary possibility and an ecological necessity."[155] Leopold called the budding environmental ethos the "land ethic," which he explained simply: "A thing is right when it tends to preserve the integrity, stability, and beauty of the biotic community. It is wrong when it tends otherwise."[156] Aldous Huxley reached a similar conclusion: "People have got to understand that the commandment, 'Do unto others as you would that they should do unto you' applies to animals, plants and things as well to people," he stated. "It seems to me that, if we are to have a better policy toward nature, we must also have a better philosophy."[157] Demonstrating a keen sense of cultural and intellectual change, Leopold realized he was only making inchoate ideas legible and providing shape for a process that would happen with or without him. His role—as with those at the ITCPN and other writers—was nudging the process forward: "I have purposely presented the land ethic as a product of social evolution," he said, "because nothing so important as an ethic is ever 'written.' "[158]

A Yale-educated forester who specialized in wildlife management, Leopold had cofounded the Wilderness Society in 1935. Over the course of his career he went from being a progressive, utilitarian conservationist, in the tradition of Gifford Pinchot—managing nature for optimal economic efficiency—to an ecologist who viewed humans as only one part of a complex biotic system that needed all of its parts in order to function healthily.

Leopold viewed environmentalists as part of an oppositional culture that was, at least for the time being, outside the mainstream. During the postwar era when consumers were making up for the deprivations of the Depression and the war, those who agreed with Leopold truly were in the minority. However, the belief that something had to change was in the air. "The case for a land ethic would appear hopeless but for the minority which is in obvious revolt against the 'modern' trends," said Leopold.[159] Over the course of the next two decades, the number of those in revolt, in whatever measure, expanded exponentially.

The land ethic was a significant thread in the fabric of environmentalism, an alternative vision for the United States and the world. Like all ethics, it was an ideal that might be continually strived for but never achieved, a goal to both inform and measure behavior. Leopold's time in nature had conditioned him to be a realist. "I have no illusions about the speed or accuracy with which an ecological conscience can become functional," he said. "It has required nineteen centuries to define decent man-to-man conduct and the process is only half done; it may take as long to evolve a code of decency for man-to-land conduct. In such matters we should not worry too much about anything except the direction in which we travel."[160] However, for many of those who outlived Leopold and witnessed the intensity of postwar industrialization and the growing power of corporate capitalism, it appeared increasingly unlikely that humanity had the luxury of taking centuries to change its conduct.

Critics like Leopold represented an advance guard in believing that there were significant threats to culture, democracy, and the environment from the inflated role of corporate capitalism in American life. In their anxious search for some means to redress its ever-expanding power and influence they developed ideas that—though the term did not come into popular use until some two decades later—became the foundations of "environmentalism." They hoped American culture would increasingly embrace environmental values that supplanted mere economics: "The 'key-log' which must be moved to release the evolutionary process for an ethic is simply this: quit thinking about decent land-use as solely an economic problem," said Leopold; "examine each question in terms of what is ethically and esthetically right, as well as what is economically expedient."[161]

That was the heart of the matter. Not all Americans had blind faith in corporate capitalism. Indeed, some feared that its governing logic did not bode well for the long-term health of the environment—or the culture. When Leopold read a portion of his friend William Vogt's manuscript for *Road to Survival*, he replied: "The only thing you left out is whether the philosophy of industrial culture is not, in its ultimate development, irreconcilable with ecological conservation. I think it is." Given that industrial culture dominated American life and was poised to spread throughout the world, the future looked grim. "Industrialism might theoretically be conservative," Leopold commented to Vogt, "if there were an *ethic* limiting its application to what does not impair (a) permanence and stability of the land [and] (b) beauty of the land. But there is no such ethic, nor likely to be."[162]

How, after all, could environmental ethics compete with corporate ethics, where managerial performance was measured strictly in terms of profits, not environmental health? Thinkers like Leopold and Vogt nevertheless continued to hope that environmentalism might convince corporate leaders that the long-term health of the planet was in the best interest of all, even if it did not register on short-term profit statements. Given corporate capitalism's ubiquitous and unsustainable presence they clung to the hope that it could, somehow, be made compatible with life on the planet. Vogt replied to Leopold: "You are, of course, correct in what you say about industrialism. I don't know how you would define ethic, but I am hopeful that horse sense may some day replace [industrialism] as a limiting factor to preserve the permanence and stability of the land."[163]

Lacking the term environmentalism, but speaking of something significantly more expansive than "conservation," Vogt reached for the phrase "horse sense." When Leopold defined the land ethic in his *Sand County Almanac* three years later he hoped that he was making explicit the horse sense of checking corporate capitalism by placing the environment at the forefront of all decision-making. "That the situation is hopeless," he concluded in his letter to Vogt, "should not prevent us from doing our best."[164]

As an ethos that placed nature at the center of ethics, the emerging land ethic had radical implications. The elimination of humans from the center of the ethical system was as revolutionary as Copernicus's elimination of the earth from the center of the solar system, and no less controversial. "This much is crystal clear," concluded Leopold, "our bigger-and-better society is now like a hypochondriac, so obsessed with its own economic health as to have lost the capacity to remain healthy."[165] Laws of nature governed the solar system; pursuit of profits governed the ethical system.

Daring to question purely instrumental economic thinking was liable to get one branded a communist in this era. Those planning the ITCPN conference recognized the precariousness of their position in the context of corporate capitalism's political, economic, and cultural power. When one organizer wondered aloud whether the conference should make a statement of the overarching problem of economics and the environment—"would [it] not be useful to discuss openly the problem of the almost inevitable antagonism between protective measures and the interests of economy"—the immediate response of his colleagues said it all: "A sentence could be added at the end of the programme of the Unesco-IUPN Conference which would recall this point and stress its importance."[166] One sentence, at the end, so as not to offend. Unlike traditional conservation, with its emphasis on setting aside aesthetically pleasing spaces or using resources more efficiently—things that could be negotiated and, if necessary, accommodated by big business—the emerging ideology of environmentalism posed a direct threat to the dominant ideology of corporate capitalism.

Truman's hopes for UNSCURR were largely realized, and resources were quickly mobilized. One year later the National City Bank of New York (Citibank) ran a series of magazine advertisements, wooing investors with opportunities in the Global South. One ad, for example, suggested that Francisco Pizarro's conquest of Peru, which had enriched Spain with silver and gold, could now be improved upon. "Today, minerals unknown to the Conquistadores are a source of much greater revenue," the ad promised. "Peru's chief exports to the United States are lead and copper. She has the largest bismuth and vanadium mines in the world, and produces also zinc, tungsten, antimony, cadmium, indium, and other strategic minerals." And on the other side of the ledger: "Peru buys nearly two-thirds of her imports from the United States." Those seeking a piece of the action could contact branches of the National City Bank of New York, spread throughout 19 countries in the Global South.[167] To further the cause, Truman formed a Materials Policy Commission in 1951, headed by the Columbia Broadcasting System chairperson William S. Paley, whose report one year later, "Resources for Freedom: Foundations for Growth and Security," recommended a permanent independent commission. With grants from the Ford Foundation, that group, Resources for the Future, was created in 1952 to advise the government on resource issues.

The dreams of the ITCPN were not as easily attained. Although businesses often supported conservation, many would quarrel with the broader goals of environmentalism. It was clear that the word "conservation" could no longer contain the expanding meaning that some were giving to it after the Second World War. "Let us think of Conservation as a relationship of resources and people that filters and permeates into virtually every part of the fabric of our national life," said Fairfield Osborn in 1950. "It involves processes that are social and ethical as well as material. It bears on the structures of economy and of law. Science and education are its allies. Above all, it demands understanding of the relationship of human beings to natural processes."[168] Not all conservationists would agree. Some remained locked in far more limited, traditional notions of conservation.

For some Americans, though, the postwar reality of atomic bombs, massive corporate power, and unbridled consumption simply was not tenable. It moved with such speed and power that it could not be grasped even as it raced toward cultural and environmental ruin. It was obvious that corporate capitalism was good for producing profits but less obvious that it was good for humans and the environment. Although Aldo Leopold sensed that a momentous change in both consciousness and culture was transpiring, most others had not yet grasped the deeper significance of what was unfolding. As evidenced in the 1949

UNSCCUR and ITCPN conferences, environmentalism as a discourse was emerging. It was the stirring of an ideology provoked by structural changes that would grow to have an enormous influence on the United States and the world. Environmentalism was always about more than the environment. Concerned not only with land, air, and water, it also sought to transform the culture. It emerged as an argument for an alternative—or at least reformed—American Way, one that could be grasped and sustained. It was an ideology that, although heavily freighted with many anxieties of the times, appeared both large and powerful enough to provide a means to move forward, a way to secure not only the planet but also American culture and democracy at a time when it appeared all might be lost.

2

Green Consumption in a Dangerous World

Because Aldo Leopold's focus was on making the emerging ethic accessible, his writing concentrated on ideas, and did little to address ways that the land ethic might be translated into everyday practice. Indeed, given that the ideology was only just emerging, there would have been little to point to in the way of specific actions inspired by the ideas. However, Leopold did note one concrete and practical gesture in the direction of the land ethic, and that was organic farming, a fringe movement just taking hold in the 1940s. Noting that the "food-value" of farm crops should not be measured only in tonnage since growing evidence indicated crops from naturally fertile soil had higher "food-value" than those from depleted soils artificially fertilized, Leopold suggested that the "outsiders" in the organic movement might be onto something. "The discontent that labels itself 'organic farming,' while bearing some of the earmarks of a cult, is nevertheless biotic in its direction," he argued, "particularly in its insistence on the importance of soil flora and fauna."[1] Of course, what was a "cult" during Leopold's time would eventually catch on and, joined with other forms of green consumption, become for many citizens their most powerful tie to, and expression of, environmentalism.

By the time the war ended in 1945, the local food economies that for centuries had provided sustenance and a way of life were eroding, giving way to national food corporations and a way of business. Much as ever-larger corporations dominated manufacturing in the cities during the war, farming in the countryside grew in scale and was concentrated among a dwindling number of ever-larger producers. "Agribusiness," characterized by large-scale commercial farms often operated by corporations, increasingly subsumed agriculture. The total number of farms in the United States peaked at 6.8 million in 1935; by 1954 that number was already down to 4.8 million. In 1935 the average farm size was 155 acres; by 1954 it had expanded to 242 acres. Exacerbating a trend toward corporate industrial farms that began in the 1920s, New Deal agricultural programs and tax codes privileged large, corporate farmers, pushing many tenant farmers to abandon the countryside and small farmers to sell to larger neighboring farms.[2] Farm-state senators and representatives, under the sway of pro-agribusiness lobbying from the powerful Farm Bureau Federation, made a deal to vote for controls on nonagricultural prices and wages sought by President Franklin Roosevelt in exchange for additional legislation and subsidies that favored large commercial farmers.[3] Agricultural policy was no longer the domain of either political party but was instead determined by industry.[4] Meanwhile, some feared that corporate agribusiness was threatening the environment and making food unhealthy.

Organics

Organic agriculture was at the heart of an alternative, environmental vision for postwar America. Organics were embraced by some as a means to salvage traditional family farms with a saner, noncorporate method of production, while at the same time providing noncorporate food for consumption. Aldo Leopold's thinking on organic agriculture was influenced by the first American book devoted to the practice, J. I. Rodale's *Pay Dirt: Farming and Gardening with Composts*, published in 1945, three years after Rodale started a journal called *Organic Farming and Gardening*.[5] An advertisement for *Pay Dirt* proclaimed, "Next to the Atom Bomb, nothing else in the world is so serious as Man's ravishment of the earth that sustains him and keeps him from starvation."[6] Rodale popularized the ideas of British organic pioneers, especially Sir Albert Howard, whose groundbreaking book on organics, *An Agricultural Testament*, appeared in 1940. Although born in New York City and educated as an accountant, after reading Howard's book Rodale spent the rest of his life experimenting with organic methods on his farm near Emmaus, Pennsylvania.[7] Howard wrote an introduction to *Pay Dirt* and served as associate editor and a regular contributor to *Organic Farming and Gardening* journal.[8] Organic farming existed prior to Howard and Rodale, but their works popularized and systematized a nineteenth century practice that was largely displaced by industrial agriculture.[9]

Industrial-style agriculture was a system based on the mid-nineteenth-century research of German chemist Justus von Liebig, who burned plants and, analyzing the ash, found nitrogen, phosphorous, and potassium (NPK); he reasoned that what was needed to grow crops was the correct N, P, and K balance. Thus, chemical agriculture was born.[10] British farmer and tinkerer John Bennet Lawes found that animal bones treated with sulfuric acid produced superphosphate that could be utilized by plants. He patented the product in 1842, and by the 1850s it was selling in the United States. After the Civil War potassium cheap enough to use for fertilizer was available either from South Carolina and European mines or from potash produced from wood ashes. The biggest obstacle in chemical agriculture was nitrogen. Nitrogen is produced naturally in small amounts by microbial action in soils, where it is taken up by plants to fuel their growth. In the nineteenth century, farmers used nitrogen-rich manure and guano to help replenish soils. Industrial production was finally achieved when German chemist Fritz Haber developed a process to synthesize ammonia from hydrogen and atmospheric nitrogen in 1909, and industrialist Carl Bosch perfected a system to carry it out on a mass scale in 1913. Germany used the method to produce munitions during the First World War. Following the war the process was converted to commercial production, and large quantities of nitrogen-rich anhydrous ammonia were soon made available to agribusiness as a cheap and abundant base for nitrogen fertilizers.[11]

In the United States, the New Deal's Tennessee Valley Authority created the National Fertilizer Development Center at Muscle Shoals, Alabama. After producing ammonium nitrate for munitions during World War II, it began selling it to farmers for fertilizer in 1943. Taxpayer-funded TVA research later developed new forms of fertilizer, then provided its research to private corporations.[12] The teaming of synthetic chemicals with hybrid seeds for hardier plants and higher yields, along with the mechanization of gas-powered tractors, combines, and other agricultural machinery allowed industrial agriculture to take over. As Rodale characterized it: "Farming has been too much reduced to a chemical formula by unimaginative, doctrinaire men."[13] The government subsidized the shift to corporate agribusiness. "If the farmer uses...a strong chemical fertilizer, he secures a [government] payment," Rodale protested. "But if he spreads organic compost he doesn't get a nickel for it."[14]

The industrialization of agriculture led to gains in productivity, often called the "green revolution," but some critics feared its social and environmental costs from the start. Rodale and others questioned the "NPK mentality" that embraced only what science and industry could quantify while denying the possible value of anything else.[15] For them it was a disturbing example of the level of postwar arrogance displayed by corporations and the American government, which would presume to alter the chemical makeup of the environment—and the human body. They denounced its alleged negative impacts on the environment and health but also, as Aldo Leopold noted, believed foods grown by the method lacked essential micronutrients necessary for optimal nutrition. "We cannot go on forever treating the soil as a chemical laboratory and expect to turn out *natural* food. What we are getting is more and more *chemical* food," Rodale emphasized.[16] "Artificial manures," added Howard, "lead to artificial nutrition, artificial animals and finally, to artificial men and women."[17]

Industrial nitrogen was altering the chemistry of the planet and its life, to a greater extent than even Howard imagined. The quantity of synthetic nitrogen fertilizers applied to crops often exceeded the amount that could be absorbed by the soil and used by the plants. In 1940 chemical fertilizers were applied at a rate of about seven pounds per acre. By 1950, the amount doubled to 14 pounds, before soaring to 70 pounds in 1970. Runoffs of excess nitrogen from fertilizer—animal feedlots are another source—accumulate in waterways causing blooms of algae that choke the oxygen from the water, killing fish and other aquatic life. Algae blooms can also produce neurotoxin acids that are harmful to marine life and birds, and a health risk for humans who drink or are exposed to the water, or eat tainted fish and shellfish. In addition, high levels of nitrates in drinking water can choke off the oxygen supply in the blood of infant humans and other mammals, causing brain damage and death. Finally, the excess nitrogen released into the atmosphere from pesticides and burning fossil fuels contributes to smog, ozone depletion, global warming, and acid rain.[18]

Not all of these chemicals were being used to grow food. More and more crops were being grown for the needs of industry, destroying diverse local food economies in the process. Rodale criticized this alarming trend, called chemurgy, as an "away from the land movement... extending large-scale monocultural practices to supply industry with agricultural materials, and the many-thousand acre farms for single-crop items like wheat, corn, and cotton." What some saw as an agricultural miracle Rodale called "vicious land-mining practices," warning that it threatened human survival. Like other proto-environmentalists, Rodale urged his readers to adopt an ecological perspective so that the country might right itself before it was too late.[19]

It was not only food that was in danger but also the environment and a way of life. "This collectivized plantation kind of commercial farming ends in disaster to the land," Rodale emphasized in Cold War terms that made the authoritarianism of Soviet collectives synonymous with that of corporate capitalism. "Our destruction of forests, creation of dust-bowls, ruining areas larger than many entire countries through land-exhaustion and erosion, must stop. This assembly-line, machine-run agriculture, depopulating rural areas or making them insufferably lonely, is very much a trend in some parts of the country," he observed, before posing the query: "Do we want its 'deserted villages'?" Between 1940 and 1970 more than three million farms vanished from the American landscape, and 30 million people left their rural homes for urban areas.[20] Some feared that managers of large corporations would make decisions about the land based on short-term profits rather than the long-term sustainability sought by family farmers who intended to pass their farms to their children.[21]

Nevertheless, during the postwar era many Americans accepted the corporate discourse that large-scale, system-centered, complex technologies represented progress and were superior to small-scale, human-centered, simple technologies. For environmental critics, though, it meant increasing fragmentation, with scientists, business leaders, and politicians all so focused on solving individual technical problems that they ignored the larger implications of their work. No longer able to view the big picture, "The experts, as their studies become concentrated on smaller and smaller fragments, soon find themselves wasting their lives in learning more and more about less and less," Howard complained in his introduction to *Pay Dirt*. The cool and detached logic of massive corporate and government systems was not sympathetic to the nuanced needs of citizens and the environment. "The specialized approach has to be integrated with a universal outlook," warned architectural historian Siegfried Giedion in 1948. "It is time that we become human again and let the human scale rule over all our ventures."[22] The solution was a more holistic, ecological, environmental embrace found in the intimate logic and scale of organics. "The remedy," said Howard, "is to look at the whole field covered by crop production, animal husbandry, food, nutrition, and health as one related subject and then to realize the great principle that the birthright of every crop, every animal, and every human being is health."[23]

Rodale capitalized on the shortage of many early fertilizers and lead arsenate pesticides during the war to market his magazine. The cover of the third issue, in July 1942, included the statement: "Due to the need of certain chemicals in war production the Government is gradually forbidding their use in fertilizers.... We can show you how to be independent of the 'artificials' and how you can use material on your farm which you are now allowing to go to waste."[24] Undoubtedly, many wartime "Victory Gardens" were organic.

At the same time that writers like Fairfield Osborn, William Vogt, and Aldo Leopold were popularizing an environmental ideology, citizens were putting the principles into practice through their actions as consumers. Rodale's *Pay Dirt* sold some 50,000 copies. By 1945 *Organic Farming and Gardening* had about 30,000 subscribers, and only three years later it reached 100,000 readers.[25] By 1970 *Organic Gardening and Farming* had swelled to one-half-million subscribers.[26] A solid link between the health of the environment and the health of humans had been established. The bible of sixties-era alternative consumption, *The Whole Earth Catalog*, later called Rodale's *Organic Gardening and Farming* magazine the most "subversive" publication in America.[27]

DDT and 2,4-D

Rodale was among those who voiced early warnings about the dangers of DDT. Readers of *Pay Dirt* learned that doctors and the US Public Health Service had found that DDT killed animals and declared it a "health hazard." Citing a 1944 article in *Science News Letter* about synthetic insecticides, he stated: "They may at the same time destroy both useful and harmful agricultural insects. They may rid your dog of fleas but insidiously, and perhaps fatally, damage his liver or paralyze him through nerve damage. They will rid your house of mosquitoes, flies and vermin, but the price may turn out to be high in human health and life."[28]

The chief of the USDA's Entomology Bureau, Dr. P. N. Annand, testified to Congress in 1947 that DDT could be harmful to humans, animals, and the environment. In an act that chemist and organics enthusiast Leonard Wickenden termed a "courageous declaration" for departing from the USDA's usual obedience to agribusiness, Annand warned that DDT could poison the soil and sometimes had the unintended consequence of increasing the number of pests relatively immune to DDT because it killed the predators that normally kept them in check. Cows feeding on crops sprayed with DDT produced meat, milk, and butter that contained the chemical. The milk and butter were of particular concern, he cautioned, because the chemical concentrated in milk. Wickenden lamented the fact that Annand's "voice and those of a few others [were] drowned out by the chorus of approval from other experts of the U.S.D.A." who could be counted on to support corporate interests.[29]

When Congress, in consultation with manufacturers, passed the Federal Insecticide, Fungicide, and Rodenticide Act in 1947, which required companies to register farm chemicals with the Department of Agriculture, it was aimed more at legitimizing and defending chemical agribusiness than protecting citizens and the environment. Even if the Secretary of Agriculture believed that a chemical did not meet the requirements of the act, the law required the secretary nevertheless register the chemical if the manufacturer demanded it. As the general counsel for the Grocery Manufacturers of America summed it up, "It is an economic law to aid the farmer rather than a health law to protect the consumer."[30]

New synthetic herbicides were another source of anxiety in the postwar period. During the war over 1,100 compounds were tested by the Chemical Warfare Service for their ability to kill plants. The idea of using them to wipe out enemy food supplies through biological warfare was first conceived in a 1941 plan by University of Chicago botanist Ezra J. Kraus. The global conflagration ended before "field trials in an active theatre" could be conducted, but soon after the war companies sold the chemical compounds domestically at lower doses to destroy unwanted plants. One of the first to be widely applied, beginning in 1945, was a broadleaf herbicide called 2,4-D (2,4-dichlorophenoxyacetic acid), marketed under such names as "Weedone" and "Dandy Kill."[31] *Audubon* magazine warned in 1946 that the herbicide, being used to control unwanted plants in Florida waterways, would also kill desired plants and upset plant ecology. Further, as plants decayed, they "may be expected to release chemicals that might well have a direct poisoning effect on some of the animal life."[32] "We look at our fields and see weeds flourishing," said Wickenden, speaking of 2,4-D in his 1949 book *Make Friends With Your Land: A Chemist Looks at Organiculture*, "and because cultivation means hard labor we smother them with a drug that destroys them, with no thought at all as to what that drug will do to the health of our soil."[33] The main ingredient in Agent Orange defoliant that the United States later dumped in massive quantities on Vietnam to wipe out ground cover and many of the nation's crops was 2,4-D, finally fulfilling the purpose for which the military had originally developed it.

The Ecology of Eating

Fairfield Osborn emphasized the growing environmental significance of organic agriculture in a 1948 speech at the Inter-American Conference on Conservation of Renewable Natural Resources in Denver, a regional meeting of 20 nations in preparation for the United Nations Scientific Conference on the Conservation and Utilization of Resources (UNSCCUR): "As we are well aware, the processes of natural production follow a fixed cycle whereby dying organisms, whether plant or animal, return to the earth, thus supplying the organic base upon which new life is created," he stated. Osborn then warned, "In effect we are hacking at the organic circle that is life itself. In order to offset this drain that we are placing upon the land's productivity, we manufacture chemical fertilizers which are widely accepted as substitutes for the organic materials that have been removed from the land. Herein lies a major illusion for it must now be recognized that these chemical fertilizers cannot by their very nature be considered as such substitutes. They are no more than supplements that restore to the land only *some* of the ingredients of which it has been depleted." As an alternative, Osborn advocated new methods for returning organic waste back to the land as fertilizer and urged his audience to stop viewing themselves as separate from nature. "The human race cannot save itself from this present peril unless it realizes that it is involved in it," he concluded grimly.[34]

Osborn, Leopold, Rodale, and other organics enthusiasts were speaking to an issue that transcended agriculture. In their view life itself was becoming artificial, divorced from the means of production, and manufactured by big business with the aid of government in a process that was threatening to spin out of control. Grounding oneself in the earth might not only save the planet and the food supply, it might also rescue the culture that was, as Osborn put it, "blindly marching along a road which ultimately leads only to disaster."[35] As a segment of environmentalism, organics sought an alternative postwar modernity—one that was not so much antimodern as it was differently modern.

In addition to industrial agriculture, there was also concern about the "unnatural" treatment of farm animals. Rodale criticized the growing trend of raising chickens and producing eggs as "Big Business." He described the living conditions of chickens in which thousands of birds were packed together in "factories" so tightly that they began pecking one another, becoming "cannibals." The sight of blood only made the chickens peck more, so whole flocks of chickens were outfitted with spectacles that either blocked them from seeing or had lenses tinted red so that they could not distinguish the sight of blood. "The average commercial flock is penned up indoors all year round and never gets the feel of grass or earth," much less sunlight, he noted, calling such chickens "artificial poultry." Consumers had already been trained to think of eggs from free-range chickens, whose diets included grass that produced yolks with a darker color, as inferior to the nutritionally poorer eggs of commercial flocks with pale yolks. These flocks were trapped indoors and fed a low-quality feed designed to get the hens to lay eggs as quickly as possible. "It is rather ironic that the public by its own fickle whim encourages practices which give it foods of dubious nourishing qualities," Rodale observed. Of course, it was not just the public's whim. With the addition of hormones, producers discovered they could reduce the usual 26-hour pace of egg production to 17 hours, resulting in more eggs and greater profits.[36]

The practice of injecting a synthetic estrogen called *diethylstilbestrol* (DES) into the necks of chickens, especially old roosters, to tenderize their meat weeks before slaughter was also exposed by Rodale. The drug, an endocrine disruptor, was first synthesized by Sir Charles Dodds in 1938 and became popular with the poultry industry in the early 1940s when Fred W. Lorenz, University of California, Davis professor of poultry husbandry, discovered that subcutaneously injecting large amounts of the drug in male chickens gave them female characteristics and made their meat far more succulent. But from the start laboratory rodent studies in 1938 showed increased incidences of cancer in mammals injected with DES.[37] Rodale warned that if any portion of the pellet had not been fully absorbed by the chicken by the time it was eaten the diner would become sick, and he argued that such chickens should carry a warning label at the market.[38]

Corporate-focused science geared toward expedience and ever-greater efficiencies was damaging the land, its produce, farm animals, rural communities, and human health in the process. Farmers received instructions about what quantities of chemicals to apply to their land and farm animals from sales agents representing the chemical companies, or from their proxies, university extension agents espousing research bought and paid for by chemical corporations, or by taxpayers for use by corporations. One way or another nearly all farms were, with the exception of those following the organic gospel, corporate.

A Revolutionary Way of Life

Americans, it appeared, were in danger from their own food—and so was the planet. James Rorty, a poet and journalist, and N. Philip Norman, a nutritionist and physician, took up where Rodale left off with their 1947 book *Tomorrow's Food: The Coming Revolution in Nutrition*. Rorty worked as an advertising writer and was involved in leftist and communist causes during the 1920s. During the Depression and Dust Bowl, his thought began linking capitalism to the exhaustion of the earth's resources. By the late thirties, disillusioned by communist authoritarianism, he was confronting corporate capitalism as an activist in the era's consumer movement. He began collaborating with Norman, leading to articles in *Harper's* and *Commonweal* on chemicals and food and the possibilities that co-ops presented for transforming capitalism and *Tomorrow's Food*.[39]

The organic movement was the beginning of a radical response to postwar American culture that urged an alternative model for living—one that emphasized the total health of the planet. The difficulty of getting such alternative views heard, much less acted upon, given that corporations aided by government aligned against them, pushed dissenting citizens to seek another path. Speaking of organics, Rorty and Norman proclaimed, "It is a revolutionary way of life. It is a critique of our technological civilization."[40] Like Rodale, they noted what they believed were disastrous trends in industrial chemical agriculture and stressed the need for organic agriculture—as well as its more spiritual cousin, Rudolf Steiner's "biodynamic agriculture"—as both a producer and consumer response.[41] "The food problem is not merely nutritional, they emphasized, "but also economic, political, and social."[42]

By 1958, 80 percent of food companies would be classified as oligopolies by the Food Marketing Commission. Rorty and Norman argued that the large corporate food manufacturers and processors that were doing away with local and regional food economies which had long tied cities to their hinterlands were not doing nearly as good a job of feeding the public. After comparing the health of unindustrialized peoples on "natural" diets to that of Americans on "processed" diets—the fact that nearly one-third of army recruits during World War II were deemed "unfit" for active duty featured prominently in their analysis—the authors concluded that American food habits had become "perverted." Though heavily fed, citizens were nevertheless often malnourished.[43]

Through clever marketing, corporations succeeded in convincing much of the public that their nutritionally inferior products were superior to the wholesome unprocessed foods of days past. "Provident Nature has given us foodstuffs that are perfect for man's utilization, but we are not content," Rorty and Norman observed. "We mutilate the original food pattern; refine, polish, and separate it into fractions; hold it in undated cans or packages for indefinite periods; add chemical preservatives; cook it carelessly; and, finally, add vitamins and minerals to make it fit for human consumption." And why would Americans choose to live so? "Can there be any explanation for this meddling and mutilating of our food," they asked, "except huge profits to processing concerns?"[44]

The shift to enormous national food processors marked the end of most local produce and food manufacturing. With monoculture replacing polyculture, less crop variety and rotation necessitated ever more chemical pesticides, herbicides, and fertilizers. Greater distance between field and table meant more transportation and increased processing, as well as chemical preservatives and stabilizers used to give foods the illusion of freshness. Citing, for example, the trend of national breakfast cereal brands, Rorty and Norman noted, "Establishment of these empires involved the approximate liquidation of our grandmothers' nutritionally sound habit of buying oatmeal—as oatmeal—by the pound or barrel from the grocer, and whole corn grits or wheat from the local water mill."[45]

Grandma's wisdom, based on generations of experience and cultural traditions, was being replaced by corporate boards of directors. As a result, Americans were well-fed in terms of calories, yet poorly nourished and suffering from endemic diseases like obesity, diabetes, and heart disease. To make matters worse, the synthetic chemicals used in growing crops and processing foods were implicated in increasing incidences of cancer. From the field to the dinner table corporations were controlling the food supply—along with the body and the environment.

Vanishing Checks on Corporate Power

Organic food was an act of resistance in a society where the institutions that were formerly counted on to protect citizens and the environment had been compromised by corporate capitalism. Corporate power, challenged during the populist and progressive eras, had emerged triumphant. Like Osborn and Vogt, Rorty and Norman warned that corporate lobbyists had unmatched influence with Congress and government departments. "At present," they warned, "half the 'consumer' representatives who show up at Food and Drug Administration hearings and on similar official and unofficial occasions are phony in the sense that they are directly or indirectly financed by commercial food processors or distributors."[46]

Journalism, which had earlier exposed corporate malfeasance with impassioned muckraking, was also tamed by corporate control. Although Upton Sinclair's *The Jungle*, published in 1906, contributed to the passage of the Pure Food and Drug Act the same year, Rorty revealed that "business took over the crusading magazines one by one through the advertising office. Thus, in subsequent pure-food battles the daily and periodical press, since it now received most of its income from advertising angels, could rarely afford to be on the side of the consumer-angels." As a result, citizens often lacked the necessary information to properly understand issues and demand political change.[47]

Censorship was no longer chiefly the purview of government, but instead occurred more often at the hands of corporations. In his 1946 study of the media, Morris L. Ernst found that they were increasingly being controlled by fewer and fewer companies. "Fourteen individual and chain publishers own a total of forty-eight papers and control about one third of our total daily circulation," Ernst revealed, and there are "a thousand less owners than a few decades ago." Thirty-nine advertisers accounted for half the advertising in the country's newspapers. Further, one-third of all radio stations were owned by companies that also owned newspapers, and four networks dominated the industry. The motion picture industry was virtually controlled by five corporations. "Government is not the sole enemy of freedom," he warned. "Concentrated economic power also acts as a restraint of thought. Monopolies of the mind have calmly entered into our folkways."[48] In 1947 the Commission on Freedom of the Press, a panel of thirteen academics convened five years earlier by *Time* editor Henry Luce, released its report that corroborated Ernst's conclusions. The commission concluded: "We have the impression that the American people...have not yet understood how far the performance of the press falls short of the requirements of a free society in the world today." Journalist Louis M. Lyons stated the report's findings succinctly: "The commission recites the communications revolution that has made the press big business and shows it acting increasingly like a big business and increasingly in alliance with the interests of other big business."[49] Although many Americans were concerned about the shape of the postwar world, mainstream media seldom reflected their anxieties. Instead, such fears were contemplated by smaller audiences through alternative sources and fringe movements like "organics."

Similarly, the scientists who were relied on to protect the public from chemical dangers also appeared compromised by corporate influence. For scientists in academia, more and more of their research, formerly funded by the government, was financed by private industry grants. As reported in *Organic Gardening and Farming*, state agricultural experiment station research budgets received over 10 times more from private industry in 1952 than they had in 1939, and the trend was accelerating. Industry dollars meant university research was increasingly being done to develop and test products for business, at the expense of university time and resources that instead might have been devoted to independent, less commercial alternatives. Whether they worked in private industry or universities, more scientists were working for corporations.[50]

Research that was still being funded by the government nevertheless often proved immensely beneficial for corporate profits. Frozen orange juice, instant mashed potatoes, aerosol cans, and a number of pesticides and herbicides were all developed in USDA laboratories. At the North Carolina station alone, for example, the university was conducting "Field Testing of Insecticides" sponsored by the Taylor Chemical Company; Buckeye Cotton Oil Company had station scientists conducting "Investigations in Animal Nutrition"; and Dow Chemical Company was financing "Weed Control in Cotton." Corporate research grants were often preferred by scientists because they were more generous than government grants, permitting more lavish expenditures by researchers for equipment and staff.[51] Critics wondered whether researchers seeking industry dollars were always capable of objective, independent research when pleasing a corporate sponsor could lead to future funding. Rorty and Norman concluded that it was unlikely that scientists would challenge the "holders of power" because "they know that they would be fired if they did."[52]

Given that watchdog institutions had been undermined, some clung to the hope that changes in education might provide the means for a brighter environmental future. "Perhaps the most serious obstacle impeding the evolution of a land ethic," Aldo Leopold emphasized, "is the fact that our educational and economic system is headed away from, rather than toward, an intense consciousness of the land."[53] He argued that education, so tightly focused on scientific values, must also emphasize ethical values. Fairfield Osborn concurred.[54]

But even education's objectivity and ability to illuminate an alternative path appeared jeopardized by unbridled corporate influence.[55] For example, when major commercial bakers and flour mills discovered that elementary school physiology textbooks contained positive references to whole wheat flour, they took steps to suppress the claim and provided "free" pamphlets, charts, and other materials touting processed white flour. Inadequate funding for schools provided opportunities for big business to infiltrate curriculums. Business leaders who sat on school boards often welcomed the flood of educational materials that, no matter how successful they might have been in teaching basic lessons, never failed to promote corporate interests. "Food advertisers have in recent years come to provide much of the content of the nutritional education furnished by elementary school teachers and home economists," reported Rorty and Norman. "There is scarcely a major food corporation in America that does not attempt to use the school system to promote its products."[56] Thomas J. Sinclair, manager of the school and college service of the Association of Railroads, boasted to a gathering of teachers in 1948 that businesses were spending about a million dollars annually on educational materials.[57] Increasingly, students were learning not from textbooks written by academics but from materials produced by corporations and their trade associations.

In January 1953, Natural Food Associates was organized to create a national organization for the purpose of teaching "the advantages of natural, poison-free food and natural organic farming methods." Toward that end it published a monthly magazine called *Natural Food and Farming Digest* that featured articles on a wide variety of environmental topics including the hazards of chemicals; food additives; diethylstilbestrol; converting a chemical farm to organic; and the advantages of breast feeding over formula. The group's stated objectives were "To teach people the values of natural food grown on fertile soil" and "To tell them how and where to get this food."[58] By 1960 it had chapters in every state and a membership of more than 10,000.[59] There was, in the postwar era, a growing network of alternative production and consumption carried out by citizens opposed to the mainstream of American corporate commercial life and its political sponsors, a budding community of citizens with an alternative vision for America.

Consumer cooperatives were one of the ways that they put that alternative vision into practice. During the postwar era large supermarket chains that first appeared in the 1930s began doing away with the mom-and-pop shops that had long served neighborhoods. Between 1948 and 1958 the number of supermarkets doubled to approximately 2,500, and by 1959 they accounted for 70 percent of grocery sales.[60] Small organic markets and cooperatives would retain the local economy and scale of neighborhood grocery stores, resisting corporate dominance as they promoted an alternative economy.[61] The cooperative movement dated back to at least 1845 in the United States, when mechanics in Boston established a network of cooperative stores and buying clubs called the Working Men's Protective Union throughout New England and New York. By 1900 there were thousands of cooperative stores and factories in the United States.[62]

Although the urban cooperative movement lagged somewhat during the early twentieth century, it enjoyed something of a boom during the 1930s, reflecting a distrust of businesses during the Depression era. By the mid-1940s, some hoped that an international movement of co-ops might even help to assure world peace.[63] In 1945 purchasing co-ops boasted some 1.5 million members in the United States, and a year earlier co-op-owned manufacturing plants produced $65 million worth of goods, a trend that led even Secretary of Commerce Henry A. Wallace to conclude that eventually a "co-operative commonwealth" would constitute a "bloodless revolution."[64]

With cooperatives geared toward altering structures of consumption, and organics intended to change the structures of production, together they promised a potent response aimed at loosening the grip of corporate control. Because they eliminated the expenses of advertising, marketing, and packaging, co-ops could pay their employees above-average wages, pay farmers a higher rate than commercial buyers, and still charge lower prices than commercial markets. In the dream vision or Rorty and Norman, co-ops would not only distribute food but would provide essential objective information from central co-op research labs staffed by scientists and nutritionists paid by the co-ops, not by corporations. Co-op sales, although modest compared to those of commercial businesses, were rising steadily. In addition to providing finished products, they were increasingly doing their own processing. Successful co-op bakeries, for example, produced whole grain breads.[65]

Part of the plan was that co-ops, liberated from national corporations, would help support local food economies. Local and regional produce would mean less transportation cost and vitamin loss, and less danger of tainted food being distributed nationwide. When fresh produce was unavailable, locally frozen fruits and vegetables would supply the markets as much as possible. The wisdom of local seemed so readily apparent that Rorty and Norman speculated that in the future, "perhaps two-thirds of our food will be locally grown and stored in individual or community food lockers." They envisioned cities planned for optimal efficiency of distribution of food and other commodities. Neighborhood warehouses would be supplied from central warehouses, linked by arteries of giant "chutes" that would eliminate the need for a great deal of trucking, freeing up both resources and the streets.[66]

Ultimately, the co-ops that some thinkers dreamed would counter corporate capitalism could not withstand the power of giant national producers and supermarkets, their support from government, and tremendous difficulties in getting financing.[67] As Murray Lincoln, president of the Cooperative League of the United States, summed it up in 1954, "President Eisenhower, under the guise of getting the Government out of business has handed it over only to great corporations—and not to the people."[68]

Alternative (Green) Consumption

Organics, however, continued to grow in popularity and became increasingly significant. Remarkably, Rodale anticipated what would become a major cultural movement. In his first issue of *Organic Farming and Gardening* in 1942 he stated: "One of these fine days the public is going to wake up and will pay for eggs, meats, vegetables, etc., according to how they were produced. A substantial premium will be paid for high quality produces such as those raised by organic methods.... The better-earning class of the public will pay a high price if they can be shown its value, and that they will save on doctor bills."[69] And, he further stated in *Pay Dirt* three years later, "The time is not far off when grocers will offer special grades of organically-grown fruit, guaranteed to be unsprayed, at higher than regular prices and they will have difficulty meeting the demand."[70] Rodale was correct, of course, and such markets soon developed in something of an alternative "green" underground. He was also prescient in recognizing that this consumer environmental movement would be limited to those who could afford to pay.

As damning evidence continued to build, more and more citizens began to exercise their political beliefs through the consumer activism of alternative consumption. Just as colonial Americans had done when shunning British goods in favor of homespun, they sought to punish some producers by avoiding their goods and reward others through their purchases, while simultaneously demonstrating their identification with the cause. Further, their actions echoed earlier consumer activists who, as historian Lawrence Glickman has noted, beginning in the nineteenth century, "stressed the hidden dangers of some products, and the equally hidden virtues of others." Products contained hidden social conditions, including slavery, child labor, and horrendous working and living conditions.[71] But, it was now understood, they also contained hidden environmental conditions, including pollution, resource depletion, and horrendous treatment of animals. More fundamentally, environmentalists recognized that products were embedded with the system of corporate capitalism that created those conditions.

Citizens who embraced environmentalism believed it unlikely that, faced with enormous corporate power and influence, government could be persuaded to protect the well-being of themselves, their children, or the environment. Most held little hope of reforming American capitalism through traditional politics after the government showed its unwillingness to continue to intervene in the economy on the consumer's behalf as it had during the war. In addition, some of them, having emerged from earlier failed experiments in radicalism, did not think it realistic to overthrow the structure of American politics. Instead, unable to gain leverage in the arena of electoral politics, these citizens practiced politics in the marketplace.[72] Environmentalists sought to reform the system or, at least, establish a separate alternative space within the larger system, a green economy where they might take shelter from the storm of corporate capitalism.

Already in 1948, when journalist Mary McGrory asked William Vogt, "What can the individual do to prevent the menace of exhausted natural resources?" he argued that citizens could have the greatest impact through their actions as consumers. "An educated public," Vogt maintained, "could boycott certain goods made from certain ill-spared products [resources]," and purchase other products deemed less environmentally harmful. Significantly, he said nothing about contacting their elected representatives or other traditional political actions. Asked for examples from his own life, Vogt replied that he "drives a small car, which required less steel to build and which consumes less gas than a large one. And he always turns out lights not in use and turns off dripping water faucets."[73] In the postwar era citizens concerned about the environment did what they could to effect change through their actions as consumers.

In a speech at a symposium on natural resources held during the annual meeting of the American Association for the Advancement of Science in 1948, Yale zoologist and limnologist George E. Hutchinson urged producers to develop techniques to preserve natural resources and, when successful, promote that environmental benefit in their advertising as a way to differentiate their products to an increasingly concerned public. "I should like to see a small systematic experiment, on the part of some such concern, in advertising in which it is pointed out that by buying this product one is letting the industrial skill behind the product operate for the benefit of one's children," Hutchinson said in a speech that was later published in *The Scientific Monthly*.[74] Less than a year later an ad for a new innovation, "particleboard," featured a headline that boasted: "Not Guilty! Of Wood Waste Any Longer." It went on to explain that the 50 percent of every tree that was formerly wasted in sawdust, chips, and endings was now being bonded into laminated boards, marking "another step in the conservation of our timberlands."[75]

By 1949, Gandy's Restaurant in Buffalo, New York boasted on its menu, "These vegetables are organically grown on our own farm. No chemical fertilizer, dusting powder or spray materials used in our gardens." Because he could not find enough organic produce, the restaurant's owner purchased a 267-acre farm to grow his own and was making additional plans to produce organic meats.[76]

That same year Frazer Products, headed by automobile manufacturer Joseph W. Frazer (Kaiser-Frazer), sought to expand organic agriculture and gardening when it began marketing organic compost produced from municipal, farm, and industrial waste using a method developed by his son-in-law, biochemist Eric Eweson. The Frazer "digester" broke organic matter down into compost in just five days. It was sold at retailers and by mail order. As reported in the *New York Times*, not only would Frazer Compost "compete with commercial chemical fertilizers," but use of the process also promised to "prevent continued contamination of rivers and waters now made impure by dumping these materials." A single digester at its main plant near York, Pennsylvania could produce 250 million tons of compost each month, and a second plant located at the Chicago stockyards added more.[77] Organic farming, said Frazer, "is of vital importance to plant health, animal health and human health. What can be more important?"[78]

When Vogt read the *New York Times* article he wrote to Frazer: "I was tremendously interested in the story in yesterday's TIMES on your development of a means of converting organic wastes into fertilizer. If you have happened to see my book ROAD TO SURVIVAL you will understand my interest."[79] Frazer replied: "Your book 'Road to Survival,' together with Fairfield Osborn's book, and J. I. Rodale's book 'Pay Dirt,' had a great deal to do with my interest in going into this development."[80] Like others, Frazer recognized the power of corporate capitalism and the inevitable difficulties involved in confronting it. "We realize that in getting its wide spread [sic] acceptance we will probably run into opposition from the chemical cartel in America," he acknowledged, "which has so successfully misled the agricultural schools and agriculture departments in our government, both state and national, into embracing the idea of chemical fertilizer."[81]

In March 1951, Leonard F. Haseltine opened the first organic food market in Los Angeles, "Organic-Ville," and business was so good that three years later he moved into a larger space. A grand-opening circular for that store boasted "luscious strawberries, peaches, plums, figs, nectarines, boysenberries... 8 varieties of fresh crisp lettuce... kale, chard, spinach, dandelion, turnip, peas, sorrel, beets and carrots... foods grown in high mineral content soil without the use of chemical fertilizers and harmful sprays." Eggs sold at Organic-Ville were laid by hens fed balanced feeds and allowed to run free outside.[82] Although it would be decades before the market Rodale saw "waiting to develop" would finally emerge as a mainstream force in American culture, it nevertheless continued to grow incrementally.

Popular nutritionist Adelle Davis helped further the trend. In her 1951 book *Let's Have Healthy Children*, a guide to prenatal and child nutrition, she advocated organic, unprocessed foods like the ones she grew in her own garden.[83] The chemically grown and processed foods from the average supermarket "cannot support the health of parents or children," she warned. Davis nevertheless found some cause for optimism in the organic movement she saw growing in response. "One of the most encouraging trends today," she noted, "is the number of young parents who are buying a small plot of land, enriching the soil, and growing much of their own food."[84]

Writers like Leopold, Rodale, and Osborn revealed that health concerns associated with food tainted by agricultural chemicals and livestock drugs, along with ethical questions concerning the living conditions of farm animals, were becoming closely tied to apocalyptic anxieties about the environment. Food provided the most intimate connection to land and the environment that most citizens experienced on a daily basis. Progressive era objections to food additives like sodium benzoate and formaldehyde were mostly limited to complaints about upset stomachs and minor ailments. And concern about the environment was narrowly focused on the efficient use of natural resources, or conservationists' campaigns to protect those natural landscapes deemed aesthetically pleasing from developments they considered inappropriate, the types of crusades led by groups like the Sierra Club.[85] During the postwar era, however, tainted food and the environment that produced it took on a much greater significance as an apocalyptic metaphor for corporate, and government, malfeasance.

The fact that those drawn to environmentalism tended to be middle class may have been one of the reasons that many on the left, accustomed to thinking of radicalism only as the province of the working class, artists, and intellectuals, were slow to recognize environmentalism's radical potential. The homogeneous, intensely conformist middle class that was constructed during this era by sociologists penning books like *The Organization Man* and *White Collar*, and popular media images like the radio and television series *Father Knows Best*, did not represent the middle class in its entirety. Alternative middle-class consumers and small organic producers refused to listen to corporate and government experts and instead filtered their consumption through their concern for the environment. Shopping at organic markets and growing their own food, all the while seeking to establish an alternative "green" economy, they were anything but conformist.[86]

Environmentalism is Un-American

Because it was perceived as subversive, the organic movement was the subject of growing controversy and the target of increasingly savage attacks designed to marginalize and discredit it. In his 1954 book *Gardening with Nature: How to Grown Your Own Vegetables, Fruits and Flowers by Natural Methods*, a very traditional how-to book, chemist and organic gardener Leonard Wickenden felt it necessary to include a concluding chapter entitled, "Why? Why Does the Advocacy of Organic Methods Stir Such Emotional Opposition?" Wickenden protested that those who dared question the wisdom of chemical agriculture were often deemed "cultists," as they had been a short time earlier in a *Reader's Digest* article entitled "Organic Gardening—Bunk." It accused organic gardeners of being "unscientific" and "emotional" and characterized them as a "cult of misguided people" operating under "pure superstition and myth," and "faddists" who subscribed to "ridiculous dogma." "The Organic Farming Myth," written by R. I. Throckmorton, dean of Kansas State College, put forward the same argument in the farming magazine *Country Gentleman*. Throckmorton protested: "In recent years there has grown up in this country a cult of misguided people who call themselves 'organic farmers' and who would—if they could—destroy the chemical fertilizer industry on which so much of our agriculture depends." He called organics enthusiasts "cultists" who "apparently believe that by a play on words such as 'natural,' 'chemical,' and 'organic,' they have the key to an immortal truth." It was clear that he viewed them as a threat to agribusiness work being done at Kansas State. Throckmorton explained that the "antifertilizer crusade" had grown in popularity to the point that he feared "such misinformation could damage the status of important agricultural research."[87] In another article, written by two leaders of a non-profit organization supported by the food industry called Nutrition Foundation, published in the American Chemical Society's *Journal of Agricultural and Food Chemistry* and condensed in the *New York Times*, the authors called those who warned of the dangers of eating foods from chemically treated soils "food faddists and quacks, successors to old-time medicine men." The viciousness of such attacks, Wickenden explained, stemmed from the pecuniary fears of the numerous stakeholders in the billion-dollar chemical agriculture industry.[88]

Wickenden was surely correct that those who felt financially threatened by organics did all that they could to discredit the movement. But the intensity of the opposition stemmed too from organics and environmentalism striking at the heart of how the United States defined itself during the postwar era. Chemical agriculture was central to the United States's project of liberal capitalism both at home and in numerous development projects abroad. It was a time of unprecedented prosperity for more Americans than ever before. With European and Japanese factories devastated during the war, the United States was producer for the world, reaping enormous windfalls for its good fortune. Calvin Coolidge's 1920s notion that "The business of America is business" appeared elevated to gospel truth during the postwar era. For many Americans—due in no small measure to concerted propaganda efforts by business organizations like the Advertising Council, Chamber of Commerce, and the National Association of Manufacturers—big business had become inseparable from the idea of the United States. During the McCarthy era, questioning the American Way was not what the nation's political leaders had in mind when they boasted of the right to free speech that distinguished it from those nations locked behind the Iron Curtain. Framing critiques in organic and environmental terms, however, provided some measure of protection from being summarily dismissed, if not prosecuted, as a communist. Instead, one could take relative comfort in being called a cultist and a quack.

Big Business attacked environmentalism with the goal of eliminating it, much as it attacked the threat of labor unions. Business feared that the move by some conservationists to expand the movement's traditional concerns to encompass the ecological health of the entire environment posed a threat to corporate interests. Efforts to expand conservation regulations were "fought at every step by private monopolies just as they fought collective bargaining," writer and political activist Judson King observed in 1948. Corporations justified these attacks on conservation laws and agencies with the slogan: "Restoring Confidence in the American System of Free Enterprise." In the climate of the times there appeared to be little hope for substantive political change. King lamented, "only the united political power of organized labor, of organized agriculture, and of organized small businesses backing up the knowledge and activities of men and women of science can save the day for ourselves and our posterity." But he conceded, "the tide is running against us."[89]

None of this is to say that most Americans saw much wrong with the central place of corporations in American life. They provided jobs, after all, and for many citizens in the postwar era who wished to consume like never before, corporations were fulfilling their desires. But shielded by their characteristically optimistic, if not blind, faith in progress and the distance, both physical and bureaucratic, that lay between themselves and what economists term "factors of production"—the natural resources, labor, and capital involved in producing goods or services—Americans were often rendered unable to discern the hidden social, cultural, and environmental costs of consumption until they became a serious threat to the nation's well-being. Early critics, though dubbed alarmist or anti-progress, anxiously searched for some means to redress ever-expanding corporate power and influence, whether through scaling back consumption or altering methods of production.

Apocalyptic Pollution

Sources of doom multiplied in the aftermath of the Bomb. In addition to the food that they ate, other biological necessities, including the air that humans breathed and the water that they drank, mutated from being a secure basis of sustenance to provoking insecurities as a potential cause of death. Little or no regulation over industrial waste, combined with increased industrialization during World War II, proved particularly devastating to the water quality of some regions. During the war the US navy refused to take ships down the Delaware River because it was so laden with chemicals that it corroded the sides of boats and produced a nauseating stench.[90] Although sanitation codes regulated bacterial counts in water, they said nothing about chemical pollution. In California, for example, the sanitary engineer for the Department of Water and Power reported that "wartime industrial wastes dumped into storm drains, streams, and on the ground form a threat to water supplies in certain areas by reason of seepages which may not come to light for years."[91] In 1948 one official termed San Francisco Bay "the world's largest cesspool," and a large stretch of beach in Los Angeles's South Bay area was condemned.[92]

Local pollution laws appeared in some cities, but without national laws polluters could simply relocate to another city where ordinances and enforcement promised to be less intrusive.[93] The Water Pollution Control Act passed into law in 1948 provided federal grants and loans to states to cover a portion of the costs to construct sewage treatment systems, and $5 million to be spent over five years to study methods for controlling industrial waste. The states, however, were left to police violators; the Justice Department could take action against a polluter, but only if the state granted consent. Although a very modest act that placed the onus on states for industrial waste cleanup rather than the companies most responsible for them, it was at least an official acknowledgment of the problem. Even at the time, however, critics derided it as a "sell-out to industry and the states" that put no real pressure on either of them to clean up."[94]

Passing water pollution regulations was somewhat easier than regulating air pollution. Massive quantities of water were needed for industrial production, and it was even argued that it was essential for national defense. To manufacture a ton of synthetic rubber required 320,000 gallons of clean water. The Truman administration worried that it took 250 tons of clean water to make a ton of steel and 18 barrels of water to refine a single barrel of oil. An administrative investigation found that at least 300 industrial or military establishments either could not be built or had to be modified during World War II for lack of adequate clean water supplies. "Industries must learn increasingly to recycle," the report concluded. "Even where water is today plentiful the available supply is often unfit for industrial purposes because of contamination."[95] A severe drought, and water shortages in both the Northeast and Southwest in 1949 and early 1950, furthered anxieties.[96] By 1951, industry was so concerned about adequate clean water for its needs that it pressed Congress to grant large tax cuts to subsidize its building of wastewater treatment facilities. To refuse, warned financial vice president of the Weyerhaeuser Timber Company David Graham, would be to hinder the nation's economic expansion and accompanying increase in standard of living.[97]

Although air pollution had long been a cause of apprehension for the way smoke dirtied cities and affected health, because clean air was not a vital factor of production for most industry, air pollution regulations tended to lag behind. Anxieties toward dirty air began to escalate, however, after reports about possible links between air pollution, cancer, and respiratory infections began circulating in 1948.[98] Air pollution took on apocalyptic overtones after 22 people were killed, and about 50 more died within the next month, when lethal smog set in on the small town of Donora, Pennsylvania in October 1948.[99] The smog was so thick that it reduced visibility to almost zero and left a layer of grime on houses, roads, and sidewalks. Automobiles stalled for lack of oxygen to their carburetors.[100]

The main culprit in the deadly smog that choked Donora was fumes from the smokestack of a local zinc smelter owned by the American Steel and Wire Company (a subsidiary of the United States Steel Corporation), although the company insisted it was not the cause of the disaster. "We are certain," it emphasized, "that the principal offender in the tragedy was the unprecedentedly heavy fog which blanketed the borough for five consecutive days."[101] But Dr. William Rongaus, a physician and member of the Donora Board of Health, would have none of that. "It's murder," he exclaimed, "there's nothing else you can call it. There was smog in Monessen [four miles away], too, but it didn't kill people there the way this did."[102]

A government investigation revealed that a total of 5,910 residents of Donora, or 43 percent of the population, reported being ill from the smog, with nearly all of them gasping for air and complaining of unbearable chest pains. The investigation also found that the first 10 ingredients of the smog were from industrial sources and that Donora had likely experienced a previous deadly smog in April 1945, when the town's death rate doubled. Those deaths had not been attributed to atmospheric pollution.[103] But in the atomic age three years later the new consciousness regarding deadly air made certain that such errors in attribution were not repeated. *Life* magazine ran a pictorial feature on Donora's environmental disaster. "Around the zinc works no grass grows," the article read. "Even up on the hill, where a few farmers try to make a living, vegetables are covered with soot and all the sheep are black. At bedtime, when Donorans put out their lights, they can still see smoke swirling across their ceilings."[104]

Before the Donora incident, "air pollution," J. J. Bloomfield of the Public Health Service told a women's club, "for years was considered to be merely a nuisance."[105] Doctors, in fact, began voicing concerns about pollution's impact on health early in the century, but such fears were routinely discredited by businesses that insisted the public's concerns were merely "folklore," and that smoke was a small nuisance to put up with in return for progress and jobs. In Donora itself there were lawsuits against U.S. Steel dating back to at least 1918, but very few were successful, and even when they were payouts were generally small.[106]

The tragedy of Donora changed the public's perception of the problem of air pollution. Reports and scientific investigations, once hesitant to assert suspicions that evidence pointed to pollution as a cause of disease and death, now had, as historian Scott Dewey has stated, "a smoking gun with air pollution's fingerprints all over it."[107] Federal Security Administrator Oscar R. Ewing observed afterward that Donora "has proven—for the first time—that air pollution in an industrial community can actually cause serious disabling diseases."[108] Such dangers were now publicized nationwide.[109]

Indeed, air pollution had changed, not only in quantity but also in quality. Humans had long polluted the air, but the spread of modern industrialization meant more noxious and toxic chemicals, like the ones that overwhelmed Donora, were now spewing forth from smokestacks. In addition, the internal combustion engine pumped increasing quantities of "photochemical" pollution into the mix—the volatile ozone-producing pollution that made eyes sting, throats burn, and noses grow irritated, and led to respiratory diseases and lung cancer. It also stunted the growth of plants. Modern industry and internal combustion engines also increased levels of carbon dioxide, carbon monoxide, and black carbon that contributed to global climate change. Like the Bomb's radiation, many of air pollution's most lethal elements were invisible.[110]

Controlling the new pollution proved difficult in the face of corporations that believed greater profits could be had by fouling the environment. Already in 1949, at the first of what became annual air pollution symposiums after Donora, Dr. Louis McCabe of the United States Bureau of Mines argued that a main reason campaigns to control pollution failed was "because industry believed that air-pollution control costs too much," and businesses took elaborate steps to delay or avoid any reforms. As McCabe explained, "There were 'cooperative' programs with the dual objectives of delay and defeat. Industry engineers were assigned to write diverting papers on the minutiae of the problem, and trade journals editorialized on the unreasonableness of 'do-gooders'" pushing for stricter environmental regulations.[111] *Business Week* concurred: "Undesirable gases and fly ash can be taken out of smokestack fumes," it admitted. "But cleaning up smoke is an expensive job." Even though the byproducts reclaimed in the cleanup were sometimes valuable and in the long run would make the installation of smokestack cleaners profitable, businesses more concerned about quarterly profit statements proved reluctant to make the initial investment.[112] Confronted with demands to change their polluting ways, the favorite stalling tactic of business and its allies in government became predictable, a call for additional, extensive research before any real action would even be considered.

The Donora episode was followed by a series of other smog incidents and tragedies that heightened public anxieties about the air they breathed. *Newsweek* featured a piece in May 1949 about a report in the *Journal of Occupational Medicine* that found that "Each year in Chicago, at least 700 deaths from cancer of the lungs, pneumonia, and pulmonary tuberculosis can be traced to the respiratory hazard of living in the city's dirtier districts."[113] In November 1950 smog descended on Detroit's West Side just before dawn; it was so intense that it awakened many residents with burning eyes and throats.[114]

In Los Angeles, smog became a problem when industry began expanding exponentially during World War II and a rapidly increasing population meant more automobiles on the roads. By 1944 it was causing damage to crops.[115] When the district attorney tried to prosecute polluting industries he ran up against an industry-friendly state law declaring that if manufacturing was permitted in a zoning ordinance a manufacturer's pollution could not be declared a nuisance and be subject to a lawsuit unless it could be proved that it resulted from "unnecessary" operations. The district attorney responded by trying to have the law changed by the state legislature in 1945, but his amendment was killed in a Senate committee after intense pressure from the Los Angeles Chamber of Commerce and the Merchants and Manufacturers Association, which insisted that voluntary policing by industry would be best and that officials should "leave industry alone to work out its own problems."[116] It soon became evident that voluntary policing was not effective. Although some state and local regulations appeared as early as 1947, such rules were typically watered down through the influence of powerful local business interests and chambers of commerce.[117] Late in 1949 persistent smog attacked the city for two weeks straight. After Donora, pollution was no longer seen as a mere "nuisance." Pasadena residents protested to the county board of supervisors, demanding they shut down all industries contributing to the problem.[118]

Fearing that the citizens' growing unease with chemicals might lead to increased pressure for regulations, the chemical industry's leading trade association moved to sway the public with propaganda assaults and control the government with increased lobbying. In its public relations campaign, the Manufacturing Chemists' Association (MCA) insisted that the atmosphere should be thought of as just another natural resource to be used by industry. Further, pollution was not a national issue that posed a health threat, but instead a local "nuisance" that should be dealt with locally.[119] The industry moved to place representatives on government committees, and enter into joint research pollution studies with government agencies under the condition that the government could not publish any interpretation of the results—permitting industry to better shape public opinion.[120] "Industry and the public health services," said a representative from chemical conglomerate American Cyanamid, "should get together to prevent harmful legislation."[121]

Without strict federal legislation, companies could respond to pollution ordinances and lawsuits by simply relocating, and a community would lose its needed jobs. Some believed that was the case in Donora. The Public Health Service's 173-page report on the disaster did not point to any single cause.[122] Critics assailed it for giving the impression that Donorans heating their homes shared equal responsibility for the tragedy with industries spewing toxic pollution. But most residents of Donora did not complain. As *Life* magazine reported, "Donorans were cautious about getting tough with the industry that provided their living."[123] Dr. Rongaus recalled after the disaster, "The odd thing was that two days later some of the people whom I had treated while they were gasping for breath denied they had been ill." It was a devil's bargain that working people had long been conditioned to making: trade your health and life in the long term to provide for your family in the short term. Said one resident, "That smoke coming out of those stacks is bread and butter on our tables."[124]

In the aftermath, Donora refused to pass any ordinances to control smoke and pollution. Even so, in 1957 U.S. Steel closed the zinc plant, and in 1960 it shut down more of its operations in Donora, laying off 1,700 of its 4,400 workers in the town. Although the company reported it had been planning to shut down the antiquated plants with open blast furnaces in favor of more efficient designs elsewhere for some time, many Donorans believed it was because U.S. Steel was angry about the lawsuits.[125] The push for environmental regulations was complicated by communities and governments that worried that unilaterally imposing environmental laws would leave them vulnerable to the whims of corporations that might relocate to a place where they were freer to pollute. By stifling robust federal pollution laws, corporations could continue to play communities against one another.

Who Is Driving the Machine in the Garden?

During the postwar era, then, the apocalyptic environmental anxieties unleashed by the Bomb, World War II, and the Cold War, as well as growing concerns about corporations, began coalescing in fears associated with the basic ingredients of human life. Considerable thought was devoted not only to understanding the enormous changes in the structures of modern life, but also to figuring out how to best deal with them. Should citizens fight the Bomb as a threat to all of life or, more poetically as Gregory Corso suggested in his poem "Bomb," embrace its potential to make humans cherish existence in a way that they too often failed to do when they took life and the planet for granted?

And what about corporations? For most Americans concerned about the environment the problem was not so much that the machine had entered the garden. Fairfield Osborn was suspicious of true believers, whether "nature worshipers" or "science cultists," and argued: "Dependence on the processes of nature does not, in any sense, exclude science and its vast benefits."[126] Even many cultural critics remained fascinated, if not enamored, with technological progress. Who can forget, after all, the affectionate enthusiasm for the automobile in the form of a 1949 Hudson Hornet found in Jack Kerouac's *On the Road*?[127] For them the concern was not so much with the machine, but rather who was driving. As T. K. Quinn summed it up in his 1953 book *Giant Business: Threat to Democracy*, "The existing corporations enjoy what amount to substantial, indirect subsidies from the government and are able through costly lobbies to bring pressure upon our legislators." After working for General Electric for 24 years, where he rose to the rank of vice president, Quinn was not so naïve or unsophisticated as to suppose that corporate power was gained through some sort of grand conspiracy. In fact, it was all the more frightening because the corporation's quest for ever more power was simply in its blood, and it had managed to transfuse that blood into the lifeblood of the nation. "No question of evil or even damaging intent is involved," Quinn noted. "Each monster-big corporation is proceeding in self-interest to extend its operations and security. Unfortunately, this security is being gained at the expense of all the rest of us."[128] And, others added, at the expense of the environment as well. "We are building a world antipathy to our capitalistic excesses that promise more power for America," Quinn concluded, with startling prescience.[129]

Could government be convinced to implement tougher regulations on big business to protect citizens and the environment? Could democracy survive the further unleashing of corporate power in postwar America? Should citizens, fueling corporate influence and resource depletion with their unprecedented levels of consumption, do as Leopold urged and develop "contempt" for material things and curb their desire to consume? Would it be better to leave postwar modernity behind and seek a premodern existence in the countryside? Or might citizens be better off, as Rodale and Rorty appeared to suggest, continuing to consume in this new era, but consuming differently? As time passed and the challenges posed by the Bomb and big business became increasingly pronounced, such questions loomed ever larger.

An answer was already emerging: environmentalism. "It is becoming more and more evident," wrote Fairfield Osborn in 1952, "that conservation is concerned not only with natural resources but equally with people, their actions and their numbers, as well as with the procedures and activities of government, of education and of industry. In this broad concept conservation is becoming, as it must, an integral function of modern society."[130] Conservationists turned proto-environmentalists were bringing additional people around to recognize that they were an integral part of the natural world, and everything they did in their daily lives impacted the health of their environment and the well-being of all life. And the way that ideology was being carried out by many of its adherents was through their habits as consumers, resulting in the growth of green consumption's appeal as a means for an alternative American Way.

3

Downwinders

Americans' atomic anxieties were kept alive through news reports of continued testing of nuclear weapons in the Pacific's Marshall Islands after the war, the USSR's first successful test of an atomic bomb in 1949, and, between 1951 and 1963, explosions at the Tonopah Bombing and Gunnery Range northwest of Las Vegas where approximately 100 aboveground tests were conducted.[1] During the Cold War era the emerging environmental consciousness was confronted with a relentless stream of potentially apocalyptic threats to stoke its fears. If Americans sensed that the very existence of the world and its inhabitants was more precarious than ever before, that feeling would multiply exponentially as waves of chemicals and nuclear fallout hit home.

On November 1, 1952, on the island of Elugelab at Enewetak atoll in the Pacific Marshall Islands west of Bikini, the United States tested its first prototype of a fusion thermonuclear, or "hydrogen," bomb three months after the Soviet Union had tested its own thermonuclear device. *Newsweek* described the event in an article titled "How to End a World: The Truth about the Bomb," that explained how fusion-style bombs were hundreds of times more powerful than the older fission-style bombs that were dropped on Hiroshima and Nagasaki.[2] It was only later learned that the blast, some 750 times more powerful than the bomb dropped on Hiroshima, was so powerful it eliminated Elugelab and left a crater in the ocean floor one mile in diameter and 175 feet deep. The United States conducted five underwater and 101 above ground atomic bomb tests in the Pacific from 1946 to 1962.[3]

For greater ease and efficiency, beginning in 1951 most testing was moved from the Pacific to the Nevada Test Site, between Las Vegas and Reno, where 119 above ground nuclear tests were conducted during the next seven years.[4] Residents as far away as Utah who were inundated with pinkish clouds of fallout following the tests began referring to themselves as "downwinders." Many of them were descendants of Mormons who settled the area in the 1840s, and they initially cheered the nearby tests. "I never saw a prettier sight," wrote one Utah journalist after observing the first series of blasts in early 1951. "It was like a letter from home or the firm handshake of someone you admire and trust."[5]

Downwinder sentiment began to change after the first aboveground hydrogen bomb test in the United States took place in May 1953. Atomic test shot Harry, later called "Dirty Harry," was exploded at the Nevada test site and soon inundated residents of St. George, Utah, east of the site, with a dose of radiation equal to the amount nuclear workers were permitted in a year. Local radio stations broadcast Atomic Energy Commission (AEC) warnings to residents to stay indoors and keep their windows closed for several hours. A number of people became ill. Thousands of sheep, approximately 25 percent of the herds in southern Utah and Nevada, died, and when ranchers blamed fallout, the AEC autopsied some sheep and declared that the deaths were due to "unprecedented cold weather," not radiation. In 1956, the government successfully fought off a suit filed by the ranchers on the grounds that they had not provided "scientific" evidence to back their claims.[6]

Finally, in 1981, with evidence revealed under the Freedom of Information Act, Judge Sherman Christensen ordered a new trial, charging the government with fraud for withholding evidence from his court in 1956. In that trial, Frank Butrico, a government radiation safety monitor stationed in St. George during the 1953 tests, testified that "instruments were off the scales" after Dirty Harry, but he was instructed to report only that "radiation levels were a little bit above normal but not in the range of being harmful."[7] Government officials merely told area residents not to consume local milk or other dairy products. "But nobody told us kids not to eat our mud pies," Jacqueline Sanders, who was suffering from cancer, later recalled. "We found out they were waiting until the wind was blowing this way instead of toward Los Angeles before they set off a test," added St. George City Director of Utilities Rudger McArthur, "because they knew what was in the cloud."[8]

Fallout

Government denial became considerably more difficult after March 1, 1954, when the United States detonated a hydrogen bomb code-named "Bravo" in the Pacific's Bikini Atoll.[9] The blast was the first test of a true "dry" hydrogen bomb, and it was more than twice as strong as scientists had calculated, some 1,000 times more powerful than the bomb dropped on Hiroshima and so powerful it destroyed the instruments set up to measure the blast. During the next four days American ships evacuated 236 residents and 28 US observers from nearby Marshall Islands who were exposed to radioactive fallout after the explosion.[10]

Nearly all the island residents suffered hair loss and severe radiation burns. Even worse was the fate of the crew of the Japanese fishing boat *Fukuryu Maru*—"Lucky Dragon"—that had been tuna fishing some 85 miles east of Bikini, about 20 miles outside the American restricted area around the "testing grounds."[11] Crew members aboard the boat reported that they were putting out their nets in the early dawn when there was a "sudden brilliant sunrise" that lasted about eight seconds, followed by a shockwave a few minutes later.[12] Ninety minutes later, as they were working to bring in their nets, they were showered with a drizzle of "snow-white ashes" that lasted until noon the next day. They brushed themselves off and kept working, and at the end of the day washed down the boat to clean off the ash. Three days later, though, red blisters appeared on the fishermen's skin that eventually turned black. "We became frightened and headed straight for home," the boat's captain, Isao Tsutsui, reported.[13]

By the time they reached their harbor, crew members were battling nausea, diarrhea, bleeding gums, hair loss, and fever. Tokyo doctors were quick to recognize the signs of radiation poisoning, and Japanese newspapers ran large front page headlines informing readers that the 23 fishermen aboard the *Lucky Dragon* had been sickened by an American atomic test. Two days later the Associated Press ran the story in the United States.[14]

What began as a minor story in the United States became front-page news the next day when food became the focus of environmental peril. It was revealed that Japanese police were attempting to remove some 12,000 pounds of fish from the market that came from the *Lucky Dragon* and bury them before they could be sold to the public. Reports stated that tests indicated the fish were so radioactive that just being within 30 yards of them for eight hours would prove fatal. Police discovered that about 1,000 pounds of the fish had already been sold in markets in Tokyo, Osaka, and elsewhere. Newspapers reported a panic among "Japanese housewives" who were avoiding fish markets and taking back or burying fish they had purchased the day before.[15] In the United States, where fear spread that some of the contaminated fish might find its way to American markets, federal officials in San Francisco used Geiger counters to screen boatloads of fish. In an attempt to calm nervous American consumers the Japanese government inspected 100 tons of frozen fish for export to the United States and stamped it certified "free from radioactivity."[16]

Later in the month the public learned of a further danger from the new H-bomb that soon became a major environmental concern in the United States and throughout the world. The *New York Times* reported that Japanese medical authorities treating the 23 crew members aboard the *Lucky Dragon* were concerned after discovering that "strontium-90" was found in the ash that fell on the fishermen and wide areas of the Pacific Ocean since the substance was considerably more persistent in the environment than other elements of atomic fallout. Because the element had a half-life of over 25 years, half of the level of radioactivity would still remain in the environment after that time. Further, as Dr. Masao Tsuzuki of Tokyo University explained, because strontium-90 has a chemical composition similar to calcium, it might become lodged in the bones and continually expose victims to internal radiation for years to come.[17] The United States Atomic Energy Commission, citing its own manual, "The Effects of Atomic Weapons," that reported the results of radiation experiments on animals, confirmed that strontium-90 does concentrate in the bones "in the rare event of sufficient fission products entering the bloodstream."[18] But, the AEC insisted, the increase in radiation from testing was "far below the levels which could be harmful in any way to human beings, animals, or crops." It called the reports of their condition "exaggerated" and stressed that all 23 fishermen would recover completely "in about a month."[19]

Six months later, the Japanese government announced that Aikichi Kuboyama, the 40-year-old radio operator of the *Lucky Dragon*, had died of radiation poisoning.[20] US officials insisted that rather than radiation poisoning, Kuboyama died of "jaundice" caused by blood transfusions. US Representative Carl Hinshaw of California took the denial a step further and claimed that communist influences in Asia were "magnifying" the death. Dr. Tsuzuki disputed this claim, pointing to an autopsy that revealed some of Kuboyama's internal organs were radioactive.[21] As even some in the United States granted, he would have never needed transfusions had there not been a desperate need to replace his radiation-damaged blood.[22] Kuboyama was termed "the world's first fatality from a hydrogen bomb blast."[23] The story received wide coverage in the United States and set off waves of anti-US protests in Japan.[24] The United States sent his widow $2,700 "as a token of sympathy of the American government and people."[25]

The *Lucky Dragon* incident alerted the world to a frightening new development in an already worrisome nuclear era.[26] As Thomas E. Murray of the AEC admitted, the "fishermen announced to the world the first fateful news about the lurking catastrophe that may possibly lie in wait for us all."[27] The new, more powerful thermonuclear bombs not only disseminated their own radioactive particles into the earth's atmosphere; the fireball of the blast sucked up tiny pulverized particles of the earth saturated with radioactivity that would eventually be delivered back to the ground in the form of radioactive "fallout." Through the media Americans learned that the heaviest particles descended most rapidly in rain, snow, or ash, forming "local" fallout like the kind that hit the *Lucky Dragon*. Lighter particles might ride the wind for thousands of miles, with those under the zone of precipitation of about 100,000 feet coming down in days or weeks, and others blasted further up into the stratosphere that might be held up by air currents for years before finally making their way back down to pollute the earth and its inhabitants.[28]

Unlike earlier fears that centered on the Bomb's deadly blast, fear of fallout permitted no refuge behind hopes that further earth-shattering devastation from nuclear bombs might never be known if war between the superpowers could somehow be avoided. As physicist Ralph Lapp stated, fallout "cannot be felt and possesses all the terror of the unknown. It is something which evokes revulsion and helplessness—like a bubonic plague."[29] Pope Pius XII spent most of his Easter Sunday message in 1954 discussing the environmental hazard of hydrogen bombs, noting that in addition to the previous destructive force of the atomic bomb, the new bomb gave humans the capacity for "polluting in a lasting manner the atmosphere, the land, and also the oceans."[30]

By May 1954, scientists were warning of fallout's threat to ecology and humanity. J. I. Rodale's *Organic Gardening and Farming* reported that University of California researchers found that the soil-plant-animal cycle was in danger after their study of barley, beans, carrots, lettuce, and radishes grown in California showed they had been contaminated with the radioactive isotopes cesium-137, ruthenium-106, cerium-144, yttrium-91, and, especially, strontium-90. The scientists concluded that animals allowed to feed on plants grown in contaminated soils faced a health risk from radioactive strontium.[31] Humans were no exception. Threats to the planet were immediately seen as threats to the food chain, with the potential to devastate the body.

The mysterious and terrifying nature of fallout inspired a boom in science-fiction films between 1948 and 1962 unprecedented for any genre in cinema, with titles like *The Beast from 20,000 Fathoms* (1953), *The Amazing Colossal Man* (1957), and *The Blob* (1958), expressing a range of anxieties centered on science, technology, and the Cold War.[32] The world itself suddenly felt like science fiction. What once appeared fantastical was now part of a surreal reality of melting flesh and mutating rain that constantly threatened the comfort of postwar abundance.

Scientists were embroiled in often heated disagreements over fallout from the beginning, generally divided between those associated with the AEC who defended testing and downplayed fallout's risks in the short term while contending it was harmless, and others outside the AEC who emphasized the danger of exposure to fallout over the long term while accusing the commission of hiding the truth from the public.[33] Geneticist A. H. Sturtevant, of the California Institute of Technology, insisted that fallout not only posed a risk to exposed individuals but also would have transgenerational effects on their descendants. Sturtevant emphasized what would become a widely held concern, that the issue of radiation exposure involved not only the amount of initial exposure but also the cumulative effects of chronic low-dose exposure. The public learned of his warning in a newspaper article that began, "The human race will reap a macabre harvest of 'defective individuals' because of the increase in 'background radiation' caused by only the few atomic and hydrogen bombs that have been exploded to date."[34] AEC Chairman Lewis Strauss denied such charges and insisted that reports of fallout poisoning the atmosphere were "lurid" stories originated by "Soviet propagandists."[35] For the public, the lack of agreement among experts only caused further unease. *Time* magazine captured the mood of uncertainty when it stated, "The truth is that no one knows the entire truth— not even the atomic experts.... The fact is that no one can estimate accurately the long-range effect of raising the earth's level of radioactivity by even a small amount."[36] One thing, however, was certain: growing numbers of citizens did not wish to find out.

Coming to Terms with a "Psychotic Civilization" and Its Dying Planet

All of this was transpiring as the broader debate over the extent of the total impact that humans were having on the earth continued to gain momentum. The sense that corporate capitalism was not sustainable—at least in its present form—was growing. "This is a matter of expanding industry, approaching maximum profitable use of its resource base, and finally overreaching that maximum at a time when (unless we are prepared) it is too late to alter values voluntarily, willingly abandon the dream of higher levels of living, and peacefully adapt our thinking and our ideals to another very different way of life," warned Samuel Ordway in his 1953 book *Resources and the American Dream*.[37] Ordway, who cofounded the Conservation Foundation with Fairfield Osborn and served as its executive vice president, joined the growing list of cultural critics espousing environmentalism as an antidote to the perceived ills of the growthmanship that dominated postwar policy. While others might point the finger of blame for environmental problems at a growing population, Ordway insisted the real culprit was the growing demands that the economy was placing on the environment. If corporate capitalism did not embrace environmental principles voluntarily and begin industrial planning to determine what should best be produced with the earth's limited resources, he feared it would not be long before resource shortages would necessitate some form of totalitarianism.[38] Like others, however, he recognized the extraordinary challenge involved in getting corporations to take action voluntarily.

In the face of that corporate obstinacy, Ordway urged citizens to reconsider the very basis of postwar consumer culture by cutting back on their consumption. "Faith in growth must give way to a truer, less aggressive faith that to prosper we do not need to consume more than the earth produces," he emphasized.

Added to earlier admonitions from proto-environmentalists that citizens should seek to purchase environmentally friendly products, Ordway's insistence that they should also strive to purchase less became another significant component of green consumerism. The key, in Ordway's view, was what would later be popularly termed "sustainability." "We can control our own destiny if we recognize (and face up to) the probabilities now, and gradually limit consumption to foreseeable replacements of supply," he reasoned. That could only occur if an educated public understood its power as consumers and brought tremendous pressure to bear on businesses.[39]

One of the people hoping to provide that type of education was John Storer, whose book *The Web of Life: A First Book of Ecology* was published in 1953. Storer's book, along with Eugene Odum's textbook, *Fundamentals of Ecology*, published the same year, provided more extensive exploration of the popular ecology put forward by thinkers like Osborn, Vogt, Leopold, and organics enthusiasts. "The forces set in motion by every act of man or bird, animal, insect, or bacterium move out to affect the lives of many other creatures," Storer emphasized. "The principles which govern all these interrelationships are called the principles of ecology... and on the functioning of these known principles depends the future of all human lives."[40] Storer, a Harvard graduate who spent 25 years farming before a career in wildlife photography, was president of the Florida Audubon Society.[41] He wrote his book as an antidote to corporate capitalism, to appeal to "everyone who would learn what has largely been forgotten in our machine age—how all living things fit together into a single pattern."[42] At a time when professional ecologists had withdrawn into their professional ranks, works like Storer's filled a void. In its review of the book, Rodale's *Organic Gardening and Farming* called it "one of the finest pictures given" of nature's interrelationship.[43]

The book offered an explicit statement of the correlation between the health of the planet and the fate of the human body, and Storer used the growing fear of contaminated food to make his point. "Bread, vegetables, and meat are merely vehicles for transferring to us the special properties of soil, air, and sunlight gathered and organized by the plants," he emphasized. In a case study of the Pacific salmon to illustrate the principles of ecology, he noted, after addressing the difficulty dams created for salmon attempting to spawn, "One of the greatest hazards to young fish is the pollution of water by poisonous discharges from industrial plants and city sewage."[44] Storer finally concluded: "Scientists have proved that it is possible to use the life-supporting natural resources of the world without destroying them.... The great and deciding test, however, still remains—whether man can coordinate knowledge into understanding and build within his heart the incentives and the wisdom to use the new-found powers wisely, and with responsibility, for the common good." At a time when business and technology seemed to be threatening all of existence, and when for many people modern life felt fractured and chaotic, ecology held the appealing possibility that all might be made harmonious and whole.

Geologist and atomic scientist Harrison Brown sounded a similar theme in his popular *The Challenge of Man's Future* (1954): "The development of atomic and hydrogen bombs makes it appear... that war is the greatest danger that mankind faces during the years ahead. But it is clear," Brown continued, "that... [e]ven without it we are faced with the problems of producing sufficient food, or supplying ourselves with raw materials, and of supplying our machines with energy for the purpose of converting raw materials into finished products. Long-range solution of these problems is imperative if civilization is to survive."[45] Following the deprivations of the Depression and rationing during World War II, and highly publicized severe famines in many parts of the world after the war, it was not difficult for readers to imagine a planet with inadequate resources. Like others, Brown feared for democracy in the context of growing corporate power.[46] He joined economist John Kenneth Galbraith and a growing chorus of thinkers who worried about the future of the country and its citizens unless corrective measures were taken to balance corporate power within the American polity.[47]

But the power of corporations was so ensconced that reining them in appeared farfetched. As Paul Sears, botanist and chair of Yale's conservation program, mused darkly in 1955: "In spite of the recurring abuses of power throughout history, commerce and industry were until the Reformation, in principle at least, subordinate to other cultural forces and restraints.... Today—again in principle—no one seriously questions the social responsibility of those engaged in commerce. Little would be gained if he did!"[48] To question the actions of powerful corporations appeared, if not un-American, simply futile.

Sears delivered his assessment at a symposium on "Man's Role in Changing the Face of the Earth" in Princeton, New Jersey, where he was among 70 international experts selected for their "common interest and curiosity about what man has been doing to and with his habitat." The meeting was organized by the Wenner-Gren Foundation for anthropology, and cosponsored by the National Science Foundation. Wenner-Gren's assistant director, William L. Thomas, Jr., whose idea it was to hold the symposium, cited George Perkins Marsh's 1864 classic *Man and Nature; or Physical Geography as Modified by Human Behavior*, as a source of intellectual inspiration and a model for the meeting. Marsh had recently been rediscovered by readers of Lewis Mumford's *The Brown Decades, 1865–1895*, which included a discussion of *Man and Nature*. "The only serious lack in Marsh's book was his failure to consider the exhaustion of natural resources," Mumford stated, before excusing the omission because even Marsh could not have anticipated the changes wrought by the subsequent industrial boom. The environmental impact of nearly a century of what is sometimes called the "second" industrial revolution, combined with the atomic threat, made the stakes appear much greater; attendees were eager to take up where Marsh left off.[49] As one participant put it: "No one should deny that man's mismanagement might entail atomic doom, but self-extinction might occur in consequence of other products of the contriving brain and the skillful hand of man."[50] The conference set out, then, to determine what some of those apocalyptic possibilities might be.

Participants pointed to the irony that new technologies, the source of so many postwar apocalyptic anxieties, might also be capable of producing new perspectives that would encourage citizens to take action to confront those anxieties. Thomas noted that the growing popularity of air travel was an inspiration for the symposium. "A new scale in time and space has been added to our mental and material equipment," another participant agreed. "Today we can look at the world with a God's-eye view, take in at a glance the infinite variety of environmental patterns spread over the earth, and appreciate their dynamic relationships."[51] Both developments complicated the relationship between technology and the environment, with careless technological developments seen as threatening the planet, while advances in technology paradoxically permitted new perspectives on humans' relationship to the earth. Near the end of the symposium, University of Michigan economist Kenneth Boulding sought to sum up the dichotomy of the pessimistic stance of those concerned with technology's threat to the earth and the Panglossian optimism of those who believed new technologies could continually solve all problems, with two contrasting poems:

> A CONSERVATIONIST'S LAMENT
>
> The world is finite, resources are scarce,
> Things are bad and will be worse.
> Coal is burned and gas exploded,
> Forests cut and soils eroded.
> Wells are dry and air's polluted,
> Dust is blowing, trees uprooted.
> Oil is going, ores depleted,
> Drains receive what is excreted.
> Land is sinking, seas are rising,
> Man is far too enterprising.
> Fire will rage with man to fan it,
> Soon we'll have a plundered planet.
> People breed like fertile rabbits,
> People have disgusting habits.
> *Moral:*
> The evolutionary plan
> Went astray by evolving Man.

THE TECHNOLOGIST'S REPLY

Man's potential is quite terrific,
You can't go back to the Neolithic.
The cream is there for us to skim it,
Knowledge is power,
and the sky's the limit.
Every mouth has hands to feed it,
Food is found when people need it.
All we need is found in granite
Once we have the men to plan it.
Yeast and algae give us meat,
Soil is almost obsolete.
Men can grow to pastures greener
Till all the earth is Pasadena.
Moral:
Man's a nuisance, Man's a crackpot,
But only Man can hit the jackpot.[52]

Frank Egler, of the American Museum of Natural History, despaired that even if a suitable means for limiting population growth were somehow found, organized industry, which more and more seemed like an independent "organism" acting "increasingly aggressive for its own interests, even when these appear to conflict with other interests of society," would mount a massive and effective opposition out of its selfish desire for ever more consumers.[53] Corporate capitalism and its concomitant industrialization and commercialization underlay symposium—and environmentalist—anxieties. There was speculation that the very civilization of advanced industrial states was causing marked increases in neuroses and psychoses. And, it was further argued, "The United States not only belongs to the most psychotic of all civilizations but also is the most psychotic of countries in that civilization."[54] Citing statistics indicating substantial increases in the rate of suicide during the first half of the twentieth century, when corporate capitalism was booming, Ordway concluded darkly that "the higher the level of living, the less tolerable life is."[55]

Beat poet Allen Ginsberg expressed a similar sentiment in his poem *Howl*, written the same year the symposium was held, which characterized those trapped in the corporatization of American life as having "the absolute heart of the poem of life butchered out of their own bodies."[56] Later in the poem Ginsberg reveals the source of this spiritual crisis by alluding to Moloch, a biblical idol who demanded the sacrifice of Canaanite children. Translating the icon to his own time, Ginsberg made his Moloch big business, which robbed citizens of their personalities and essential humanity—a "sphinx of cement and aluminum [that] bashed open their skulls and ate up their brains and imagination."[57] Ginsberg was not the first critic of modernity to draw symbolically on Moloch. In his 1927 dystopian film *Metropolis*, Fritz Lang showed Moloch as a giant machine below ground where the working class lives and toils constantly to power the city of elites above. When the film's protagonist, Freder, who travels from the city to witness the grim reality of the world below, sees an accident that kills several workers, he is struck by a vision of hordes of workers being fed to a giant furnace, "Moloch," to provide warmth for the wealthy in the city above.[58]

Lang's apocalyptic vision was joined by those of other cultural observers who sought to express their sense that life had been tragically altered by the period's industrial and commercial revolutions. Early in the century such images of apocalypse were largely metaphorical, meant not so much to express fears that the world was physically ending as to demonstrate that the newly evolved systems of mass production and consumption, along with the enormous corporations and the bureaucracies that made them possible, meant an end to the world as it had been known. In the atomic era, though, nothing seemed permanent.

The only hope for the future, according to environmentalists, was to let go of the false promises offered by corporate capitalism in order to embrace new possibilities for organizing the economy, society, and life. As Mumford stated, "We shall be ill-prepared to meet the real challenges of the future if we imagine that our present institutions, because of the extraordinary successes of the machine economy in production, have congealed into a final mold from which man can never hope to escape.... There is plenty of evidence at this moment to indicate that man may...be on the point of emerging onto a new plane." Mumford and other proto-environmentalists dreamed that a new consciousness might break down old patterns of living and nationalism in order to hold the entire planet in a loving, sustainable embrace.[59]

Consumer Solutions

For some, alternative technologies that promised to sustain the quality of life in the Global North while improving the quality of life in the Global South were a significant component of the emerging new plane. In November 1955 the first International Conference on Solar Energy, directed by the Stanford Research Institute and sponsored by the Association for Applied Solar Energy Research that had formed two years earlier, drew 700 scientists, including 119 from 30 different nations, to the University of Arizona to discuss their research and the prospects for solar heat, engines, and electricity.[60] Many scientists and architects enthusiastically researched new possibilities for solar energy; some solar-heated homes were built in the 1940s and 1950s. However, solar quickly lost popularity due to new discoveries of natural gas deposits that resulted in cheaper prices, and aggressive marketing of gas water heaters to homeowners with free installation and low-cost monthly leases during the postwar building boom.[61] And the solar conference could not compete with another international energy conference held less than three months earlier in Geneva.

The first International Conference on the Peaceful Uses of Atomic Energy, sponsored by the United Nations, drew some 1,800 delegates from 72 countries. The president of the conference, Homi J. Bhabha of India, caused a sensation when he boldly predicted that fusion reaction—the same type that fueled hydrogen bombs and was many times more powerful than the fission reaction used in power plants—would be tamed to power much of the world with an endless supply of energy within the next 20 years.[62] The United States revealed that for the first time ever an entire town's electricity needs had been met with atomic power. On July 17 the government had secretly switched the power grid of Arco, Idaho to an experimental nuclear reactor for one hour.[63] The country already had one major commercial nuclear power plant under construction at Shippingsport, Pennsylvania when the conference began and chose the opening day of the event to announce that plants to serve Detroit and Chicago would soon be built.[64]

Many critics of the radioactive fallout resulting from atomic testing expressed similar apprehensions about radioactive waste resulting from power plants. Nevertheless the press said very little about the problem—even though the track record of corporate capitalism on industrial pollution left little room for optimism when it came to nuclear waste. "Our contempt for health when profits are at stake, our lack of reverence for life, even our own life, continue to poison the atmosphere in every industrial area and to make the streams and rivers, as well as the air we breathe, unfit for organic life," said Lewis Mumford. Atomic waste, he warned, would be no different: "The people who are now proposing to use atomic energy on a vast scale are the same people who have not yet made an effort, technologically, to dispose of the lethal carbon monoxide exhaust of the motorcar, the same people whose factories expose the inhabitants of industrial areas to air polluted with virtually the entire number of known cancer-producing substances."[65] For critics, such concerns had no half-life.

In the United States alternative energies could not compete with the fuel industries that enjoyed large government subsidies. By 1955 the government had spent $13.5 billion on atomic research, and major corporations were already on board to translate that investment into peacetime uses and profits.[66] In contrast, federal funding for solar research in the early 1950s totaled about $200,000.[67] Government efforts to promote "atoms for peace," begun in 1953 to further nuclear development while easing public anxieties about living in an atomic age, were followed by the industry-sponsored 1954 Atomic Energy Act which assured that civilian nuclear energy would be almost entirely corporate-controlled—albeit promoted and subsidized by federal tax dollars.[68]

Neo-Romantics in the Cold War

While these new postwar environmental issues were garnering attention, the more traditional, aesthetic concerns of longtime conservationists also gained greater prominence. Atomic weapons and power plants required uranium, and early on 75 percent of it was imported from Africa. The government was anxious to establish a domestic uranium industry, and in 1948 began offering an incentive of 1,000 percent of the existing rate for 10 years to spur domestic exploration, mining, and production, a deal soon sweetened by a variety of bonuses. The move set off a uranium rush in Colorado, Wyoming, Utah, Arizona, and New Mexico, as thousands poured into the area hoping to strike it rich.[69] Combined with Los Alamos in New Mexico and the Rocky Flats plutonium-trigger plant northwest of Denver that began production in 1953, the Bomb was responsible for a significant share of the region's population and industrial boom during and after the war. In addition, at the Rocky Mountain Arsenal east of Denver the government began manufacturing chemical weapons in 1942 and by 1946 began leasing facilities to pesticide and herbicide manufacturers, which manufactured products including DDT and dieldrin. By 1952 contamination from the plant was found to be damaging nearby crops and contaminating groundwater.[70]

The uranium rush resulted in a wave of road building funded by the federal government. The Defense Department subsidized 1,253 miles of roads in the uranium-producing states of the West. Prospectors and mining companies cleared many roads too. They added to mountain roads and trails constructed by FDR's Civilian Conservation Corps. As one observer stated, "Where there had once been barren wastelands, virtually impenetrable by man, there were now well-marked jeep trails, gravel roads, and even paved highways."[71]

Formerly, wilderness treks of the type sponsored by the Sierra Club required a good chunk of leisure time and money. Ironically, although roads and the soaring popularity of the automobile and trucking after World War II meant tree-cutting, bulldozing, and increased pollution, they also permitted people of more modest means to access remote reaches of rugged terrain and experience what was, to them at least, wilderness. It was likely due in part to the greater democratization of nature travel via roads that wilderness preservation expanded from a mostly elite concern to an increasingly wider audience.[72]

That broader concern for aesthetic wilderness was evident in the era's most noted conservation controversy. The rapid population growth of the Rocky Mountain West, and the desire of local boosters to further expand development, contributed to calls for increased production of electricity and additional water supplies. By the late forties the Bureau of Reclamation, the Interior Department division in charge of water projects in the West, had formulated a plan for a series of dams in the region, including one at Echo Park on the Colorado–Utah border that triggered significant environmental opposition.[73] Although Echo Park was still accessed only by river raft, or for many others "virtual river raft" via a widely distributed film made by the Sierra Club, the larger cause of wilderness preservation had captured the imagination of many more Americans than during the Hetch Hetchy dam controversy in California's Yosemite Valley some 40 years earlier.[74]

The fight to preserve landscapes of natural beauty and wilderness was not only about aesthetics, which had long drawn conservationists to their defense, but also about citizens asserting their authority in the face of the growing power of corporations and their allies in government. The struggles to stop development, oil drilling, and resource extraction on cherished natural sites were not just about the sites themselves; they were part of a larger fight for greater democracy. Citizens who might never visit such places were passionate in their defense, believing that keeping such lands undeveloped symbolized stopping corporations from exercising absolute power.

Determined not to go down in defeat as the Sierra Club had over Hetch Hetchy, citizens waged a strong offensive to block the reservoir in Echo Park. The dam, they said, would infringe on "primeval wilderness" set aside by the government for the purpose of preservation. Almost immediately after it was proposed in 1949 the Echo Park dam drew strong opposition from conservation groups including the Wilderness Society, the Izaak Walton League, the Sierra Club, the Audubon Society, and the Wildlife Management League. As the controversy continued the protest grew to encompass more than 175 organizations.[75] Opponents feared a dam would not only damage the beauty of Echo Park but would also hamper future efforts to preserve both national parks and wilderness in the face of pressures from growing populations and industry.[76] After more than six years of struggle, in 1956 Congress reached a compromise with conservationists and agreed to prohibit the dam. It was built instead in Glen Canyon in Arizona, creating the massive Lake Powell, a reservoir of anguish for writer Edward Abbey and other lovers of the desert Southwest.[77]

Although Abbey and later environmentalists questioned the ultimate wisdom of the compromise, many conservationists celebrated it as a major victory. The final legislation declared that no dam or reservoir should be built in any national park or monument. The years of struggle and publicity drew greater attention to the cause of conservation. As stated in the *New York Times*, "Conservationists and sportsmen discovered that they can prevent the misuse of public lands and defeat unsound conservation legislation by means of strong public protests." In another article it stated, "The immense latent strength of conservation as a political force in the United States is becoming constantly more apparent." Indeed, in 1956 both Democrats and Republicans would find it prudent to include conservation planks that mentioned the need to preserve wilderness areas in their party platforms.[78] The well-publicized battle over the dam served to further sensitize the public to the conservation cause, helping push the Sierra Club's membership, which stood at 7,000 in 1950, to 10,000 in 1956.[79] However, winning grassroots conservationist victories to preserve sites of aesthetic beauty would prove easier than gaining environmentalist victories that challenged the role of corporate capitalism in American life.

The Old Scourge: Air Pollution

Fallout was not the only contaminant in an increasingly lethal atmosphere. Following Donora the public's increased sensitivity to air pollution was met with a series of lethal pollution incidents that further raised the level of citizen unease. In November 1953 thick smog covered the entire Eastern seaboard from Southern New England all the way down to Virginia, as well as most of Pennsylvania, for six days.[80] Later analysis showed an estimated 25 to 30 people a day died in New York City alone during that month.[81]

In Los Angeles smog was so bad during three weeks in October 1954—rumor had it that it was enough to take the chrome off a Cadillac—that even the membership of the Optimist Club donned gas masks for a smog protest lunch. Hanging in the dining hall was a large banner protesting government and industry inaction in a sardonic rhyme that read "Why Wait Till 1955, We Might Not Even Be Alive."[82] The League of Women Voters organized protests, and a group of "homemakers" wearing gas masks and carrying brooms called for "a clean sweep of smog" outside Pasadena's City Hall in November.[83]

By the mid-fifties research had demonstrated that automobile exhaust was a substantial contributor to Los Angeles's smog problem. But when cities like Philadelphia and San Francisco too were blanketed with smog it became increasingly evident that Los Angeles, with its smog-trapping temperature inversions, was not unique in its problems with air pollution.[84] "I would like to envision the car of the future as running by electricity," said J. I. Rodale in a 1954 article in *Organic Gardening and Farming* included in a six-part series on smog.[85] But the enormously profitable automobile and petroleum industries were much more motivated to maintain and increase their profits than they were to solve the smog "problem."

In a 1955 "Health Message to Congress," President Eisenhower finally recommended increased research on air pollution because, "As a result of industrial growth and urban development, the atmosphere over some population centers may be approaching the limit of its ability to absorb air pollutants with safety [sic] health."[86] Modeled on the 1948 Water Pollution Control Act, the Air Pollution Control Act established funds to "provide research and technical assistance for air pollution control," providing $5 million annually for five years to the Public Health Service and Department of Health, Education, and Welfare.[87]

But the $25 million the government budgeted to study air pollution paled in comparison to the $25 billion it agreed to spend to subsidize the automobile industry with the Federal Aid Highway Act in 1956, which financed 90 percent of the costs of the massive project to build limited-access highways across the United States. The act included $208 million for the construction of roads in national parks and forests.[88] Rather than using citizen tax dollars to fund significantly more efficient (and environmentally friendly) public mass transportation, the government's largesse went toward constructing the infrastructure for private corporate profits.

Some states tried to make up for the federal government's inaction by promoting a market solution that they hoped would be more agreeable to corporations. A Northeast Governors Conference on urban problems, attended by 60 public officials from six Northeastern states and the District of Columbia in 1957, urged automobile manufacturers to help cut air pollution and congestion by producing smaller cars with more efficient engines. But a spokesperson for the industry dismissed the governors' request and boasted that the auto industry had already invested $3.5 million in the last three and a half years researching the problem.[89] Such "research" was a favorite stalling tactic of the automobile industry.[90]

The situation grew graver with increasing evidence confirming that air pollution caused lung cancer.[91] The difficulty remained getting producers to take steps necessary to limit and clean their emissions. The cooperative relationship between government and industry made sanctions politically difficult.[92] Nevertheless, an increasingly aware and frightened public was demanding, without much success, that both government and industry take measures to curb air pollution. Atmospheric pollution provided many with a daily reminder of the growing need to protect the environment.

Strontium-90

One of the other daily reminders and driving forces behind the nascent environmental movement was the growing concern over atomic testing fallout. The National Academy of Sciences sought to provide definitive answers to the many questions surrounding fallout when it published its comprehensive report on the effects of the nuclear era in June 1956. Besides confirming earlier warnings that the effects of radiation are cumulative, and that any exposure to radiation carries a corresponding mutational risk, the report included a further warning that garnered the most attention.[93]

That warning was an analysis of the effect of fallout on food. "Radiation from fallout inevitably contaminates man's food supply," it read. "Radioactive elements in the soil are taken up and concentrated by plants. The plants may be eaten by humans, or by animals which in turn serve as human food." Researchers explained that the same process happened in the oceans. The report went on to warn that the most dangerous food contaminant was bone-seeking strontium-90 that had "already turned up in milk supplies thousands of miles from the site of atomic explosions." The report's insistence that the present level of contamination was "negligible" was overshadowed by its admission that "the maximum tolerable level is not known. There is not nearly enough information about the long-term effects on man or animals from eating radiation-contaminated food."[94]

Yet again it was a threat to the food supply that captured the public's attention. The dairy industry liked to boast that milk appeared on 95 percent of America's kitchen tables each day; milk enjoyed a reputation as the nation's most wholesome and nutritious beverage.[95] Within two months the AEC sought to calm the public's nerves with a report that, though admitting strontium-90's presence in milk, claimed the level of strontium-90 produced by testing was 350 times smaller than the "permissible concentration" for humans.[96] But there was only so much the AEC could do to calm the public. If the death of a Japanese fisherman from strontium-90 complications was not enough to move most Americans, the threat to the well-being of their own children was, and nothing the AEC could say would ease their fears. Strontium-90 became the first nationwide, and worldwide, popular environmental cause.

In October, Democratic Senator Adlai Stevenson made strontium-90 a central issue in his campaign to unseat incumbent Dwight Eisenhower in the 1956 presidential election, the first time an environmental issue became part of a presidential campaign.[97] Although both political parties included conservation planks in their 1956 presidential platforms, besides a brief mention of water pollution they mostly focused on traditional issues of aesthetics and conservation of natural resources.[98] Stevenson warned, "Only a tablespoon shared equally by all members of the human race would produce a dangerous level of radioactivity in the bones of every individual." He charged the Eisenhower administration with concealing its knowledge that the country's milk supply had been polluted with strontium-90 since 1954 and that the level of strontium-90 in children had already reached a level judged hazardous. He promised that his first order of business if elected would be to seek an international agreement to end all nuclear bomb testing.[99]

Crowds listening to Stevenson's speeches attacking strontium-90 responded enthusiastically, giving him what one journalist called "the biggest and largest demonstration he has had at any time on any issue since the start of the campaign." When President Eisenhower rejected Stevenson's test-ban proposal and argued that testing could continue without danger to humans, 19 scientists from the University of Rochester issued a statement citing the particular danger of strontium-90, insisting that Eisenhower's statement did "not face the important issue of the hazards of the H-Bomb testing."[100]

Any campaign momentum Stevenson received from the strontium-90 issue, though, was dashed on October 19, when the Eisenhower State Department made public a letter from Russian Premier Nikolai A. Bulganin supporting a test ban and praising "certain prominent public officials in the United States" for advocating a halt to testing. The Republican Party and the press promoted the letter as a Soviet attempt to influence the American election by endorsing Stevenson, suddenly turning the popular issue into what *Newsweek* termed "a political kiss of death." Although he lost the election, Stevenson furthered the public's awareness of the strontium-90 issue, while shaking its confidence in the government's trustworthiness to protect its citizens and the environment.[101] In the spring of 1955, only 17 percent of those surveyed knew what fallout was; by the spring of 1957, 52 percent said it was a "real danger."[102]

A Poisoned Planet and the "Dread Disease"

Shortly before the election cancer specialist William G. Cahan noted in the *New York Times* that while much had been made of the effects of radiation, there had been little attention paid to the possible role of radioactivity in causing cancer. Cahan argued that any claims by supposed experts that the amounts of radiation released by nuclear testing are "'insignificant' presupposes knowledge of what is significant, and that, explicitly, is the knowledge we do not now possess."[103]

In addition, Cahan discussed further environmental implications of fallout in the case of a wild muskrat captured in a river near the Oak Ridge, Tennessee X-10 nuclear laboratory, constructed as part of the Manhattan Project to develop the Bomb. The lab had released "insignificant" amounts of radiation into the water, but they were captured by the plants in the river and concentrated in their leaves at an amount 14 times higher than the surrounding water. The radiation found in the muskrat's cancer-ridden right hind leg was 150 times higher. Cahan concluded that the additional radiation (a known carcinogen) in the environment might combine with other carcinogens "still unknown, but which are undoubtedly present in our daily lives" and "be enough to tip the scales" at "a threshold lower than either of them acting by themselves" to cause cancer.[104] Researchers from Washington University Medical School later supported Cahan's speculation when they announced that cigarette tar and strontium-90 together caused skin cancer in mice more often than either carcinogen did.[105]

British scientists exacerbated fears when they released a report in April 1957 indicating that strontium-90 might be causing leukemia. Two weeks later, Nobel Prize–winning chemist Linus Pauling said that 10,000 people throughout the world had already died or were dying of leukemia due to testing fallout, and urged an international agreement to ban nuclear testing. The following month, California Institute of Technology biologist E. B. Lewis reported in *Science* on four different studies, including one on survivors of the bombing of Hiroshima and Nagasaki. All indicated that leukemia is caused by radiation, including that produced by strontium-90.[106]

Adding leukemia to the threat of bone cancer already attributed to strontium-90 upped the ante considerably. When asked, "What disease or illness would you dread having most?" by a Gallup poll in 1947, nothing came close to the fear of cancer cited by 67 percent of those polled. Tuberculosis registered a distant second at 15 percent.[107] "I don't want to know if it's cancer," said one patient. "I don't want to know I'm doomed."[108] Leukemia, with a fatality rate of 90 percent—was among the most dreaded of all cancers.[109] This was particularly true during the postwar era when popular attention was focused on cancer as a threat to children. A *Colliers* article entitled "CANCER, THE CHILD KILLER" was one of many magazine articles in the late 1940s to alarm readers by revealing that, other than accidents, cancer was the leading killer of children from ages five to fourteen in the United States, killing more than polio, meningitis, scarlet fever, diarrhea, dysentery, malaria, peritonitis, and diphtheria combined.[110]

Only recently had medical researchers begun moving away from the notion that diseases like cancer were caused exclusively by biological weaknesses and the hereditary susceptibilities of individual bodies, or the victim's lifestyle, and toward the idea that the environment might also play a key role. The environmental focus was led by occupational cancer studies conducted by Wilhelm C. Hueper that he first published in a controversial 1942 book. Hueper had been hired by DuPont in the late 1930s to find the reason for an unusually high incidence of cancer in the company's chemical dye workers, but was fired by the company two years later for repeatedly insisting one of the company's chemicals, beta-naphthylamine, was to blame.[111] Researchers in the fifties revealed an expanding list of other suspected carcinogens, including air pollution, asbestos, food additives, X-rays, and cigarettes, furthering the public's growing concern about the health of the environment.[112] Such evidence only added to Americans' sense that there was something fundamentally wrong with the way they were living.

Thus, when cancer became linked to fallout it was no small matter. As a letter to the *New York Times* stated, "The 'fight cancer' crusade is on. Does it not seem ironic that we...are asked to...contribute to this worthy cause, while at the same time our Government spends millions on atomic-bomb tests which have now been proved beyond a doubt to be sprinkling cancer-producing fall-out on us all?"[113] In an age when many Americans wanted to believe that science and technology could solve every problem, cancer was a source of lingering doubt.[114]

"A Worldwide Consumer Problem"

In December 1956 and January 1957 a variety of witnesses at US Senate hearings expressed growing fears of fallout's deadly potential. A St. Louis mother described being "faced with the contamination of milk, cheese and vegetables" and called it "a worldwide consumer problem."[115] The January 1957 issue of the women's magazine *McCall's* featured a picture of a baby on its cover with a banner running across it that read, "RADIOACTIVITY is Poisoning Your Children." Inside, in an article titled "Fight for Survival," writer and filmmaker Pare Lorentz warned that fallout could kill most humans and that waste from the growing nuclear industry was threatening the earth with pollution.[116] Testing continued unabated though, with both the United States and Soviet Union avoiding a test ban as long as they feared the other side might be ahead in bomb technology or they believed they needed to test bombs for new purposes such as arming airplane-fired and intercontinental ballistic missiles. But an informed citizenry was taking note, and opposition was building.

In April 1957, Nobel Peace Laureate Dr. Albert Schweitzer, ranked the fourth most admired man in the world by a Gallup Poll, issued a letter through the Nobel Committee titled a "Declaration of Conscience" that called on the public to demand an end to nuclear testing. "The radioactivity in the air...will not harm us from the outside, not being strong enough to penetrate the skin," Schweitzer wrote. "But the danger which has to be stressed above all the others is the one which arises from our drinking radioactive water and our eating radioactive food as a consequence of the increased radioactivity in the air."[117] Days later Willard F. Libby of the AEC wrote an eight-page response to Schweitzer, asking the Nobel Laureate to weigh the "small" risk of fallout against "the far greater risk to freedom-loving people everywhere in the world, of not maintaining our defenses against the totalitarian forces at large in the world until such time as safeguarded disarmament may be achieved."[118] It seemed that growing numbers of Americans were, however, questioning Libby's calculus; the threat of fallout, ingested with every meal, if not a greater threat than totalitarianism, was, significantly, more intimate, immediate, and definite.

Environmental Activism

That summer new citizens groups, such as the Committee for 10,000 Babies, whose name alluded to Linus Pauling's warning, formed to organize opposition to additional testing and fallout.[119] Fallout and strontium-90 from the bomb were convincing more citizens to view life and the planet in a new way. "The world has suddenly become a small sphere," stated an article in the *New Republic*, "too restricted in surface area for the 'safe' testing of super-bombs."[120]

The first national organization aimed at stopping tests formed in New York in June through the efforts of Norman Cousins, publisher of the *Saturday Review of Literature*, Clarence Pickett, executive secretary of the Quakers' American Friends Service Committee, and Norman Thomas, former Socialist candidate for President.[121] Called the National Committee for a Sane Nuclear Policy—later known as SANE—it took its name from the urging of psychoanalyst and Nazi Germany refugee Erich Fromm who reasoned that "the normal drive for survival" had been confused by the Cold War and that informed citizens needed to "try to bring the voice of sanity to the people."[122]

Even though many in the group's leadership were chiefly motivated by a commitment to pacifism, they quickly realized that their greatest popular appeal lay in the environmental issue of fallout and strontium-90. "Ending bomb tests is the issue" to attract public interest, wrote West Coast activist Catherine Cory to Cousins and Pickett. "At last we have an issue that the average Joe understands."[123]

That the "average Joe" understood the campaign spoke to the growing environmental concern among Americans. SANE's efforts helped to further popularize that consciousness. The group went public on November 15, 1957, when it issued its first in a series of full-page ads in the *New York Times*. Beneath a banner headline reading, "We Are Facing a Danger Unlike Any Danger That Has Ever Existed," it stated its belief that American culture and character were out of balance. SANE fixed much of the blame on corporate capitalism: "We have been concerned with bigger incomes, bigger television screens, and bigger cars—but not with the big ideas on which our lives and freedoms depend," it lamented. The group insisted: "Man has natural rights. He has the right to live and to grow, to breathe unpoisoned air, to work on uncontaminated soil. He has the right to his sacred nature." SANE maintained that if those environmental rights are impinged upon by the state, "then it becomes necessary for people to restrain and tame the nations." In addition to Cousins, Pickett, and Thomas, the ad's 48 signers included luminaries Cleveland Amory, Erich Fromm, Oscar Hammerstein II, John Hersey, Lewis Mumford, and Eleanor Roosevelt.[124]

At the bottom of SANE's ad was a coupon soliciting donations. Within three weeks the group took in almost $10,000, along with 1,700 positive responses. Typical was a Denver resident who sent $2.00 along with a note that read, "This is THE idea I have been waiting for." Encouraged, SANE began organizing local groups to run similar ads in hometown newspapers. Reprints of the original ad appeared in 32 newspapers by January 1958. There were 25,000 requests for reprints of the ad's statement. By the middle of the year there were 130 local SANE chapters with a membership totaling almost 25,000.[125] The *Denver Post* ran a condensed version of the statement to accompany an editorial that said, "It looks like the spark that could call forth the expression of one great amen of the apprehensions common to men everywhere over whether or not they will be able to survive the awesome power their species has acquired with technical knowledge."[126]

Despite such apprehensions, by the fall of 1957 the three nations testing nuclear weapons, the United States, Soviet Union, and Great Britain, had already set off 42 reported nuclear explosions that year—more than twice as many as in any other year. Opposition to testing in the United States was complicated by Cold War anxieties that the Russians had gained a lead in technology and the arms race with their successful launch of the first artificial satellite, Sputnik, on October 4. Those concerns, in turn, were challenged by the more immediate and growing threat from bomb-testing fallout.[127]

In February 1958, Columbia University scientists conducting research for the AEC revealed a worldwide study of bone samples indicating that in one year the average level of strontium-90 in humans had increased by a whopping 30 percent, and in children by an alarming 50 percent. Further, they found that in children up to age four the concentration was 20 times higher than in adults age 20 and older. The report also revealed that some children had three times the average, while some adults carried as much as seven times the average. The highest concentrations, due to jet stream patterns, were in North America. Even if bomb tests stopped immediately, the scientists said, fallout would continue to descend on the earth and increase strontium-90 levels until 1970. Still, they insisted, that level would remain below the acceptable maximum. But *Time* magazine called that claim into question when it noted that many scientists believed that maximum had been set "far too high."[128]

In March, SANE ran a second full-page newspaper ad, with a banner headline reflecting the public's feeling of political powerlessness in the face of threats to the environment that declared, "No Contamination without Representation." Among its signers was Martin Luther King, Jr.[129] Less than one week later, legendary television journalist Edward R. Murrow devoted an episode of his popular 85-minute Columbia Broadcasting System program, *See It Now*, to the issue of fallout. [130]

Residents of the earth grew weary of being bombarded with toxins and sought some way to protect themselves and their families. As J. I. Rodale nicely summed up the odd combination of fatalism and hope in *Organic Gardening and Farming*:

> Let's take a look at the common man, a person almost completely overlooked in the concerns over Foreign Ministers' meetings, Summit conferences and warlike matters in general. There really is very little that you or I can do to try to protect ourselves against hydrogen warfare, and the best course emotionally is to wipe the whole thing from our minds and try to forget what may be in store for us some day. There is no use getting all worked up about something beyond our realm of influence. But, be careful not to let that same dreamlike attitude lull you into lowering your defenses against strontium. For there are things you and I can do about strontium-90. [131]

Of course, even organic foods could not escape strontium fallout. Rodale advised eating calcium-rich foods and taking calcium supplements in the hope that such efforts might limit the body's need for calcium so that bones might not absorb strontium while seeking additional calcium. Foods like asparagus appeared to absorb less strontium than some other foods. [132]

Although American concerns remained complicated by fears of falling behind the Soviets in the arms race, such complexities did not exist for most other inhabitants of the earth caught in the crossfire of strontium-90 as the superpowers maneuvered to outdo one another. Anger over fallout escalated as countries found their levels of strontium-90 multiplying at the same time that the number of reports of its negative consequences for health, genetics, and the environment were on the rise. By May 1958, after the Soviet Union announced that it would unilaterally stop testing, world opinion soured to the point that President Eisenhower could no longer ignore it, and he determined to finally seek in earnest a test ban with the Soviets. The two countries settled on a one-year moratorium on testing beginning on October 31, when meetings would begin in Geneva to attempt to negotiate a test-ban treaty. "Unless we took some positive action we were in the future going to be in a position of 'moral isolation' as far as [the] rest of the world is concerned," Eisenhower told his Secretary of State John Foster Dulles. [133]

Between May and the end of October, all sides rushed to test as many bombs as possible before the start of the moratorium, resulting in the largest number of tests ever in one year. [134] Record testing led, inevitably, to record fallout. As fallout continued to attack the earth and the food chain long after the final blasts, evidence of its environmental impact grew. In January 1959 the Public Health Service announced that strontium-90 levels in milk had increased in 8 out of 10 cities they actively monitored.[135] The next month a Pan American jetliner that had been flying above 30,000 feet was found to be coated with radioactive fallout. Officials from Minnesota revealed that strontium-90 levels in some wheat samples in the state tested 55 percent higher than the "permissible" level, leading a member of the British Parliament to call for a ban on the import of US wheat.[136] In March, New York City officials reported that strontium-90 levels in the city had more than doubled in the last four years. The Department of Defense released preliminary findings indicating that AEC claims that strontium-90 took as long as 10 years to fall back to earth, meaning that its intensity was diminished because it fell in small quantities over a long period of time and it partially disintegrated during its duration in the stratosphere, were false. It took an average of only two years, which meant greater contamination of the earth. Given the tremendous increases in measured fallout less than six months after the final tests before the moratorium, the Defense Department's revelation made it appear that once again the AEC, the government agency that was charged with protecting the public from radiation's harmful effects, was instead, as New Mexico Democratic Senator Clinton P. Anderson charged, trying to "hush up" information.[137]

Most worrisome of all was, once again, milk. In March 1959 *Consumer Reports* magazine issued a 10-page report on the strontium-90 levels in milk from 50 different cities across the United States, a report far more comprehensive than any ever publicized by the government. It criticized the AEC's lack of research and information on public health. "The fact is that fresh clean milk, which looks and tastes just as it always did, nevertheless contains (wherever you get it these days) an unseen contaminant, a toxic substance known to accumulate in human bones," it warned.[138] In a sidebar, the report detailed exactly how strontium-90 might affect both *somatic* damage, "damage to cells not engaged in reproducing the next generation," and *genetic* damage, "damage...to the subtle molecules of genetic material which contains the blueprint for the next generation." It went on to explain that there was general scientific agreement "that genetic damage, which in humans leads to embryonic deaths, still-births, and congenital defects, has no threshold. *Every* increase in the dose which affects the genes of some person is going to appear statistically in his progeny."[139] It cautioned that the government's maximum "permissible" exposure levels were suspect, if not meaningless, as evidenced by the fact that the level had been reduced three different times since 1936 and was currently a remarkable 95 percent less than the level government scientists had originally claimed to be safe.[140]

The magazine had some 800,000 subscribers and an estimated four million readers. In subsequent weeks many newspapers carried stories about the

Consumer Reports tests, quoting the disturbing results. Although the report noted that to stop drinking milk would be as foolish as refusing a medically necessary X-ray, milk sales plunged.[141]

Consumer Reports' publisher, Consumers Union, was founded not only to test consumer products for quality but also to monitor the working conditions of laborers who produced the goods. It was soon accused by the House Un-American Activities Committee of being part of a "Consumers Red Network" and therefore disloyal. In response, Consumers Union focused solely on its product testing. But in 1957 some CU board members, frustrated with the group's circumscribed role, successfully returned the organization to its activist roots.[142] It would now monitor environmental threats. The milk report was the first study out of the magazine's "Department of Public Service Projects," established by CU in 1958 to examine "some of the inescapable problems of modern life—among them the hazards of fallout, and the health and economic consequences of air and water pollution. Such problems are inextricable parts of the environment created by an industrial society."[143] Consumer education and choices, CU hoped, might influence industrial practices to better protect the environment and life.

Women Lead the Way

The same month that *Consumer Reports* issued its investigation, the *New York Times* published a letter from a reader signed "Worried Mother" that spoke to the feelings of fear, frustration, and powerlessness being experienced by many:

> Are the learned statesmen and scientists on both sides of the Iron Curtain, tossing nuclear bombs about with the abandon of boys setting off fireworks, at all interested in how a mere mother feels as she feeds her trusting infant milk contaminated with strontium 90? Can they appreciate her anxiety when even the "experts" cannot agree on safe permissible levels? Is thought given to the fact that leukemia among young children is increasing at a disturbing rate? And may a mere mother add that whereas a nuclear attack is an uncertainty, even an improbability, the peril of increasing fall-out is a dead certainty...? Let's be sensible.[144]

As traditional family caregivers, women were often the first to be directly confronted with the disturbing realities of how damage to the environment might affect their loved ones. Women protesting for the safety of their families in the face of environmental peril, though often quite radical by Cold War standards, were able to speak with a uniquely powerful and effective moral voice against any government or industry official without being easily dismissed as "commies" and "fags."[145]

Concerns of mothers and others in the St. Louis metropolitan area intensified when the Greater St. Louis Citizens' Committee for Nuclear Information announced a program to begin an annual collection of the baby teeth of at least 50,000 area kids to track the level of strontium-90 in growing children. The committee had formed in 1958 out of a consortium of members of a number of citizens' groups including the St. Louis Consumer Federation, the International Ladies Garment Workers' Union, and faculty of Washington University such as biologist Barry Commoner, who first began working together in 1956 over concerns about strontium-90 in milk. Through their lobbying efforts, the United States Public Health Service agreed to begin testing milk in St. Louis and four other cities.[146] Citizens groups in additional cities, soon aided by Consumers Union, began collecting their own children's teeth to determine how much radiation was being stored in their young bodies.[147]

In May 1959 Dr. Edward B. Lewis, a geneticist at the California Institute of Technology in Pasadena, warned that another radioactive element in milk, iodine 131, also posed a serious threat to humans, especially children. Though it was previously thought to be of little concern because of its brief half-life of only eight days, iodine 131 "tends to concentrate in milk and it should further concentrate in the thyroid glands of milk drinkers," Lewis found. Alarmingly, infants, given the same quantity of milk, received about 18 times more radioactive iodine in their thyroid tissues than adults, and there was additional evidence that the thyroid glands of infants and children were especially sensitive to radiation-induced cancer. He estimated that, with then-present levels of fallout, as many as 1,600 children would suffer thyroid cancer because of iodine 131 in their milk.[148]

By August 1959 the issue of harm from fallout had become so unmistakably mainstream that even the staid *Saturday Evening Post* ran an in-depth, two-part series titled "Fallout: The Silent Killer." It noted, "No scientific issue in many years has so exasperatingly eluded all efforts to lay hands upon the truth," before criticizing the government for unnecessarily confusing the matter. It took particular aim at the AEC's semantic glossing effort to associate misleading "happy" terms with the issue, such as labeling the fallout-measuring program "Project Sunshine."[149] Citizens were losing faith in their government.

The monthly journal of the Greater St. Louis Citizens' Committee for Nuclear Information, *Information*, featured a four-page article in October titled "Mothers Ask—What Should We Feed Our Kids?" The author described how the article grew out of her experience of getting together with neighborhood women when the conversations increasingly turned to such questions as, "Should we still give our kids milk?" and, "How much harm will fallout cause?"[150] With all of the publicity surrounding the issue, similar conversations were taking place all over the country and around the world.

The Death of Paterfamilias?

The well-being of children was often at the center of environmental concerns and appeals. Beyond the usual desire of parents, and the broader culture, to protect children from harm, their prominence in environmental issues signified additional anxieties.[151] Children were born into a world where the air they breathed, water they drank, food they ate, and their own mother's milk, threatened their very lives. Consumers were similarly portrayed as innocents who were susceptible to the manipulative marketing of producers and their advertisers. All counted on the government to play the role of the protective parent who would shelter citizens and the environment from producers who might do them harm.

To many it appeared that the government was growing increasingly derelict in its paternal role. After all, could a government that knowingly inflicted fallout and strontium-90 on its citizenry, poisoning its milk and food in the process, be counted on to protect it from the excesses of big business? Government was not performing its expected role in assuring the welfare of nature and the nation. It seemed a new order in which government placed the welfare of corporations above that of its citizens and the environment had taken hold. What might be done to right the balance of power and give children, consumers, and the earth a fighting chance became an increasing focus of not only cultural critics but also growing numbers of citizens. Some hoped that government might be persuaded to assume its protective role, while a few in the avant-garde had largely given up on that and were voicing something else altogether.

4

Chemicals and Romance

The anxieties that grew amid the fallout of the Bomb set the stage for apocalyptic fears of other chemicals. In April 1957, a joint federal–state aerial spraying program that began in an attempt to stop the spread of the forest-devouring gypsy moth in three Northeastern states raised public concerns. Less than a year later a second controversial massive USDA spraying program began in nine Southern states in a "war" against the "imported fire ant." Like atomic fallout, chemicals dropped from converted World War II bombers drifted in the atmosphere and invaded the ecosystem, altering its ecology, poisoning the food chain, and modifying the chemistry of the body. A series of chemical mishaps during the late 1950s led growing numbers of Americans to fear that they, their families, and the environment were under deadly attack. A rising chorus of cultural critics blamed citizens themselves, arguing that it was their conspicuous consumption that was driving both corporate power and the environmental ruin that accompanied it. But many others joined the ranks of those who were faulting corporations and the government's failure to effectively regulate their actions.

The European gypsy moth was first brought to the United States from France in 1868 by Leopold Trouvelot, an artist, astronomer, and amateur entomologist, who hoped that by crossbreeding its hearty caterpillar with the delicate Polyphemus silkworm he had been trying to cultivate, mostly unsuccessfully, he could develop a robust hybrid silkworm that would make a large-scale silk-production industry possible in the United States. Trouvelot was culturing the moths beneath nets in trees in his backyard in Medford, Massachusetts when some of their larvae escaped. By 1882 a gypsy moth outbreak was killing trees in his neighborhood and beyond. The state of Massachusetts attempted to eradicate the insect, but to no avail. The actual moth was not the problem; it was its caterpillar larvae with a voracious appetite for foliage that caused massive destruction to a wide variety of timber hardwoods and fruit trees. The moths eventually spread across some 38,000,000 acres in the Northeast, where for years traps and quarantines on the borders of their habitat kept them largely contained. However, three hurricanes that hit the Northeast in 1954 were feared to have spread the moths and larvae to parts of New York, New Jersey, and Pennsylvania.[1]

In 1957 the US Department of Agriculture began a program to spray three million pounds of DDT on some three million acres over parts of the threatened states—more than 85 percent of it in New York—with 65 airplanes, including converted World War II bombers, to establish a 25-mile-wide "barrier zone" extending from the Adirondack Mountains to Long Island to prevent the spread of the moth southward and westward of already infected areas. From there they hoped to eventually make inroads into the moth's existing territory and wipe it out completely.[2] The bombers dumping DDT were an apt metaphor for the postwar era, when it increasingly appeared that technology was at war with nature. Business produced the deadly chemicals, and government dumped them on citizens who felt defenseless as the power they counted upon to protect them became increasingly allied to the one that produced the threat.

The gypsy moth–spraying plan was controversial from the start. Some New York residents protested the government's proposal to spray their land with DDT that they neither wanted nor asked for. But citizens possessed no defense, nor allies. The USDA insisted that spraying at a rate of one pound per acre would not "materially" affect bird populations, injure humans, or damage automobile finishes (they did concede that it might kill "a few fish" in small streams and ponds lacking runoff), and that any small risks were greatly outweighed by the benefits of halting the scourge of the gypsy moth.[3]

A Losing Battle to Defend the Environment

After a month of watching DDT's destructive effects, eight residents of Long Island sought a federal court injunction to halt spraying on the grounds that it violated the Fifth Amendment of the Constitution by depriving persons of their property and "possibly their lives without due process of law." Led by Robert Cushman Murphy, curator emeritus for birds at the Museum of Natural History, author of many books on ornithology, past president of the National Audubon Society, and organic gardener, who had been issuing warnings about the deadly effects of DDT since 1945, the group also included other organic farmers and nature enthusiasts. "DDT is a cumulative poison," said Murphy. It "throws the entire balance of nature out of whack. Last time we had a big spraying here...we had to *shovel up* the dead birds."[4]

Arguments against the spraying were often grounded in the principles of ecology and the growing consciousness that humans were not separate from nature. As reported on the front page of the *New York Times*, the group's proposed injunction noted that DDT is "recognized and admitted by the defendants to be a delayed-action, cumulative poison such as will inevitably cause irreparable injury and death to all living things, including human beings, animals, birds, insects and the predators and parasites of harmful insects, if ingested, inhaled or brought into contact therewith in sufficient quantities over a sufficient period." The complaint further stipulated that the spray would likely act "upon predators and parasites more powerfully than upon the pests themselves, upsetting nature's balance and defeating its own object." Among the objections was that it would be harmful to bees that were vital to the pollination of fruit trees on Long Island. Dairy farmers complained that milk from cattle grazing on sprayed pastures showed traces of DDT. In an additional brief filed in the case, the group's attorney, Roger Hinds, argued that organic farming was almost "a religion" with some people threatened by the spray. "One spraying of DDT on plaintiff's land," he emphasized, "will forever destroy its utility as an organic garden or orchard."[5]

One of the protesters was Daniel McKeon, a former Wall Street broker turned organic farmer in Fairfield County, Connecticut. As journalist William Longgood reported in a front-page story in the *New York World-Telegram*, McKeon had farmed for 20 years. Ten years earlier, concerned about human health and the environment, he decided to quit using chemical sprays and go organic on his 225 acres where he raised crops and milked about 75 cows whose milk he sold to a nearby dairy. He conscientiously raised most of his own feed to prevent chemicals from contaminating the milk. On May 24, 1957, McKeon and his wife, Louise, were awakened by the sound of a low-flying plane and soon smelled the pungent odor of chemical spray. The McKeons lived one mile east of the New York state line in an area that was not supposed to be sprayed. The pilot later admitted the error, but the damage to McKeon's land was done. "I feel angry and heartsick," said the devastated McKeon. "I feel that all of our efforts of patiently trying to avoid poisons have been wasted."[6]

McKeon charged that the spraying was undemocratic. Pointing to a plaque on the front of his house that identified it as the former home of a Revolutionary War veteran, Captain Henry Whitney, McKeon noted with some bitterness, "I feel there has been a violation of our Constitutional and state's rights. When the government forces its will upon private citizens against their wishes—especially when they don't even have a chance to express their opinion—it is nothing more than the tyranny of dictatorship." Robert Cushman Murphy agreed. "In all our history," he said, "there is no more flagrant case of a bureaucratic attitude signifying 'The Public Be Damned!'"[7] The *New York World-Telegram* ran a full-page ad in the *New York Times* promoting its newspaper on the basis of Longgood's story on DDT, with a headline quoting a letter from a reader that read, "*World Telegram's* DDT warning is a vital public service."[8]

Organic farmer Hanes Fried of Spring Valley, New York, complained about the spraying to his congresswoman, Katherine St. George, prompting a visit to his farm by A. E. Weyl of the USDA's Agricultural Research Service. Weyl answered the farmer's concerns about his unpasteurized milk being tainted with DDT by assuring Fried that "the material would break down rapidly in the sun and dissipate," even though it was well known that chlorinated hydrocarbons persisted in the environment for a very long time. A frustrated Weyl protested, "All in the area seem to be organic farming enthusiasts."[9]

Some of the loudest and best-organized protests against DDT came from the group of consumers often referred to as "outdoorsmen." In this instance the 1,000-member Beaverkill–Willowemoc Rod & Gun Club, headquartered in the Catskills town of Roscoe that billed itself as "Trout Town USA," protested that spraying DDT would kill fish and damage the life of streams and rivers. They cited the precedent of Yellowstone National Park spraying in 1953 and 1955. During the 1955 spraying DDT drifted into the Yellowstone River, resulting in, as the Rod & Gun Club stated it, the deaths of "tons of fish." An *Outdoor Life* magazine article entitled "Insecticides and Dead Fish," reported that the Rod & Gun Club hired biologists to measure fish and fish-food life in trout streams before and after spraying to monitor its effects. Evidence showed that the spray was devastating to both.[10]

The Federal Court in Brooklyn denied the request of Long Island residents for a temporary injunction to stop the spraying.[11] As evidence of the spraying's harmful effects continued to mount in New York, including swimming pools in Westchester covered with films of oily DDT, apple orchards saturated in Bedford, and dead birds all around, the eight plaintiffs who filed the injunction were joined by six others, including the son of Theodore Roosevelt, Archibald R. Roosevelt, and Marjorie Spock, younger sister of famous pediatrician Benjamin Spock and a longtime practitioner of Rudolf Steiner's biodynamic organic gardening, in a new suit filed to block all future spraying.[12] Following the completion of 1957's spraying Robert Cushman Murphy reported significant damage to Brookhaven, where he lived. "There is scarcely a fish alive in the still waters. There are few if any frogs," he said. "I myself have seen bumblebees fall. We counted ninety-three dead trout in half a mile of stream." In a nearby marsh blue crabs and fiddler crabs were killed, and an organic farmer who bought thousands of ladybugs for natural plant-lice control found all of them dead. In a pre-trial deposition, Murphy asserted that the widespread spraying necessarily meant that some of the city's food supply had been poisoned, and consumers were ingesting DDT-tainted milk and produce.[13] Indeed, by 1957 DDT was present in much of the nation's food supply, the body fat of its citizens, and the milk of its mothers.

Additional concerns were raised at the trial, including the specter of cancer. Doctor Malcolm M. Hargraves of the Mayo Clinic testified that DDT sprays might actually be encouraging the dread disease. He argued further that estimates of human tolerance for the chemical were narrowing, just as they were for atomic radiation. Most of the blood specialists at the clinic, he told the court, agreed with him. To make matters worse, it was increasingly difficult to avoid the poison in one's daily diet. Organic farmers testified that years of hard work had been undone by the spraying. Much of the criticism, as had Murphy's, focused on the broad implications for ecology and the environment. As an article on the trial in *American Forest* magazine summarized: "Actually, this comes down to a question of whether we are slowly committing suicide by killing off so much of our wildlife as to drastically upset the balance of nature by arbitrarily removing certain predators."[14]

The government countered with the testimony of Dr. Wayland J. Hayes, chief of the toxicological division of the US Public Health Service, who boasted that two prison experiments had shown that inmates exposed to large doses of DDT suffered no health problems. In one experiment he insisted that 51 prisoners who received 200 times the amount of DDT typically swallowed daily by individuals for a period of 18 months had demonstrated no adverse effects.[15]

On June 23, 1958 the Federal District Court upheld the right of the federal and state governments to spray DDT from airplanes. The case was appealed to the United States Court of Appeals, which upheld the lower court's decision in October 1959. In March 1960 the US Supreme Court refused to hear the case, over the protest of Justice William O. Douglas, who noted that DDT may have been causing "mounting sterility among our bald eagles," negative effects on other birds and wildlife, as well as human blood diseases. The FDA had ruled that milk could not contain even a trace of DDT, an outraged Douglas argued, and the plaintiffs had produced evidence that milk, as well as fruits and vegetables, were contaminated.[16]

Although the lawsuit was unsuccessful, the fight over DDT spraying brought together like-minded constituencies. And it established a precedent for using court action for environmental purposes. Publicity surrounding the lawsuit further awakened the public to a darker side of corporate capitalism. Rodale's *Organic Gardening and Farming* concluded: "It was the most significant and widely-publicized law suit [sic] yet fought on this vital point. The general public was made to realize that spray programs killed wildlife, fish, birds; contaminated unsprayed gardens; upset the balance of nature; constituted a trespass on private property and a threat to human life."[17] Lest there be any confusion about the source of the threat, J. I. Rodale added, "The highly populated northeastern area of the United States had dramatized to its populace the extent to which the chemical industry is today influencing our environment."[18]

In 1959, even *My Weekly Reader*, a four-page mini-newspaper read by schoolchildren across the United States, carried an article proclaiming DDT a poison that kills many birds. *Croplife*, a newspaper for the farm chemical industry, immediately protested that *My Weekly Reader* was part of a deliberate attempt to make American children hate insecticides.[19]

While national news was spreading the stories of the massive gypsy moth spraying controversy, for many Americans those reports only confirmed the environmental hazards of DDT that they discovered through much smaller spraying programs in their own communities throughout the East and Midwest to control mosquitoes and combat Dutch elm disease. Until the advent of DDT, cutting down the infected elm trees and carefully disposing of them appeared to provide the only hope for containing the disease that had broken out in the 1930s. DDT offered the possibility of killing the disease-carrying elm bark beetles before they could spread their damage. In the earliest community-spraying campaigns in the late 1940s, residents of cities including Princeton, New Jersey, Cleveland, Ohio, and Indianapolis, Indiana, complained that their streets and yards were littered with dead birds.[20] As Dutch elm disease continued to spread, communities in additional states sprayed their trees, and everywhere dead birds followed; mortality rates were as high as 80 percent. Protests were lodged in some communities, especially by conservationists and birdwatchers, but many residents were torn between their love for the elm trees and their concern for the birds.[21]

By the late 1950s Americans were noting a "serious and mysterious" decline of bald eagles, the nation's symbol and national bird. Scientists and the National Audubon Society cited widespread sterility among the eagles that was likely caused by the great birds feeding on DDT-tainted fish that had been feeding on poisoned insects.[22] Other research indicated that in some areas sprayed with DDT "robins and other birds are dying like flies." In early 1959 zoologist George J. Wallace reported in *Audubon* magazine that more than 140 kinds of birds were believed to have been killed by insecticide poisoning. It was found that DDT accumulated in earthworms, and when birds ate the worms they suddenly died. The chemical pesticides that were supposed to kill insects were killing the birds that naturally helped to keep insect populations in check.[23] Rodale's *Organic Gardening* noted, rather grimly, that these birds and other animals were protecting humans because, living closer to nature, they were providing advance warning to how humans were making the environment toxic. "The song bird in the field is now serving the same purpose as the canary in a cage carried down into a gas-filled mine," Robert Rodale said. "When the canary in the mine died, the miners knew that dangerous gas was present. We are now watching the birds in the fields to see how long *they* can hold out."[24] But, unlike miners, citizens could not exit the mine to escape the deadly gas; chemicals were fast permeating the entire ecosystem.

Waging Chemical Warfare on Fire Ants

While the gypsy moth–spraying program was causing growing controversy in the North, the South was also falling victim to aerial attack. The nerve agent pesticides heptachlor, from the Velsicol Chemical Corporation, a subsidiary of the Chicago & North Western Railway, along with DDT and the Shell Chemical Corporation's dieldrin (roughly 40 times as toxic as DDT), were deployed in a massive USDA aerial- and ground-spraying program covering some 20,000,000 to 30,000,000 acres in nine Southern states beginning in early 1958. It was a "war" against the "imported fire ant," a South American insect believed first introduced into the United States as a stowaway on a freight ship in Mobile, Alabama in 1918. The spraying campaign hoped to not just control the insect but "eradicate" it.

Supporters of the spraying singled out the fire ants for destruction because their homes, consisting of foot-and-a-half-tall mounds that numbered as many as 200 to an acre, jammed and broke mower bars when farmers were attempting to harvest. Children and farm workers were sometimes the victims of painful stings from the insects, resulting in swelling and scarring or, for a few particularly sensitive ones, even hospitalization. Furthermore, the fire ants were purported to have attacked and killed calves and pigs. Crops, lawns, and gardens were all said to have been damaged by the ants feeding on seeds and young plants.

Some insisted that these claims were alarmist and fostered by corporations to sell more chemicals. As J. I. Rodale summed it up, "Much of the journalistic furor about [the fire ant] is propaganda-induced. It means sales of more 'control' chemicals."[25] The Alabama Department of Conservation added that in years of research no evidence of the fire ant being responsible for the death of a wildlife species had ever been observed. Dr. F. S. Arant, head entomologist at Alabama Tech, reported, "Research proves that the imported fire ant feeds largely on other insects and is not ruinous to crops, although it does pose a nuisance by building mounds which interfere with harvesting." Nevertheless, the agribusiness-friendly USDA set out on an aggressive campaign to halt the insect's advance by applying two to four pounds of pesticide per acre, an amount Dr. M. R. Clarkson of the Agency's research service assured had been carefully planned to "do the least possible damage to wildlife and other insects."[26]

Although the USDA insisted the spraying was safe, increasing evidence to the contrary led many to oppose the program on environmental grounds. In its protest of the spraying the National Audubon Society noted that the California Department of Fish and Game reported that a pound and a half of dieldrin per acre had caused the death of pheasants, quail, gophers, snakes, rabbits, dogs, chickens, geese, and turkeys, while the government's own Fish and Wildlife

Service demonstrated that a pound of the chemical had "sufficient toxicity to kill approximately 4,000,000 quail chicks." The Conservation Foundation and New York Zoological Society issued a joint 57-page report summarizing "the present knowledge of the dangers of mass spraying of pesticides to control insect infestation and plant diseases" that emphasized the hazards of the many unknown qualities of pesticides.[27]

The gypsy moth and fire ant spraying campaigns occurred at the same time that British ecologist Charles S. Elton's book, *The Ecology of Invasions by Insects and Plants* (1958), was alerting the public to the differentiated organisms having evolved for millions of years on isolated continents that were being introduced to nonnative environments, intentionally and unintentionally, through increasing international travel and trade. Upsetting the balance of ecological systems, the environmental consequences of these "invasive species" were often disastrous. Invasions by synthetic chemicals that upset the ecological balance were, the Audubon Society noted, having similarly catastrophic effects.[28]

Opposition to mass spraying programs continued to multiply, encompassing a wide variety of constituencies. Some traditional conservation organizations began to expand their focus to include environmental issues. Three Harvard scientists, including famed biologist Edward O. Wilson, backed the position of the National Wildlife Federation that the spraying of heptachlor and dieldrin would harm wildlife, and added that it might also result in "the emergence of new insect pests once they have been freed from the natural enemies that held them in check." Audubon Society president John H. Baker added that the insecticides also left birds unable to reproduce. "When you realize that the poisons may well have similar cumulative effects on the human system," he continued, "it is unthinkable that a widespread program be undertaken in the absence of proof that there is no risk of such a result." He urged society members to petition Congress to put a halt to the spraying of DDT, heptachlor, and dieldrin until further study of the poisons was completed. Wilhelmine Waller, president of the Garden Club of America, called on members to lobby Congress "just the same way the chemical industry does," to stop the spraying. Insecticide hazards, warned Baker, "may well rank" with those of radioactive fallout.[29]

James Hancock was among those who viewed the spraying as an affront to democracy. After noting that spraying had killed many fish in his Madisonville, Kentucky farm pond, yet his protests to government officials did not stop the planes from returning, Hancock wondered, "As an American citizen, is there nothing I (or we) can do before it is too late?... I'm proud of my country, but it is hard to feel so toward... organizations that force aerial spraying on those of us who despise it and its terrible consequences."[30] There was a growing sense among Americans that their environment was under threat but there was little, if anything, they could do about it, a sense that the chemical industry held greater sway than citizens.

Although one scholar who searched USDA records found "very little material connecting the chemical industry to the campaign," by this time there was no effective separation between the chemical industry and the USDA.[31] USDA officials were usually educated at land-grant universities, where they learned, based on research funded by chemical companies, that chemical-industrial agriculture was the best way to grow. Upon arriving at the USDA they were lobbied relentlessly by the agribusiness-friendly American Farm Bureau Federation.[32] Entomologists, who had formerly received a broad education in biology and understood the insect as a part of a vast natural ecology, were instead now trained as technicians in economic entomology and taught to narrow their view of the insect to a profit threat that needed to be eradicated—with a chemical insecticide. The few entomologists still employed by the USDA to seek biological control of pests rather than chemical eradication found their division bled dry via staffing and funding cuts. "It is apparent to us," they complained, "that the Bureau's personnel as a whole are insecticide minded and that the insecticide industry is exerting a tremendous influence on the Bureau even to the extent that it dictates the character of much of its research."[33] Thus, chemical companies did not need to be directly involved in the spraying campaigns. Agribusiness dominated research and development at land-grant universities, assuring that its interests were paramount in the products they developed. Faced with a problem, the corporate-educated agents put forward corporate solutions.

Some of the biggest fire-ant spraying protests came from outdoor recreationists. Leading hunting and fishing magazines strongly questioned the spraying's environmental impact. *Field & Stream* charged that the spraying took place even though lab tests by the US Fish and Wildlife Service had shown dieldrin and heptachlor were 10 to 20 times more toxic than DDT. "No one really knew the answers," the magazine charged, "but this big control program got off the ground *with no provision for finding out*."[34] After noting that nearly all of the "6,000 brand name insecticides, herbicides, and fungicides used in agriculture... *are in some way harmful to fish and game*," *Outdoor Life* quoted the Wildlife Management Institute, which warned, "This program could be the biggest boomerang in the controversy-studded history of mass insect-poisoning campaigns." The magazine concluded, "Lack of scientific knowledge of how chemical insecticides introduced in the past 10 years affect fish and game makes their large-scale use as dangerous as leaving a loaded shotgun, its safety off, in the rumpus room."[35]

The *Field & Stream* article included a gloomy photograph of a red fox, cottontail rabbit, black bass, chuck-will's-widow, meadowlark, bobwhite quail, and mourning dove, laid out together on the ground with the caption, "Casualties of fire-ant spray war," and provided a detailed inventory of the birds and animals found dead in an area sprayed in Alabama. Earthworms, food for many birds, were found to contain heptachlor in "significant amounts." Both dieldrin and heptachlor were designed to have a three-year lethal "residual" effect. The magazine stopped short of calling for a ban on all pesticide spraying but urged that if deemed absolutely necessary it be done in localized areas and on the ground.[36] During the spring of 1959, Northerners who spent the winter in Florida reported that the massive flocks of birds usually seen migrating north in February and March were nowhere to be seen; the *Washington Post* reported that spraying programs were to blame.[37] Yet again, citizens were made to feel powerless in the face of environmental destruction.

After more than a year of the USDA's insisting that the spray was safe, on October 27, 1959—the same month an appeals court ruled against the New York plaintiffs in the gypsy moth DDT case—the other government agency charged with regulating chemicals, the FDA, finally issued an order that placed restrictions on the use of heptachlor. It discovered that an unexpected, more toxic and persistent new product, heptachlor epoxide, formed after heptachlor was applied and was accumulated in the liver, kidneys, and fatty tissues. By then heptachlor was being used not only on fire ants but as a soil pesticide on fruit, vegetables, and grains. The FDA moved from permitting small residues of the chemical on crops to zero tolerance until its manufacturer, Velsicol Chemical Corporation of Chicago, could prove that trace residues were not harmful to humans. Despite evidence that it was a carcinogen and caused liver damage, heptachlor was used in agriculture until the late 1970s, and its commercial sale was not banned until 1988. A persistent organic pollutant, heptachlor epoxide could be found in soil 15 years after application, where it continued to poison crops.[38]

It was yet one more example of how little understood and potentially dangerous the new postwar chemical world was, and along with the controversy surrounding DDT spraying heptachlor helped convince many that the use of chemicals posed a real and serious problem not only to human health but also to the health of the total environment. A few years later Louisiana and Florida both had more fire ant–infested acres than before the program began. The journal *Sugar Bulletin* reported that where heptachlor had been aerially sprayed for fire ants over sugar cane fields, there was an increase in crop damage from the sugar cane borer, whose predators had apparently been killed in the process.[39] Only days after the toxic effects of heptachlor were finally revealed, fears fostered by the massive spraying programs grew to alarm when an iconic American food was found to contain dangerous chemical poison.

The Great Thanksgiving Cranberry Affair

In November 1959, the Food and Drug Administration warned the public about yet another reason to fear their food. In what some would later term the "Great

Thanksgiving Cranberry Affair of 1959," Secretary of Health, Education, and Welfare Arthur S. Flemming announced only 17 days before the holiday that cranberries grown in Oregon and Washington might not be safe to eat due to contamination by a weed killer called aminotriazole that had been shown to cause thyroid cancer in rats.

Cranberries, legendary food of the first Thanksgiving, had been commercially harvested in the United States since 1816.[40] In 1947 a *New York Times* editorial expressed the significance of the cranberry in American life: "President and Mrs. Truman have struck pumpkin pie from the holiday menu," it noted, "but not cranberries, never. It's a Presidential Citation."[41] If milk was the symbol of pure and wholesome food, then cranberries symbolized "American" food, and both might now contain additional humanmade substances unleashed in the environment that might kill any who ingested them.

Aminotriazole, produced by the American Cyanamid and Amchem corporations, had been approved by the Food and Drug Administration in early 1958 for use in cranberry bogs, but only if used within a few days after the cranberry harvest. If used during the growing season it would be incorporated into the cranberries. But the ruling came after cranberry growers had already used aminotriazole during the growing season in 1957. When the FDA warned producers that year that the pesticide was not yet registered and the practice might not be safe, growers agreed to set aside three million pounds of contaminated berries that would have been subject to seizure for further FDA testing. Thus in 1958 the FDA, seriously understaffed and believing its warning from the previous year would stop the use of aminotriazole on cranberries, did not check any berries going to market. When FDA scientists concluded in 1959 that aminotriazole was a carcinogen and none of its residue could be on crops, the cranberry association destroyed the 1957 berries that were held over. That autumn, though, the FDA began hearing rumors that the chemical was still being widely used during the 1958 and 1959 growing seasons. When tests confirmed those rumors, Flemming issued his statement. It was clear that, in the interim, the public had consumed contaminated berries.[42]

Ocean Spray Cranberries, Incorporated, the growers' cooperative that controlled over 75 percent of the country's cranberries, protested that it required sworn affidavits from all of its growers certifying that they had used the chemical only as directed. Of 1,079 growers "only ten or eleven declined to sign," who immediately had their crops impounded along with some others that were suspected of being contaminated by drift from nearby areas. To make matters worse for the growers, 1959 was a record cranberry harvest. But Secretary Flemming was unmoved. When asked by reporters how consumers would know if the cranberries they were buying were safe, he replied that if a "housewife" was unable to determine the point of origin of cranberries "to be on the safe side, she doesn't buy." Of course, because it was an undifferentiated crop, determining a cranberry's point of origin in the market was generally impossible. A panic ensued. Many grocers responded by pulling their entire inventory from store shelves, restaurants removed cranberries from their menus, and some municipalities banned their sale.[43]

Ten days later the FDA announced that it would begin a program to examine cranberries and cranberry products. Those that passed inspection would be released to the market and labeled "Examined and passed by the Food and Drug Administration."[44] An advertisement for the Safeway grocery store chain boasted, "Fresh and Canned Cranberries Tested and Cleared."[45] Even so, cranberries were in short supply that Thanksgiving, and many families did without or substituted lingonberries from Scandinavia.[46] Even some of those able to find cranberries may have regretted their good fortune when the government later announced that more than 2,000 packages of contaminated berries were accidentally sold in Kansas City markets, and in addition to those grown in the Pacific Northwest some cranberries sold from Wisconsin were also found to be bad.[47]

Industry officials derided the entire incident as a boondoggle. Charles Shuman, president of the agribusiness-friendly National Farm Bureau, called Flemming "irresponsible" and sent a telegram to Eisenhower urging the President to fire him. An effigy of Flemming was hanged, and the "corpse" then carried to a waiting ambulance by the winner of the "Miss Cranberry" contest, Joan Aliamus of Modesto, California, who sported a long strand of cranberries, like pearls, around her neck. To demonstrate his unwavering support for agribusiness, Secretary of Agriculture Ezra Benson ate a bowl of cranberries while visiting a farm in Maryland. Presidential hopeful John F. Kennedy drank a couple of glasses of cranberry juice in Wisconsin. Not to be outdone, Republican candidate Vice President Richard Nixon downed four helpings of cranberry sauce and proclaimed they were just the "way mother made them." Wisconsin Democratic Senator William Proxmire denounced the FDA's "blanket condemnation" of the entire industry, and New Jersey Representative Frank Thomas called it "irresponsible government at its worst."[48]

Much of the public took a decidedly different view. Letters sent to FDA headquarters favored Flemming's action by a ratio of 7 to 1, with comments that included, "Please take my thanks as a consumer and be assured we appreciate your bravery"; "You are to be commended for sticking your neck out for the 170,000,000 population"; and, "We applaud your concern for the American people despite heavy pressures from commercial interests." In addition, a number of organizations expressed public support for the FDA's action, including Consumers Union, the General Federation of Women's Clubs, the National Wildlife Federation, the American Home Economics Association, the Federation of Homemakers of Washington, DC, and the American Nature Association. In a letter to the editor of the *New York Times*, Armand Oppenheimer, dentist, anthropologist, and ecologist, thanked Flemming and the FDA, noting, "While radioactive fallout is a dramatic and present danger, peril from food additives, chemical poisons and quack remedies is equally grave."[49]

"Pesticide violations are occurring every day with no one knowing of them but the offending farmers," wrote *Washington Post* reporter Milton Viorst. "With its meager network of inspectors," he warned, "FDA has no clear idea of the pattern of violations and is virtually powerless to stop them." Even if inspectors did send crop samples to a lab for inspection, by the time long and complex testing was completed the crop had usually already gone to market. The ecosystem and food chain were being inundated with toxic chemicals.[50]

The article also left the unmistakable impression that many other similar hazards existed, as yet undiscovered by the overmatched FDA. Much of the public must have been feeling the same way. In December 1959, the FDA admitted that a 1958 study of 17 cities across the United States revealed that some milk in 11 of them was tainted with "substantial amounts" of DDT and other pesticides.[51] By 1960 over half the products being sold by the chemical industry had not been in production 20 years earlier, and more than 90 percent of drugs and pharmaceuticals had been developed only in the last 10 years.[52] As *Consumer Reports* concluded, "There seems little doubt that if the FDA had the resources and authority to undertake testing of its own, it would find many other instances in which harmful chemicals are permitted in dangerous amounts on common foodstuffs."[53]

Of course, that assumed that the FDA desperately wanted to protect the public but merely lacked the resources to do so. Its often cozy relationship with the industries it was supposed to regulate called such assumptions into question, and even when it did move to act it was frequently thwarted by relentless corporate pressure. Herbert Ley, who served as FDA Commissioner in the 1960s, later complained about badgering from big business: "The bugging was unmerciful at times," he said. "Some days I spent as many as six hours fending off representatives of the drug industry." The agency's budget of about $74 million, he noted, "was less than the cost of one nuclear submarine or one tank missile program," even though the FDA was supposed to "regulate hundreds of billions of dollars' worth of products a year.... The thing that bugs me is that the people think the FDA is protecting them—it isn't," Ley concluded. "What the FDA is doing and what the public thinks it's doing are as different as night and day."[54]

None of this would have surprised readers of a 1955 book by chemist and organic gardener Leonard Wickenden entitled *Our Daily Poison: The Effects of DDT, Fluorides, Hormones and Other Chemicals on Modern Man.*[55] As Wickenden stated, "Most of us have become uneasily aware, in recent years, that we are living in a poisoned world. Pesticides are sprayed over the fruit and vegetables that we eat; we cannot buy beef or poultry with any assurance that the meat is free from hormones that may produce profound changes in our bodies; the flour used in making our bread is 'aged' with chemicals and doctored in other ways; the air we breathe in hotels and public halls is impregnated with poisoned vapors... cosmetics are on the market which may bring lasting injury to the masses."[56]

After detailing these and other concerns, Wickenden suggested that the most promising response from citizens was political action. "The first and most obvious action is for the reader to spread the alarm among his friends and neighbors," he urged. "If we want unpoisoned food, unpoisoned water, unpoisoned air, we can have them," he optimistically predicted, "provided we are prepared to insist upon our rights and to sweep from office those who condone present practices.... The vote is still a powerful weapon." Perhaps it was, but was it more powerful than corporate lobbying and campaign funding? Secretary of Commerce Frederick Mueller urged business leaders to "engage much more actively in public affairs at every level—to share with government the responsibility of economic statesmanship." "At our disposal," said Mueller, "is an American heritage of priceless worth—a wealth of resources of immeasurable value."[57] For those citizens who found it difficult to compete with the combined forces of business and government, and who were able to find neighborhood growers, Wickenden suggested consuming organic vegetables.[58] Barth's of Long Island, a mail-order marketer of natural foods, thought Wickenden's book was so important that in 1959 it offered a free copy of *Our Daily Poison* with each ten-dollar order.[59]

Increasing numbers of citizens and scholars wondered if the ballot box could really compete with corporate power. In the 1958 edition of his popular textbook *Parties, Politics, and Interest Groups*, political scientist V. O. Key observed, "The power wielded by business in American politics may puzzle the person of democratic predilections: a comparatively small minority exercises enormous power."[60] "The cure cannot come through political leadership because every politician is bound to promise 'bigger and better,'" said Fairfield Osborn that same year. "The cure cannot come from business and industry because the aim of every business is to 'beat last year's record.' Times call for a tremendous readjustment in our national point of view."[61]

Along with the controversies surrounding the gypsy moth and fire ant sprayings, the Great Thanksgiving Cranberry Affair seemed to confirm fears that American democracy was distorted by corporate power, while simultaneously validating the wisdom of an alternative path like the environmental vision Leopold termed "the land ethic." It lent additional credence to earlier warnings from writers like J. I. Rodale and James Rorty regarding the growing hazard of chemicals in food. As former General Electric Vice President T. K. Quinn had argued in his 1956 book, *Giant Corporations: Challenge to Freedom*: "To the extent that we, the consumers, are not represented, with our consent, in the control over the production of what we consume, freedom is restricted and the democratic process violated."[62]

Among the most significant outcomes of the late 1950s chemical controversies was the further mainstreaming of environmentalism discourse. The *New Yorker* was moved to begin an occasional feature the month after the cranberry scare called "These Precious Days: The New Yorker's fever chart of the planet Earth, showing Man's ups and downs in contaminating the air, the sea, and the soil." It was a collection of paragraphs—factoids—on a wide variety of environmental issues from around the world.[63] Friends drew Rachel Carson's interest to both the gypsy moth and fire ant spray hazards which, combined with the decade's other chemical threats, convinced Carson that the environment was under unprecedented attack. She set to work researching and writing her seminal book, *Silent Spring*, which would be published in 1962. It was a powerful work that convinced many who still held doubts that threats to the environment were, indeed, threats to all.[64]

The Delaney Clause

The restrictions on heptachlor and the Great Thanksgiving Cranberry Affair were the FDA's first enforcements of the "Delaney Clause," a 50-word addition to the Food Additives Amendment of 1958 to the 1938 Federal Food, Drug, and Cosmetic Act which stated: "That no food additive shall be deemed safe if it is found to induce cancer when ingested by man or animal, or if it is found, after tests which are appropriate for the evaluation of the safety of food additives, to induce cancer in man or animal." The amendment was the culmination of congressional investigations into the effects of chemicals used in the production, processing, preparation, and packaging of foodstuffs from 1950–1954. "What we are seeking," said New York Representative James J. Delaney as the study began, "is information on all chemical substances used in processing and manufacturing foodstuffs, about the contents of insecticides and pesticides and chemical fertilizers and their effects on the human system."[65]

According to Delaney the genesis of the hearings was a conversation he had with Wisconsin's Republican Representative Frank R. Keith in 1949, who told the House Rules Committee that Delaney sat on about his decision to have the area surrounding his Wisconsin lake home sprayed with DDT after he was inundated by hordes of mosquitoes. Following the spraying he returned to the lake to find the mosquito population reduced, but he was alarmed to discover many fish that ate the insects also became poisoned and died. Keith's testimony helped push Congress to create the House Select Committee to Investigate the Use of Chemicals in Food and Cosmetics, chaired by Delaney.[66] Representatives wondered if chemicals used on crops and in processed foods were having a similar effect on humans that the DDT-tainted mosquitoes had on fish.

When the Delaney Committee held its first round of hearings the FDA list of food additives included 124 preservatives, antioxidants, and mold inhibitors; 189 insecticides, fungicides, herbicides, and plant growth regulators; 90 emulsifying agents, wetting agents, "improvers," maturing agents, and flour bleaches; 51 wax coatings, resins, plasticizers, and other components of packaging materials; 24 acidulants, buffers, and neutralizers; 274 flavoring materials and solvents; 24 artificial colors; 33 vitamins and minerals; 4 sugar substitutes; and 29 "miscellaneous" chemicals, for a total of 842, of which 704 were known to be in use.[67] Prior to the war, sales of agricultural chemicals, including pesticides, herbicides, and fungicides, totaled about $35 million. Within twenty years, the total had soared to $278 million.[68]

The committee soon determined that this explosion in the use and complexity of chemicals necessitated a law that would place the burden of proof on producers to demonstrate that a new chemical was safe for consumption before it could be used, instead of the current arrangement that forced the FDA to first find an additive in a product and then prove the ingredient was harmful before it could halt its sale. In all, some 217 witnesses testified at the hearings. F. J. Schlink, president of Consumers' Research, founded in 1929, appeared before Delaney's committee to complain that the USDA was promoting the use of chemicals and appeared "little concerned" about possible dangers to consumers. The head of the American Home Economics Association, Cornell University professor Faith Fenton, testified, "the present chaotic situation is cause for anxiety."[69] J. I. Rodale submitted a 32-page statement to the committee detailing the history of the organic method and why he believed it was superior to chemical agriculture.[70]

In an interim report released in January 1951, Delaney said the widespread postwar use of chemicals in foods was an "alarming" situation that raised "a serious problem as far as the public health is concerned." The committee noted that of the 704 chemicals being added to food, "only 428 are definitely known to be safe as used. Thus, there are approximately 276 chemicals being used in food today, the safety of which has not been established to the satisfaction of the Food and Drug Administration and many other groups concerned with the health and safety to the public."[71]

When the Delaney Committee took up hearings again in 1952, it heard from an executive of Beech-Nut, a major manufacturer of baby food, who demonstrated that not all companies were complacent about chemical pollution. In testimony reported by the press, L. G. Cox emphasized that his company was concerned about experiments indicating that younger animals were especially susceptible to the chronic toxic effects of chemicals like DDT, and additional data indicating that newborns may already have DDT stored in their tissues and be receiving additional amounts from their mothers' milk. He testified that Beech-Nut believed "that any insecticide residue which tends to accumulate in fatty tissue should be eliminated in so far as possible from the baby's diet," and his company had already spent $688,000 in the past six years in an effort to keep pesticide residues and crop chemicals out of the baby foods and peanut butter it manufactured. In 1948 alone Beech-Nut rejected squash from Florida, peaches from Pennsylvania, and celery from Florida; in 1950 it rejected $15,000 worth of contracted vegetables; the next year it refused contracted apples from New York. All the rejections were due to residues of DDT and BHC, another persistent pesticide that, like DDT, was later banned. Nevertheless, he told the committee, some chemical residue was likely making its way into baby foods. Cox took a pointed jab at the chemical industry by noting that although it accused his company of "being hysterical about the problem," it nevertheless put together a fund of about $119,000 "to counteract unfavorable publicity." Cox's testimony provided both Congress and citizens with alarming details about environmental threats to babies' health.[72]

Concerns and frustrations mounted as details of the Delaney hearings were made public. In a 1952 letter to the *New York Times*, Louly Bare complained, "It is nothing short of moral lassitude on the part of government to have permitted the development of such wholesale use of drugs and chemicals in the production and processing of foods, livestock and poultry. It is a grave lack of responsibility on the part of producers and processors who ignore the implications and potential dangers of their methods. Practically everything we eat is being subjected to commercial fertilizers or pesticides of varying degrees of toxicity." All of this was, in Bare's view, a threat to the nation's democratic system. "It will be impossible to correct this condition adequately until we plan and execute a program of readjustment in our economic thinking and in our actions," she said. "If we refuse to accept our responsibilities as individuals we shall forfeit our freedom as individuals. We are forced to eat drugs in foods against our will."[73]

Attempts at regulation were fought every step of the way by the lobbying efforts of powerful industry trade associations like the Manufacturing Chemists' Association and the National Agricultural Chemicals Association, which were protecting a lucrative pesticide industry that had grown in sales from $40,000,000 in 1939, before the era of synthetics, to a staggering $260,000,000 in 1954 when DDT and other synthetic compounds dominated the market. Powerful corporations like DuPont, Shell, and Olin Mathieson were intent on doing whatever was necessary to maintain their markets and profits.[74]

The committee's initial investigation lasted two years until finally, on June 30, 1952, Delaney concluded: "Reasonable testing should be required. And that includes testing the unknown latent affects [sic] that chemicals may have if consumed over a long time."[75] Researchers had been expressing concerns about long-term exposure to small amounts of DDT since the mid-1940s.[76] Delaney later summed up the proceedings by stating, "Our food supply is being doctored by hundreds of new chemicals whose safety has not yet been established. Many of these chemicals were developed during and after World War II. Most of them may be harmless, but enough have been proved dangerous and even deadly to make us wonder if your health is threatened." He wondered if there was a connection between the growing number of mental illnesses and the many new chemicals used in food. And doctors testified that there was further evidence that these substances were implicated in some diseases, including cancer.[77]

Committee testimony continued until 1954. Although legislation was proposed in the following years to force producers to prove the chemicals they used were safe—eleven bills were introduced during the 84th Congress in 1955–1956 alone—it stalled in the face of intense industry lobbying. Finally, the level of concern increased dramatically, and Congress was pushed to demonstrate action after August 1956 when media attention given to the Symposium of the International Union Against Cancer in Rome focused increased public attention on the issue.[78]

At the symposium a number of food additives used in the United States and Europe were declared cancer-producing. Its report listed 20 groups of suspect additives including dyes, thickeners, synthetic sweeteners and flavors, bleaches, oils, fat substitutes, and preservatives. In addition, it identified 17 groups of suspect food contaminants, including antibiotics, estrogen used in fattening animals, pesticide residues, soot, chemical sterilizers, antisprouting agents, wrapping materials, and radiation.[79]

The paper that served as the basis for many of its recommendations was delivered by Wilhelm C. Hueper, chief of the Environmental Cancer section of the National Cancer Institute since 1948, who spent his life researching cancer after being fired by DuPont back in the late 1930s for telling his bosses one too many times that some of the company's chemicals were giving their workers cancer. After discussing the explosion in the use of chemicals in foodstuffs he noted, "A disturbing aspect of this development is that there exists no mandatory provision for assuring, *a priori*, the biologic contaminants, particularly long term or delayed effects, have adequately been studied. The circumstances suggest the virtual certainty that many have not."[80] He concluded by emphasizing the undemocratic nature of the situation and the vulnerability of each citizen "to potential, long delayed health hazards which he has neither consented to nor is able to avoid."[81] The symposium included cancer experts from 21 countries who agreed unanimously on the "urgent necessity of international collaboration for the protection of mankind" against the hazards of carcinogenic food additives.

The report the symposium produced had tremendous influence in the United States. William Smith, a New York physician involved with the symposium, met with Delaney after the meeting in early 1957 to press for an anticancer provision in the additives law. In a letter to Delaney, Smith compared the protection of American bodies from attack by foreign chemicals to protection of American lands from foreign enemies.[82] The Delaney anticancer clause in the amendment, with its controversial zero tolerance for carcinogens, was modeled after the symposium's recommendations. All other known poisons were permitted in food, as long as they did not exceed tolerances deemed safe by the FDA. Since it was not known if there were safe tolerances for cancer-producing substances in food, none were permitted.[83]

The popular Delaney almost did not remain in Congress to finally see the amendment pass in 1958. In 1956 "the chemical lobby spent $90,000 to defeat me," he recalled. "I usually carry the district two or three to one, but that year I was down 40 votes on election night." After he demanded a recount Delaney was ultimately declared the winner by only 145 votes.[84] The message, nevertheless, was plain. Lawmakers who dared take on corporate power were liable to see their careers cut short.

Corporate Lobbying and Legislative Loopholes

Although the Delaney clause appeared to reflect a Congress and FDA both determined to protect consumers from developing cancer from chemicals in the foods they were eating, a loophole in the legislation to satisfy corporate interests limited its effectiveness. A corporate cost–benefit analysis determined that the corporate profits that stood to be lost was greater than the value of the citizens who were likely to become ill or die from chemicals in processed foods. The amendment was supposed to shift the burden of proof from the government to the producers, who now had to demonstrate that an additive was safe before they could use it.[85] Chemical manufacturers waged vigorous protests on the grounds that free-market principles were being violated. As stated in the *Journal of Commerce*, "The chemical industry objects strongly to the idea of having to ask permission to market each new additive. It can be counted on to fight Rep. Delaney's bills or any others like them." Cosmetics manufacturers called the Delaney bill "dictatorial."[86] A top official from an agricultural chemical company complained, "In order to meet Government requirements we must now spend up to $2,000,000 in research over a period of up to five years before a new product can be marketed," and "any further restrictions would make our research costs prohibitive." In addition, the agricultural chemical industry was already weathering continual opposition from wildlife and conservation groups who believed their products were damaging the environment, as well as from pure food enthusiasts who believed they were damaging human health. Somehow, chemical manufacturers managed to carry on. The cranberry culprit aminotriazole had alone been grossing about $1 billion annually for American Cyanamid.[87] And when the government agreed to pay cranberry producers about $10 million to offset their losses from the aminotriazole scare, it was taxpaying citizens who footed the bill.[88]

Although business derided it, critics pointed out that compromises in the final wording of the Delaney clause bore the unmistakable imprint of big business's power over Congress. Prior to the amendment chemicals were classified as either "poisonous" or "non-poisonous," and those deemed poisonous to humans could not be used. With the amendment, a chemical additive known to be poisonous in large doses could be used as long as it could be shown to be "safe" in the quantities and conditions used in a given food, and it was not a known carcinogen. Thus, many substances formerly prohibited were now permitted. Industry claimed this was only reasonable, given that even many substances generally thought benign were harmful if ingested in large enough doses. Further, the FDA had already been giving de facto approval of poisonous chemicals in quantities deemed safe to humans after consulting with industry representatives for at least a dozen years, according to the FDA's director of the division of pharmacology, Dr. Arnold J. Lehman. "What we have been doing all along has been pretty illegal," admitted Lehman, "until Congress bailed us out." Detractors also protested that 188 additives already in use when the amendment was passed, and believed safe by the FDA, were given a "grandfather" exemption, placed on a GRAS ("generally recognized as safe") list, and exempted from testing. They appeared to have some grounds for concern. Ironically, the same *New York Times* article that reported the 188 "cleared" chemicals also noted that seven food dyes "long considered safe" had recently been found harmful thanks to improved testing technology.[89]

Further, critics of the amendment wondered whether industry testing done by scientists under the employ of producers could be trusted to be accurate and objective. Under the amendment, producers with a new chemical additive were required to submit a petition to the FDA with the name of the additive and its chemical identity (if known), explain how it would be used and its intended effect, and then describe the quantitative testing methods along with a complete account of investigations made to test its safety. The FDA would post the petition in the *Federal Register* for 90 days, during which time objections could be submitted. As *Science* journal noted, "Scientific experts will thus have a large responsibility under the terms of the amendment. If they raise objections to the proposal, the FDA will take them into account and hold hearings or otherwise gather additional information before making a ruling." Would scientists be keeping close watch on the *Federal Register* to monitor petitions, raising objections to new substances developed by producers and tested by their scientists? "If, on the other hand, scientists do not object, the FDA will assume there is general scientific agreement and will put the regulation into effect," the amendment concluded.[90]

Finally, the title of the amendment itself was seen as symbolic and significant. What had been called the *chemical* additive amendment was changed to the decidedly more innocuous *food* additive amendment, leaving the impression that it could just as well be addressing salt and pepper as polyoxyethylene monostearate. "A small matter, it might seem," noted *Consumers' Research*, "but a vitally important one when one realizes that the aim was to get the public's mind off *chemicals* and to bring in the implication to the nontechnical public that the additive is itself a food, not a *chemical added* to food."[91]

Chemical Meat

In the following months apprehensions about chemicals and cancer continued to escalate. In December 1959, only a month after the cranberry scare, Secretary Flemming announced a halt to the production and sale of chickens treated with the synthetic estrogen diethyistilbestrol, commonly called stilbestrol or DES, because it caused cancer. It was the drug J. I. Rodale had warned about nearly 15 years earlier. Speaking of its residue in chicken, Dr. Don Carlos Hines, a researcher for its manufacturer, Eli Lilly and Company, assured Delaney's Committee in 1952 that it was "neither helpful nor harmful, but neutral," when consumed by humans.[92]

By the time the FDA banned DES, "finishing" chickens was no longer its only use, or even its primary use. In 1954 Iowa State University ruminant nutritionist Wise Burroughs discovered that the hormone sped up weight gain in cattle by more than 10 percent when added to their feed or implanted in their ears, allowing stilbestrol-enhanced cattle to reach market about 35 days sooner while consuming about 500 pounds less feed than untreated cattle. In the opinion of executives from the Rath Packing and Wilson Packing companies, stilbestrol cattle had "better finished" meat to boot, making it more aesthetically appealing to consumers. Opponents pointed out that what this really meant was that the meat had increased fat marbling. Consumers who ate the meat of stilbestrol-treated beef were not only subject to possible chemical contamination, but increased fat intake that could lead to heart trouble.[93] Nevertheless, the FDA gave its approval to stilbestrol for cattle the same year, and the drug soon received a patent as the first artificial animal growth stimulant.[94]

This increase in cattle "productivity," as well as the largest and most intensive marketing campaign in the history of animal agriculture by Eli Lilly and Company which held an exclusive five-year patent from Iowa State University, marked a shift to confined feeding in massive commercial feedlots that soon began dotting the landscapes of the major cattle-growing regions in the South and across the Plains to the West. Feedlots not only pulled cattle off grazing land, they altered the landscape as miles of corn—and its accompanying crop chemicals—replaced native grazing grasses. Corn became the cattle feed of choice. Although it was not a natural part of the bovine diet and proved difficult for cattle to digest, it did promote rapid weight gain in livestock. Lilly billed stilbestrol as "the most important advance in animal nutrition since the introduction of antibiotics as growth stimulators." *Farm and Ranch* magazine reported that 16 cents of stilbestrol meant an extra 12 dollars in beef for cattle producers. By 1960 the power of the profit margin triumphed over concerns about cancer and resulted in some 90 to 95 percent of cattle receiving diethyistilbestrol.[95]

Beef treated with stilbestrol escaped the FDA's 1959 ruling that banned it from chickens, despite a study by the National Cancer Institute that found the synthetic hormone caused cancer in mice, rats, rabbits, and guinea pigs and produced a residue in poultry and livestock that might cause cancer in humans. The two leading producers of stilbestrol in cattle feed were Quaker Oats and Ralston Purina; Quaker was a particularly large financial contributor to Eisenhower's 1952 presidential campaign. Indeed, shortly after the election one Quaker Oats executive was named Ambassador to Canada, while another was appointed Assistant Secretary of State. Represented by the industry trade group American Feed Manufacturers Association, the companies hired Bradshaw Mintener to lobby against a stilbestrol ban in cattle. Mintener, a former Assistant Secretary of the Department of Health, Education, and Welfare, now lobbied the department to keep its Food and Drug Administration from imposing a ban on stilbestrol for livestock. He succeeded.[96] In congressional hearings in 1960, Thomas P. Carney, vice president for research of Eli Lilly, argued that DES was obviously safe because it was given to 300,000 women in 1959, with no ill effects. The same synthetic estrogen hormone used in chickens and cattle had been given to women after World War II in various doses both to prevent miscarriages and as a pill to induce chemical abortions.[97]

In 1959, tests began demonstrating that an average of 63 percent of DES given to cattle was excreted in urine and feces, raising some questions about what had become of the missing 37 percent of the carcinogen left unaccounted for. Decades later, concerns about the DES remaining in food were joined by alarm over DES which made its way into the ecosystem when excreted by farm animals, and the endocrine disruptor's effect on aquatic life and humans.[98]

Although it remained highly controversial, the FDA did not finally ban stilbestrol for cattle until 1979, and then only after a study published in the *New England Journal of Medicine* revealed that seven young women between the ages of 15 and 22, suffering from a form of vaginal cancer very rare for patients so young, were all daughters of mothers who had been given large doses of DES by their doctors. The young women had been exposed to the drug in utero.[99] Rodale's warnings about the drug a half-century earlier were, yet again, remarkably prescient.

By the close of the 1950s, Americans had been inundated by chemicals, along with news reports detailing their dangerous toxicity. The planet, their environment, and their bodies were being chemically altered, with consequences nobody could fully know or predict. Government actions to protect the public from the onslaught continued to appear inadequate, pushing growing numbers of citizens to do what they could to protect themselves, the planet, and their families through their choices as consumers.

PART TWO

A NEW RESPONSE

I'm gonna clean up my earth
And build a heaven on the ground
Not something distant or unfound
But something real to me.
—Paul Weller, *"Brand New Start,"* 1998

5

"A Ground Swell of Public Indignation"

By the end of the 1950s anxieties unleashed by the Bomb, pollution, and poisoned foods were moving increasing numbers of mainstream Americans to seek concrete solutions that could spare themselves and their families from the perils of postwar culture and its increasingly toxic environment. A number of authors were moved to further question the outsized role of corporate capitalism and consumer culture in the United States, echoing concerns that Aldo Leopold and others began raising a decade earlier. They worried that producers, through manipulative marketing, were seducing the middle class into never-ending consumption by convincing them that acquisition was the greatest path to pleasure, to the detriment of both personal and social improvement, not to mention the environment.

Most prolific was Vance Packard, who published a trilogy of best-selling nonfiction books from 1957 to 1960—*The Hidden Persuaders*, *The Status Seekers*, and *The Waste Makers*—all claiming that market researchers and advertisers were turning middle-class Americans "into voracious, wasteful, compulsive consumers." The new pressures to consume, said Packard, "are bringing forward such traits as pleasure-mindedness, self-indulgence, materialism, and passivity as conspicuous elements of the American character."[1] What Packard described could have more accurately been explained as the democratization of those character traits.

But it was not only the American soul being corrupted by consumer culture, he counseled; the natural environment was being compromised as well. "United States industrial firms are grinding up more than half of the natural resources processed each year on this planet for the benefit of 6 percent of the planet's people," Packard observed, before prophesying: "In the lifetime of many, if not most, of us, Americans will be trying to 'mine' old forgotten garbage dumps for their rusted tin cans."[2]

In his own 1958 bestseller, *The Affluent Society*, economist John Kenneth Galbraith had also warned of the cultural and environmental threats posed by corporate capitalism and consumer culture. For Galbraith, marketing and advertising branches of corporations manufactured desire to accompany their often-unnecessary products, blinding the nation to the possibility of better, more rational uses for its tremendous productive capacity. Like Packard, he feared that all of this was not only corrupting the American character but also polluting and threatening its natural environment.[3]

At a "Resources for the Future Forum" in Washington, DC that same year, Galbraith attacked the tendency of traditional conservationists to be stuck in outdated modes of concern focused on remote sites selected for their pleasing romantic aesthetics at the expense of almost everything else. He assailed many in his audience by stating a "law of conservationists": "The conservationist is a man who concerns himself with the beauties of nature in roughly inverse proportion to the number of people who can enjoy them." The environment would be much better served, Galbraith insisted, if traditional conservationists shifted their focus from breathtaking vistas to the more mundane issue of consumption. "Surely," he insisted, "this is the ultimate source of the problem." Galbraith encouraged conservationists to follow the lead of proto-environmentalists like Samuel Ordway, who urged citizens to confront the issue of consumption and the quantity consumed.[4]

Like Ordway, Galbraith did not mean that consumer culture should (or could) be entirely curtailed.[5] Restricting consumption of profligate products could be accomplished through government's means of social control: "Taxation; specific prohibitions on wasteful products, uses, or practices; educational and other hortatory efforts; subsidies to encourage consumption of cheaper and more plentiful substitutes are all available," Galbraith counseled.[6] Following such edicts would instill new economic sensibilities, and patterns of economic growth much less dependent on resource-intensive personal products. The emphasis could then shift to public, post-materialist goods that demand less from the environment but do much to enhance society, such as: "Education, health services, sanitary services, good parks and playgrounds, orchestras, effective local government, a clean countryside."[7] If conservationists truly care about the environment, Galbraith concluded, "There is no justification for ruling consumption levels out of the calculation."[8]

But such actions were, he realized, exceedingly unlikely. Confronting consumption required confronting the tenet of the nation's postwar civic religion that equated free markets, consuming, and economic growth with fundamental American freedoms. "Freedom is not much concerned with tail fins or even with automobiles," Galbraith countered. "Those who argue that it is identified with the greatest possible range of choice of consumers' goods are only confessing their exceedingly simple-minded and mechanical view of man and his liberties." Nevertheless, daring to raise questions about the wisdom of uninhibited consumption would lead to uncomfortable questions about the basis of postwar American culture. In addition, the postwar conservative backlash against both the New Deal and an expanded role for government in American life meant, "Since consumption could not be discussed without raising the question of an increased role for the state, it was not discussed."[9]

Indeed, just raising these issues that called into question the basis of liberal corporate capitalism was judged risky, even by those sympathetic to Galbraith's views. "Galbraith has, in putting his questions and suggesting the answers, pointed to additional places in our economic and political order where departure from neo-classical economic postures may be indicated," commented sociologist, demographer, and former Assistant to the Secretary of Commerce Philip M. Hauser. "In suggesting additional areas of federal interventionism, Professor Galbraith is, even in this present post–Senator McCarthy climate, indulging in possibly dangerous forms of economic and political heresy."[10]

In the face of that danger, and government inaction, green consumers were already practicing alternative politics by restraining their consumption with the environment in mind. Although many Americans would have suffered no harm by consuming less, the moralizing tone of critics like Packard and Galbraith sometimes failed to acknowledge that consuming is ensconced in the conduct of modern life. They did not see that consumers are not merely pathetic strivers manipulated to buy through marketing and advertising that they are powerless to resist. It requires a certain credulity to insist that consumption is a never-ending process of consumers being duped into purchasing things they do not want. Consumer culture is fostered not only by a desire to emulate social superiors, elevate status, compete, or gain respectability through material display, but also by a yearning to realize an inner life of daydreaming of a better, or at least different, existence.[11] The implications of the interior dream world of consumption have had enormous significance for environmentalism. The same daydreams that imagine that consuming perfect products might result in a better life also imagine living on a perfect planet and how that might be achieved.[12]

Thus did environmentalism tied to consumerism—a vision of idealized individuals in an idealized world—become increasingly aggregated during the postwar era and foment a movement. Environmentalists recognized that products were embedded with myriad assumptions regarding resources and the environment. They envisioned something of a consumer-driven cultural revolution marked by a shift in what people bought, how much they bought, as well as how those products were produced. Environmentalists insisted that consumers had a moral responsibility to the natural environment. Before making a purchase buyers should factor in how the natural environment that produced the product was treated and avoid those products that were produced by businesses that treated the environment poorly.

For those associated with it, environmentalism and its outward expression in green consumption also held the appeal of providing an identity that positioned one's self in opposition to what, for many, was the vulgarity of postwar modernity's corporate excess, not to mention corporations' outsized role in the polity. Environmentally minded consumers constituted a far-flung imagined community. Their ideas were finding increasing expression in actions that marked one of the most significant responses to the cultural, political, and environmental challenges of the postwar era. Citizens would not stop consuming, but they would consume differently. Feeling themselves denied representation in electoral politics, they asserted their political beliefs about a better society and environment through their actions as consumers.

The Growing Appeal of Green Consumption

In reaction to government actions perceived to be inadequate, an alternative green marketplace continued to grow. By the late 1950s organic foods were a Hollywood "craze," praised by a host of acting luminaries including James Arness of the popular television series *Gunsmoke*, Gloria Swanson, and Red Buttons. They often dined at the organic restaurant Aware Inn on Sunset Boulevard in Los Angeles, which also served hormone-free meats. They purchased organic foods at Organic-Ville, or Balzer's grocery on Larchmont Boulevard, which advertised fresh organic fruits and vegetables in 1955: "Free from forced growth chemical fertilizers; free from toxic sprays or poisonous insecticides." "Hollywood is on a new kick," joked television writer Larry Gelbart. "The same men who used to sit around Schwab's drugstore eating cheesecake and laughing at their boss' [sic] jokes are now eating weed sandwiches at the Cavendish health bar."[13]

Indeed, Representative James Delaney, perhaps only half-jokingly, credited the power of celebrity for finally getting his amendment to the Food, Drug, and Cosmetic Act passed. He had introduced the bill in Congress for five successive years, "but it was completely ignored," he said, until a 1956 speech on the subject by actress Gloria Swanson to a group of congressional wives. Swanson was a vegetarian and organic-food advocate who opposed additives, to the extent that she frequently brought a brown paper bag with her own meals to various dinners and functions. When Delaney heard she was going to be in Washington he asked his committee aides to meet with her and describe his bill. Vincent A. Kleinfold, counsel to the select committee, later recalled discussing the bill with Swanson several times. "Miss Swanson had quite a grasp of the subject herself and when she got before the Congressmen's wives she was a spellbinder," Delaney said.

After her speech a number of congressmen stopped Delaney in the Capitol to tell him that their wives ordered them to vote for the amendment. "I had never been able to arouse any interest in the bill until her speech," Delaney claimed, "but then it gained momentum and was passed two years later."[14]

The growing anxieties associated with postwar corporate capitalism, and the corresponding appeal of alternative, green consumption, were also evident in the popularity of journalist William Longgood's 1960 book, *The Poisons in Your Food*. Three years earlier Longgood documented the plight of the McKeon family whose organic Connecticut farm had been ruined by gypsy moth spraying. He began his book with a quote from Dr. Lionel James Picton, a British pioneer in linking organics to improved physical and environmental health: "We are natural beings and are trying to live in an artificial world. It cannot be done." Longgood then set out to prove as much, emphasizing the unknown risks of small amounts of synthetic chemicals ingested over a long period of time. "Those apples you bought at the supermarket for the children's lunch today—you made sure they were red, succulent, unblemished. But did you suspect they were probably shot through from peel to core with some of the most powerful poisons known?" he asked. "The list is endless," he concluded bleakly after detailing the artificial contents of a wide variety of foodstuffs. "Virtually every bit of food you eat has been treated with some chemical somewhere along the line."[15]

And what about meats? "In addition to being laced with pesticides," he warned, "the average steak or roast probably comes from a cow born through artificial insemination, raised with an artificial sex-hormone implant in its ear, fed synthetic hormones, antibiotics, and insecticides, and shot with tranquilizers; even its natural pasturage is contaminated with radioactive fallout. If the animal survives this chemical onslaught it is slaughtered—usually by an inhumane method—and sold as meat."[16] An advertisement by Longgood's publisher, Simon & Schuster, noted that the book was already in its second printing and called it "An urgent report to every American adult who eats and can read—on the powerful chemicals being fed to us three meals a day.... It is must reading for everyone who is serious about his responsibilities as a parent and as a citizen."[17]

Much of Longgood's book updated earlier works by writers like James Rorty, Philip Norman, and J. I. Rodale. The trends those writers identified more than a decade earlier had only worsened during the intervening years. Among those was the issue of excessive corporate power continuing to pervert scientific research. The one area that many believed was a bastion of independent thought was, in reality, also increasingly under the control of industry. "The problem of trying to retain scientific freedom in universities becomes more acute as industries 'own' increasingly larger shares of such institutions through grants, fellowships, scholarships, donations, subsidies and other direct and indirect handouts," Longgood cautioned, "bringing a rich harvest in loyalty from the beneficiaries." Under such conditions, strictly objective work from university scientists was increasingly unlikely because, "They, like others who serve industry as consultants, are seldom unaware of the source of their bread and butter or supplementary income."[18]

And if scientists did dare to publish work that conflicted with corporate interests, they might suffer consequences—as Colorado State University entomologist Joseph Moffet learned. In 1959 Moffet reported in the *American Bee Journal*, a newsletter for beekeepers: "Bees massacred in grasshopper spraying in Larimer County." Lending further credence to concerns that entomologists had put forth in professional journals since the 1940s, Moffett stated, "Large numbers of honey bees were killed in Larimer County when 15,091 acres of cropland were sprayed to control grasshoppers." He went on to detail how white cloths that he had placed in front of four colonies collected a total of 3,220 dead bees. Moffet was quickly informed by his superior that he could not report things like that because it "gave the people of Colorado a bad impression of the Spray program." He later resigned from the university to sell real estate. "Once you start a controversy at a university," he explained, "you're through."[19]

Corporations also had an increasingly tighter grip on government. Citing the "revolving door" trend of former corporate executives being appointed to the very government agencies charged with regulating their industries, Longgood concluded that the government citizens counted on to protect them appeared increasingly overwhelmed and not up to the task or, even worse, guilty of placing the interests of corporations before the needs of citizens and the environment. "Because of the enormous power industrialists exert, they have been able to get control of the Government agencies that are supposed to regulate them," he warned. "They are able to place their own men in key spots and dictate policy."[20]

In the few instances when business practices were exposed that were shown to be damaging the environment or placing profits before the health of consumers, companies often appeared to be less concerned about changing their harmful behaviors than about waging massive public relations campaigns to alter perceptions of those behaviors and construct a favorable public image. For example, when medical researchers reported that hydrogenated (trans) fats might cause heart disease, producers pooled $300,000 to wage a public relations campaign aimed at convincing the public that such fats were harmless.[21]

Such PR offensives were typical by 1960. Corporate public relations divisions proliferated and became central to company operations during World War II and after. In the words of General Motors Public Relations Director Paul Garrett, "production *plus* interpretation" became the corporate mission. That mission, as defined by the PR director of United States Steel, was to win the "competition with the government for the greatest prize of all—the good will of the public."[22]

Among the most concerted of such corporate public relations efforts during the postwar era was Keep America Beautiful (KAB), organized as a nonprofit corporation by an alliance of beverage, cigarette, and container companies in 1953 to promote litter prevention. With an ever-growing list of corporate sponsors KAB maintained a large and persuasive voice in the postwar discourse on litter and pollution. In 1961 it began a partnership with the Advertising Council, a cooperative of advertising agencies during World War II that transitioned into designing and executing government-approved "public service announcements." Together, KAB and the Advertising Council produced a series of clever publicity campaigns with themes like "Every Litter Bit Hurts," and a character named "Suzy Spotless" who constantly got after her father for littering. KAB always emphasized the responsibility of individual consumers for litter and pollution, shielding corporations that were using more and more disposable packaging from blame in an effort to retain "the good will of the public." Its most famous ad, featuring an Indian moved to tears by the nation's pollution, debuted on television on the first anniversary of Earth Day, in 1971.[23] The advent of KAB in the 1950s as a systematic effort by corporations to frame and control environmental discourse was sure evidence of environmentalism's increasing influence, as well as its perceived threat to corporate capitalism.

The intensity of the attacks waged against Longgood and other advocates of alternative, green consumption in an attempt to marginalize and discredit them betrayed the threat that many of those in power believed green consumers posed to both the status quo and profits. Some critics in the scientific community denigrated Longgood's book as the naïve work of a layman who was trying to understand modern science and technology that were beyond his grasp. William J. Darby, a biochemist from Vanderbilt University, waged a vicious attack on Longgood in *Science*. After accusing him of a "fascination with the cult of 'natural' versus 'synthetic and artificial,' " Darby at least acknowledged that the book "deals with the important question of chemical additives." However, he condemned it for doing so "from the bias of the nonscientific, natural food—organic gardening cult—the followers of J. I. Rodale . . . of Natural Food Associates Inc., and others of the same convictions."[24] One medical doctor snubbed Longgood for having a "b.s." degree in journalism.[25] *New York Times* science reporter John Osmundsen stated in his review of the book, "William Longgood has written a selectively documented, sometimes inaccurate, frequently hysterical tract against the use of any chemicals in food unless they are 'proved to be safe for all persons who must eat them.' "[26] These types of attacks leveled on those who questioned corporate capitalism were hardly limited to Longgood. When not screened out entirely, environmentalism and green consumption were trivialized as the practices of quacks and extremists, or disloyal citizens. But mounting evidence spoke to the validity of the new movement's concerns, and the alternative environmental vision gained a growing following in the margins of American culture.

"This is an organized movement representing a ground swell of public indignation," Longgood enthused, "which gains momentum as people learn that the Government has sacrificed them to commercial interests."[27] Five years before Ralph Nader was credited with starting the sixties consumer movement when he published *Unsafe at Any Speed*, Longgood advised that "the housewives of the country begin to seek and demand pure foods without additives or pesticide contaminants... and insist upon their right to such foods."[28] Again, it was women who were charged with defending the family from corporate malfeasance (and the men perpetuating it) when government (and the men who ran it) was derelict in its duty to protect.

Another book appeared later in 1960 supporting most of Longgood's contentions and adding some criticisms of its own, further solidifying the link between environmental degradation and diminished human health. Franklin Bicknell's *Chemicals in Your Food and in Farm Produce: Their Harmful Effects* began: "Americans consume more chemicals in their food than any other nation. At the same time American forecasts are the gloomiest in the world about the continued rise of cancer, high blood pressure, heart disease, congenital abnormalities, etc.—in fact all the degenerative diseases. The United States leads the world in chemicalized food and in degenerative diseases."[29] It was a correlation that was raising doubts for citizens.

In addition to the familiar warnings about the hazards posed by chemically contaminated foods and the dangers DDT presented for the environment and wildlife, Bicknell also posed stark warnings about antibiotics being used "not only to treat illnesses in cows, but as a routine addition to the feed of all farm livestock both to increase their rate of growth and to permit them to be kept in tightly crowded and infectious conditions."[30] This overuse of antibiotics "led not only to resistant strains of bacteria being increasingly common in food," he warned, "but also to food itself now containing antibiotics," with milk being the outstanding example. He pointed to evidence that this overuse of antibiotics was already leading to increasingly resistant strains of bacteria.[31] Because he and others could not successfully overcome the power of corporations, the problem continued to escalate. A 2001 World Health Organization report cited antibiotic use in animals as a contributor to growing numbers of microbes that had become resistant to antibiotics.[32] Critics had a tougher time attacking Bicknell's credibility than Longgood's. He was a British physician and expert on vitamins, and his book cited substantial evidence from medical and scientific literature, with a bibliography of nearly 300 sources.

While Longgood appeared to have little faith that government could be persuaded to truly place the interests of citizens before those of corporations, Bicknell still hoped that by better understanding the dangers of the chemicals in their food and environment Americans would insist on improved government protection. "The Food and Drug Administration makes great efforts to protect its public," Bicknell stated in a view not shared by a growing number of his colleagues in the United States, "but there is little active support from the average citizen. Were there more understanding of how chemicalized food is insidiously eroding away health in the United States even faster than in Europe, then more and better legislation would not only be tolerated but demanded," he optimistically concluded.[33]

Bicknell's faith that the government and FDA could be persuaded, with a little nudge, to assume their roles in protecting citizens appeared overly optimistic. Instead, in response to the increasing popularity of organics, the Food and Drug Administration moved to protect agribusiness by publishing a widely distributed pamphlet titled "Food Facts vs. Food Fallacies." Described by an FDA official as "Our catalogue of current quackery," the pamphlet warned consumers to "beware of 'natural' and 'organic' foods."[34] By the 1960s it appeared that it was easier for experts outside of the United States to possess a degree of optimism that the American government might be persuaded to genuinely get out in front on the issues affecting the environment and the food chain than it was for Americans like Longgood who had grown accustomed to watching their government kowtow to corporate interests. For some citizens, then, consumer activism appeared more viable than traditional political activism.

An Expanding Green Marketplace

The increasing popularity of environmentalism was evidenced in an increasing number of green consumers. The group emerged from seeds sown during World War II that took root during the 1950s; it would finally reach full bloom with Earth Day in 1970. Members of the green middle class constructed a world of their own within the existing society.

In addition to growing organic gardens, by the early 1960s green consumers purchased produce from an increasing number of organic farms. In California they also shopped at supermarkets that carried an expanding number of naturally grown products, or they might buy them from Farmer Dick Kidson's Organic Produce stand at the Los Angeles Farmers Market.[35] In larger cities, naturally grown products were found at "health stores" like Radio City Health Shop in New York City, which advertised, in 1960, a fruit and vegetable juice bar along with "natural, organic foods," or at an organic cooperative that also operated in the city.[36] In Washington, DC, residents had their choice of six stores, including Modern Natural Foods, which sold organic produce from local gardens and farms in Maryland and Pennsylvania. Stores there reported a doubling in sales in 1959 compared to a decade earlier.[37] In Chicago, citizens formed an organic cooperative that contracted with area farmers for foods free of artificial chemicals.[38]

Green consumers not living in cities turned to mail-order businesses like Nature Food Centers in Cambridge, Massachusetts, which advertised "natural, organic foods"; Walnut Acres Farm, a pioneering organic farm near Penns Creek, Pennsylvania, started by Paul Keene in 1946; and Welsh's Natural Foods in Laguna Beach, California which featured organic produce and meats and offered to ship fruits anywhere.[39] And there was Globe Hill Farms in Pine Plains, New York, which was producing "natural" beef by growing its own chemical-free feed and pastures, then shipping cuts of frozen meat all over the United States.[40] Arrowhead Mills was founded in 1960 to produce organic, stone-ground flour.[41] Green consumers ordered "Pure Cosmetics 100 percent Organic & Natural" from Orjene of New York.[42] Some purchased "Tap Sprite," a charcoal filter that when attached to a home water faucet promised to put "mountain freshness into your drinking water."[43]

Parents sent their children to places like the Wildwood Nature Camp, operated by the Massachusetts Audubon Society, which aimed not only to "stimulate interest & develop skills for enjoying and understanding our environment" but also to emphasize "natural and unrefined foods."[44] Families camped at some 45 "organic" campsites spread across 22 states in every region of the country, where no chemical sprays or insecticides had been used; many offered organic fruits, vegetables, and even prepared meals to campers.[45]

Family pets were not left out. Pet owners could care for their animals "naturally" with products from MBF Products, Inc., of Wilton, Connecticut, which sold a variety of goods for cats and dogs under the advertisement: "Your Pets Need Protection, Too! To Stay In Top Health, Year 'Round With Natural Organic Products."[46]

The growing green marketplace evidenced resistance to assurances by the FDA and others that the American Way was best. Biologist and environmentalist René Dubos—perhaps best remembered for later coining the phrase "Think globally, act locally"—argued that although humans were genetically similar to other animals in so many ways, it was the ability to dream of a better future that set humans apart.[47] Dubos's environmental hopes for the future resonated with a postwar generation where little seemed permanent: "Among the obvious responsibilities toward the future are those concerning the preservation of natural resources," he urged in his 1962 book, *The Torch of Life*. And there was no time to waste. "We are already suffering from the problems posed by crowding, by air pollution, by automobile traffic," he cautioned, "and by countless products of industrial life. The least we can do," Dubos concluded, "is to leave for those who will follow us a world as good as that which we have inherited from the past."[48]

Dubos and others remained optimistic that the threats of cultural and environmental apocalypse could be overcome, or at the very least that humans would find meaning and enjoyment in trying and failing to overcome them. These "expectations, from visions of the mind, indeed from dreams, they are so real and powerful that they can sway human behavior and are thereby the most effective forces in changing the face of the earth," he emphasized.[49] Increasingly, with some measure of irony, these human dreams of a better world were being acted out in alternative shopping.

Old-Line Conservationists and Politicians Struggle toward Environmentalism

Traditional conservationists were also expanding their fields of vision. In its first in a series of lavish coffee-table books, *This Is the American Earth* (1960), the Sierra Club aimed at broad middle-class appeal. Filled with striking photographs, many by longtime Sierra Club board member Ansel Adams, *American Earth* expressed the concern for aesthetic wilderness areas for which the Sierra Club had long been known, but it also demonstrated that the club's vistas were beginning to extend beyond romantic landscapes to encompass the broader concerns of environmentalism. The book began with a question that appeared aimed at an apocalyptic mood among its readership: "Now in an age whose hopes are darkened by huge fears—an age frantic with speed, noise, complexity—an age constricted, of crowds, collisions, of cities choked by smog and traffic—an age of greed, power, terror—an age when the closed mind, the starved eye, the empty heart, the brutal fist, threaten all life upon this planet—What is the price of exaltation?"[50]

Exaltation for the Sierra Club, clearly, lay in experiencing nature at its most pristine and aesthetically pleasing. However, in words and photographs the book illustrated how fallout, air pollution, water pollution, suburban sprawl, careless use of natural resources, the conduct of imperialism to gain more resources, population growth, synthetic agricultural chemicals, and extinction were threatening all life and the planet.[51] The answer for all of these ills, the book argued, was an alternative postwar consciousness that reconnected humans to the spirit of nature.[52] As traditional conservation encompassed broader environmental concerns it expanded its appeal to citizens who were viewing nature as something vital and present in their everyday lives. The Sierra Club increased its membership to 16,000 in 1960, 60 percent higher than it had been just four years earlier.[53]

Politicians were pushed to take notice. In the 1960 presidential election race, Democrat John F. Kennedy sought to appeal to the nation's growing environmental concern. *Life* magazine asked both Kennedy and Republican candidate Richard M. Nixon to write essays defining the national purpose. Nixon's reply did not address the environment, but Kennedy's response demonstrated a keen sense of the shifting political winds. "Even in material terms, prosperity is not enough when there is no equal opportunity to share in it; when economic progress means overcrowded cities, abandoned farms, technological unemployment, polluted air and water, and littered parks and countrysides."[54]

Although Kennedy spoke to environmental concerns and later voiced support for a Wilderness Act bill that had been languishing in Congress for years, his environmental vision remained locked mostly in the progressive conservationist mode. Kennedy had a dual approach to the environment that, while acknowledging environmental problems, never shied away from a belief in the "wise use" of resources. As he said while campaigning in 1960, "our forests are vanishing, our wildlife is vanishing, our streams are polluted, and so is the very air we breathe. Yet America is rich in natural resources. Our impending resource crisis is not due to scarcity. It is due to under-development, despoilment and neglect."[55] Three years later, as evidenced by his comments at the dedication in Hanford, Washington of the largest nuclear reactor to date, during a five-day "conservation tour," his attitude had not changed:

> There are two points on conservation that have come home to me in the last two days. One is the necessity for us to protect what we already have, what nature gave to us, and use it well, not to waste water or land, to set aside land and water, recreation, wilderness, and all the rest now so that it will be available to those who come in the future. That is the traditional concept of conservation, and it still has a major part in the national life of the United States. But the other part of conservation is the newer part, and that is to use science and technology to achieve significant breakthroughs as we are doing today, and in that way to conserve the resources which 10 or 20 or 30 years ago may have been wholly unknown.

The President went on to detail some of these new "conservation" uses for science and technology, including nuclear power, solar power, extracting coal and oil from shale, and new techniques for mining and harvesting from the ocean so "we get all the resources which are there."[56]

For growing numbers of Americans, trust that politicians would place the protection of citizens and the environment above the desires of corporations was optimism that they simply could no longer muster. Although writers like Rodale, Rorty, Norman, and Longgood might hope government regulations would provide some badly needed safeguards, in the end they believed it naïve to think that government alone could be counted upon to protect its citizens against the power and influence of giant corporations. They sought surer influence, and protection, through their consumer choices.

The Push for a Test-Ban Treaty

Environmental shopping was further spurred by the growing threat of nuclear fallout in food. That the public had reached a point where it was dreaming of a brighter environmental future free of poisoned food and other life essentials was further suggested by a November 1959 Gallup poll—the same month as the Great Thanksgiving Cranberry Affair—that showed 77 percent of those asked wanted the one-year nuclear test ban, which officially expired on October 31, extended for another year. The editors of the *Bulletin of Atomic Scientists* welcomed the results as hopeful evidence that the tipping point where the public was concerned enough about environmental threats to support an end to nuclear arms testing had been reached. "The general agreement that the air we breathe is the common property of mankind and not to be polluted at the will of sovereign nations," they reasoned, "is a step forward in the education of the human race."[57] *Bulletin* editors recognized that public support for a testing ban was based upon the threat of environmental peril much more than it was the issue of nuclear weapons themselves, which most Americans were willing to tolerate out of Cold War fears of the Soviet Union.

Anxieties about fallout continued to be an enormously effective vehicle for SANE's antinuclear campaign, once again demonstrating environmentalism's growing appeal. By 1960 the group had 150 local chapters, among them a Hollywood group headed by Steve Allen, comedian and former host of NBC television's popular *The Tonight Show*, whose membership included Milton Berle, Marlon Brando, Sammy Davis Jr., Kirk Douglas, Henry Fonda, Gene Kelly, Groucho Marx, Shirley MacLaine, and Gregory Peck—one of the early attempts by Hollywood to raise its political voice after being thoroughly bullied by the House Un-American Activities Committee beginning in 1947. In addition, there were over 25 Student SANE committees on college campuses.[58]

When SANE held a celebrity-studded rally at New York's Madison Square Garden in May 1960 in hopes of igniting the test-ban treaty talks that had stalled in Geneva it drew some 20,000 people. For authorities, such an overwhelming display of environmental concern meant it was time for aggressive action.[59]

Senator Thomas J. Dodd, Democrat from Connecticut, temporary Chairman of the Senate Internal Security Subcommittee, and strong opponent of the proposed nuclear test ban, responded by accusing the chief organizer of the rally, Henry Abrams, of being a veteran member of the Communist Party, and charged that "the Communists were responsible for a very substantial percentage of the overflow turnout" at the rally. Though careful to concede that SANE's national leadership, including Norman Cousins and Eleanor Roosevelt, consisted of upstanding citizens, he warned that his subcommittee had uncovered evidence of "serious Communist infiltration at chapter level throughout" and urged them to "purge their ranks ruthlessly."[60] He demanded that Linus Pauling name those who helped him collect the signatures of the 11,000 scientists who signed the atomic test–ban petition he submitted to the United Nations in 1958, and he subpoenaed 37 SANE members. SANE nervously responded by suspending the charter of its New York chapter and kicking out the 37 members in question. The red scare proved temporarily crippling for the organization, setting off an internal political struggle that threatened to tear the group apart and pushing some to quit SANE out of disgust with its timid leadership.[61] However, significantly, it did not derail public interest in the environmental impact of fallout and strontium-90.

In June, *Consumer Reports* again raised concerns when it issued the first-ever study of strontium-90 in the total diet, done by analyzing the three meals per day plus snacks typically eaten by US teenagers in 24 cities across the country and one in Canada. The tests found "the level of strontium-90 in the diet of young Americans significantly higher than has been indicated by tests on milk alone." Contrary to the popular belief that milk was supplying about 80 percent of total intake, it was instead furnishing half, indicating that other foods were posing their own dangers. The report chastised the government for not taking a more active role in monitoring food safety and the dangers of fallout. "The pride that CU takes in having been first to make total-diet tests for strontium-90 levels," it stated with some sarcasm, "is tempered by the bleak circumstances that permit CU that distinction."[62]

During the same month the Izaak Walton League of America, a conservation group founded in 1922 mostly by fishers and hunters, extended the reach of concern over fallout in the environment when it issued a resolution urging the government to not only monitor the fallout danger in food and water but also take greater measures to detect and eliminate fallout and other pollutants from the air. The League espoused an environmental view that valued the entire ecosystem by arguing that the air we breathe deserves the same safeguards as the food and water we consume.[63] Given the state of laws to protect food and water, it might have done well to aim a little higher.

Anxieties over nuclear testing and fallout eased somewhat between the summers of 1960 and 1961. It had been two years since the last testing, and there were indications that the level of strontium-90 in the environment was leveling off. Although the Geneva test-ban treaty talks remained deadlocked, neither side had resumed testing, and there was relative calm between the superpowers.

No sooner had the sense of urgency begun to ease than events conspired to raise public fears to unprecedented heights. Only months after John F. Kennedy's inauguration, conflict with the Soviets over the future of East Germany led to the Berlin Crisis, resulting in the building of the Berlin Wall in August. Kennedy called for a massive fallout-shelter program as the threat of a superpower clash and nuclear apocalypse seemed to draw nearer. In September the Soviet Union resumed nuclear-bomb testing, ending the nearly three-year-old moratorium.[64] Tests started on September 1, and by September 18 the Soviets had already set off 18 blasts. In the United States 12 Eastern and Northern states recorded record increases in fallout.[65] The United States resumed its own testing but for the time being limited it to underground tests. In October, Canada announced that its level of fallout had increased 400 times since the Soviets resumed tests.[66] The US Public Health Service revealed that iodine 131, associated with thyroid cancer, had increased in milk and fresh food, particularly around Minneapolis and Des Moines where quantities approached the government's maximum permissible levels.[67]

The public reacted passionately, if not angrily, to the renewed testing. It was as if all of the earlier dire predictions of atomic testing were coming true. Later in the month the president of the American Cancer Society warned that the new wave of Soviet testing may have already produced a level of fallout dangerous to humans and revealed that the rate of deformed births and childhood cancer had, for reasons unknown, already increased sharply during the past two decades.[68] The *Washington Post* ran a mock obituary on its editorial page for the "unnumbered hundreds of thousands" who would die due to the testing of a large Soviet bomb the day before.[69]

For the downwinders, there were no "mock" obituaries. By 1961, 10 years after testing started at the Nevada site, residents began to notice unprecedented clusters of childhood leukemia in their communities. The small town of Parowan, Utah, saw four teenagers die from leukemia in 1960 alone, the first ever in the area to die from the disease, and a rate five to seven times greater than the national average. A Centers for Disease Control study in 1961 found there were 11 deaths from leukemia in 1959 and 1960 in the southwestern Utah counties of Iron and Washington. The Utah Cancer Registry later reported that, although the incidence of all cancers in the Southwest was 20 percent below the national average, in the four counties downwind of the Nevada test site between 1957 and 1974 the incidence of acute childhood leukemia was one-and-a-half times greater than the national average. Fredonia, Arizona, with a population of 643, had four cases from 1962 to 1965, about 20 times the national average.

Residents who had initially embraced the bomb testing had a change of heart. "Our government lied to us," became a common refrain in the region, one that increasingly echoed throughout the country.[70]

The Fellowship of Reconciliation, an international interfaith pacifist group dating back to World War I, published a newspaper ad on October 29, 1961 denouncing the new round of Soviet tests on environmental grounds: "Across the world the food that men eat, the milk their children drink, the earth from which humans and animals alike draw their sustenance, are being contaminated anew," it read. "It is time to speak. Soon it may be too late."[71] The next day, though, the Soviets defiantly exploded the largest bomb in history—a 50-megaton bomb 3,000 times more powerful than the bombs that destroyed Hiroshima and Nagasaki and more than three times as large as the infamous US Bravo test in 1954.[72]

Students became irritated with the slow pace of change from the reorganized SANE's strategy of newspaper ads signed by prominent individuals, speeches, and lobbying of sympathetic politicians. They believed a more urgent, direct-action route of demonstrations, marches, and mass action would prove more effective. But SANE paid little attention to its own student branch. "We weren't looking for help from the youthful *polloi*," one SANE leader later admitted. Students, coalescing in a New Left movement, criticized the group for what it viewed as a naïve stance against civil disobedience. "SANE will not challenge the Government, and therefore can accomplish very little," said Norman Uphoff of the University of Minnesota's chapter of the more activist Student Peace Union, which boasted 70 chapters across the nation. In addition, individual campus groups like Tocsin at Harvard-Radcliffe and Students for Peace and Disarmament at the University of Wisconsin formed in opposition to testing. Students from 12 colleges in the Midwest and East picketed in front of the White House in November to protest the resumption of tests, some carrying signs which read "Don't Poison the Air!" In February 1962, Tocsin's Todd Gitlin and Peter Goldmark organized a march on Washington and enlisted the cosponsorship of Student Peace Union, Student SANE, and the then fledgling Students for a Democratic Society. The two-day event drew an estimated 4,000 to 8,000 demonstrators.[73]

Women Strike for Peace Wages an Environmental Consumer Campaign

Even more influential than the students was another newly formed group frustrated by SANE's approach. It called itself Women Strike for Peace, and it waged its first nationwide strike on November 1, 1961. Although the date had been selected weeks in advance, the coincidence of it falling on the day after the public learned of the Soviets' record blast served to strengthen the determination of the estimated 50,000 women in 68 cities who left their homes and jobs that day to make their voices heard on the issues of bombs and atomic testing. Some pushed baby carriages while holding signs that read "Save the Children" and "Testing Damages the Unborn." At a public square in Detroit they held up enlarged photographs of their own children. In Washington, DC, more than 750 women, some with their children, and a collie dog wearing a bib with the message "Please No More Strontium 90," marched in front of the White House. In Los Angeles, 4,000 women joined to demand an end to nuclear testing.[74]

Women Strike for Peace had formed about five weeks earlier. Dagmar Wilson, a children's book illustrator and mother of three in Washington, DC, met with five of her friends who, like her, were frustrated with the failure of male-dominated institutions like the government and SANE, a group they all belonged to, to respond with sufficient urgency to the growing threat to the planet.[75] As Wilson later recalled, "We were worried. We were indignant. We were angry. The Soviet Union and the U.S.A. were accusing each other of having broken a moratorium on nuclear testing. What matter who broke it when everyone's children would fall victim to radioactive Strontium 90?" They determined direct action was needed and decided to wage a one-day strike to register their fears and gain media attention. They called on women across the nation to leave their routines to "Appeal to All Governments to End the Arms Race—Not the Human Race." Word circulated through word of mouth, personal phone lists, PTAs, church and temple groups, and women's clubs. The organizers, who would identify themselves only as "concerned housewives," were sick of top-down organizations and carried out a self-consciously grassroots effort.[76]

Though the women who initiated WSP were committed pacifists, they recognized that their most powerful popular appeal, particularly as mothers, lay in the issue of the environment. Unlike SANE, their actions were focused not on producing advertisements but instead on the power of their role as consumers. "Pure Milk Not Poison" was their most effective slogan, which did much to draw other women who were struggling daily with whether it was safe to give milk and other contaminated foods to their children to the cause. To sustain public pressure, they decided to strike on the first day of each month until testing stopped. On December 1, 3,500 women marched in front of the United Nations headquarters in New York, led by a woman carrying a large placard in the shape of a milk bottle emblazoned with skull and crossbones.[77]

The group urged women to boycott milk during periods of nuclear testing. Many women organized boycotts of local dairy companies until milk was free from strontium-90, well aware that the means to that end was to stop nuclear tests. WSP coupled its boycotts of local, contaminated milk with "buycotts" of powdered milk that its careful research assured was from areas with no recorded fallout contamination. Its newsletters included tips for making powdered milk more palatable for children.[78]

The issues of nuclear fallout, chemicals in food, and environmental pollution were increasingly bleeding into one another and seen as one overriding issue. Around the same time that WSP marched on the United Nations, a 12-page article in the 1961–1962 "Annual Edition" of the conservationist *Consumer Bulletin* stressed that fallout was only part of a much broader problem. "Some hold that the *chemical* hazard to the future of man and his progeny is greater than the danger from radioactive fallout from tests of nuclear weapons," the magazine stated.[79]

Significantly, threats from environmental pollution were now believed to pose a greater risk to the body than were infectious diseases. "Germs are no longer the chief enemy of man," *Consumer Bulletin* concluded. "Rather it is the disturbance of the inner balance of our tissues, as determined by the chemical pollution of the air we breathe, and the smoke, fumes, and dusts we inhale, and the presence of approximately 3000 chemical additives and modifiers in the water we drink and the food we eat. These chemical additives are made by some 6500 manufacturers, and utilized in about 75,000 food processing plants. Perhaps not 10 of the 3000 are in common use in home food preparation and cooking."[80] The weight of multiple environmental threats was being increasingly felt, and corporations were increasingly bearing the blame.

By late 1961 an undeniable shift in the zeitgeist had occurred. A *Saturday Evening Post* editorial warned that insecticides "can be dangerous enemies if used by *zealots*." The fact that those who were using chemicals were now being referred to as "zealots" in mainstream publications, rather than the organic and environmental enthusiasts who were typically characterized as such, represented a sea change. That an "orthodox mass magazine" was now judging those in the chemical mainstream as emotional and irrational, and by contrast those espousing environmental views as more rational, did not go unnoticed by Robert Rodale, son of the founder of *Organic Gardening and Farming* and the magazine's editor at the time. He commented: "It is a strange feeling for me...to see the chemical people being called 'zealots.' For so long it has been the other way around. Organic gardeners were characterized as misguided revolutionaries, while the spray people were looked on as cool and precise guardians of the public's welfare."[81] The warnings of Rodale's father and others had proven prescient, giving growing credence to their ideas for alternatives to mainstream industrial, commercial, and corporate life.

The membership of WSP recognized the power of a boycott uniting the issues of fallout, the environment, and consumption. It was a stance that had particular meaning given that the FDA had implicated women who dared leave the traditional domestic sphere as being partly, if not mostly, to blame for the chemicals in foods that might be threatening the well-being of their families. "Today approximately 22 million women are employed outside the home in our country and the reason that many of them can be so employed is that they have convenience foods available that can be made ready for the table quickly," stated an FDA report. "Many of these convenience foods would not be possible without the chemicals that are being incorporated in the food today."[82] In the estimation of the FDA, then, it was not the corporations producing the harmful chemicals that were to blame but women who dared work outside the home.

Shopping, often denigrated as superficial and meaningless, if not harmful, was instead shown to be a potent tool for cultural and political change by WSP. The group recognized that the power of consumer culture in the United States was double-edged, and producers were not the only ones who could manipulate it for their ends. Like the working-class women who led consumer boycotts during World War I and those from the middle class who joined them during the Great Depression, these middle-class women recognized their own power in the marketplace. Significantly, it was a power that could be exercised not only to affect prices but to influence the much broader cultural and political goals of stopping atomic testing, shielding the environment, and protecting the food chain while sparing the body from harm.[83]

WSP boycotts, combined with the frightening reports of radioactive fallout in milk, led to a 700,000,000-pound decrease in milk consumption in 1961 compared to its 1960 level—even in the midst of a baby boom—meaning that Americans drank 326,000,000 fewer quarts. Dairy industry officials sought to downplay contamination fears and the WSP boycott by citing concerns about weight gain and cholesterol as contributing factors, but in the end they acknowledged that the fear of radiation in milk was hurting sales.[84] In January 1962 President Kennedy, in support of the dairy industry, issued an address urging Americans to keep drinking milk and pledging that henceforth milk would be served at all White House meals. Kennedy explained that his purpose was to "reassure on radiation, and also to see if we can stimulate [consumption] by example." He argued that milk did not constitute a health hazard and that dairy companies did not need to use "strontium removal plants."[85]

But when the President announced in a March 2 televised address that the United States would resume its own aboveground, atmospheric testing if an agreement with the Soviets was not reached by April 1, 1962, WSP called for a one-week boycott of fresh milk if testing resumed. The threat prompted a warning from the Public Health Service that mothers should not stop feeding their children milk to protest the renewed tests. Pediatricians reported that mothers were stockpiling powdered milk from regions believed safest in anticipation of increased fallout contamination in fresh milk. WSP had 40 radiation committees around the country pressuring dairies, the Department of Agriculture, and Congress for measures to remove radiation from milk. At a time when many middle-class families had milk delivered to their homes in glass bottles, women left notes in empty return bottles threatening to cancel their order unless decontamination of milk started immediately.[86]

President Kennedy sought to calm national anxieties by announcing a major conservation initiative in March. In a message that bore the unmistakable imprint of his close advisor, Secretary of the Interior Stewart Udall, he first asked Congress to authorize a $1 billion, eight-year plan for conservation, which he defined as "the wise use of our natural environment...the prevention of waste and despoilment while preserving, improving and renewing the quality and usefulness of all our resources." Focused on the traditional conservation concerns of aesthetics and resources, the plan included nine new national parks, a Youth Conservation Corps modeled after Franklin Roosevelt's Civilian Conservation Corps, and a Land Conservation Fund financed by entrance and user fees at federal recreation areas to acquire more recreational and wilderness lands. In addition, he urged Congress to approve pending legislation to establish a national wilderness preservation system. Finally, he announced that he would soon convene a White House Conference on Conservation.[87] Two months later some 500 invited conservationists and business leaders met to discuss the future of the nation's natural resources. "Social values must be equated with economic values," said Udall. If not, "we face an austere rationing of even those things which have been traditionally free in America—its waters, wilderness and space."[88]

"What Have They Done to the Rain?"

Despite such assurances, SANE issued its own strong response to Kennedy's announcement of the possible resumption of atmospheric testing, running three full-page newspaper ads in April. An ad featuring famed pediatrician Dr. Benjamin Spock drew the most attention. Spock was the author of the wildly popular *The Common Sense Book of Baby and Child Care* (1946), which sold 4 million copies by 1952 and at least 1 million copies a year in 29 languages for 18 years.[89] The ad was reprinted in some 700 newspapers around the world and printed in poster form 25,000 times; the poster appeared in places like store windows and on the walls of doctor's offices. An additional 20,000 copies were sent individually to the White House, addressed to President Kennedy. The advertisement was so important that it was a news item in *Newsweek* and *Time*.[90]

The campaign was the brainchild of William Bernbach, of the giant advertising firm Doyle, Dane, and Bernbach, who offered the services of his agency to place a full-page ad in the *New York Times* to publicize Spock's views after he became a contributor to SANE. Spock submitted a 4,000-word essay for the ad, but Bernbach realized the image of Spock, the caregiver to all children, would supply the ad's real power.[91] In the end his message was cut to about 200 words to leave more space for a large picture of a bespectacled Spock standing behind a toddler girl, gazing down at her with a look of concern. Beneath the picture a headline read, "Dr. Spock is worried." His message began, "I *am* worried. Not so much about the effect of past tests but at the prospect of endless future ones. As the tests multiply, so will the damage to children—here and around the world."[92]

If she was like many other youngsters, the girl Dr. Spock gazed down on might have shared his apocalyptic concerns. When a mother found her six-year-old boy destroying the lawn by digging a hole in their front yard and asked, "What are you doing?" he replied while still frantically digging, "I'm digging a big hole in the ground to hide from the Bomb!" One 10-year-old girl reported that she and her friends often discussed fallout shelters and radiation, while another who was watching President Kennedy talking about the future on television said to the cat she was stroking, "I wish I were you so that I wouldn't have to think about such things." Reading the morning newspaper's headlines after the Soviet Union's record 50-megaton blast, yet another young girl asked, "Mother, is it going to be the collapsification of the whole world?"[93] Seeing fallout shelter signs at the entrances of public buildings and participating in "duck and cover" nuclear bomb attack drills in school, children absorbed, along with DDT and strontium-90, the anxieties of the era.

To make matters even worse, the fear that infants might be deformed by chemicals was made powerfully real when officials in the United States confirmed for the first time that a sedative and treatment for morning sickness widely prescribed in Europe since 1958, thalidomide, had been proven responsible for thousands of severe birth abnormalities (especially phocomelia, in which limbs are stunted or missing) and many infant deaths. As *The Nation* stated in an article lamenting that Cold War pressures were preventing some in the media from openly decrying the perils of strontium the way they did thalidomide's dangers, "If a horror that will last for a year is unendurable, what about a horror which will go on for 10,000 years, or till the end of time? If a few thousand malformed or stillborn children can make us wring our hands, why not a few hundred thousand, or millions?"[94]

During that same spring of 1962 a powerful British apocalyptic film, *The Day the Earth Caught Fire*, debuted in American theaters. In the film the United States and Soviet Union conduct simultaneous thermonuclear tests that are followed by strange weather with severe shifts in temperature and a series of environmental catastrophes, including inexplicable floods, droughts, and tornadoes. A journalist named Pete Stenning soon uncovers that the superpower governments are withholding information that the simultaneous blasts have forced the earth off its orbit. "Never mind the data on leukemia, or infant mortality, or strontium, or any of the other clinical facts of mass suicide," Stenning says upon discovering the catastrophe, faulting humanity for not acting sooner. "The human race has been poisoning itself for years with a great big smile on its fat face." Later he attributes the inaction to a repressed desire by many humans, overcome by the pressures and uncertainties of postwar modernity, to commit suicide. "A lot of people don't want to live," he says. "It's too difficult; they're tired, they're frightened. They'd rather it was all over than go on worrying and being frightened, losing a bit more hope every day. So they want to finish it." Scientists decide to set off all hydrogen bombs at once in a desperate effort to right the planet. In the end the audience is left wondering if the solution worked. Whether or not the earth survived is never revealed. The film was a dramatic, if not melodramatic, depiction of escalating environmental fears and a public that had had enough. As the *New York Times* said in its review of the film, "the scientific theories involved in the climax could be questioned by atomic Pooh-Bahs, but its pleas make sense in a world awesomely aware of possible destruction."[95]

"What Have They Done to the Rain?", a folk song written by Malvina Reynolds, also appeared in 1962 and focused on atomic fallout's threat to both the environment and children: "Just a little boy standing in the rain / The gentle rain that falls for years / And the grass is gone, the boy disappears / And rain keeps falling like helpless tears / And what have they done to the rain?" It was the "they" in the lyrics that was most significant. Who was this "they" that was so careless and crass as to kill the grass, and so unfeeling and cold as to kill a child? "Just a little breeze with some smoke in its eye / What have *they* done to the rain?"[96] By the early 1960s Malvina Reynolds did not have to explain who "they" were; everybody knew that it referred to the military-industrial complex. Most significantly, "they" were not "us"—a troubling trend for democracy.

The next year, at the age of 21, Bob Dylan was already making a name for himself as the greatest folk musician since Woody Guthrie. One of his popular tunes was "A Hard Rain's a-Gonna Fall," a song full of apocalyptic images whose title and refrain seemed to fold the biblical Deluge into a portent of nuclear fallout and environmental doom. Dylan sang of stepping "in the middle of seven sad forests," and being "out in front of a dozen dead oceans," and walking "to the depths of the deepest black forest...Where the pellets of poison are flooding their waters."[97] One reviewer of an April Dylan concert said the song "about the pollution of the atmosphere with fallout generated...tension through repetition and an inexorable guitar beat."[98] The song's real power came not only from its beat, though, but by tapping the enormous tension over pollution that was already in the air. When Allen Ginsberg heard the song he wept, and realized that the torch was being passed from the Beats to a new generation.[99]

Despite the public's apprehensions and WSP's threat of a milk boycott, with no agreement in Geneva the United States resumed atmospheric testing on April 25, 1962, and set off an additional 32 blasts before the end of the year. Fallout soon reached dangerous levels. Two months later iodine 131 levels were already so high in parts of the Midwest that the Public Health Service estimated the absorption by thyroids of children in Minneapolis and Des Moines had already approached four-fifths of the maximum level set by the Federal Radiation Council.[100]

Decentralization

There was no escaping this fallout, Murray Bookchin stressed in a new book, *Our Synthetic Environment*, published that spring. As with chemicals sprayed from planes that drenched the land whether residents wanted them or not, "radioactive wastes that enter man's environment through nuclear weapons tests and the activities of nuclear reactors are essentially beyond human control. They contaminate everyone, irrespective of age or health," he warned.[101] With that remark Bookchin, who wrote under the pen name "Lewis Herber," hit upon what was becoming a central concern in the modern, postwar era, that much of life seemed somehow to be "beyond human control." Between governments damaging the environment with fallout and insecticides, and corporations adding chemicals, pollution, and processes that continually posed additional threats, citizens felt beleaguered and frustrated.

Bookchin deliberately spoke to that frustration and gave voice to many proto-environmentalists: "[W]e cannot fatalistically bend our knee to the historic eventuality of basic social change while the environment deteriorates before our eyes. The environmental crisis must be attenuated now, as much as possible, if the exploitative practices and zealous 'chemo-mania' of an utterly immoral business community, acting in collusion with equally immoral governmental institutions, are not to damage the government irreparably and expose the public to increasingly hazardous pollutants."[102] At heart, Bookchin did not believe the myriad environmental threats he detailed in his comprehensive book could be satisfactorily solved within a market economy. However, he was practical enough to recognize that until the structural changes he hoped for arrived something had to be done about the rapidly deteriorating environment.

Bookchin's work provided a comprehensive treatment of environmental themes that had appeared elsewhere, but he also considered the psychological effects of environmental choices. "By oversimplifying the natural environment," he concluded, "we have created an incomplete man who lives an unbalanced life in a standardized world. Such a man is ill—not only morally and psychologically, but physically."[103] He joined those who believed environmentalism held the promise of a solution for all of these ills.

Like others before him, Bookchin emphasized that some of these downsides of postwar modernity could be avoided through careful shopping and living, and he urged his readers to do so. However, he also joined others in recognizing that class inequities, and geographic variables, often made it difficult to avoid the negative effects of corporate capitalism. "Any serious attempt to limit the diet to pure foods, free of pesticide residues, artificial coloring and flavoring matter, and synthetic preservatives, is well beyond the financial means of the average person," he soberly assessed. "Even if the individual can afford it, he will find that untreated foods are difficult to obtain, for relatively few pure foods are grown in the United States and those that reach urban centers are rarely sold in large retail markets."[104] To permit everybody to live well, Bookchin proposed a plan he called "decentralization."

Echoing many thoughts expressed by J. I. Rodale some two decades earlier, but years before economist E. F. Schumacher's seminal *Small Is Beautiful*, Bookchin attacked problems associated with the monster scale of modern industry and institutions. Assailing corporate capitalism, Bookchin put a name to the problem afflicting agriculture and society that many now lamented: "giantism." As a review of the book in *Consumer Bulletin* stated, "Mr. Herber [Bookchin] traces the changes in food character and quality that have grown out of the transfer of food production from small-scale farms and home industry to large-scale farm and factory operations." "American farming must be reduced to a more human scale," Bookchin said. "It will become necessary to bring agriculture within the scope of the individual, so that the farmer and the soil can develop together, each responding as fully as possible to the needs of the other."[105]

Much as James Rorty and Philip Norman had earlier, he anticipated the local economy and foods movement as a response to corporatized production. Bookchin envisioned a "decentralized, moderate-sized city that combined industry with agriculture, not only in the same civic entity but in the occupational activities of the same individual," an "urbanized farmer" or "agrarianized townsman." A community well-integrated with the resources of its region, he reasoned, could "promote agricultural and biological diversity." "What is really important," he emphasized, "a decentralized community holds the greatest promise for conserving natural resources, particularly as it would promote the use of local sources of energy." Solar and wind power might be better developed, allowing conservation of the remaining petroleum and coal, which would permit the use of energy from environmentally dangerous nuclear reactors to be delayed or avoided altogether. "This seems to be the only approach to the task of creating a long-range balance between man and the natural world," he concluded, "and of remaking man's synthetic environment in a form that will promote human health and fitness... by restoring the complexity of man's environment and by reducing the community to a human scale."[106]

In its review, *Consumer Bulletin* recognized that Bookchin's book was necessitated by the fact that the institutions counted on to place a check on corporate power had failed. He had "done a job that academic institutions and governmental agencies have long neglected," the *Bulletin* emphasized, "of speaking for the 'consumers' of smoke and smog, foul waters of rivers and the seaside, food chemicals, and residues of pesticides."[107] Although they did not grow to the scale of a "moderate city," Bookchin's principles were an inspiration and model for many of the rural communes that soon began dotting the American landscape.

Averting Apocalypse

A few months after Bookchin's book debuted, SANE ran another full-page ad, this one featuring a large picture of a glass milk bottle with a skull-and-crossbones logo stamped on its side where the name of a dairy might normally be found. Beneath a headline that read, "Is this what it's coming to?" the ad stated, "As if we weren't having problems enough with Strontium 90 in our milk, something new has been added. Iodine 131. From the atomic tests." After citing the evidence of children at risk in the Midwest, the ad urged action, "Raise hell; it's time you did."[108] Minnesota instituted a program to pay milk producers a premium price for milk from herds fed with feed aged at least 21 days rather than pasture grasses to assure that any iodine 131, with a half-life of eight days, would be mostly gone.[109]

Concerns over nuclear-testing fallout were temporarily eclipsed as the Cuban Missile Crisis occupied the nation's attention during the second half of October 1962. The world held its collective breath during the superpower showdown until the Soviets finally agreed to halt their plans to install nuclear missile bases in Cuba in exchange for a secret promise from the United States to remove its Jupiter ballistic missiles from Italy and Turkey where they had been deployed in 1961. In the aftermath of the crisis, citizens pushed for a test-ban treaty with greater determination than ever before.

In November the government sought to undermine those efforts when the House Un-American Activities Committee issued subpoenas to 14 members of Women Strike for Peace charging that communists had infiltrated the movement. But, embracing their power as mothers, the group not only successfully fended off HUAC's attack, their defense so discredited HUAC that it provided the crucial blow that finally destroyed the credibility of the controversial congressional group.[110] At the HUAC hearings the next month the first WSP witness, Blanche Posner, a retired Bronx high-school teacher, took her seat and immediately turned the tables on the committee. "You don't quite understand the nature of this movement," she chastised. "This movement was inspired and motivated by mothers' love for children.... When they were putting their breakfast on the table, they saw not only the Wheaties and milk, but they also saw strontium 90 and iodine 131."[111] The committee adjourned under criticism from much of the press for attacking the concerned mothers. WSP emerged vindicated and strengthened in its quest.[112]

The Public Health Service reported in November that iodine 131 levels in Palmer, Alaska and Salt Lake City had exceeded the government's radiation protection standards during the last year, and had neared that level in a number of Midwestern cities.[113] In addition, Alaskan caribou had a strontium-90 content that exceeded the government's maximum level. The lichen caribou ate received their nutrients from the air, and because that air was heavy with fallout strontium-90 became concentrated in the lichen. Ultimately, the Alaskans who ate the caribou had strontium-90 levels four to thirty times higher than those of other Americans. Wolves also dined on caribou, with an individual wolf killing as many as 100 a year.[114]

On Easter Sunday April 1963 thousands of people, mostly women and children, marched on the United Nations and demonstrated in cities across the country for a test-ban treaty. In Hartford, Connecticut, 170 people marched to the state capitol. Nobel-laureate geneticist Hermann J. Muller proposed the precautionary measure of storing sperm from males relatively early in their lives and holding it in underground deep freezers to be used later for procreation because it would be freer of genetic defects than it would if exposed to prolonged fallout.[115]

The US government was under unprecedented pressure, both domestically and internationally, to put a halt to testing. Both superpowers, shaken by how quickly things escalated toward nuclear war during the Cuban Crisis, finally showed more willingness to listen to worldwide public outcries and to compromise to reach an agreement in the long-stalled Geneva talks.[116] On July 25, a Partial Test Ban Treaty was signed in Moscow by the United States, the Soviet Union, and Great Britain that banned all atmospheric and underwater tests (underground testing was still allowed). The US Senate ratified it on September 24, 1963. Kennedy's science adviser, Jerome Weisner, later commented that credit for moving the president toward the test-ban treaty should go to WSP, SANE, and Linus Pauling.[117]

With the treaty's curbs on atmospheric testing the issue of fallout receded. The *Bulletin of the Atomic Scientists* clock that had been sitting at seven minutes until midnight eased back to twelve minutes before twelve.[118] "Writers rarely write about this subject anymore, and people hardly ever talk about it," wrote a *Saturday Evening Post* columnist in 1967. "In recent years there has been something of a conspiracy of silence about the threat of nuclear war."[119] Following the treaty many of those concerned about the environmental impact of atomic testing switched the focus of their activism to other environmental issues.

Of course, atomic fear did not disappear. Like the testing itself, it merely went underground. While the magnitude of its force on individuals was difficult to detect and measure, its power was often intense. In his book *Life After God*, Douglas Coupland recalled a series of horrific nightmares and visions of nuclear apocalypse while growing up during the Cold War, as when sitting in his high school "physics class hearing a jet pass overhead, turning around surreptitiously and waiting for the pulse of light to crush the city." Later, many conversations convinced him that apocalyptic visions of a nuclear end were common to his generation, but often unspoken.[120] Todd Gitlin reached a similar conclusion. "There may not have been a single master fear," he conceded, "but to many in my generation...the grimmest and least acknowledged underside of affluence was the Bomb.... [W]e could never quite take for granted that the world we had been born into was destined to endure."[121]

The Persistence of Environmentalism

But although concerns about the Bomb moved underground, the issue of environmentalism that the Bomb helped bring to life remained. Americans might accept the Bomb, especially after the crises of Berlin and Cuba, but they would no longer accept its environmental costs, nor would they accept, by extension, the environmental destruction that characterized corporate capitalism. Certainly, they would not accept having to give their children milk laced with environmental toxins. Life in the nuclear era might mean the constantly lurking threat of instant mass slaughter, but that was enough. Being forced to await that grim possibility in an ever more damaged environment with its accompanying agonizing deaths and gruesome genetic defects was not seen as a foregone conclusion.

In July 1962, as anti-testing sentiment was reaching a fever pitch, Rachel Carson's *Silent Spring* was published, further awakening the world to the fact that strontium-90 and iodine 131 were not the only World War II chemicals threatening the earth and humanity. She dedicated the book to Albert Schweitzer, and its frontispiece included his apocalyptic prediction: "Man has lost the capacity to foresee and to forestall. He will end by destroying the earth." Because she was already a beloved best-selling writer of nature books on the ecology of the sea, it was assured that anything Carson wrote would receive notice.

Silent Spring, about half of which was first serialized in the *New Yorker* in June, drew enormous attention and helped legitimize environmentalism for some readers for whom the ideology may have previously appeared overly radical. As Robert Rodale observed a year later, "Even those who didn't read the book read about it in the papers or saw it discussed on television."[122] As a trusted authority Carson quieted many lingering doubts regarding the legitimacy of environmental concerns, reinforcing that—despite claims to the contrary by government and business officials—such apprehensions were warranted. She reviewed the environmental tragedies of the fire ant and gypsy moth sprayings in compelling, if not alarming, terms. However, much of the authority of *Silent Spring*'s narrative was due to the power of its prose and the wisdom of its central metaphor that compared DDT to nuclear fallout.[123] Carson wrote:

> In this now universal contamination of the environment, chemicals are the sinister and little-recognized partners of radiation in changing the very nature of the world—the very nature of its life. Strontium 90, released through nuclear explosion into the air, comes to earth in rain or drifts down as fallout, lodges in soil, enters into the grass or corn or wheat grown there, and in time takes up its abode in the bones of a human being, there to remain until his death. Similarly, chemicals sprayed on croplands or forests or gardens lie long in soil, entering into living organisms, passing from one to another in a chain of poisoning and death.[124]

Through these comparisons, Carson recognized, her readers could readily comprehend the nature and seriousness of the chemical threat of substances like DDT. In the eerie glow of the atomic blasts humans could never again view life and their planet with the level of confidence they had previously known. On the popular television program *CBS Reports* Carson stated ecologically, in terms that echoed the writings of Fairfield Osborn and William Vogt some 15 years earlier, "We still talk in terms of conquest. We still haven't become mature enough to think of ourselves as only a tiny part of a vast and incredible universe. Man's attitude toward nature is today critically important simply because we have now acquired a fateful power to alter and destroy nature. But man is a part of nature, and his war against nature is inevitably a war against himself."[125]

When it could no longer be seen as indestructible, the earth instead became vulnerable and in need of protection from a multitude of ever-increasing human threats. Chief among these threats was, Carson made clear, corporate capitalism. "This is an era...dominated by industry, in which the right to make a dollar at whatever cost is seldom challenged. When the public protests, confronted with some obvious evidence of damaging results of pesticide applications, it is fed little tranquilizing pills of half truth."[126]

In a chapter aimed at the growing anxieties toward big business, Carson made an allusion to Vance Packard's popular book on advertising and marketing, *The Hidden Persuaders*, when she stated: "Lulled by the soft sell and the hidden persuader, the average citizen is seldom aware of the deadly materials with which he is surrounding himself; indeed, he may not realize he is using them at all.... A few minutes research in any supermarket is enough to alarm the most stouthearted customer."[127] She denounced the FDA's "tolerances" for levels of chemical poisons in foods, insisting that "to establish tolerances is to authorize contamination of public food supplies with poisonous chemicals in order that the farmer and the processor may enjoy the benefit of cheaper production—then to penalize the consumer by taxing him to maintain a policing agency to make certain that he shall not get a lethal dose."[128]

Silent Spring is often credited with inspiring the environmental movement, but it entered an already active environmental discourse and nascent movement. Indeed, the book's rhetorical power resonated through that existing discourse. Four months before *Silent Spring* appeared in the *New Yorker* Fairfield Osborn summed up how widespread the concerns of (some) conservationists—not yet termed environmentalists—had already become. "As each year passes, conservation becomes an evermore pervasive subject involving not only the condition and use of a specific natural resource, whether animate or inanimate," he stated, "but also a disparate host of related or near-related subjects such as regional planning, urban sprawl, air and water pollution, fundamental ecological research, recreational programs, the preservation of scenic and other natural areas, the rights of public versus private ownership, the responsibilities of large corporations and of governments, and, finally, the ethic of man's trusteeship for the ultimate welfare of human society.... The last decade has witnessed a great surge forward in the conservation movement."[129] When Carson's editor, Paul Brooks, read her manuscript, he wrote to tell her, "the parallel between effects of chemicals and effects of radiation is so dramatic that people can't help getting the idea. In a sense, all this publicity about fallout gives you a head start in awakening people to the dangers of chemicals."[130]

Nevertheless, serious doubts remained regarding whether even the increased publicity resulting from Carson's book would be enough to overcome the power of big business and its control over the government that was supposed to regulate it. A *New York Times* editorial that ran during *Silent Spring*'s serialization expressed skepticism that, in the end, the government would actually take meaningful action against corporations: "If her series helps arouse public concern to immunize government agencies against the blandishments of the hucksters and enforces adequate controls," the editorial stated, "the author will be as deserving of the Nobel Prize as was the inventor of DDT."[131] With the flood of publicity surrounding the issue some form of government action was almost certain. The real question, as the editorial suggested, was whether any level of public concern was capable of moving Congress to place the welfare of citizens before that of big business: would government's action be "adequate"? Business did all that it could to assure that it was not.

As they had been doing for more than a decade with pioneers in organic agriculture, officials from industry sought to undermine *Silent Spring*. Its popularity inspired harsh attacks from chemical companies and agribusiness aimed at discrediting or silencing Carson. After portions of the book appeared in the *New Yorker*, Versicol Chemical Corporation sent a threatening letter to Houghton Mifflin telling the publisher that it should reconsider issuing *Silent Spring* in view of Carson's "inaccurate and disparaging statements" about Versicol's pesticides heptachlor and chlordane. "Unfortunately, in addition to the sincere opinions of natural food faddists, Audubon groups and others, members of the chemical industry in this country... must deal with sinister influences," complained Versicol. At their core, the company insisted, questions regarding the safety of chemicals were in reality a thinly veiled communist plot to undermine the free world. "Attacks on the chemical industry have a dual purpose," Versicol insisted, "(1) to create the false impression that all business is grasping and immoral, and (2) to reduce the use of agricultural chemicals in this country and Western Europe, so that our supply of food will be reduced to east-curtain parity. Many innocent groups are financed and led into attacks on the chemical industry by these sinister parties." When scientists hired by Houghton Mifflin verified the accuracy of Carson's statements, publication proceeded. The book was quickly met by a wave of vicious industry-funded public relations attacks that assailed both Carson and her message.[132]

In *Silent Spring* Carson attacked the government's failure to protect citizens from chemical threats produced by big business. A former biologist for the US Fish and Wildlife Service, she sought political solutions and legitimized the issue of the environment to such an extent that politicians could no longer dodge the public's concern. President Kennedy appointed a special panel of his Science Advisory Committee to investigate the pesticides issue. In its 46-page report issued in May 1963 it recognized Carson for helping to "make people aware of the toxicity of pesticides," as if all the lawsuits, congressional testimony, investigative journalism, and research warnings prior to the publication of the book somehow never happened. Linking environmental peril to the postwar era, the report continued: "During two decades of intensive technical and industrial advancement we have dispersed a huge volume of synthetic compounds, both intentionally and inadvertently. Many, such as detergents, industrial wastes, and pesticides are now found far from the point of initial dispersal."[133] Dr. Jerome B. Wiesner, chair of the committee, told a Senate subcommittee that the uncontrolled use of chemicals is "potentially a much greater hazard than radioactive fallout."[134] The only real action the report called for was additional research. Corporations were successful in holding off a government ban on DDT for another nine years—twenty-five years after Fairfield Osborn questioned its "ultimate and net result to the life scheme of earth."[135]

The environmental concern that took root in the fallout of the Bomb and was later fertilized by *Silent Spring* continued to grow, until it became a cultural force when millions poured forth for Earth Day in 1970. For many who gathered that day the ethos that began stirring in the shadows of the Bomb had fought its way through the din and pollution to become a powerful presence, providing answers for many of the questions of the 1960s and holding forth the promise of avoiding both environmental and cultural apocalypse. With the Test Ban Treaty, fallout's threat to the earth was finally eased. The question of how to deal with the planetary, cultural, and political threat posed by the other source of untamed postwar power, big business, remained. In the years that followed, efforts to strike some sort of balance between the power of corporate capitalism and the desire for a healthy planet continued.

6

The "New" Conservation

Beyond the Test Ban Treaty, not a great deal of significant environmental legislation occurred during Kennedy's abbreviated administration. A Clean Air Act, amending the Air Pollution Control Act of 1955, was enacted in 1963—"an Act to improve, strengthen, and accelerate programs for the prevention and abatement of air pollution"—after a Senate study confirmed existing research that linked urban air pollution to increasing rates of pulmonary emphysema and lung cancer. It received final congressional approval just two days before Kennedy's assassination and was signed into law by President Lyndon Baines Johnson. Although somewhat tougher than earlier versions, it nevertheless reflected corporate influence. Focusing more on additional research and voluntary compliance than on expanded enforcement, it provided little to substantively address the larger environmental ethos.[1]

Amid Johnson's antipoverty programs, civil rights, women's rights, gay rights, Vietnam, and other issues of the tumultuous 1960s, the environmental concern that had taken hold during the Cold War nevertheless forced its way onto the crowded political radar. Signs of a deteriorating environment built increased pressure for political action, as evidenced in statements by the celebrated writer and author of the dystopian novel *Brave New World*, Aldous Huxley, in a speech published in 1963: "Do we propose to live on this planet in symbiotic harmony with our environment?" he asked. "Or, preferring to be wantonly stupid, shall we choose to live like murderous and suicidal parasites that kill their host and so destroy themselves?" Huxley saw only one solution: "Only when we get it into our collective head that the basic problem confronting twentieth-century man is an ecological problem," he concluded, "will our politics improve and become realistic."[2]

LBJ's Environmentalism

In many respects, environmentalism *did* enter the nation's "collective head." And as it penetrated the mainstream of political discourse, environmentalism, in turn, further informed the larger culture. The expanded vision of environmentalism to serve as a check on corporate capitalism and reconnect humans to the natural world, a vision that had been building incrementally during the postwar era, finally made its way into the mainstream of political rhetoric with President Johnson's "Great Society" speech at the University of Michigan graduation in May 1964.

Although best remembered for its emphasis on combatting poverty and ensuring civil rights, in that speech Johnson defined a great society as an environmental society. "The Great Society," he emphasized, "is a place where man can renew contact with nature. It is a place which honors creation for its own sake...." Addressing the outsized role of materialism, he added, "It is a place where men are more concerned with the quality of their goals than the quantity of their goods." The President linked traditional aesthetic conservation with newer environmental concerns. "We have always prided ourselves on being not only America the strong and America the free, but America the beautiful," he observed. "Today that beauty is in danger. The water we drink, the food we eat, the very air that we breathe, are threatened with pollution. Our parks are overcrowded, our seashores overburdened. Green fields and dense forests are disappearing. A few years ago we were greatly concerned about the 'Ugly American.' Today we must act to prevent an ugly America."[3]

Johnson began unveiling his plan for what he termed "new conservation" four months later. "Three changing forces are bringing a new era to conservation," he argued:

> The first is growing population.... Increasing pressures will take our resources, and increasing leisure will tax our recreation. The second is the triumph of technology. The bright success of science also has a darker side. The waste products of our progress, from exhaust fumes to radiation, may be one of the deadliest threats to the destruction of nature that we have ever known. The third force is urbanization. More of our people are crowding into cities and cutting themselves off from nature. Access to beauty is denied and ancient values are destroyed. Conservation must move from nature's wilderness to the manmade wilderness of our cities. All of this requires a new conservation.[4]

What did he mean by this "new" conservation? "It is not just the classic conservation of protection and development, but rather creative conservation of restoration and innovation," Johnson explained. Then, neatly summarizing how the new conservation reached beyond traditional conservation ideals, he stated, "Its concern is not with nature alone, but with the total relation between man and the world around him. Its object is not just man's welfare, but the dignity of his spirit."[5] Johnson was influenced by his wife, Lady Bird, who made "beautification" her focus, his economic advisor John Kenneth Galbraith's views on profligate consumption, and also by Secretary of the Interior Stewart Udall, whose 1963 book, *The Quiet Crisis*, lamented the fact that while the nation's wealth was increasing, its environment was in decline.[6] It was clear that he understood the more holistic environmental consciousness that was taking over from the traditional conservation of days past.

The President's first great environmental deed was to sign into law the Wilderness Act, which its supporters—including Kennedy and its author Howard Zahniser, who was executive secretary of the Wilderness Society—had been trying to move through Congress since the first draft of the bill in 1956.[7] At first glance, the Wilderness Act appeared to be a throwback to the goals of traditional, aesthetic preservation that had long preoccupied conservationists. Although it may have been difficult to separate nature from those late-nineteenth-century associations with wilderness, in the era of postwar modernity the meaning of nature was not limited to those romantic connections.

Wilderness: Conservative or Liberal?

Large corporations were threatening local and regional variety. National brands, chain stores, and media conglomerates fostered corporate homogeneity. Urban renewal was extinguishing organic diversity in the cities. Mass-production architecture in sprawling suburbs meant the houses all looked the same. The varied architecture of downtown retail cores was being replaced by suburban big-box shopping centers and strip malls. Local diners were being displaced by cookie-cutter fast-food franchises. It seemed self-sufficiency and craftsmanship were nearly subsumed by specialization and mass production. Agriculture was increasingly becoming monoculture agribusiness. It all combined to produce a fear that some timeless wisdom might be carelessly lost in the process of the corporate overhaul.

In the early 1960s nobody better articulated the growing concern over decreasing diversity and the need for wilderness as a counterpoise than conservation biologist and ecologist Raymond Dasmann. In his book *The Last Horizon* (1963), Dasmann noted, "The most alarming single trend on earth today is the trend toward uniformity. It extends through all of life: vegetation, wild animals, human cultures." On the physical level wilderness was to be a storehouse and museum, preserving biological diversity in the face of ever-encroaching development. But just as important was the cultural component of wilderness. Dasmann could see that the power of corporations, and their never-ending desire to increase their markets to satisfy shareholders, meant their forceful homogenizing tendency would continue to spread. In Dasmann's words, "We are thus faced with the prospect of a future in which little Americas or little Europes, and the two are becoming disturbingly similar, will displace all other kinds of human settlement, whether we seek to accomplish this or try half-heartedly to avoid it."[8] It was a process Arthur Koestler had pithily characterized in 1960, referring to the ubiquitous American soft drink, as the "cocacolinization" of the world.[9] "The present trend is toward a world-embracing human monoculture," Dasmann feared, "in which only one kind of people, adapted to an industrialized culture, can survive."[10] He joined growing numbers of Americans in looking to environmentalism to arrest the trend toward corporate homogeneity.

Dasmann drew on Tibet for an analogy to explain why preserving unique spaces was becoming increasingly urgent. When the Chinese People's Liberation Army invaded Tibet in 1950, he observed, many Americans, even though they had never been there and likely never would, "felt a deep and personal loss." "There was a satisfaction in knowing it was there," Dasmann noted, "remote in its high plateaus and mountains, stubbornly resisting influences from the outside, holding to its old ways through the turmoil of the twentieth century."[11] Such places held the promise of models of other ways to live. "We have already gone so far in grinding down separate human cultures into the same bland meal that it seems hopeless to arrest the process," he argued. "But," he nevertheless maintained, "it would be worthwhile to try." Even if it proved impossible to stop the march toward sameness, Dasmann nonetheless insisted that the effort was necessary, for to do nothing to stop the trend would mean the tragic end of the world as humans had known it.[12]

Like Dasmann, many feared that the rapid environmental and cultural transformations brought about by corporate capitalism were transpiring at the cost of organically evolved characteristics in the environment and culture being lost that, should the new corporate model of living prove unsatisfactory, might never be regained. In the Cold War era unfettered capitalism was equated with Americanism, while different notions of freedom tied to wilderness traditions and nature struggled to compete and, worse, were often condemned as un-American.

Although most Americans might never visit the wilderness, many nevertheless derived comfort and satisfaction from knowing it was there. As long as such spaces continued to exist individuals could imagine escaping to the wilderness. If wilderness spaces continued to decline they would be increasingly relegated to mere fantasy, greatly diminishing the power of both their literal and figurative impacts. In the midst of the Cold War and corporate homogeneity, the need for wilderness never seemed greater. As Admiral Hyman Rickover lamented in 1957, in an echo of Frederick Jackson Turner's frontier thesis, "Much of the wilderness which nurtured what is most dynamic in the American character has now been buried under cities, factories and suburban developments where each picture window looks out to nothing more inspiring than the neighbor's back yard."[13] Although the American wilderness was diminished, it was still large enough to contain the most sacred national myths like freedom, rugged individualism, and self-reliance, all the while holding forth the promise of both personal and national renewal.

At a time when Americans measured their existence against the totalitarian standard of the Eastern Bloc, wilderness represented a victory for liberty and freedom not only from corporate hegemony but from government's gaze. As Dasmann observed, wild places "have helped to guarantee a measure of freedom, an opportunity for change, that might otherwise have vanished. So long as they remain, such freedom and opportunity will stay with us."[14] Along with the abundance of consumer goods that Vice President Richard Nixon had insisted defined life in America during his legendary "Kitchen Debate" with Soviet Premier Nikita Khrushchev in 1959, for many citizens the notion of what it meant to be an American was also tied to wilderness.

We can see, in wilderness, the broad appeal of the "nature" aspect of environmentalism as a palimpsest for a variety of actors. It was attractive to those who found modern life too circumscribed and confining and believed that it inhibited creativity and expression; it was a quest for "authenticity" and an embrace of the Dionysian in a world of corporate artifice and control. But wilderness also held appeal for conservatives and libertarians who cherished it as a space free from government intrusion. Others—especially white males—took that notion even further and romanticized a social Darwinist fantasyland where only the strongest and fittest could, without government to look out for the weak and undeserving, survive. For them, wilderness was a space outside LBJ's Great Society where they could playact scenes of rugged individualism and self-sufficiency. For these white males it was not so much a site of creativity and expression as it was a place to reassert "natural" laws that had been corrupted (and feminized) by modern civilization.[15]

As first drafted by Howard Zahniser, the Wilderness Act was to set aside 50 million acres of federal lands "where man himself is a visitor who does not remain." Wilderness areas would be free from any commercial development, including resorts, mining, and hydroelectric power projects. Opposed by business—especially timber, mining, livestock, and power companies—the act finally made it through Congress thanks to a concerted effort by traditional conservation groups like the Wilderness Society, Sierra Club, and Audubon Society, which teamed with civic groups like the Jaycees to lobby Congress to the point that, by 1962, senators and representatives received more mail about wilderness than any other legislative proposal.[16]

Nevertheless, by the time it finally achieved congressional approval the final version of the Wilderness Act was the victim of corporate compromises. Of the 310 million acres available in public and Bureau of Land Management lands, only 54 areas totaling 9.1 million acres were designated as wilderness. In addition, cattle grazing was still permitted, a president could still authorize dams and power plants in the designated areas, and mining and lumber interests were appeased by retaining exploration and extraction rights for at least 25 years before the land would be closed off as wilderness. Even so, the Wilderness Act marked another hard-fought victory for conservationists, even if government foot-dragging in the aftermath meant that it was not until 1968 that additional parcels of land were finally entered into the wilderness system.[17]

The Endangered Species Preservation Act of 1966, inspired in part by the sad plight of the whooping crane, marked an additional victory for diversity.[18] But the broader environmental threats posed by big business nevertheless remained largely unresolved.

Increasing Evidence of Environmental Ills

Even wilderness preserves could not hide the fact that environmental damage was posing an increasing threat to the planet and its inhabitants. In November 1963, US Surgeon General Luther L. Terry told the annual meeting of the American Public Health Association that DDT had "invaded the water environment of the world," noting that, like radioactive fallout, DDT had spread over the planet and was now found in fish caught off the coasts of Iceland and Japan, as well as aquatic plants in the Arctic.[19] Two months later biochemists at Rutgers University discovered why consumers who ate fish caught in ocean waters near metropolitan areas often complained of a peculiar flavor called "harbor taste." The scientists, who were able to recreate the taste in laboratory fish, traced the flavor to petroleum distillate from industrial wastes that was in the fish but had not (yet) killed them.[20]

The heartland of the nation was hardly immune. In Omaha it was revealed that even seven years after the Federal Department of Health, Education, and Welfare first warned the meat-packing industry to clean up its act in 1957, the city's packing plants were still dumping some 300 tons of untreated solid waste into the Missouri River daily, endangering the drinking water of downstream citizens in Nebraska, Iowa, Missouri, and Kansas. Although Omaha had pledged to take care of the problem, some of the 19 meat-packing companies there, claiming the expense was just too great, later reneged on their promise to the city to properly dispose of their own waste. Instead of forcing the corporations to comply, the city subsidized the packing houses by building a taxpayer-funded $1.6 million incinerator to dispose of the solid waste produced by the meat-packing companies. But even that would take at least another two years.[21]

The early sixties were also a time of growing alarm over massive fish die-offs in polluted waters. Agricultural pesticides draining into the Mississippi River basin first began showing up in huge numbers of dead fish in 1960. In late 1963 Louisiana asked Washington for help after it found more than five million dead fish, including shad, mullet, bass, trout, catfish, and gar, as well as large numbers of dead and dying ducks. Chemists with the Public Health Service found endrin (most often used on cotton, but also on rice and sugar cane), dieldrin, DDT, and DDE (a chemical formed when DDT breaks down and which is stored in body fat) in the dead fish.[22] Many of the fish appeared to be suffocating. The fish, wrote Harry McHugh in the Franklin, Louisiana *Banner Tribune*, "will stick his head completely out of water and just breathe in the air for a while until he breathes in so much that he cannot submerge again." Further, reported McHugh, he saw only five live crows in the swamps in 1963 "where there used to be millions," and "countless thousands" of white cranes had died.[23] Large numbers of shrimp were also found dead in the river, and Louisiana commercial shrimp in the Gulf of Mexico were found to contain endrin, dieldrin, heptachlor, DDT, and DDE. Oysters from the Mississippi Delta area were also tainted.[24] The drinking water of New Orleans and other cities that took their water from the river was found to contain pesticides, even after treatment.[25] Oregon was hit with a similar tragedy, in which some 70,000 dead steelhead trout in the autumn of 1963 were found to contain 50 times the amount of chemicals, including dieldrin, known to kill a trout. Around the country fishermen protested, and consumers were forced to wonder whether it was safe to drink their water or to eat fish and seafood.[26]

Shell Chemical Company, maker of dieldrin, sought to defend itself by arguing that unexplained fish kills had been occurring since the beginning of recorded history. The company insisted that judgment should be withheld until more evidence could be gathered, and even then the benefits of the insecticides should be weighed against any hazards.[27] University of Cincinnati professor of industrial medicine Dr. Mitchell R. Zavon testified before a 1963 Senate hearing on a President's Scientific Advisory Committee Report critical of pesticide use that the panel of scientists responsible for the report did not know what they were talking about. The reason laboratory mice got more tumors from food containing dieldrin, he maintained, was that they ate more food than mice eating a dieldrin-free diet. Zavon, a paid consultant for Shell Chemical, neglected to explain why mouse food fortified with dieldrin was so much tastier.[28]

Given that there was seemingly no end to environmental threats, it was little wonder that in 1963 Robert Rodale could declare, "The demand for organic food is here, and it is a bigger demand than we have ever had before. The commercial food industry is worried that the organic food idea will catch fire and make their refined, packaged foods look like something second rate. Continued and intensified attacks of food industry spokesmen on organic food and health foods is testimony to their concern."[29] Increasing numbers of citizens who dreamed of a different world were shopping for change. Politicians could ignore them for only so long.

Government Pushed to Act

The "new" conservation promoted by President Johnson was not a disavowal of traditional conservation but rather an expansion of its boundaries. Government was finally catching up with the shift from conservation to environmentalism that had been growing for about 20 years. Traditional conservation goals remained important, especially because they were a focus of the First Lady. Following her lead, as conservationists had long done, Johnson emphasized aesthetics. "Above all, we must maintain the chance for beauty," he said. "When that chance dies, a light dies in all of us...."[30] He was not talking only about the beauty of wilderness.

By February 1965, his new conservation had evolved into a special message to Congress on the "Conservation and Restoration of Natural Beauty." Playing to traditional conservation interests, he called for acquiring more parklands and announced that he had asked Secretary of the Interior Udall to work with state and local governments to develop a program of national trails for walking, hiking, horseback riding, and bicycling. He urged Congress to establish a National Wild Rivers System to preserve remaining stretches of free-flowing rivers not yet dammed. Johnson emphasized the impact that ever-growing numbers of automobiles were having on the environment and argued that care should be taken that roads not destroy natural beauty, that landscaping should be included in all federal road building, and that roadside billboards should be limited. Nevertheless, he said that more roads should be constructed to access scenic and natural recreation areas.[31] In May 1965, there was a White House Conference on Natural Beauty, attended by conservationists, business leaders, and concerned citizens, headed by Laurance Rockefeller.

Other proposals in LBJ's new conservation clearly reflected the expanded concerns of postwar environmentalism, chief among them pollution. "This generation has altered the composition of the atmosphere on a global scale through radioactive materials and a steady increase in carbon dioxide from the burning of fossil fuels," said Johnson. "Entire regional airsheds, crop plant environments, and river basins are heavy with noxious materials.... Every major river is now polluted," resulting in waterborne viruses, mass deaths of fish, and abnormalities in wildlife. Furthermore, the President noted, changes in manufacturing, packaging, and marketing of consumer products meant that "In addition to our air and water we must, each and every day, dispose of a half billion pounds of solid waste." Johnson also issued warnings about pesticides and recommended additional funds for research. "Pollution," the President concluded, "destroys beauty and menaces health."[32] After decades of government evasiveness and hedging, in one address Johnson had come clean on strontium 90, air pollution, water pollution, solid waste, and pesticides and, furthermore, linked the problems to the practices of corporate capitalism. Significantly, Johnson touched upon issues of equity and the environment that foreshadowed the environmental justice movement. "Beauty must not be just a holiday treat," he said, "but a part of our daily life. It means not just easy physical access, but equal social access for rich and poor, Negro and white, city dweller and farmer."[33] Environmentalism had, clearly, made its way to the White House.

LBJ acknowledged that environmentalism was closely tied to consumer culture. In March 1965 he declared in a "Consumer Interest" message to Congress, "Every domestic program of the Federal Government in a very real sense is directed toward the consumer.... When we work to stem pollution, improve transportation, or rebuild our cities, we promote the welfare of the American consumer."[34] Three years later the Johnson administration further demonstrated its recognition that in daily living environmentalism often played out in concerns people had about what they consumed when it created the Consumer Protection and Environmental Health Service (CPEHS), made up of food and drug, national air pollution control, and environmental control administrations within the Department of Health, Education, and Welfare (HEW).[35] As the Public Health Service explained, it was decided that "man's environmental milieu consisted of the products he consumed and used, as well as the elements of nature; therefore, it was felt that the FDA and the environmental health aspects of the DHEW should be brought together."[36] But CPEHS was short-lived; Congress did not fund it.[37]

A presidential panel raised an alarm about the threat of climate change brought about by industrial processes in the fall of 1965, noting that massive additions of carbon dioxide from heating, lighting, and transportation "will modify the heat balance to such an extent that marked changes in climate could occur." The Environmental Pollution Panel, established by the President's Science Advisory Committee and composed of 15 leading scientists, physicians, and engineers, issued the warning in its report on *Restoring the Quality of Our Environment*, which also detailed dangerous levels of air, water, and soil pollution that threatened humans, animals, and the planet.[38] The report assailed the effects of corporate capitalism on the environment. Upon its release President

Johnson acknowledged: "Ours is a nation of affluence. But the technology that has permitted our affluence spews out vast quantities of wastes and spent products that pollute our air, poison our waters, and even impair our ability to feed ourselves."[39]

Scientific theories about increased carbon dioxide from industrialization in the atmosphere causing climate change dated back to the early nineteenth century but took on greater urgency in the late 1950s when advances in technology that permitted improved scientific modeling and testing confirmed an increase in carbon dioxide in the atmosphere due to industrialization and its propensity to alter the global climate.[40] Repeating research first reported by Swedish meteorologists Bert Bolin and Erik Eriksson in 1962, estimating that there would be about 25 percent more carbon dioxide in the atmosphere by the year 2000, the Pollution Panel's report forecast: "This will modify the heat balance of the atmosphere to such an extent that marked changes in climate, not controllable though [sic] local or even national efforts, could occur. Possibilities of bringing about countervailing changes by deliberately modifying other processes that affect climate may then be very important."[41]

In all, *Restoring the Quality of Our Environment* put forward 104 recommendations to confront the causes of the environment's deterioration and urged citizens to demand a healthy environment as a "human right."[42] Defending the message against charges that the proposals lacked any real enforcement powers, administration officials claimed that the plan was to first rally the nation to combat "ugly America," then back it up with expanded federal authority later if necessary.[43] Although often lacking in substance, the Johnson administration's rhetoric surely contributed to increasing public awareness of environmental issues. The Sierra Club's membership climbed to 33,000 in 1965, more than doubling from what it had been just five years earlier.[44]

By the mid-1960s the environment had grown into a mainstream concern. In 1967 a National Research Corporation poll revealed that 53 percent of those asked believed air pollution was a "serious problem" in their area, while 52 percent believed the same thing about water pollution. Forty-four percent said they would be willing to pay higher taxes to fund a pollution-control program (pollsters did not ask if they would prefer to see government impose tougher regulations on corporations to reduce pollution instead). By 1969 "pollution control" was the area of government spending that 38 percent of those asked in a Louis Harris poll would "least like to see cut." (With the publicity surrounding Earth Day in 1970, that number jumped to 55 percent one year later.)[45] Politicians were moved to demonstrate that they heard their concerns.

Johnson's rhetoric was accompanied by some environmental legislation. The Solid Waste Disposal Act of 1965 provided funds to research more effective methods to deal with the rapidly increasing quantities of solid waste resulting from the consumer boom. The Highway Beautification Act of 1965, championed by Lady Bird, regulated and limited billboards along the nation's interstate highways, required that junkyards along the highways be removed or screened from view, and encouraged the development of natural scenery along the roadways. A 1965 amendment to the Clean Air Act gave HEW the power to establish pollution standards for new motor vehicles. The Water Quality Act of 1965 mandated that the states establish adequate clean water standards and authorized the Secretary of HEW to establish them for any state whose benchmarks were deemed inadequate; the Clean Waters Restoration Act followed in 1966 to provide grants to state and local governments to help them meet the new water standards; the Air Quality Act of 1967 provided federal grants to assist states in meeting more stringent ambient air-quality standards, mandated that the Secretary of HEW impose regional air-quality standards for coal-burning industries if state efforts were inadequate, and established the President's Air Quality Advisory Board at a time when the Public Health Service said some 7,300 communities had air-pollution problems. President Johnson said when he signed the Act, "We are pouring at least 130 million tons of poison into the air each year.... Either we stop poisoning our air or we become a nation in gas masks, groping our way through dying cities and a wilderness of ghost towns."[46]

Traditional conservation's emphasis on aesthetics was expanded to include urban concerns. In addition to the Wilderness Act, in 1965 Congress appropriated $310 million for parks and urban beautification. There was also the National Historic Preservation Act of 1966, which authorized the Secretary of the Interior to establish the National Register of Historic Places and list buildings, sites, cultural resources, and entire districts deemed historically significant. Once listed they were eligible for federal matching grants and tax benefits for acquisition and preservation, providing funds to refurbish old buildings in the core of the nation's cities.[47] A National Wild and Scenic Rivers Act was passed in 1968 to prohibit dams from rivers, or segments of rivers, deemed to have particular scenic, recreational, geologic, fish and wildlife, historic, cultural, or other outstanding values. Finally, the National Trails System Act of 1968 provided for scenic and historic trails, designating the Appalachian and Pacific Crest Trails as the charter trails of the system.[48]

The Limits of LBJ's Environmental Legislation

Although the new laws and agencies established some important precedents, most of the environmental legislation during the Johnson years was watered down by industry influence and proved less than robust. In December 1967, even an article in *Sports Illustrated* magazine protested that the administration was focusing too much on beauty at the expense of more serious environmental problems that were plaguing the nation.[49] The Endangered Species Act did little more than authorize the creation of a list of endangered fish and wildlife, and their protection was largely discretionary, with the Secretary of the Interior powerless to stop the taking of any animal declared endangered. The Air Quality Advisory Board of the Air Quality Act of 1967 included many industry leaders, with the end result that corporations helped draft the air-pollution legislation that was supposed to regulate them and a Clean Air Act that many derisively referred to as "coal's law" due to the influence of industry leaders. It failed to establish national emission standards for industries, including paper mills, steel mills, chemical plants, and oil refineries that were some of the biggest polluters. Its regional ambient standards were difficult to monitor with existing technology and personnel, and even if a pollutant was found to exceed the standards there were often hundreds of industrial sources and no provisions to force all of them to reduce their emissions. Rather than ambient standards, what was needed, Secretary of the Department of Health, Education, and Welfare Secretary John Gardner and other experts told Congress, was enforceable emissions standards for all businesses in specific industries to stop pollution at the source. Instead, with the help of corporations, Congress delivered a law that delayed meaningful regulation.[50] In 1967 George R. Stewart noted in his book *Not So Rich as You Think* that each American produced an average of 1,600 pounds of solid waste a year while polluting the air and water to a point where the country was on a path to becoming uninhabitable. Americans had, Stewart emphasized, thus far been living better than they deserved by "living in more or less blissful ignorance" of the costs of environmental damage and avoiding the "bills" for proper disposal.[51]

One of the major environmental issues largely ignored by the Johnson administration was lead pollution. The 1967 Clean Air Act required only that manufacturers identify the quantity of lead and other additives in fuel so that research might assess their effects on humans and the environment. But lead's toxic qualities had long been known.[52] The administration's own 1965 *Restoring the Quality of Our Environment* report noted: "In persons heavily exposed to automotive exhausts, the body levels [of lead] approach the concentration known to have deleterious effects."[53] Children are most vulnerable to lead's effects, which can hinder brain development, leading to lower IQs, learning disabilities, hyperactivity, attention disorders, and hearing loss. Adults are not immune either: for them it is the cause of elevated risks of hypertension, heart disease, and stroke. Most of the lead was delivered to the environment from automobile exhaust pipes. Lead is not a natural element in gasoline. General Motors developed gasoline with a lead additive in order to prevent engine "knock" in the more powerful engines it was using in the larger and faster cars it designed. It first went on sale in 1923; by the end of the century an estimated seven million tons of lead were burned in gasoline in the United States, most of which still remains in the environment and living organisms. Unlike strontium-90, lead has no half-life; it does not break down in the environment and disappear over time.[54]

It did not have to be so. GM's own research confirmed that ethyl alcohol was an excellent antiknock additive. But DuPont owned over 35 percent of GM's stock in the early 1920s, and Pierre DuPont served as its president. Neither DuPont, nor GM, stood to profit much from ethyl alcohol that could not be patented, but both the chemical giant and GM stood to profit handsomely from a patented lead additive—tetraethyl lead (TEL). With its patent GM now not only profited from the sale of automobiles, but also got a royalty from every gallon of gasoline sold. It soon partnered with Standard Oil, which had found a faster method to synthesize TEL.[55]

From early on, public health officials, research scientists, medical experts, and labor leaders all expressed serious concerns about leaded gasoline's threat to humans. However, although GM knew TEL was dangerous, it managed to quell opposition by funding its own government research with the Bureau of Mines in 1923. That research contract stipulated that research had to be submitted to GM "for comment, criticism, and approval" before publishing. Not surprisingly, the final report claimed that leaded gasoline posed no health risks.[56] Thus over 40 years later, in 1965, when geochemist Clair C. Patterson of the California Institute of Technology was moved to warn, "There are definite indications that residents of the United States today are undergoing severe chronic lead insult," it was hardly the first warning, but it may have been more frightening in the context of the era's other chemical disasters. Like strontium-90 and DDT, Patterson warned, lead was stored in the body and accumulated over time where it might shorten lives, trigger nervous-system disorders, and cause developmental disabilities in children.[57]

Nevertheless, the automobile and petroleum industries continued to fight regulations to remove lead from gasoline on the basis that it would be too costly, an estimated penny a gallon. The level of control that corporations were accustomed to wielding over the government that supposedly policed them was further revealed when a 1966 Department of the Interior press release to announce research on lead-free antiknock additives noted that "lead is toxic." An outraged executive of the American Petroleum Institute trade association blasted the Interior Department for "grabbing headlines" without first submitting the press release to his organization for vetting. The government finally moved to phase out leaded gasoline in the mid-1970s; it was completely banned in 1996.[58]

Johnson's environmental legislation was aimed not only at providing environmental safeguards but also expanding the appeal of the Democratic Party among the white middle class. Since the New Deal, the Democrats had mostly been associated with the bread-and-butter issues of the working class and the poor, and more recently the civil rights movement. By the mid-1960s, though, they were seeking to broaden their appeal to the expanded postwar middle class.[59] Environmental issues became an increasingly important component of that effort. Presidential aide and speechwriter Ben Wattenberg argued, in a February 1967 memo regarding talking points for an upcoming Johnson speech to an AFL-CIO policy committee, that the biggest problem for the President among middle-income workers was the perception that they were being "lost in the shuffle" among the pressing concerns over the war in Vietnam and the War on Poverty. Wattenberg outlined several keys that Johnson needed to highlight, explaining how the administration was looking out for "middle-class working people," including its efforts to improve recreation and curb pollution. Emphasizing the need to stress the administration's preservation of wilderness and parklands, Wattenberg added, "Working class Americans have cars. They have roads. They have vacations. But where are they going to go? Only presidential assistants and union leaders can afford Majorca or a cruise to the Caribbean."[60]

The Democrats' traditional emphasis on redistributive justice increasingly gave way to a new conception of justice focused, instead, on environmental preservation. Unlike redistributive justice, which could be measured concretely in dollars and cents, environmental preservation was often complex and difficult to quantify. So long as the Democrats appeared to be more concerned about the environment than Republicans, they could claim the mantle of the "environmental party," along with the votes of the growing block of citizens who named care for the environment among their chief concerns. It did not, however, require them to do too much in the way of powerful legislation and enforcement.

Beneath the surface of the Johnson administration's environmentalism remained political realities that made clear why, although making gestures toward environmentalism was relatively easy, deep and genuine political change was unlikely. Television meant increasingly expensive campaigns, and Democrats moved to woo corporate donors. Although big business might have continued to align more readily with the ideology of the Republican Party, it nevertheless realized that it could reap significant benefit by funding both political parties, especially when it meant backing the likely winner. In the 1964 election, for example, the 4,000 members of the "President's Club," nearly all of whom were corporate executives or their representatives, contributed at least $4 million to the Johnson campaign. Corporate lobbyists also shelled out as much as $1,000 per plate for numerous fund-raising luncheons and dinners. In all, business paid at least 75 percent of the bill for Johnson to remain president.[61] Given that corporations were financing American politics, it is hardly surprising to find that government gave greater priority to their desires than to the needs of average citizens and the environment.

Only days after assuming his first full term as president following the election, Johnson held a private dinner for corporate leaders at the White House. The Business Council, made up of 62 top executives, had been consulting privately with top government and Cabinet officials to influence policies since its founding in 1933. During those meetings top corporate officials often received information that was not available to either the public or even lesser business leaders. Gatherings often included recreation activities for the government officials and corporate executives, paid for by the Business Council. The relationship between the corporate elite and the Johnson administration was so cozy that even his own Commerce Secretary, John Connor, protested that when President Johnson "wanted to know what business was thinking, he would pick up the phone and call members of the Business Council," not the Commerce Secretary. Richard Barber, an attorney who served as counsel to the Senate Anti-Trust Subcommittee during the Johnson years, said of the intimate relationship between corporations and the government that citizens counted on to place a check on their power: "It is a cozy club, bringing together the top policy makers of government and business in an elitist environment that may be foreign to our traditional ways of making public policy but that is now coming to be an accepted way of life for the new partnership."[62] Corporate power had altered American democracy.

For example, in 1968 Congress passed a water-pollution bill that was significantly tougher than existing legislation. It passed the Senate unanimously, and a slightly watered-down version made it through the House on a 277-0 vote. Despite the overwhelming support in both houses the two versions of the bill were never reconciled, due mostly to intense lobbying efforts by oil, power, paper, and other industries that were profiting by polluting water.[63] "Revolutionaries must begin to think in ecological terms," wrote one writer in New York's *Rat* newspaper in an article later reprinted elsewhere in the underground press. "The people, as represented by Congress, have no power. Even when Congress does try to curb the 'excesses' of environment destruction, industry and military pressures water the controls."[64]

Through sophisticated lobbying and unrivaled access, corporations had an unmatched voice regarding potential legislation. In a seminal 1965 study economist Mancur Olson found that the size and power of business lobbying groups had grown substantially since World War II. Their extreme wealth gave them advantages in collective action that other groups simply could not match, affording them access to political leaders and the policymaking process that allowed them to effectively control issues that impacted their industries. "Often," Olson pointed out, "a relatively small group or industry will win a tariff, or a tax loophole, at the expense of millions of consumers or taxpayers in spite of the ostensible rule of the majority."[65] In addition, by means of powerful legal teams they often successfully combated legislation that did manage to make its way into law. With former corporate executives dominating high-ranking government positions, they effectively controlled the enforcement of environmental regulations. As political scientist Grant McConnell concluded in a 1966 study of corporate power and American democracy, "the problem of the corporation becomes much more visible when the character of governmental agencies is considered.... The web of relationships between the regulators and the regulated and the influential committees of Congress is so complex and strong that it is unrealistic to expect reform except after great effort and much determination."[66] Such effort and determination was bound to be lacking when the "regulated" were financing the political campaigns of their "regulators" in both major parties, effectively determining who gained and retained office.

Although new environmental legislation gave the impression that the government was taking the steps necessary to regulate corporations, doing whatever needed to be done to protect citizens and the environment, in reality corporations with their White House access and congressional lobbyists were generally successful in framing issues and controlling the outcomes of legislation. "These measures met with considerable resistance," President Johnson admitted. "Powerful special interest groups, particularly in industry, foresaw that it would be expensive to change their methods of operation in order to meet strict new federal pollution standards." Larry O'Brien, Johnson's special assistant for congressional relations and personnel, noted, for example, that "up to this time, there hadn't been any major effort to impose rules and procedures on the auto industry, which is contributing tremendously to the problem of our air. Now you're getting into big lobbying, a powerful group with supporters in Congress."[67]

Those regulations that did manage to make it through were generally tamed and even then often poorly enforced. "Nothing much has changed," observed New York Times architecture critic Ada Louise Huxtable, "except the statements of Federal policy that somehow get lost in the translation at the local level, and the increasingly pious use of the word environment—a poorly understood concept at best."[68] Although attempting to talk a better talk, government was still mostly failing to address the nation's environmental needs.

Consumer activist Ralph Nader argued that pollution standards like the ones passed by the Johnson administration were largely meaningless unless they were "adequately drafted, kept up to date, vigorously enforced, and supported by sanctions when violated." Environmental acts drafted during the Johnson era generally fell short on all counts. The problem, Nader and other critics maintained, was that experts counted upon to protect the public usually showed more loyalty to corporations than they did to citizens. Sanctions were seldom invoked, and when they were they did not have enough bite to really matter.

In addition, requirements for public disclosure of corporate wrongdoing were too often skirted by companies insisting that to divulge such information would be giving away "trade secrets." Finally, there was too little protection for corporate whistle-blowers who wished to inform the public about the environmentally harmful acts and practices of their employers.[69] Business financed politics because it received a healthy return on its investment, even as the health of citizens and the planet suffered in the process.

Nader's landmark 1965 study of the automobile industry, *Unsafe at Any Speed: The Designed-In Dangers of the American Automobile*, which contained a scathing chapter on automobile pollution, further shook American confidence in corporations as well as the ability of the government to effectively regulate them. His book's focus on business's disregard for the health and safety of consumers in its pursuit of profits led *Science* to call it "the *Silent Spring* of traffic safety," further solidifying the link between consumerism and environmentalism in the public consciousness.[70] The book generated substantial interest in the sometimes abusive relationship of business toward consumers, and Nader followed its success with numerous exposés of corporate wrongdoing, popularizing the consumer movement during the sixties.

The links between the consumer culture of corporate capitalism and the deteriorating environment had become increasingly clear since World War II. As Hugo Fisher, administrator for the Resources Agency of California, summarized in 1966, "The rest of the world is going to take a dim view" of our level of consumption. They will recognize not only that we are using more than our fair share, he warned, but they will also note that the United States is "consuming the earth's resources at a rate that requires us to fill foothill canyons with refuse, fill our ocean bays and offshore waters with garbage, line our highways with junked cars and discarded beer cans, incinerate billions of tons of wood fiber wastes with one hand while denuding our forests with the other, and strip our rivers and beaches of sand while covering some of the world's most productive agricultural lands with freeways, airports and 'slurbs' and go-cart runways."[71]

Insufficient Laws Inspire Increased Activism

The limited gains achieved through the political process inspired renewed grassroots efforts for environmental protection. SANE founder and editor of *The Saturday Review*, Norman Cousins, became a leading voice protesting pollution problems. In May 1965, his magazine published a special section on "The Fouling of the American Environment." Less than a year later he was chosen to lead an Antipollution Task Force in New York to study pollution and recommend solutions for the crisis.[72] In 1967 the St. Louis Committee for Nuclear Information, which had formed in 1958 and quickly became a leading voice in the fight against strontium-90 and nuclear testing with measures like the children's-teeth study, changed its name to the Committee for Environmental Information to mark its shift in focus to the broader issues that still threatened the environment in the wake of the Test Ban Treaty.[73] Despite the Treaty a host of other threats inspired ongoing environmental anxieties and activism.

The limits of LBJ's "new conservation" soon became apparent in a flood of environmental issues that captured media and public attention in the second half of the decade. Little, if any, real change was felt by citizens as they went about the conduct of their daily lives, even as the increasing rhetoric and publicity served to further environmental awareness and legitimize existing environmental concerns, all the while raising expectations for a clean, healthy, and aesthetically pleasing environment. Frightening evidence of a deteriorating environment continued to mount. A 1966 study published in the journal *Industrial Medicine and Surgery* and reported in the popular press confirmed for the first time that earlier findings of pesticides in infant animals, absorbed from the mother while a fetus, were also true of humans. Research on stillborn and unborn babies of mothers killed in accidents found pesticides in all of those tested.[74] In addition to their mother's DNA, babies were emerging from the womb with mom's DDT.

One of the most symbolic conservation fights during the sixties was the effort to stop the building of two dams on the Colorado River in Arizona's beloved Grand Canyon as part of the Colorado River Basin Project. Although both dams, at Marble Gorge and Bridge Canyon, were to be built outside of the National Park, they nevertheless would greatly slow the flow of the river, backing water into part of the park and causing significant changes in the area's ecology. Further, the scenery in the gorges outside of the national park's borders, including Bridge Canyon's 3,000-foot sheer walls and the stunning colors of Marble Gorge, would be severely altered. The dams themselves were not necessary for Arizona's water needs but instead were claimed to be "cash register dams" reaping profits from the sale of hydroelectricity that would help defray the costs of reservoirs and waterworks that would be located elsewhere on the river to aid in Arizona's economic development. However, it was later learned that the dams were not even needed to finance the Central Arizona Project and that their real purpose was to supply a fund for the future importation of water into the Colorado River from the Columbia River, if and when it became politically and economically feasible.[75]

Secretary of the Interior Udall, an ex-congressman from Arizona, and his brother Morris, a sitting Congressman from Arizona, both took pride in their reputations as leading conservationists. But in the end they placed their concern for Arizona's corporate interests and development ahead of their cares for conservation and fought for the dams with all of their political might. When the Sierra Club ran a full-page newspaper advertisement in early June protesting the dams and urging the public to "save the Grand Canyon," it was notified by the Internal Revenue Service less than 24 hours later that its tax-exempt status might be revoked pending an investigation into whether a "substantial" portion of its funds was used to influence legislation. As the *New York Times* stated, "The Internal Revenue Service's action looks suspiciously like harassment and intimidation."[76] Nevertheless, those opposing the dams ultimately emerged victorious, and the Grand Canyon was spared. But there were many other battles to be waged.

The second half of the sixties was a time of numerous controversies over proposed developments that threatened cherished sites of aesthetic nature. Many of these struggles found citizens desperately trying to stave off powerful corporations, developers, and their allies in government from inflicting environmental damage. In part these efforts were in the tradition of preserving aesthetically pleasing natural spaces. But, the environment also served as a surrogate issue for citizens seeking some means to combat corporate hegemony. In New York, residents waged a protracted battle to keep Consolidated Edison from building a hydroelectric dam on the Hudson River at Storm King Mountain that protestors called "one of the most beautiful river scenes in the entire world."[77] Dams were also opposed in a number of other states, including Kentucky, Idaho, and Alaska.[78] In New Jersey conservationists fought to save the Great Swamp and surrounding wetlands and prevent Chatham Township from using it as a dump.[79] Plans by the Walt Disney Corporation to build a major ski area and year-round resort in the Mineral King Valley of the Sierra Nevada Mountains in Sequoia National Forest in California aroused bitter opposition and prompted bumper stickers around the state that read "KEEP MINERAL KING NATURAL."[80] In Oregon, citizens successfully contested the location of a highway through sand dunes near the edge of the Pacific Ocean.[81] The Sierra Club and others defended giant, 300-foot redwood trees in California from the saw blades of the Georgia-Pacific Corporation.[82]

But industry fought opposition to its environmental encroachment at every turn. Corporations often framed environmental protesters as irrational. As stated by Don Cave, the co-chair of a timber industry group that fought the proposed Redwoods National Park: "Every time there is mention of cutting a redwood tree the extremists go into a spiritual fit."[83] A government attorney representing the Federal Power Commission in hearings over Consolidated Edison's proposed Storm King project complained that the Sierra Club was bullying utility companies. "They [the utilities] have to have real temerity these days in view of the opposition of the Sierra Club," said Federal Power Commission attorney John Lane.[84] Just as they had done to those touting the benefits of organic foods, corporations attempted to marginalize any who dared question their actions, branding those seeking to protect the environment as unreasonable, irrational, and "extremists."

The Lingering Problem of Outsized Corporate Power

Beyond the threat they posed to aesthetic wilderness, corporations continued to make their presence felt in nearly every walk of life, and concerns about their outsized role in the American polity were spreading and intensifying. In 1967 John Kenneth Galbraith published *The New Industrial State*, a bestseller in which he warned that the nation was becoming increasingly antidemocratic as the power once vested in the people of the United States was further monopolized by "mature corporations" operated by a "technostructure" of highly specialized managers that took on something of a life of its own as it manipulated and controlled, in an alliance with government, all of society to meet its ends.[85]

By 1968 the government funded some 60 percent of research conducted in the United States, but 70 percent of it was carried out by industrial corporations. Of the roughly 570,000 scientists and engineers doing research in the United States, 469,000 received federal funds, and 359,000 of these were employed by private companies. A good deal of corporate research was being carried out at universities.[86] Many of the technological advances and resulting profits of corporate America were subsidized, at least in part, by the tax dollars of American citizens. As government, corporations, and universities became increasingly conjoined in the years following World War II, traditional balances of power were severely altered. "In the past the university was relied upon to serve as a social critic, insulated from the kinds of pressures that inevitably dictate accommodation in business and government," Richard Barber observed. "Today that independence is rapidly being lost as the universities join with industry and government in mutually appealing endeavors."[87] Corporate capitalism increasingly infiltrated the culture and conduct of American universities.

Environmentalism and the War in Vietnam

The protests that began in 1965 to voice opposition to the war in Vietnam grew to become a majority opinion by the end of the decade, but citizens were unable to move the government to end the war. Some blamed the cozy ties that the military and politicians maintained with corporations—the "military-industrial complex" that President Eisenhower had warned about in his farewell address in 1961—for the government's stubborn refusal to get out of Vietnam.[88] One of the most noted incidents was the April 1969 student occupation of the Applied Electronics Laboratory at Stanford University, protesting its secret military-related research for the US government under the theme, "Research Life, Not Death!" Student president Denis Hayes, who only a year later would lead the organization of Earth Day, was pushed to broker a peace between student protestors and the administration.[89]

The war in Vietnam raised additional environmental concerns. By the late sixties the environmental damage being inflicted on that nation by the American government was enormously controversial, adding to the growing environmental awareness of American citizens and deepening the nation's antiwar sentiment. Vietnam was devastated by relentless "carpet" bombing. More bombs were dropped on Southeast Asia than were dropped during all of World War II, by war's end quadrupling that earlier war's tonnage. Beyond the devastating human toll, the result on the landscape was craterlike holes so numerous that in some areas it resembled a moonscape. In 1968 alone B-52 bomber airplanes created an estimated 3,448,000 craters as large as 30 feet deep and 45 feet in diameter that often filled with water and became breeding grounds for malaria-carrying mosquitoes. "The devastation of Vietnam," concluded 1967 Nobel Prize for Physiology or Medicine recipient Dr. George Wald, "has been as complete as world opinion will allow."[90]

In addition to conventional bombs, continual dumping of chemical "defoliants" transformed the lush, tropical nation into an environmentally devastated piece of land beginning in 1962. At the same time that Johnson was promoting his new conservation at home, he was creating an environmental nightmare in Vietnam. By the end of the decade, low-flying C-123 cargo planes, equipped with tanks and high-pressure spray nozzles, had showered some 13.5 million gallons of chemicals on the country at concentrations up to 10 times those recommended for safe use in the United States. The military explained that the purpose of the program—code-named Operation Ranch Hand and given a slogan that was a sardonic twist on a popular Smoky Bear advertising campaign, "Only we can prevent forests"—was to remove the thick canopy of the tropical forests to expose enemy troop movements and to kill brush along roads and waterways that might provide cover for ambushes. In all, some 7,000 square miles were sprayed, including 500,000 acres of rice and other croplands. Vietnam went from being a nation that, prior to 1967, exported $134 million worth of rice annually to one that, in 1968, was forced to import 800 thousand tons. The chemical sprays were commonly known by the color of the bands around the 55-gallon drums they were shipped in, and included "agents" purple, pink, green, blue, and white. The most infamous, strongest, and widely used, "Agent Orange," was a mixture of 2,4-D (Dichlorophenoxyacetic acid), first developed during World War II to eliminate enemy crops, and 2,4,5-T (Trichlorophenoxyacetic acid), whose manufacturers included Dow Chemical, Monsanto, Diamond Shamrock, and Uniroyal, along with a few other companies. A scientific investigation reported in *Science* magazine in the autumn of 1968 revealed that 2,4,5-T caused widespread chromosomal defects in plants, and that it was impossible to claim that the chemical was safe because it might take generations to fully determine its damage. Vietnamese citizens had complained for years that the spray was causing birth defects, miscarriages, and stillbirths. Manufacturers and the military, however, continually insisted it was safe.[91]

Critics, including Harvard biologist Matthew S. Meselson in *Scientific American*, called the spraying "chemical-biological warfare" and often referred to the environmental results in heavily symbolic and gendered terms, as in "the rape of Vietnam," and "ravaging Vietnam."[92] Attacks sometimes occurred at the height of the rainy season, when increased runoff contaminated sources of drinking water. President Nixon announced a ban on germ warfare in 1969, but did not extend the ban to chemical weapons and defoliants like the ones that were devastating Vietnam.[93] Arthur W. Caston, biologist from Yale, pointed out that it was the first time that chemicals designed to damage or kill plants had been used in war. "When we intervene in the ecology of a region on a massive scale we may set in motion an irreversible chain of events," he warned, "which could continue to affect both the agriculture and the wildlife of the area—and therefore, the people, also—long after the war is over."[94] For increasing numbers of citizens, the United States's actions were unjustifiably aggressive, callous, and morally indefensible. The spraying not only called into question the environmental treatment of Vietnam but also served to further discredit the corporations producing chemicals for the domestic market, as well as the government that supported them.

In October 1969, after years of pressure and denial, the federal government finally announced that it was taking a series of actions to limit the domestic use of one of the major components of Agent Orange, 2,4,5-T, because research by Bionetics Research Laboratories indicated it caused birth defects in the offspring of laboratory animals. The government announced that it would cancel registration of the herbicide for use on food crops as of January 1, 1970, unless the FDA could establish a "safe" tolerance before then. Even though this gave credence to the protests of Vietnamese citizens who for years complained that it was causing birth defects and miscarriages, the government refused to ban its use in Vietnam. Dr. Lee A. DuBridge, science adviser to President Richard Nixon and executive secretary of the President's Environmental Quality Council, argued that it was saving American lives in Vietnam by reducing the number of ambushes. The government did, though, say it would no longer be used in populated areas in

Vietnam. However, as critics pointed out, with Vietnam's widely dispersed rural population it was almost impossible to spray anywhere that would not have an impact on people.[95]

It was increasingly clear that many Vietnamese civilians were suffering and dying from the effects of Agent Orange, and American troops were likely suffering long-term damage too. By December, even the notoriously conservative Council for the Association of the Advancement of Science called for an immediate halt to the use in Vietnam of both 2,4,5-T and 2,4-D, the active ingredients in Agent Orange, by a vote of 114 to 51 at its annual conference. Said Professor John T. Edsall of Harvard, "The use of these compounds is much more seriously questionable than the use of cyclamates [an artificial sweetener banned by the FDA two months earlier after long-running controversy]. If one applies the same criteria one would consider the risks unacceptable."[96] An investigative report issued in 1970, entitled "What Have We Done to Vietnam?" erased some of the mystery surrounding the refusal to completely ban the use of the deadly chemical compounds. "Part of the answer," it concluded, "may lie in the fact that 2,4-D and 2,4,5-T production contributes over thirty-five million dollars annually to the herbicide industry."[97]

Meet the New Boss, Same as the Old Boss

Despite the legislation and regulations that accompanied Johnson's new conservation, the number of perceived environmental problems appeared to grow unabated. As a seemingly endless stream of environmental maladies made the news, the inadequacy of environmental legislation became increasingly clear to the American people. The public's increased sensitivity to its environmental plight and a growing countercultural sense that the damaged environment was evidence of a sick society were met with a slew of catastrophes that continued to result from the advanced corporate capitalist age. The resulting fears and frustrations led to some renewed pushes for greater political action. However, the ranks of those who lost faith in the government's willingness and ability to act to protect its citizens against corporate environmental abuses seemed to grow with the discovery of each new crisis.

Water pollution was an inescapable source of concern by decade's end. Phosphates in laundry and dishwasher detergents, which helped soften water, suspend dirt particles, and enhance "surfactant" action, were found to be a major water pollutant, causing increased eutrophication (aging) of lakes that resulted in decreased oxygen and the death of animal and plant life. Lakes Erie and Ontario provided the most dramatic and disturbing evidence of the process.[98] Nitrates from agricultural and lawn fertilizer runoff were also singled out for playing a major role in oxygen-robbing algae blooms polluting water around the country and, most notably, the "death" of Lake Erie.[99] Each day Detroit, Cleveland, and some 120 other municipalities dumped 1.5 billion gallons of inadequately treated waste containing phosphates, nitrates, and a variety of toxins that made its way to Lake Erie. Of 63 beaches along the lake's US shore, only three were judged completely safe for swimming. Those who ventured into the lake might be greeted by as many as 30,000 sludge worms per square yard on the lake's bottom.[100] Yet, at a federal Lake Erie cleanup hearing in Cleveland in October 1969, the Republic Steel Corporation appeared more concerned about its image than how it was contributing to the death of Lake Erie when it protested that its deficiencies in wastewater treatment were being revealed publicly rather than negotiated in private.[101]

Making the air pollution crisis even worse—in 1969 some 140 million tons of contaminants were forced into the atmosphere every year, 10 tons more than just two years earlier—was the revelation that US automobile companies had been conspiring to block the development and use of air-pollution-control devices on cars. Ten days before leaving office the Johnson administration filed a lawsuit against the Big Four automakers and their trade association, the Automobile Manufacturers Association, Inc., accusing them of violating the Sherman Antitrust Act by secretly agreeing that none of them would market a car with new pollution control devices until all of them agreed to use the device. The administration charged that emissions-reducing "positive crankcase ventilation" could have been put in all cars in 1962, but due to the conspiracy it did not happen until after 1963. The Big Four were also charged with lying to California officials when they claimed they did not have the technological ability to place new exhaust controls on cars in 1966; they mutually agreed to try to delay the change until 1967. The Nixon administration's Justice Department, much to the chagrin of environmental groups, settled the case out of court, sparing the automobile companies the humiliation of having damning evidence against them appear in public and denying private litigants seeking to sue the auto companies volumes of evidence that could have been used in civil cases.[102]

The Uneasy Relationship between Population Control and Environmentalism

Another issue that crowded its way onto the nation's congested environmental radar toward decade's end was population. The FDA's approval of the Pill in 1960 dramatically changed the dynamics of the debate. Stanford entomologist Paul

Ehrlich's *The Population Bomb*, first published in 1968, caused a sensation about population, though the issue was anything but new by the late sixties. Both William Vogt's *Road to Survival* and Fairfield Osborn's *Our Plundered Planet* in 1948 put forth neo-Malthusian anxieties about the planet's resources being overrun by humans, and both followed with later books devoted to the "population problem."[103] In 1965 even the US Department of the Interior published a small book titled *The Population Challenge: What It Means to America*, which cautioned: "The greatest threat to quality living in this country is overpopulation and we need a lot more public education on this subject."[104] The Task Force on Environmental Health and Related Problems convened by John Gardner, Secretary of Health, Education, and Welfare in the Johnson administration, proclaimed in a 1967 report: "Virtually every assessment of environmental problems attributes them, in substantial measure, to the combined effects of increasing population."[105] Such pronouncements served to deflect blame from corporate capitalism. Ehrlich's book, from its title and the picture of a baby inside a bomb on the outside cover to the rhetoric on its pages, was even more sensational and apocalyptic than most. It went through a half-dozen printings in its first year, and Ehrlich rocketed into being something of a pop culture idol, even appearing on Johnny Carson's *The Tonight Show*. He also helped found the popular group Zero Population Growth.[106]

Environmental problems, Ehrlich said, were chiefly attributable to a population that had become too large. Even if the abundance of the United States kept it from suffering the fate of less well-off nations, he warned, it still would not be immune from unpleasant environmental effects. Speaking of those in the nonindustrialized nations of "spaceship earth," he stated, "If their end of the ship sinks, we shall at the very least have to put up with the spectacle of their drowning and listen to their screams. Communications satellites guarantee that we will be treated to the sights and sounds of mass starvation on the evening news.... Will we be willing to slaughter our dogs and cats in order to divert pet food protein to the starving masses in Asia?"[107]

Even some environmentalists were uncomfortable with such pronouncements, as well as Ehrlich's broader argument on the dangers of population. For them it was not so much population that was the problem but rather the structural systems of power that controlled technology, production, consumption per person, and distribution. Former Peace Corps worker Rachel Cowan observed, after two years working in a birth control clinic in Ecuador, that although International Planned Parenthood and the Agency for International Development (AID), which funded the clinic, both believed that people in the Global South were poor simply because they had too many kids, it was more complicated than that.

It became increasingly clear to Cowan and others that the real culprit was not so much the number of children women were having as it was distortions in the distribution of land and wealth brought about by corporate capitalism. Instead of being used to grow food crops for residents, most of Ecuador's fertile land was owned by wealthy families who grew bananas for export on plantations under contract with multinational corporations like United Fruit Company, with poorly paid workers providing the labor. Most people were going to be desperately poor regardless of the number of children they had. As Cowan summarized it, limiting family size in order to get ahead "only makes sense if you're middle-class in a mobile society. Poor people in Ecuador know that even if they only have two children, the children won't be educated or have adequate health care. There's no more possibility for two than for ten." The real goal of organizations like AID, she concluded, was not to help women and families but rather to "help the country's economic development by keeping the population growth down."[108] As one underground-press writer summarized the typical critique of zero-population-growth advocates, "It's easy to blame all of the earth's problems on overpopulation. It has the advantage of spreading the blame over about three billion people, most of them non-white, non-Westerners. It places the blame equally on all political, social, and economic systems."[109]

Those in the environmental movement who supported efforts to control human populations in the belief that it would result in less strain on natural resources were often in tension with the mainstream of the population-control movement, led by organizations like AID and the World Bank, which were attracted to managing population precisely because it promised to aid the cause of economic development. As historian Matthew Connelly argues, "conservationists offered a very different argument for population control: the economic development necessary to support growing populations was already destroying the environment."[110] Nevertheless, he points out, environmentalists were often inadvertent "foot soldiers" for the cause of population control led by pro-development forces.[111] Biologist and environmentalist Barry Commoner famously criticized Ehrlich, arguing that the misuse of technology was a far greater problem than population.[112] The issue of population control continues to divide environmentalists to the present day, but in the late Sixties Ehrlich and his book were influential in further alerting the public to the apocalyptic threats of environmental destruction.

Awash in Oil

One of the incidents to draw the greatest national attention to the environment at the close of the decade happened six miles off the coast of Santa Barbara, California on January 28, 1969, when a "blowout" of an offshore Union Oil Company well released millions of gallons of crude oil that formed an 800-square-mile oil slick that devastated some 45 miles of mainland beaches and surrounded Anacapa Island, a national monument and wildlife sanctuary. Extensive television coverage broadcast powerfully disturbing images of shorelines covered in black ooze, as birds covered in oil lay dead or dying.[113]

Many residents of Santa Barbara and the surrounding area had opposed the offshore oil rigs in federal waters from the start. In 1966 the Interior Department began auctioning oil-drilling rights to nearly 1,000 square miles of federal waters off the coast to a dozen major oil companies for $603 million, although the real price was reduced by a government rebate of a 27.5 percent oil-depletion allowance to subsidize the industry. Residents' objections were largely ignored. Oil companies profited from the subsidies, while the government profited from leasing the waters that it was also trusted to protect. After the oil spill, outraged citizens of Santa Barbara formed grassroots resistance groups, including GOO (Get Oil Out). As one person stated, "How far do we go in sacrificing the pleasantness of everyone's surroundings for short-term economic gains for a relative few?"[114]

Among those who spoke out was pioneering environmental historian and Santa Barbara resident Roderick Nash, who called on government officials to obey an "eleventh commandment" that he defined as "an extension of ethics to include man's relationship to his environment: Thou shall not abuse the earth."[115] Drawing obvious inspiration from Aldo Leopold's land ethic but imbuing it with a tone of religious authority, Nash's commandment, in the words of two Santa Barbara writers, "gave the aroused community an ideology and a creed, and attracted national attention." As a response to the crisis he and some colleagues started the country's first environmental studies program at the University of California, Santa Barbara.[116]

In the aftermath of the spill citizens sued the government to get all oil development out of the Santa Barbara Channel. Their frustration might have been eased by a greater federal cleanup effort, but the Federal Water Pollution Control Administration could not proceed unless requested by a state governor. California's Governor Ronald Reagan, who had appointed an oil-company executive to head his Fish and Game Division, made no such request.[117] In early June, after the oil well had been leaking for over 120 days, a panel of scientists and engineers appointed by President Nixon's science adviser, Lee DuBridge, decided that the best way to stop the leak was to drill even more wells and pump out the underlying oil.[118]

Santa Barbara residents were outraged that the decision was made without citizen input, as only government and oil-industry witnesses were invited to testify at closed meetings of the panel. Adding to their frustration was the fact that there was no published record of what was said because, the government claimed, most of the testimony came from Union Oil and other industry sources and therefore was considered proprietary and secret. A group of

Santa Barbarans, with the aid of the American Civil Liberties Union, filed suit in federal court (*Weingand v. Hickel*) claiming that Secretary of the Interior Walter J. Hickel had unconstitutionally exceeded his authority in granting drilling rights, that their "rights to a decent environment had been impaired by Secretary Hickel and his aides, and by the oil companies, and that this was done without due process of law." The complaint, which further stated that the government's decision to resume drilling had been reached in secret with the oil companies, pressed the plaintiff's concept of basic human and property rights: "The personal right is the right to live in, and enjoy, an environment free from improvident destruction or pollution. The property right is the right to ownership, use and enjoyment of property, free from improvident invasion or impairment."[119]

In March 1969, in the midst of the oil spill, ABC television aired a two-hour prime-time documentary, *Three Young Americans in Search of Survival*, which interwove three stories of individuals trying to improve the environment and indicated how diffuse and varied such efforts had become. One was Gary Smith, who explained the challenge of trying to protect the Western Canyonlands from commercial development and exploitation; another told the story of Harold Haskins, who organized members of a street gang in North Philadelphia to work on improving the environment of their neighborhood; the third followed Margaret Godwin as she investigated industrial water pollution in the United States. It was an ambitious effort to get at the interconnected nature, and importance, of all environments—whether rural, urban, or industrial—that served, as one reviewer put it, to "successfully raise one more needed warning that society cannot long go on ignoring the earth's treasures, which include the interdependence of man and nature."[120]

The Issue of Nuclear Power

Atomic power was another source of growing environmental anxiety by the decade's close, when 79 nuclear power plants were either in the process of being built or on order. By 1968 the number of people living within 30 miles of an existing or proposed nuclear plant had grown by 150 percent, from 14 million to 37 million, in just three years. Power companies were attracted to nuclear power both by federal incentives and, ironically, by a desire to avoid the environmental controversies of coal combustion. In its seminal 1962 Port Huron Statement, even the radical Students for a Democratic Society stated, with optimism not uncommon at the time for the potential of peaceful nuclear power, "With nuclear energy whole cities can easily be powered, yet the dominant nation-states seem more likely to unleash destruction greater than that incurred in all wars of human history." But the public grew leery of the discharge of radioactive waste into the atmosphere and water, and following the controversy over atomic testing and fallout often did not trust the Atomic Energy Commission, the agency in charge of developing and promoting atomic power, to also regulate it.[121]

In Minnesota, Northern States Power Company was building a plant on the banks of the Mississippi River at Monticello, just north of Minneapolis-St. Paul, and applied for a waste permit from the newly formed Minnesota Pollution Control Agency. The state, at the urging of its citizens, placed tighter limits on radioactive discharge than the AEC's federal standards. Northern States Power, with the support of nuclear plant builders Westinghouse and General Electric, sued the state of Minnesota in both state and federal courts, charging that its restrictions were illegal. Republican Governor Harold LeVander strongly supported the tougher restrictions, but the ranking minority member of the congressional Joint Committee on Atomic Energy, Illinois Representative Craig Holifield, insisted that nuclear regulation was too complicated for states to attempt and, further, took the state's residents to task for their audacity in trying to make their voices heard as citizens. Radiation standards are "not a subject for public rallies and placard makers," he said. "You can't have 200 million people deciding them."[122] The state ultimately lost its suit when the US Supreme Court rejected its arguments in 1972, only months after a storage facility at the plant overflowed in November 1971, discharging tens of thousands of gallons of radioactive waste into the Mississippi River and causing Minneapolis and St. Paul to close their municipal water systems in an effort to save their citizens from drinking radioactive water.[123]

A River Ablaze

Perhaps no environmental calamity during a year that overflowed with them was more symbolic and emblematic than the Cuyahoga River going up in flames in Cleveland on June 22, 1969. It was not the first time the Cuyahoga, repository of wastes from Cleveland's many industries, had caught fire, but with a nation now environmentally sensitized, this time it gained national notice. A *Time* magazine story titled "The Price of Optimism" expressed in grim terms the state of the river: "Some river! Chocolate-brown, oily, bubbling with subsurface gases, it oozes rather than flows. 'Anyone who falls into the Cuyahoga does not drown,' Cleveland's citizens joke grimly. 'He decays.' " The Federal Water Pollution Control Administration added its own characterization: "The lower Cuyahoga has no visible signs of life," it reported, "not even low forms such as leeches and sludge worms that usually thrive on wastes."[124] The story of a river catching fire in 1969, in the midst of all of the other environmental disasters, contained sufficient apocalyptic symbolism to further stir the nation's growing environmental concern.

The Cuyahoga River fire created one of the nation's largest organic producers. "I became an environmentalist at 17, when I saw a river catch on fire from a chemical spill," Stonyfield Organic Yogurt founder Gary Hirshberg later recalled. "In college a few years later I learned that those same chemicals were being used on New Hampshire farms and realized that organic was not only earth-friendly, but also far safer and healthier for farm families. I've never looked back."[125] Hirshberg was not alone. The environmental catastrophes of the late sixties pushed many more Americans into the ranks of environmentalists, and, feeling little hope for traditional political change, many of them practiced their new ideology in the green marketplace.

Desperate Measures for Desperate Times

Some Americans had not given up on trying to correct the perceived imbalance in the nation's polity through established political and legal channels. The Environmental Defense Fund, founded by attorney Victor Yannacone after the unsuccessful bid to stop DDT spraying on Long Island, formed in 1967. With dozens of lawyers and scientists leading its membership, its aim was to use the courts to force the government to enforce laws and carry out its responsibilities to ensure a healthy environment.[126] Its theoretical foundation was the Ninth Amendment statement that "The enumeration in the Constitution of certain rights shall not be construed to deny or disparage others retained by the people." Spraying, they argued, was not in the public interest.[127]

Traditional conservation groups like the Sierra Club, whose memberships had been increasing incrementally during the postwar era, experienced an explosion in memberships as they further shifted their focus from traditional conservation to lobbying for the broader concerns of environmentalism. In its earlier days the Club was, according to Michael McCloskey, its executive director from 1969 to 1986, "a private exclusive club that dealt more with socially prominent people than it did in its devotion to public policy changes."[128] Nevertheless, as it began to extend its interests into policy and the larger environmental realm from its conservationist past its membership continued to grow. By the end of 1967 it had nearly 60,000 members, more than doubling in size with an increase of 31,500 in six years.[129] Although that was impressive membership growth for the club, the overall numbers were still relatively low by design. Prior to 1970 membership of the Sierra Club was exclusive by its country club–like requirement that new members had to be sponsored by two existing members for admission.[130]

By the late sixties growing numbers of citizens were left frustrated that traditional legal, political, and even protest efforts were failing to produce adequate change, and some grew weary of working within a political system that appeared to offer little hope for altering the march to apocalypse. In 1969 the music duo Zager and Evans had the number one song in the country for six weeks running and scored *Billboard* magazine's number one record of the year with their apocalyptic "In the Year 2525." Each stanza of the song peered further into an increasingly grim future until, finally, humanity's ultimate collapse was envisioned in environmental ruin: "In the year 9595 / I'm kinda wondering if man is gonna be alive / He's taken everything this old earth can give / And he ain't put back nothing."[131] For many Americans 9595 seemed overly optimistic.

7

"Striking Back at the Goddam Sons-of-Bitches"

By the late 1960s, despite LBJ's gestures toward new conservation, for growing numbers of citizens the only solution appeared to be taking matters into their own hands rather than waiting for government, too beholden to corporate interests, to finally take substantive action on the environment. In the aftermath of the Santa Barbara oil spill a conference was held at Santa Barbara City College to discuss what citizens could do. There was an entrance fee, and during the conference attendees were asked for additional contributions. The focus of the meeting quickly turned to the need to educate the community on a variety of environmental issues and offer effective solutions. With the money raised from the conference the non-profit Community Environmental Council was founded. It quickly went to work achieving its two inaugural objectives. First, they planted an organic community garden in a vacant lot in the heart of the downtown business district to prove that chemical fertilizers, pesticides, and herbicides were not necessary to produce food. They also opened an Ecology Center with a film library, bookstore, and meeting space in order to provide environmental information to the community.[1]

As was so often the case, the space where citizens felt they could assert the most meaningful measure of control was in their choices as consumers. In echoes of the environmentalism and green consumerism that had been building since the late 1940s, those consumer choices were at the heart of the sixties counterculture. Many Americans, especially the young who felt trapped in the suffocating confines of one giant corporate tent, sought alternatives to a mainstream culture and its environment that seemed ever more polluted. If the culture was unwilling to change, they would simply form their own.

The popularity of communes during the era was great, and media fascination made their influence on the larger culture far greater. The trend boomed sometime around late 1967, fueled in part by shared information in the wildly popular underground press network that by then covered the nation. As Timothy Miller has estimated in the most comprehensive study of sixties-era communes, there were "thousands, probably tens of thousands" of communes during the decade, occupied by "probably hundreds of thousands, conceivably a million" people.[2]

Although they varied widely in philosophy and purpose, the one characteristic almost always present across the various communes as theaters of dissent was a heightened concern for the environment. Organic gardening was very common. As Jeanie Darlington advised in an underground press article on organic fertilizers: "Gardeners! You've got to get your manure together. Otherwise your garden won't be worth shit."[3] Although some communes were early experimenters with alternative energy sources like solar, wind, and hydro, others chose to live a premodern existence and eschewed all modern technologies, while others still used modern technology but sought to tie its use to an alternative, more environmentally harmonious consciousness.[4] Martin Jezer, activist and editor of the radical magazine *WIN* (Workshop in Nonviolence), characterized the communes as "A back to the land movement to ease the pressure off the cities [through] decentralization, community, small-scale and organic farming." It was, in short, an effort to break free from a postwar modernity that had seemingly been overtaken by corporations and the corporate model by establishing a viable alternative.[5] As one member of a commune summarized it, "After the Bomb who's going to know how to be? We here are trying to learn how to be."[6]

Garnering less publicity, though substantial numbers, was a "back-to-the-land" movement during the sixties whose practitioners shared the anti-corporatism of their commune brethren but lacked their desire for communal living. These "new pioneers," as they liked to call themselves, and who have been estimated at over one million, set up individual homesteads on small acreages. Like many in the counterculture and those on the communes, they rejected mainstream corporate capitalism and consumer culture as both spiritually and environmentally degrading and sought a way of life that was more meaningful and sustainable.[7]

The spirit of the rural communes and the sixties back-to-the-land movement was captured in the popular 1968 Canned Heat song "Going Up the Country":

> I'm going up the country, baby don't you wanna go
> I'm going up the country, baby don't you wanna go
> I'm going to some place where I've never been before
> I'm going, I'm going where the water tastes like wine
> Well I'm going where the water tastes like wine
> We can jump in the water, stay drunk all the time

I'm gonna leave this city, got to get away
I'm gonna leave this city, got to get away
All this fussing and fighting, man, you know I sure can't stay.[8]

It has since been argued, correctly, that the efficiencies gained by living tightly packed together in metropolitan areas offer considerable environmental advantages compared to the resources required to live in dispersed rural (and suburban) settings. But for many of those taking to the land in the sixties, nature and the countryside held the promise of escaping a mainstream culture that they had grown to distrust, if not despise.[9]

The Dawning of the Age of Aquarius?

On Broadway, the hit musical *Hair* opened to critical and popular acclaim. Its 1968 song "Aquarius," which soon became the most popular recorded song in the country, made fashionable the notion that the world was witnessing the "dawning of the age of Aquarius," an astrological epoch characterized by: "Harmony and understanding / Sympathy and trust abounding / No more falsehoods or derisions / Golden living dreams of visions / Mystic crystal revelation / And the mind's true liberation." Environmentalism was central to this new consciousness, which would finally save the planet from the type of threat described in another of the play's songs, titled "Air": "Cataclysmic ectoplasm / Fallout atomic orgasm / Vapor and fume / At the stone of my tomb / Breathing like a sullen perfume / Eating at the stone of my tomb / Welcome! Sulfur dioxide / Hello! Carbon monoxide / The air, the air / Is everywhere / Breathe deep, while you sleep / Breathe deep / Deep, deep, deep, (cough, cough)."[10]

The optimism of the "age of Aquarius" was not limited to musical fantasies. In March 1968, historian Theodore Roszak began a series of four articles in the *Nation* magazine that, one year later, he expanded into his book, *The Making of a Counter Culture: Reflections on the Technocratic Society and its Youthful Opposition*. In it Roszak bewailed, in echoes of John Kenneth Galbraith, the technocratic corporate system that had insidiously spread its influence into all facets of contemporary life. It was, he said, like an "umpire" in a baseball game that because it is not the center of attention often goes unnoticed but nevertheless is most important because it sets the "limits and goals" of the society, as well as its boundaries and rules. But unlike an umpire, who is supposed to be impartial, the technocratic corporate system set the rules and boundaries to assure that its own interests would win.[11]

Roszak found hope in the growing numbers of young people who were simply refusing to partake in a mainstream culture that they believed was harmful to individuals and the environment. What made the counterculture so meaningful, Roszak believed, was that it represented a fundamentally different way to look at the world. "What makes the youthful disaffiliation of our times a cultural phenomenon, rather than merely a political movement," he said, "is the fact that it strikes beyond ideology to the level of consciousness, seeking to transform our deepest sense of the self, the other, the environment."[12] Roszak popularized the phrase "counter culture," in the process forever linking the concept to the sixties generation. In reality, of course, proto-environmentalists, organics enthusiasts, and green consumers already constituted a counterculture years before the sixties.

Roszak's book was soon joined by the similarly optimistic *The Greening of America*, by Yale law professor Charles A. Reich. "There is a revolution coming," he proclaimed. "It will not be like revolutions of the past. It will originate with the individual and with culture, and it will change the political structure only as its final act." Reich assumed that the movement would eventually reach a critical mass, the weight of which would crush the status quo and ultimately result in a restructured American polity. Like Roszak, Reich located the cause of the revolt in the corporate capitalist state. "Democracy," Reich argued, "has rapidly lost ground as power is increasingly captured by giant managerial institutions and corporations." [13] Like others, Reich saw the counterculture and its associated environmentalism as a response to crises in American politics and democracy, an attempt by citizens to regain control as individuals in a society where they felt they no longer had a real voice.

Shopping for a New World

Although most Americans' lives remained centered in mainstream culture, many nevertheless shared the counterculture's concerns and embraced at least some of its values. Consumer alternatives like organic food and vegetarianism practiced by the counterculture were features that could be readily adapted to daily living, and they resulted in a further expansion of environmentalism. Even the wife of William J. Levitt, the builder of the seminal suburb Levittown on Long Island, New York was running her own organic farm by 1967. "I started the farm because I couldn't stand what they were doing to the tomatoes you found in stores—all those chemicals," Alice Levitt explained.[14] By 1968 there were an estimated four million vegetarians in the United States, and many people were seeking organic produce.[15] Organic food held the attraction of permitting one to exist within the mainstream of culture while simultaneously, in daily habits of living, resisting and protesting the methods of production and consumption central to that culture. As harried citizens increasingly turned to foods prepared by corporations rather than preparing them at home, food ways were not only a personal choice but a political statement. Citizens avoiding foods manufactured by giant corporations were trying to keep "the system" from killing them—and the environment.

By the second half of the decade, green consumers were cultivating a growing number of environmentally focused businesses. Among them were "Far Fetched Foods," which opened in Haight-Ashbury in 1966. Its ideals extended into its structure with employees organized as a commune and an owner, Jerry Sealund, who took only $20 a week for expenses. It sold produce from area organic truck gardens. A year later Erewhon opened in Boston. Founded to supply those following the macrobiotic diet espoused by Michio Kushi, it soon supplied both organic foods and advice to large numbers of area residents in a loosely structured, informal store.[16] Some natural markets included restaurants. An advertisement for a natural-foods store in Santa Cruz, California advised: "Man must cease polluting his environment if he is to continue existing on the earth for any period of time. The first step in halting pollution is to stop consuming the devitalized, plastic, psuedo [sic] foods which turn men into walking cesspools." Emphasizing the natural foods store as a space promoting alternative consumption and production, the ad concluded, "Stop supporting the parasites who make a living producing the modern trash called food." The store's logo included a slogan that summed up one of the things many people were seeking through the consumption of natural and organic foods: "A communion with nature through diet."[17] The movement did not stop at food. In Philadelphia a store called Gulliver's Travels advertised in the underground *Philadelphia Free Press* that it "Deals Organic Clothes."[18]

Some took the consumer protest against corporate capitalism even further and held that a retail establishment profiting from something so fundamental as natural food was necessarily wrong in principle. As one writer in the San Francisco underground newspaper *Good Times* said of the city's organic food retailers, "They traffic in something too essential to be trafficked in."[19] In response they turned to the model of the Diggers, an anarchist community activist guerilla theater group that ran Free Stores in San Francisco, giving away food and kitchen utensils that had been donated—or stolen. But theirs was a difficult model to emulate on a mass scale.

By the late sixties there were, however, many organic buying clubs, sometimes called "conspiracies" to denote their intent to subvert the corporate system, springing up around the country. They purchased natural, organic foods in bulk that were often stored in garages before being divided among their membership.[20] As the idea expanded, many of these groups became natural-foods co-ops, like the Mifflin Street Community Co-op in Madison, Wisconsin, which years later sported the slogan: "Food for the Revolution Since 1969."[21] Natural foods co-ops often set up shop in buildings that had previously housed neighborhood grocery stores put out of business by corporate supermarkets. "Today's corporations, with their monolithic prices, are like the royalty the colonists overthrew," said the Exploratory Project for Economic Alternatives. "Co-ops are a practical, self-reliant alternative—they are a declaration of independence from the corporation."[22]

Co-ops sold not only natural and organic foods, but also served as community centers. Their focus was on creating and nurturing an alternative to mainstream corporate capitalism. Bulletin boards were a clearinghouse of information about yoga classes, local music, midwives, politics, area communes, and any other information that might appeal to those who were shopping for change. In addition to groceries, they often carried local artisan-made pottery, crafts, and jewelry. "We could be on the brink of the greatest period of human history," stated Wallace Stegner in December 1969. "And it could begin with the little individuals, the kind of people many would call cranks, who insist on organically grown vegetables and unsprayed fruits, who do not pick the wild flowers, who fight against needless dams and roads."[23]

Writing about Rodale's *Organic Gardening and Farming* magazine in the *Whole Earth Catalog*, Gurney Norman stated: "It has occurred to me that if I were a dictator determined to control the national press, *Organic Gardening* would be the first publication I'd squash, because it is the most subversive. The whole organic movement is exquisitely subversive. I believe that organic gardeners are in the forefront of a serious effort to save the world by changing man's orientation to it, to move away from the collective, centrist, super-industrial state, toward a simpler, realer, one-to-one relationship with the earth itself."[24] The movement had been quietly subversive for over two decades. The flamboyance of the counterculture raised its volume, leading many others to take notice.

The Whole Earth Catalog, founded by Stewart Brand and first published in 1968, was something of a combined Sears catalog and *Consumer Reports* for communes and the counterculture which came out twice a year, with four additional "supplements."[25] Brand hoped the catalog would provide a means for revolutionary citizen empowerment, free from the influence of giant corporations that were corrupting the potential for fulfilling, meaningful lives. Like the organic movement, its appeal was to those who dreamed of a better world through alternative consumption. As an advertisement for the catalog stated, "All our lives big corporations have been taking care of business for us; they have been cobbling our shoes, sewing our clothes, building our cars, constructing our dwellings, finding our ways in wilderness, printing and producing our newspapers and television, growing our food and teaching us our three R's.... The Whole Earth Catalog, however, is the beginning of our attempt to teach ourselves."[26] It was a notion of self-sufficiency that was familiar in American history, but one derived from an overwhelming sense that the institutions of the dominant culture, all shaped by large corporations, not only were no longer functioning for the greater good of citizens, but were actually hampering human progress.

The cover of the publication carried its own powerful message. Stewart Brand was convinced that the image of earth from space would inspire a new human consciousness about the planet. Covers featured images of the planet taken by satellite or the NASA Apollo moon mission, only recently made public for the first time, on a black background. Suspended alone in space the earth appeared particularly vulnerable. Images of the earth from space, Brand and others believed, supported and amplified an existing sense of the planet's vulnerability and fragility.[27] Just as the perspective gained from an airplane had helped inspire the 1955 Symposium on "Man's Role in Changing the Face of the Earth," images of the earth from space and the spaceships used for travel permitted a more holistic view of the planet that broke away barriers of locality, and even nation-states, and permitted a concrete understanding of the earth as an interconnected, fragile system in need of care.

Like many environmentally minded Americans, Brand and the editors of *Whole Earth* did not disdain technology, nor consumption per se. Instead, their concern centered on the consciousness that was carried into the creation and use of technologies and how the control of technology related to power in a democratic system. The first edition carried an ad for ready-made tipis, as well as the first-ever desktop scientific calculator, a 40-pound, $4,900 machine from Hewlett-Packard.[28] Many environmentalists envisioned an alternative modernity but were not necessarily antimodern. The dream for *Whole Earth* was to provide a manual for circumventing the hegemonic power of large corporations in American life by empowering individuals and communal groups through their actions as consumers. As Brand later summed it up, "At a time when the New Left was calling for grassroots *political* (i.e., referred) power, *Whole Earth* eschewed politics and pushed grass-roots *direct* power—tools and skills."[29] It was a familiar strategy for environmentalists, dating back to the Second World War.

In addition to purchasing products that they believed were less damaging to the environment, in their effort to alter corporate capitalism green consumers also boycotted goods. In November 1969, timed for the holiday shopping season, Friends of the Earth launched a campaign to stop the sale of fur coats. The new environmental group, founded by the controversial former head of the Sierra Club, David Brower, kicked off the campaign with a pledge signed by a number of prominent women who declared that they would not buy fur coats or any clothing made from skins of wild animals. "It must be made unfashionable for these clothes to be worn or used on walls and floors," said Natalie

Stevenson, daughter of architect Nathaniel Owings and daughter-in-law of Adlai Stevenson.[30]

People's Park: A Real Gathering of the Tribes

The issue of the environment crossed the divide between the counterculture and the political left with the events surrounding People's Park in Berkeley, California, in the spring of 1969. Although the New Left and "hippie" counterculture sometimes came together, they should not be confused as the same movement. The leaders of the New Left believed their actions would lead to revolutionary social change; the hippies typically did not share their optimism and held little hope that their personal actions would translate into political transformation. Instead, they sought personal liberation by carving out their own space within the existing culture.[31] As Melody Kilian summarized the difference between the counterculture and New Left in the Palo Alto underground newspaper *Peninsula Observer*, "To all of us the system is ugly and frightening, but the 'hippies' believe that if they themselves practice beauty and love, others will see the way, by example, and will understand.... But for the political revolutionaries there can be no beauty for individual people as long as we know that most of the world is so quickly being polluted and cut down and people are being napalmed by capitalists."[32] The New Left, focused on social justice, was suspicious of environmentalism as a means for radical change.[33]

In 1967 the University of California bought a 270-by-450-foot piece of land four blocks south of the campus through eminent domain where some old, low-income houses sat. In June 1968 it condemned the houses and tore them down, leaving a muddy, trash-filled vacant lot in their place. The following April local residents, tired of the eyesore, organized a community gathering that, with donations from storeowners near campus, bought sod, vegetable seeds, and plants to convert the space into a community park. A sign was erected that read "PEOPLE'S PARK: POWER TO THE PEOPLE." Within days the original group was joined by hundreds of other residents from all walks of life—as many as thousands on weekends—who put in a good deal of work planting trees, landscaping, constructing a bandstand, and installing swings, slides, and playground equipment for children, all the while eating from communal pots of soup and stew, drinking, and smoking marijuana.[34]

For the University of California, however, People's Park was an act of defiance. At 4:45 a.m. on May 15, 1969, some 250 police and highway-patrol officers blocked off eight square blocks around the park, moved out 70 street people sleeping around a bonfire in its midst, and arrested three others. Crews then constructed an 8-foot-tall wire fence around the perimeter while workers began bulldozing the gardens, trees, and playground equipment. By noon thousands had rallied on campus in response, and upon hearing student president-elect Dan Siegel say, "Let's go down there and take the park," began a march toward the fence, shattering a Bank of America window as a symbolic act along the way. When they neared the police the protestors were met with tear-gas canisters; they hurled rocks and bottles at the officers in return. Special Alameda County Sheriff's squads arrived and, after a reported stabbing (nonfatal) of an officer near the fence, police fired shotgun blasts into the crowd in an assault that lasted for hours. Witnesses testified that they fired indiscriminately. About 200 people were injured and 920 arrested. One died, and another was permanently blinded. Sixty-four police officers were injured. By nightfall, Governor Ronald Reagan had called in the National Guard and banned public assembly. Nevertheless, 85 percent of the 14,969 University of California students who voted in a special referendum approved "the preservation of the land currently known as People's Park as it was prior to May 12," as did 81 percent of residents surveyed from a 35-block surrounding area.[35]

On May 28, while the National Guard occupied the park, the American Federation of Teachers sponsored a campus teach-in—a type of alternative education gathering made popular a few years earlier to provide information and discussion about the war in Vietnam—on "Ecology and Politics." A pamphlet the AFT prepared for the event cut straight to the heart of how growing numbers of citizens were connecting the issues of American democracy and the environment: "The questions raised by this issue reach into two worlds at once: the world of power, politics and the institutional shape of American society on the one hand, and the biological shape of our environment on the other," it stated. "Ecology and politics," it concluded, "are no longer separate or separable issues."[36]

Beat poet Gary Snyder read his "Smokey Bear Sutra" for the first time. Snyder imagined Buddha returning to earth in the form of a giant Smokey Bear, "Trampling underfoot wasteful freeways and needless suburbs; smashing the worms of capitalism and totalitarianism." The poem was later widely copied in underground newspapers and elsewhere.[37]

Snyder was not the only writer to draw on Smokey Bear to express frustration with big business and the government's policies designed to serve it. *WIN* magazine imagined a disgusted Smokey Bear quitting the Forest Service. "Smokey the Bear, big, brown and furry (ursus groovious) with a funky brown hat is now a free bear," reported *WIN* in 1969. "He's dropped out of the employ of the US Forest Service where his job was carefully restricted to urging people to prevent forest fires." Smokey, *WIN* insisted, had come to realize that his job was to prevent fires not so the forests' beauty could be enjoyed by all but so that their timber would be preserved for corporations that leased logging rights from the Forest Service—yet another example of the teaming of government and big business that left citizens, and Smokey, feeling marginalized in the American polity. "All the time I was telling people to keep America green... I thought I was talking about trees and shrubs. But all the US Forest Service is interested in is maximizing the profits of those who exploit the land for profits," *WIN* quoted Smokey. "After dropping some acid" with freaks he stumbled upon in the forest "living communally with nature," with a new consciousness Smokey finally saw it all clearly and quit the Forest Service in order that he might truly defend the environment. "I was at Berkeley to defend People's Park," he said, "and I'll be wherever the ecological struggle needs me."[38] In the estimation of Smokey Bear and others, then, traditional conservation was not only no longer adequate, it was often regressive and controlled by and for corporate capitalists.

In the aftermath of the incident, People's Park fast became a symbol of dashed hopes for political change. In the estimation of Yippie cofounder and New Left leader Stew Albert, because "the repression was so brutal," People's Park marked the beginning of the end for sixties New Left activism. Former Students for a Democratic Society (SDS) leader Todd Gitlin agreed. "For those who paid attention to Berkeley, the sense of white exemption died there," he acknowledged. Violence had long rained down on civil rights activists; now, it was clear, it would also be visited upon white youth activists.[39] Burned out from fruitless fights in the political trenches, and especially after SDS broke apart in 1969, many young people who had been political activists moved away from politics and instead sought refuge in the counterculture.[40] "The thrust is no longer for 'change,' or 'progress' or 'revolution,'" said journalist Hunter S. Thompson, "but merely to escape, to live on the far perimeter of a world that might have been—perhaps should have been—and strike a bargain for survival on purely personal terms."[41]

Upon reading Snyder, Gitlin was taken by the notion that the ideals of the shattered New Left might be joined together with environmentalism in a united front for genuine change. Gitlin believed it important for the New Left to avoid alienating environmentalists, and he hoped that the two sides might inform one another and work toward mutual goals. "Snyder can help us do one thing we've scanted," he said, "which is to understand how American capitalism rips up *everything* of value, to taste the concreteness of the loss and to broadcast visions of a new civilization which knows coexistence with the earth."[42] Gitlin imagined the environmental goals of the counterculture and the political ideals of the New Left coexisting.

Part of the strength of the environmental vision was always that it held forth a concrete alternative to corporate-dominated mainstream American culture; for many it appeared to be a space capable of containing a variety of abstract ideals to offer a seemingly workable solution to a wide array of cultural, political, and economic ills. In large, bold print the cover of the San Francisco underground newspaper *Good Times* captured the dream: "AFTER THE REVOLUTION WE WILL ALL HAVE MANURE ON OUR STRAWBERRIES."[43]

A Familiar Foe with a New Twist: Globalization

Many agreed with Smokey Bear that the environmental problems, along with a host of others, that vexed the sixties generation had a common origin: corporations. They were right. As Ned Groth stated in Palo Alto's underground *Peninsula Observer*, "Many of us believe that the changes needed to avert total ecological disaster are massive—pervading the political, economic, and philosophical foundations of American capitalism." And there was only one real power at the foundations of capitalism: "Many people are learning, moreover, that the men most responsible for pollution and the rape of the environment are essentially the same men who promote wars of counterinsurgency and racist social institutions," Groth concluded; "that is, the men who own and control the giant corporations."[44]

By the late sixties it was clear that the trend toward megacorporations earlier aided by World War II had intensified, allowing them to further dominate the American polity and culture. At the end of World War II the 100 largest manufacturing corporations produced a remarkable 23 percent of the value of manufactured goods; by the end of the sixties the share of the top 100 had increased to an astonishing 33 percent. They employed 25 percent of all manufacturing employees and accounted for one-third of total wages. In all, the 100 largest manufacturing corporations controlled nearly as much wealth and economic activity as the 300,000 next largest manufacturers combined; their power to influence the environment was enormous. Although there had earlier been some belief that, following World War II, market forces and competition would result in a flurry of small companies that would balance the corporate giants, it soon became apparent that the huge corporations, with their many advantages and massive power, would not be displaced or challenged.[45] "Our institutions have become one critical mass," warned Charles Ross, who was a member of the Federal Power Commission under presidents Kennedy and Johnson. "The checks and balances which each institution provides for the others are no longer as effective. The unholy three [corporations, government, and universities], in their eagerness to rearrange nature, have failed to appreciate the dangers to the environment."[46]

Business had further secured its hold on power during the Cold War years not only by means of its unrelenting growth but also through its continually evolving nature. By the late sixties American corporations had moved many of their operations, especially manufacturing, to other countries, and the United States had become the world's first postindustrial nation, with more workers earning wages in service industries than in production. Whereas prior to the war most American corporations produced their goods in the United States and exported to other countries, now they supplied foreign markets, and increasingly the domestic one as well, from factories located outside the United States whenever, and wherever, it was most cost-effective to do so. In 1969 direct investment abroad by corporations based in the United States, which had been $19 billion in 1955, surged to more than $65 billion, and between 1958 and 1968 American corporations increased their overseas manufacturing capacity by 471 percent, compared with 72 percent domestically.[47]

Having operations around the globe gave corporations the ability to quickly shift capital and production, making them progressively more difficult to regulate. Just as individual states in the United States were reluctant to impose environmental regulations on businesses for fear that companies would simply leave for a different, more accommodating state, individual countries were slow to impose environmental regulations on corporations for fear that they would respond by moving their facilities to another country that either did not have environmental regulations or, if it had them, did not enforce them. As Richard Barber noted in his examination of the changing nature of corporations from World War II through the end of the sixties, "today the global scope of commercial activity by major US and foreign companies is rendering national regulation obsolete." Big corporations had effectively become, he concluded, "immensely powerful political states... [and] the colonizers of the twentieth century."[48]

Frustrated by their inability to rein in corporate power through electoral politics, by the end of the decade some young Americans turned to destructive strategies in desperate efforts to advance their cause. The Weather Underground broke from SDS in 1969 and began a bombing campaign that it hoped would foment revolution. In the year between March 1969 and March 1970, there were hundreds of bombings across the United States. In Seattle, there were 32 blasts. San Francisco reported 62 bombings during the same period. In New York there were 93 explosions in 1969 alone. The *New York Times* reported that targets of the bombs were usually "symbols of the 'establishment' and the Vietnam War," including corporate offices.[49] In one case, early in the morning of March 12, 1969, a group identifying itself as Revolutionary Force 9 bombed three buildings in Manhattan, doing extensive damage to the offices of Mobil Oil, IBM, and General Telephone and Electronics. The group explained that the businesses were targeted because they profited from the war in Vietnam, racism, sexism, exploitation, and destruction of the environment. "IBM, Mobile [sic] and GTE are enemies of all life," the group declared. Revolutionary Force 9's frustration centered on corporate America's conflation of corporate capitalism with the

American way of life: "These corporations seek to enslave us to a way of 'life' which values conspicious [sic] consumption more than the relief of poverty, disease and starvation, which values giant cars as status symbols more than the purity of our air.... This way of 'life' is a way of death."[50] Businesses responded to such attacks with stepped-up protection measures and expanded private security forces.[51]

By the end of the sixties no solution had emerged to effectively deal with corporate power and its threat to the American environment, culture, and polity. Government regulations were rendered insufficient through corporate pressure and lobbying. Counterculture efforts in rural communes and the cities changed the lives and consciousness of many individuals, but all around them the larger environment continued to deteriorate. Most Americans did not support domestic bombing as a means to effect change. For some the next logical step was an attempt to systematically fuse the spirit and enthusiasm of the green counterculture with the practical power of the political, in the hope that the combined force might be enough to effect genuine and meaningful change.

Environmental Teach-Ins

One group that tried to forge counterculture environmentalism with revolutionary activism was Ecology Action, founded in Berkeley, California in 1968 by archeology student Cliff Humphrey who became inspired while writing a paper on the Cheyenne Indians. "That was the switch right there," he said. "I realized the importance of ecology—and the relation of the Plains Indians to their environment." A veteran of many campus protests against the war and the university at Berkeley, Humphrey decided to form an activist group. Within two years Ecology Action inspired over 100 autonomous local groups across the country.

Like many others, Humphrey saw corporate capitalism at the root of environmental problems. "We have a vested interest in our own destruction," he warned. "When the stock market goes up it is a signal device warning us of the imminent destruction of some part of the environment." And he did not believe traditional politics would bring about needed change. "Survival can't be voted into existence," he emphasized, "it has to be lived."[52]

Toward that end Humphrey, with his wife Mary and 10 volunteers (most of whom were conscientious objectors doing alternative service), joined with environmentalists and focused on their consumer choices in the house where the group lived and worked in Berkeley; they urged others to do the same. The group took their own reusable shopping bags to the market and, to avoid wasteful packaging, purchased foods in bulk whenever possible. Paper and envelopes were reused. Their organic waste went into a compost heap in the backyard, and all cans, bottles, and paper were recycled. Plastics, "virtually indestructible," were avoided. Clothing was worn and repaired until it would no longer hold together, and when the weather was cool sweaters were worn to avoid using the furnace. Bricks were placed in toilet tanks so that each flush would use less water. In the process of individuals doing these personal acts, they believed, a constituency for larger political acts would be built. Until then, Humphrey emphasized that citizens using their power as consumers, or nonconsumers, could influence corporate decision-making. "There's no way they can make us consume," he reasoned.[53]

Those who viewed environmentalism and green consumption as not only a means to personal liberation in the midst of corporate capitalism but also a way to save society and the planet sought to translate the enthusiasm and popularity that attended it in the counterculture to all of society. At an "Ecology Fair" in June 1968, the Humphreys, with the help of 60 others and a sledgehammer, transformed their 1958 Rambler station wagon into an artwork that they called "a monument to the gods of clean air," hoping it would be an inspiration for others to use alternative transportation. In September they organized an alternative-transportation "Smog-Free-Locomotion Day" in Berkeley, and a "Damn DDT Day" in San Francisco where Ecology Action volunteers, one dressed as the Grim Reaper, handed out pamphlets as they walked through the city's financial district during the noon hour.[54]

Ecology Action and the American Federation of Teachers were not the only groups to organize environmental teach-ins and demonstrations prior to Earth Day. On April 19, 1969, effigies of 15 major polluting corporations, including Union Oil, Permanente Cement, and Leslie Salt, were hanged from a gallows at an "Anti-Pollution Fair" in Palo Alto, California. Painted across the gallows was a sign that read "These Companies Kill Your Air." The fair was organized by People Against Pollution, which grew out of a class at the Midpeninsula Free University taught by writer, organic farmer, and former forester Gurney Norman called "Striking Back at the Goddam Sons-of-Bitches." Norman was a friend and former Stanford graduate creative writing program classmate of both Wendell Berry and Ken Kesey. He also became friends with Stewart Brand when both lived in Haight-Ashbury in 1967, and he worked as an editor and writer for Brand's *Whole Earth Catalog*. Fair-goers were encouraged to sign petitions to automakers in Detroit saying they would boycott gasoline-powered vehicles. Three electric cars and an electric motorcycle were on display. Discussion groups were organized to talk about future actions to try to curb pollution, and more than 20 area environmental groups presented exhibits on issues like smog, pesticides, and noise pollution.[55]

Other ideas for environmental teach-ins germinated prior to Earth Day. At the University of Wisconsin in July 1969, students from most of the nation's larger universities met to plan how to raise environmental awareness on their campuses.[56] In an article in the August issue of *WIN* magazine Tony Wagner wrote, "In our personal lives, we should avoid food which is not organically grown, useless possessions which will soon break down or become obsolete, and goods which have more wrapping than contents.... Use only *bio-degradable* detergents. We should seek alternative means of transportation...." To provide education on all of those fronts, he suggested, "We can have ecology teach-ins. We can have fairs in city parks, which might include displays on pollution, street theatre, and action workshops."[57]

On Labor Day weekend 1969, environmental activists held a march and teach-in at Lake Tahoe, California, to oppose any further building of subdivisions that they believed were already destroying the lake's ecology. About two weeks later over 70 environmental groups were invited to a march and teach-in held at San Francisco's Union Square on September 18 to protest the Stanford Research Institute's "International Industrial Conference" at the Fairmont Hotel, where, as one writer in Palo Alto's underground *Peninsula Observer* put it, "top executives from some of the nation's most offensive polluting industries" would be gathering, including "corporate elites" like U.S. Steel, Owens-Corning, Standard Oil, and Monsanto.[58]

Contrary to Wisconsin Democratic Senator Gaylord Nelson's statement that the idea for an environmental teach-in, eventually known as Earth Day, was his "brainchild," the idea to hold teach-ins to further environmental awareness and action was, by 1969, already in the air. At San Fernando State College (now Cal State Northridge), the Mountaineering and Conservation Club formed in the spring of 1969 and quickly decided to have a teach-in the following year on environmental issues. The college agreed to sponsor the event. As club member Ronald Eber recalled, by the time Nelson announced his plan for a teach-in the group already had $2,000 in hand, speakers lined up, and a teach-in planned. "It should be no surprise that the event [Earth Day] was so successful," concluded Eber, "since if you line up all lead-up events, there was tons of stuff going on right up to the big event."[59]

It was Nelson's friend Fred Dutton, former Assistant Secretary of State and advisor to President Kennedy, who proposed the idea of an environmental teach-in to Nelson.[60] Nelson hoped a teach-in might draw enough public support to solidify environmentalism as a mainstream cause to a point that it would force the political system to finally address environmental issues in earnest.[61] "The same concern the youth of the nation took in changing the country's attitude on the war in Vietnam and on civil rights can be directed toward the problems of the environment," he believed.[62] His announcement of a plan for a teach-in on "The Crisis of the Environment" during a speech to the Washington Environmental Council in Seattle on September 20, 1969, tapped the nation's cultural, political, and environmental anxieties and, with enthusiastic media coverage, quickly gained widespread national interest. As Nelson put it, "Once I announced the teach-in, it began to be carried by its own momentum."[63]

Concern for the environment was nothing new for Nelson. As a boy in Clear Lake, Wisconsin, he spent much of his time hunting and fishing in the surrounding wilderness. Nelson's time in the woods led to a lifelong passion and commitment to conservation. After ten years in the state senate, in 1958 he was elected governor of Wisconsin; one of his greatest lasting achievements was the Outdoor Recreation Act Program, a penny-a-pack tax on cigarettes to fund purchases of recreational and conservation lands.[64] He was elected to the first of three terms as a United States Senator in 1962, and immediately began pushing for traditional conservation legislation. By the middle of the decade his vision expanded toward environmentalism. As his concerns about pollution, strip-mining, and the chemical poisoning of wildlife grew, he became increasingly frustrated in many of his efforts to get stricter conservation bills passed by Congress and enforced by the government.[65]

Bipartisan and House of Representatives support for Earth Day was secured when Representative Paul (Pete) N. McCloskey, Jr., a Republican from California, agreed to cochair the event. McCloskey's concern for the natural environment came from witnessing the rapid corporatization and urbanization of his home state. "I grew up in Southern California in the Depression," he recalled, "when we had the cleanest air in the world. People came from all over the world to the tubercular sanitariums in the Santa Clara and San Fernando Valley. In my lifetime, I saw it turn to the worst air in America."[66]

Soon after Nelson's Seattle announcement, requests for information about the teach-in overwhelmed his Senate office and its staffers. Acting on a recommendation from Dutton, Nelson and McCloskey started a Washington-based nonprofit coordinating committee, called Environmental Teach-in, Inc., to organize the event.[67] Not long before their meeting, Nelson had met with Denis Hayes, who read about the teach-in and wanted to be an organizer both because he was interested in ecology and because he had to complete a project assignment for Harvard's Kennedy School of Government that was required to intersect with the public sector. After meeting with him Nelson had granted Hayes a charter to organize Boston's Earth Day activities. In need of somebody to head the new national organization, Nelson subsequently called Hayes to ask if he would consider putting school on hold to organize all of America's Earth Day events. Hayes jumped at the opportunity.[68]

Like Nelson and McCloskey, Hayes acquired his love for nature early in life. Growing up he was struck by the contrast of the "pristinely beautiful" world of streams, forests, and Cascade Mountain foothills that surrounded his home in Camas, Washington, and the Crown Zellerbach paper mill, where his father worked, that polluted the Columbia River as it ran through town and caused a stench in the air. The summer after his junior year in high school he gained perspective on his town by attending an ecology seminar at Dennison University sponsored by the National Science Foundation.[69]

As leader of Environmental Teach-in, Inc. (which he and other organizers soon renamed Environmental Action, Inc.), Hayes landed in the middle of controversy as national coordinator for Earth Day, viewed with suspicion by factions on both the right and the left. On the right, in addition to long-standing concerns over environmentalism's threat to business interests and the American Way of Life, several newspapers warned that it was no mere coincidence Earth Day was scheduled on the anniversary of Vladimir Lenin's birthday, and the Daughters of the American Revolution labeled it "one of the subversive element's last steps."[70] Others, on the left, were convinced that Earth Day would detract from activism aimed at other pressing issues, including Vietnam, even though Senator Nelson was an early and vocal opponent of the war. "The American political process," stated Barry Weisberg in the leftist magazine *Liberation*, "has for some time been looking for an 'issue' that might patch up the strains created within both political parties, between young and old, and draw attention away from the seemingly insoluble problems of race, poverty and militarism. The long sought potion promises to be the environment."[71]

Some African Americans, Native Americans, and poor Americans feared Earth Day would undermine what they viewed as the more urgent issues of civil rights and poverty. As University of Michigan architecture student James Williams put it, "I'm too tied up in being black to give a damn about the environment." Edwin Fabre, a law student and officer in Michigan's Black Action Movement, gave a speech condemning Earth Day as "a white middle class toy." "There are 50 bills in the legislature on environmental problems," he pointed out, "but none on the rats in Detroit, Flint, and Jackson that are feeding on black children." Michigan event organizers Douglas Scott, a forestry student, and zoology student David Allen, who thought the teach-in was "a neat idea" when they first heard about it, discovered that not all groups shared their enthusiasm when they asked the Black Action Movement to participate. "The blacks looked at what we had to offer and told us to shove it," Allen recalled.[72] Encountering such opposition moved organizers to listen to the concerns of the Black Action Movement and other campus groups—"Guilt whipped across everybody," said Allen—and Earth Day organizers across the nation took care to emphasize that theirs was a broad definition of "environmental" that included issues like Vietnam, corporate abuse of power, poverty, racism—"the system."[73]

Nevertheless, the legacy of the association of conservation with privileged white Americans was still glaringly present in some of Earth Day's events. At the University of Wisconsin, members of the Wisconsin Student Indian Movement (WSIM) staged protests during the school's weeklong Earth Day symposium,

"Survival—Fourteen Years to 1984." They demanded to know why they had been excluded from the program. WSIM member Sandra Waubanaseum charged, "the Indian gave up our lands to you—you have taken it and destroyed it." She continued, "We know what our problem is, it's the white man, the Kemo Sabes who don't know anything about our people.... The Menominees would like to have the white man get the hell out of here."[74]

Some critics on the left believed Earth Day would provide not only a distraction from other pressing problems, but a distortion of the real issues afflicting the environment. The problem, as they viewed it, was that Earth Day would "point the finger of guilt at the consumer," when it instead must be understood that corporations were the real problem. "As long as society organizes production around the incentive to convert man's energies and nature's resources into profit," argued *Ramparts*, a leading magazine of the left, "no planned, equable, ecologically balanced system of production can ever exist. Teach-ins which fail to confront this fact of life do worse than teach nothing. They obstruct knowledge and stand in the way of a solution." The solution? "We must, in short, junk the business system and its way of life, and create revolutionary new institutions to embody new goals—human and environmental," the magazine urged.[75]

Although many Earth Day enthusiasts surely agreed with the spirit of *Ramparts*' notion, they might have also noted that the magazine was short on specifics for how to achieve such a herculean goal. For the most part, reservations held by the political right and left did not seem to be of much concern to the thousands of student groups and citizen organizations that heeded Nelson's call and began planning for Earth Day.

For many, the time was clearly ripe to embrace nature and the environment, even if government solutions and political revolution seemed unlikely—perhaps because government solutions and political revolution seemed unlikely. In its "Manifesto," printed in many underground newspapers, the group Ecology Action East stated, "We hope that ecology groups will eschew all appeals to the 'heads of government' and to international or national state institutions, the very criminals and political bodies that have materially contributed to the ecological crisis of our time. We believe the appeals must be made to the people and to their capacity for direct action that can get them to take control of their own lives and destinies."[76] Many Earth Day organizers shared a belief that corporations and growthmanship were ruining the environment while government mostly just stood by and watched, or, even worse, subsidized the destruction. Said Boston University sophomore Gary Herbst, "Industry is a giant funnel taking in nature and turning out garbage for its own profit. The government doesn't police them—they say growth's not just good, it's God."[77]

The local and campus organizations mirrored the national organization of Environmental Action, which Hayes characterized as "half a staff that was sort of old political organizers, and half of them who were, and I'm caricaturing a bit, but who... didn't want to have anything to do with politics because it was corrupting."[78] Both groups were represented by Environmental Action's ad promoting Earth Day, which read: "It is a day to challenge the corporate and governmental leaders who promise change, but who short change the necessary programs."[79]

What had been a minor issue on most college campuses began to eclipse other sixties concerns, especially with the decline of other causes and the breakdown of the New Left. Crucial among Earth Day organizers, as they had been with the fight against atomic fallout, were women. Even many women who did not venture to the frontlines of the battles for civil rights and to stop the war in Vietnam stepped forward as environmental activists.[80] "This environmental thing touched them, disproportionately to the way that it touched men," said Hayes. "They tied it to their children. And just a huge number of organizers in cities across the country were these 25- to 35-year-old women whose husbands held jobs that gave them the flexibility to go out organizing things."[81]

Indeed, for some women environmental exploitation was readily understood in terms of their own exploitation in a male-dominated culture. As an editorial in the Washington, DC underground women's newspaper, *Off Our Backs*, protested, "We women know that our bodies, our minds and our souls have been raped by that same excessive pride, that same brutal inhumanity that has raped the land, the water and the sky. We are all alike its victims." Even more than other citizens, women often felt powerless to change the corporate practices, backed by government, that were threatening their families. Responding to numerous studies that detailed the presence of DDT in human milk, *Off Our Backs* continued: "We must nurture our babies with our milk made toxic with DDT. If we were to carry that milk in bottles rather than our breasts we would not be allowed to cross state lines. And we know we have no control over those industries which produce and use the poisons our bodies now store. We women suffer the tragic irony of a system which makes us responsible for the health and well-being of our families and yet provides no means for us to meet those needs.... We discover that we are to carry the burden of responsibility for lives and lands maimed by institutions and policies we are powerless to affect."[82] Combatting that sense of helplessness, many women turned to environmental activism.

Ecotage

Shortly before Earth Day, on April 6, 1970, under the cover of night at a sewage treatment plant in Miami, six black-clad "commandoes" from a group calling itself "Eco-Commando Force 70" made it past a security fence and a night watchman. Each then deposited a colored dye bomb in individual giant waste vats. Before daybreak they did the same thing at two additional plants. By the time the sun rose the next day half of the Miami area's inland waterways were bright yellow, and a communiqué from Eco-Commando Force 70 explained that they had dyed the sewage to show how it is carried through area waters and prove that it was not, as claimed by officials, carried far out into the ocean by the Gulf Stream. Leadership of the clandestine group included a marine biologist, medical technician, nurse, teacher, landscape architect, print shop owner, and medical student. They later carried out additional daring feats to further expose Miami's inadequate sewage disposal, which often left sewage washing up on area beaches. If they ever got caught and arrested, they planned to plead "self defense."[83]

Another eco-guerilla operated in the Chicago area and was known as "Fox." Among his most notorious stunts was climbing a very tall industrial smokestack and sealing it so that it could no longer release toxic smoke; hanging a 60-foot banner from a railroad bridge that read "WE'RE INVOLVED IN KILLING LAKE MICHIGAN—U.S. STEEL"; and collecting a container of discharge from U.S. Steel's drainage system, dumping it on the carpeting of the company's Chicago office, then telling the *Chicago Daily News*, "They keep saying that they aren't really polluting our water. If that's true, it shouldn't hurt their rugs."[84] "I got tired of watching the smoke and the filth and the little streams dying one by one," he told *Time* magazine in 1970. "Finally I decided to do something—the courts weren't doing anything to these polluters except granting continuance after continuance." Upon Fox's death in 2001, at age 70, his family revealed that his true identity was James F. Phillips, a middle-school science teacher from Aurora, Illinois.[85]

A Day for the Earth

As if all the publicity for the event had not been enough, a troubled NASA mission to the moon, the inauspiciously named *Apollo 13* spaceship whose plight the nation had nervously followed as it struggled to get home, finally splashed down safely only five days before Earth Day. President Nixon declared a national day of prayer and thanksgiving. The near-tragedy further shook the nation's faith in technology and created a greater sense of urgency regarding the environment. A *New York Times* editorial noted that the spaceship's perilous return home, when the malfunctioning craft nearly ran out of oxygen and water, stirred "passionate worldwide interest in its 'consumables.'" It was clear that the *Apollo 13* crew survived only by making the most careful and efficient use of its resources. "Earth

Day next Wednesday," said the *Times*, "aims above all to convince the American people that similar prudence is required on Spaceship Earth." *Los Angeles Times* syndicated political cartoonist Paul Conrad pictured the earth floating in space beneath the headline "Another Spaceship Low On Water, Oxygen, And Other Life Support Systems."[86]

At last the day itself arrived. It surpassed almost everyone's expectations. On April 22, 1970, some 20 million Americans took to streets, rivers, lakes, oceans, parks, campuses, and lecture halls across the country with a wild mix of demonstrations, parades, protests, guerilla theater, marches, music, and an endless variety of talks to participate in what was billed as an Environmental Teach-In: Earth Day. *Newsweek* magazine tabbed it the "biggest street festival since the Japanese surrendered in 1945."[87] Nobody really knew what Earth Day was, yet nearly everybody seemed to know what it meant. The broad range of actions and concerns put forth reflected the depth and breadth of the environmental concern that had been building since World War II, as well as the variety of constituencies attracted to the cause: the hippies, outdoor recreationists, vegetarians, hunters, birdwatchers, sport fishermen, organics enthusiasts, anticorporatists, those concerned about population growth, romantics, antipollution advocates, preservationists, atomic-energy opponents, traditional conservationists, consumerists, parents, children, and family pets, to name just a few. Though a celebration, Earth Day was a day of reckoning, a day of atonement, a day of repentance. More than anything else, though, it was a day of reconciling how to best go about living in a state of postwar modernity.

Various types of pollution drew the most attention during the day's speeches, but many Earth Day speakers also tried to assure audiences that environmentalism would not detract from other, established liberal concerns—especially ending the war in Vietnam. Union representative Charlie Hayes pushed the boundaries of environmentalism and emphasized environmental justice. "Our program to protect the environment must include feeding the hungry, healing the sick, building homes and schools, eradicating racism and discrimination, and finally making the national welfare program adequate to lift people forever out of the degradation of poverty," he said, arguing that black people and poor people would support environmentalism if it addressed the whole range of environmental concerns.[88]

Many of the speeches sounded an apocalyptic tone, including a warning about global warming. Dr. J. Murray Mitchell, of the Federal Environmental Science Services Administration in Washington, DC, issued a dire prediction that "air pollutants—mainly carbon dioxide—may cause the earth's temperatures to rise to levels that will threaten life itself."[89] It was a warning that, despite all evidence, corporate and government leaders would still be trying to deny 40 years later.

When it came to assigning blame for the host of problems identified under the expanded definition of environmentalism, the usual suspects were corporations. "To many of us it seems that individuals have lost control over their lives, that they are manipulated by a system with an inherent death wish rather than one in which enhancement of life is the primary goal," said Earth Day's Midwest coordinator Barbara Reid outside a General Electric shareholders' meeting in Minneapolis. "The major symbol of this death culture is the institutionalized violence perpetrated upon people and the land by corporations such as General Electric."[90] George Wiley, director of the National Welfare Rights Organization, concurred in a speech at Harvard: "I would say if you are a serious movement you must be prepared to take on the giant corporations who are the primary polluters and perpetrators of some of the worst conditions that affect the environment of the country and indeed the world."[91] University of Michigan students dumped 10,000 empty cans on the lawn of a Coca-Cola bottling plant, and another group of students spread tar and feathers on the steps of a building where Alaska oil developer Atlantic Richfield Corporation was on campus recruiting employees. A political-science graduate student challenged the notion that individual consumers were most responsible for pollution: "The major cause of pollution," he argued, "is the structure of society—I mean the corporations."[92] As Denis Hayes later summarized it, "An awful lot of things that we were concerned about, and I guess the vast majority of the things that we were putting on the agenda with Earth Day, were the behavior of companies themselves and the nature of the products the companies were manufacturing."[93]

As with earlier efforts by Women Strike for Peace, Denis Hayes and others in Environmental Action operated the organization as a clearinghouse of information for those who wished to plan local Earth Day events around the country but mostly left it up to them to decide exactly what they were going to do to mark the day. There were, however, some notable exceptions to this mostly hands-off strategy.[94] Because many of those on staff were savvy veterans of the civil rights and antiwar movements, the group made sophisticated use of the media. For big cities and media markets like Washington, Chicago, and especially New York City, Hayes and his staff spent considerable time and effort helping orchestrate Earth Day's events. This was especially true for New York. "Before cable," noted Hayes in a 2006 interview, "New York was the *New York Times*. It was *Time, Newsweek, U.S. News and World Report*. It was ABC, CBS, and NBC. If it didn't happen in New York it wouldn't have happened. And if it did happen in New York it almost didn't matter what happened elsewhere. That's where you got the big photographs. That's where the people who decided what *was* news would either notice it or not notice it."[95]

Earth Day was a front-page story in newspapers across the nation that often detailed both local and national events, and all of the television networks had extensive coverage along with special Earth Day programs. Like television producers, Earth Day organizers skillfully staged spectacles (guerilla theater, marches, protests, music, demonstrations, etc.), to lure the attention of cameras and viewers, then joined the images with numerous speeches and panel discussions to get their message out. It was a potent formula.[96]

Earth Day Brings New (and Limited) Environmental Laws

Earth Day realized Senator Nelson's intended effect of dramatizing the nation's concern for the environment, making it easier to get environmental legislation passed into law. President Nixon and Congress responded to the growing environmental fervor in the buildup to Earth Day and shortly after with some of the most significant environmental legislation in the nation's history. Although Nixon once told John Ehrlichman, his assistant for domestic affairs, that the issue of the environment was "just crap," he was a savvy political operator who recognized that the public mood required some sort of action.[97] The fact that Democratic Senator Edmund Muskie of Maine, a vocal conservationist, was a likely challenger in the 1972 presidential election also factored into Nixon's political calculation. On January 1, 1970, the National Environmental Policy Act (NEPA) was signed into law. In order to push the environment into federal decision-making, it required all government agencies to prepare a preliminary environmental review or impact statement for any proposed project or legislation, and it established a three-member Council on Environmental Quality to review environmental-impact statements and administer the act. Nixon followed NEPA with strong environmental rhetoric. On January 22, in his State of the Union Address, he proposed making "the 1970s a historic period when, by conscious choice, [we] transform our land into what we want it to become." The National Environmental Education Act, which mandated environmental education in public schools and provided funds for teacher education and materials, introduced by Gaylord Nelson, was signed into law on October 30, 1970. Nelson deemed the act, and its potential to effect lasting change through education, even more important than Earth Day itself.[98] By President Nixon's executive order the Environmental Protection Agency came into being in December 1970, charged with overseeing the enforcement of federal environmental policies by setting and enforcing environmental standards. The Marine Mammal Protection Act followed in 1972.[99]

Even established conservation groups, some of which were leery of Earth Day, admitted afterward that it had a significant effect. Michael McCloskey, executive director of the Sierra Club, said the Club had had a very ambivalent attitude toward the event. "We believed in lobbying day in and day out, and lifetime commitments to conservation," he said. "And so our thought was, this is not just a thing that you go out and do a stunt about once a year.... This all just seemed like childishness." But following Earth Day, when it became apparent that the Sierra Club no longer had to work just to convince lawmakers that there was vast public support for greater environmental protection, McCloskey realized that Earth Day had a more profound effect than he previously imagined. "To some extent I was wrong," he admitted. "I didn't realize the extent to which it would catalyze a lasting change in public opinion.... Industrial lobbies were just thunderstruck. The other side knew that something like a whirlwind had come out of nowhere. Suddenly there was tremendous support for our positions and they could no longer assume we were a few crazy people who could be disregarded."[100] Of course, the whirlwind hardly came out of "nowhere."

The Best Environmental Laws Money Can Buy

Senator Nelson discovered that there were limits to the legislation that could sail through Congress in the slipstream of Earth Day. In an effort to force technological innovation, Nelson attached an amendment to the Clean Air Act that would have prohibited the sale of any automobile with an internal combustion engine after January 1, 1975, and a resolution to reallocate the $1.5 billion that automobile manufacturers spent annually on style changes toward conversion to a new type of engine. The proposal fell victim to what drove Nelson to introduce the legislation in the first place. The automobile industry "has skillfully filibustered and sweet-talked the nation out of forcing them to do anything meaningful," he complained.[101]

"Sweet talking" was just one of the ways that corporations dealt with the prospect of tougher environmental legislation. Stronger environmental laws inspired a fierce backlash, most of it corporate-sponsored, designed to limit the effectiveness of new regulations and avoid further threats to the status quo. In addition to ramped-up PR campaigns, companies also funded research institutes and think tanks like the Heritage Foundation (1973) and Cato Institute (1977) that published floods of anti-environmental position papers widely disseminated by the media.[102] Before long, companies also employed a new tool called "corporate front groups" to do their bidding. Some of these groups had false or misleading names to shield their anti-environmental intent. The Global Climate Coalition included over 50 trade associations and corporations bent on convincing government and the public that global warming was not real. Others—often derided by critics as "Astroturf"—were designed to appear to be "grassroots" groups, even though in reality they were closely tied to industry. They included groups like the National Wetlands Coalition, funded by Amoco, ARCO, BP, Chevron, and at least nine other major oil companies, to secure rights for oil and gas drilling in wetlands.[103] Like the government's misinformation campaigns designed to confuse the public's perception of the war in Vietnam, corporate misinformation did not necessarily have to "win" the debate on environmental issues. Rather, it often sought to manufacture just enough confusion and doubt in the public sphere to justify inaction or ever more research, in the process maintaining the (profitable) status quo of environmental degradation.

Business also stepped up its efforts to control elections and the courts. In 1970 there were fewer than 100 corporate Political Action Committees in the United States; 10 years later there were over 1,100. Efforts to block or tie up environmental rules and regulations in the courts also expanded. Corporations soon created what they termed "public interest" law firms (PILFs) throughout the country, designed to wage legal battles and conflate the interests of citizens and the environment with the interests of big business. By 1975 the umbrella National Legal Center for the Public Interest was established in Washington, DC. Its founding president, Leonard Theberge, summed up the organization's sardonic twist on environmentalism when he stated, "What we cannot accept are mindless proposals that would sacrifice the people of the US on the altar of nature." Brewery magnate Joseph Coors, whom *Reader's Digest* called "one of the country's leading anti-environmentalists," sat on the board of the National Legal Center and, with oil companies Amoco, Chevron, Phillips, and Shell, was a major contributor to the powerful Mountain States Legal Foundation PILF.[104] That organization was a leading force in the antistatist "Sagebrush Rebellion" of Westerners who, in the spirit of the mythical Old West, fiercely resented any governmental regulations that got in the way of their doing what they pleased to the environment. Mountain States and other sagebrushers often pushed for state and local rights to circumvent federal environmental regulations. Coors appointed as Mountain States's first president his friend James Watt, who was later appointed—much to the dismay of environmentalists—Secretary of the Interior by President Ronald Reagan.[105]

The Earth Day era's seemingly robust environmental legislation was not immune to the political process in the aftermath. The increased number of corporate PACs was countered by surges in growth for existing citizen groups (Sierra Club, Wilderness Society, etc.) along with the creation of a slew of new groups (Greenpeace, Friends of the Earth, etc.) to pressure lawmakers. But while such groups assured that lawmakers devoted more attention and time to environmental issues, they had more trouble assuring that new laws were not, in the end, watered down through corporate influence.[106]

In addition, enforcement of environmental laws varied widely, depending on the political climate of the times and the environmental attitude of the president who made key appointments to agencies like the EPA, FDA, and Department of the Interior, not to mention the federal courts. Laws and regulations that worked well initially were often not as effective once corporate lawyers went to work figuring out how they could be exploited, and corporate lobbyists and lawyers aimed their skills at softening their impact. "It wasn't until the next year [after Earth Day], in 1971 or '72," the Sierra Club's McCloskey recalled, "that they [corporations] began finding ways to counterattack."[107]

Indeed, in 1972 Nixon made a secret deal with the Ford Motor Company to undermine the EPA, the agency he had established only two years earlier. The president told Ehrlichman to have the EPA "say a number of things designed to shock the consumer that the cost of the environment will be very high and that the air quality laws are very impractical." The EPA complied, shaking the public's confidence enough to reduce or delay a number of antipollution regulations opposed by Ford and the automobile industry.[108] "Whether it's the environment or pollution or Naderism or consumerism," President Nixon once assured a gathering of Ford Motor Company executives, "we are extremely pro-business."[109] As Denis Hayes said of the promise and the reality of the environmental policies ushered in during the era of Earth Day, "It all became kind of nice, in this political science text way, if you don't think of a world in which there's graft, corruption, huge campaign contributions, friendships forged on golf links, and all of the other stickiness in the system, it should work pretty well in a mechanical sense to pass a tough law and have an enforcement mechanism, and have a fallback for citizens if the rest of it doesn't work."[110]

But, of course, the real political world bore little resemblance to a political-science text. For example, the 1970 Clean Air Act established 247 air-quality-control regions in the United States, overseen by individual states, which were required to comply with the EPA's National Ambient Air Quality Standards (NAAQS) by 1977 at the latest. Each state would submit a State Implementation Plan to the EPA for approval, detailing how it would comply with the NAAQS. When states did not comply, a new Clean Air Act in 1977 extended the deadline. Nevertheless, by 1985 less than 60 percent of states had so much as an approved plan. Another New Clean Air Act in 1990, although strengthening the 1970 Act in some respects, again extended the NAAQS deadline for compliance, depending on the geographic area, anywhere from three to twenty additional years. The promise of the 1970 law was subsequently diminished in extensions and weak enforcement.[111]

To cite another example, although NEPA set up an environmental-review process and placed the environment into the mix of government decision-making, one of its biggest weaknesses was the fact that although it required environmental assessments for federal projects, it did not require that the environment necessarily be protected. Environmental Impact Statements became just one more bureaucratic obstacle to overcome, and their initial effect on government agencies was soon muted.[112] Shortly after it became law, researchers found that inadequate funding and administrative support limited NEPA's effectiveness.[113] Subsequent years were no different. The authors of the most detailed study of NEPA thus far concluded, "NEPA has barely scratched the surface of our nation's and globe's most pressing environmental problems.... Among the biggest problems with NEPA's effectiveness is not the language of the statute, but rather the lack of judicial and presidential enforcement of NEPA policy goals." Investigations revealed that state officials were similarly lax in enforcing EPA laws.[114]

Political scientists have found that although environmental issues received much more attention than ever before from the media and public in the early 1970s, that increased popularity did little to change the attitudes of lawmakers. Policies to rein in corporations for the sake of the environment were more symbolic than substantive, and, in the end, the government's dedication to corporate capitalism and economic growth trumped environmental concerns. When they did consider environmental issues, one study revealed, members of Congress tended to view those issues through a traditional conservation lens focused on aesthetics and recreation and not with the ecological lens focused on the more expansive concerns of environmentalism. Further, lawmakers recognized that they could score political points with the voting public by passing environmental legislation, even if such laws had very limited real effect because government did little in the way of financing and enforcing them.[115] In his study of environmental policy, political scientist Matthew Cahn found that policymakers oversimplify complex environmental issues and seek to convince the public that "modest regulation will effect substantial improvement," while at the same time inducing citizens to accept that such limited regulation is the only "attainable" policy option. Legislators seek to mediate the conflict between the desires of business and the public's urgent demands to improve the environment through "symbolic politicking." But continuing environmental problems eventually give the lie to policymaking theatrics. Ongoing environmental crises bring about only a new round of theatrics and yet more symbolic politicking.[116]

Bill Mauk, who was director of research for Environmental Action, Inc. during the organization of Earth Day, wondered if the shrewd politician Nixon knew all along that his environmental policies would have less real impact than they originally suggested. "I think, in some ways, that Nixon was probably smarter than all of the rest of us," Mauk mused. "He signed a lot of that legislation, but I think he also realized that the legislation was only as good as the people who enforced it. And, if you controlled the bureaucracy and the bureaucracy was acceptable to corporations and industry and lobbyists—which it is—then that's where it will make the difference."[117] Political theorist Ralph Miliband had earlier reported as much in his 1969 study, *The State in Capitalist Society*, in which he found that government appointees tend to be people whose professional backgrounds and beliefs ensure that they uphold corporate interests.[118] Politics may be the art of compromise, but even with the EPA and new environmental legislation, for many Americans it still seemed that the compromises favored big business at the expense of citizens and the environment.

Thus, not all environmental ills were cured. Air pollution decreased, but, especially in some cities, it has remained a significant problem. An EPA water-quality survey in 1998 found that 35 percent of rivers and streams, along with 45 percent of lakes, ponds, and reservoirs, were "impaired" and not meeting minimum water-quality standards for "designated beneficial uses," including drinking water, support of aquatic life, swimming, and fishing. Runoff of agricultural, industrial, and residential pollutants, as well as persistent toxic pollutants, continue to degrade the nation's water quality.[119] At least 37 states have issued health advisories against eating fish from their polluted waters.[120]

Most significantly, the government only monitors for known pollutants. A growing body of research suggests that startling increases in rates of certain cancers and neurological disorders like Parkinson's and Alzheimer's, declining male reproductive health, and incidences of developmental disabilities including autism and attention deficit hyperactivity disorder, are due to environmental causes such as herbicides, nitrate fertilizers, phthalates, plastics, and a variety of chemicals. Research published in 2012 found that as many as 30 percent of cases of autism, and perhaps schizophrenia, are attributable to men aged 40 and older who father children. Having been exposed to more environmental toxins than younger men, these older fathers have substantially more mutations in their genetic material.[121] In 1963 Nobel laureate geneticist Hermann J. Muller advised that men might wish to freeze their sperm when they are young and it is freer from cumulative environmental damage, to use it for fatherhood when they get older; nearly 50 years later all scientists could do was offer the same advice.[122]

8

Green Consumerism Goes Mainstream

Gaylord Nelson's plan to secure environmental legislation by means of greater public pressure brought to bear through Earth Day was, to some degree, successful. Nevertheless, to many environmentalists who remained frustrated in their efforts to protect the environment and rein in corporate power through traditional politics, the limited effect of the laws spawned by Earth Day was only further confirmation of the outsized power of corporations in American life. For them, it was clear that corporate capitalism had destroyed the balance of the American polity. As ecologist Kenneth Watt observed in an Earth Day speech at Swarthmore College in Pennsylvania, "More and more people are giving up on the system. This isn't just the young people, or the poor, or the black people. I've been startled to discover the extent to which white, middle-class, suburban housewives have become so frustrated and are so full of despair about the ability to have any effect on the system that they've given up on it."[1] That attitude was evident in comments by Mary Humphrey of Ecology Action at an EcoFair in Newhall, 20 miles north of Los Angeles: "I don't think you'll find anyone who really thinks the government will do something," she said of protecting the environment. "It's a real grassroots thing."[2]

A frequent theme during Earth Day was the dream of citizens using consumption to both alter American culture and protect the environment. Perhaps the most telling admission that the political system was simply not up to the task was made by prominent Senate Democrat and conservationist Edmund Muskie of Maine, who conceded that it was no longer possible for citizens to wield effective power through the voting booth. "The power of the people is in the cash register," said Senator Muskie, acknowledging just how distorted the American polity had become, "and we can resolve to purchase only from those companies that clean themselves up."[3] Roderick Cameron, executive director of the Environmental Defense Fund, further explored why electoral politics was ineffective: "Industries who profit by rape of our environment see to it that legislators friendly to their interests are elected, and that bureaucrats of similar attitude are appointed," he said. "Our government seems extraordinarily vulnerable to the accrual of political power by representatives of narrow but powerful economic interests. Indeed, we seem to be more a democracy of economic interests than of private citizens." Like others, Cameron urged Americans to compensate for their lack of agency in electoral politics by instead asserting their political power as consumers. As citizens, he concluded, we consumers need to "crank one more factor into our buying decisions: environmental impact."[4] Ralph Nader, speaking in Philadelphia, called industries the worst polluters and concluded that change would come about only through a "radical militant ethic" by consumers.[5]

A Radical Militant Ethic?

In a special Earth Day edition of the underground newspaper *Free Spaghetti Dinner*, the Santa Cruz chapter of Ecology Action concurred, and urged citizens to not only consume with the environment in mind but also to consume less. "The cultural changes needed to prevent a depleted and poisoned planet will not have industrial or government sources, " it argued. Instead, the necessary changes would come about only through basic changes in the ways people consumed: "These cultural changes must be fostered and lived by individuals. . . . We, the consumers, must begin consuming less. Save water by not bathing every day," they recommended, "unless exceptionally dirty, and not washing shirts after only one wearing: Start digging human looks and smell. Off the cosmetics and deodorant, bottle and chemical clutter in the bathroom."

Just as planned, the largest media spectacle was in media-rich New York City. Union Square was the center of Earth Day activities; an estimated 20,000 people filled the square at any given moment. With the turnover of the crowds, as many as 100,000 different people were likely there at some point during the day. Above the crowds balloons stamped with slogans like "Stop at two" and "War is the worst pollution" waved in the breeze. About a hundred booths lined the square and adjacent 14th Street offering information on a wide array of environmental topics including conservation, wildlife preservation, clean air, peace, and voluntary sterilization.

Less than a block from Union Square, on 17th Street, Ellie and Raymond Jacobs had opened a store just weeks earlier to sell "Anne Kalso Minus Heel Shoes." Sales were slow for the unusual-looking shoes until, seeing the crowds that gathered for Earth Day, they hung a sign in their window that read "Earth Shoe." "All those kids who were demonstrating in Union Square came by, saw us, and we were swamped," said Ellie. The shoes themselves were a perfect symbol of the zeitgeist. Advertisements later explained that Kalso, the Danish yoga instructor who designed the shoe, was inspired when "She saw footprints in the sand, and realized that with every footprint the body was designing a shoe. A natural shoe. A shoe with the heel lower than the toe." Implicit in the shoe's appeal was the sense that business was so out of touch that it had not even bothered to notice how nature would design something as basic as footwear. By 1973 there were five company Earth Shoe stores and 35 dealerships across the country, with sales of $3.5 million.[6] European shoe designer Manolo Blahnik later said, "It was the first shoe, [along] with the Jesus sandals, to make a social statement!"[7]

In a study that asked those who attended Earth Day events if they learned anything that would change their behaviors, and if so, what, nearly 40 percent reported learning nothing new, leading researchers to conclude that "Most came not to be informed that there exist environmental problems, but to look for specific actions to alleviate these problems. Thus, it appears the teach-in was not serving to change attitudes (for the majority), but rather had the function... of demonstrating to the concerned attendant that others shared his concern and willingness to act.... The teach-in and the environmental furor of 1970 made it socially acceptable to be concerned about the environment."[8] Given how the environmentally minded had been demonized in the past, that in itself was very important. In addition to whatever else they might have learned, it is likely that the most important lesson citizens gleaned from Earth Day was that many others shared their concerns about the damaging effects of corporate capitalism and their dreams for an alternative, or at least modified, system.

When asked what they would do to help the environment, the plan most frequently cited by Earth Day attendees was to change their "consumer behaviors." Forty percent of those polled reported that they would change the way they consumed, including types and quantities of products. In comparison, only about 8 percent mentioned changes in interpersonal activities such as joining others to take action, and only some 7 percent said that they would make more drastic lifestyle changes, including having fewer or no children, changing living habits, or changing occupations. "It appears, therefore," one researcher concluded, "that the major impact of the teach-in will be in altering consumer behaviors, with lesser effects on more complicated or personally costly behaviors."[9] The dramatic impact of Earth Day helped to further solidify a distinct identity for the environmentally minded within American culture who sought environmental and cultural change through consumption.

The growth of this green community could be seen in the growth and number of businesses that sought to appeal to its demands. Natural and organic foods exploded in popularity. An estimated 1,500 to 2,000 natural-foods stores provided alternative sites of consumption for Americans in 1970, and in a survey

85 percent reported sales were up.[10] At Organic-ville, which had opened in Los Angeles in 1951, owners remarked in the autumn of 1970 that at least one-third of their business came from the "upper-class hippie" group, and many older customers were following the "with-it" kids into the store. The owner of another organic market, Health Food International in Lemon Grove, California, reported that sales were up 72 percent, and business from young people had doubled in the past 12 months.[11] At Sunrise Farm store in Chicago, which sold some 3,000 pounds of organic produce a week, owner Wayne Myroup did all he could to get produce locally, including contracting with growers and starting his own organic farm.[12] In Massachusetts the Boston Area Ecology Action Center's organic-food store, run cooperatively, sold most food in bulk with minimal packaging, and when packages were used they were returnable. Although much of its organic produce came from California, as much as possible was obtained locally. "The Store," as the Boston market was called, even sponsored a 150-acre organic farm at nearby Nashua, New Hampshire. Its philosophy of the alternative green marketplace was captured in one of its pamphlets that proudly proclaimed, "The Store runs independently of the agriculture-distribution-supermarket complex, buying only from organic non-exploitative farmers."[13]

In addition, the trend was continuing to spread to traditional supermarkets. In Colorado, stores in the King Soopers supermarket chain carried 25 to 30 organic produce items, and they could not get enough from their suppliers to keep up with demand.[14] Alexander's, a 10-store chain in the San Fernando Valley in California, not only carried organic produce but also saw sales increase 5 percent after a concerted environmental advertising campaign. The program centered on tagging certain products with "ecology preferred" stickers. Stores installed recycling centers for newspapers, tin, aluminum, and glass, and weekly newspaper ads included environmental news and information.[15] Frozen organic foods were increasingly popular, including breads, vegetables, fruits, ice cream, and meats free of antibiotics and hormones.[16] One of the largest distributors of organic foods registered a doubling of sales from 1968 to 1970.[17]

The expanding movement gained widespread media attention. By the end of the year, *Newsweek, Time, Life, McCall's,* and *Vogue* had all featured articles on the escalating popularity of organic foods, and CBS aired a special report on television.[18] *The Mother Earth News*, a magazine that began in January 1970 for what it called the "Gentle Revolution of the new 'Life Style,'" consisting of "organic gardening, working at home, ecology, living off the land, solar energy, tipis, water power, free transportation, domes, home canning, crafts, building and flying a man-carrying airplane, communes, macrobiotics, freelancing, free land, homesteading, herbs, getting paid for doing exactly what you want, and much, much more," in May published a list of 40 things to do to keep the spirit of Earth Day alive, the vast majority of which dealt with consumer behavior.[19]

In 1970 bottled-water sales also took off, thanks in part to a federal report that 30 percent of the nation's tap water was tainted. Water coolers with familiar five-gallon jugs had long been popular in offices, but environmental concerns broadened the market to individual-sized bottles. An article in *Advertising Age* explained, "With fears of actual water system pollution creating the demand in some areas, and the general angst about the environment and its impurities widening the market elsewhere, bottled spring water and purified water have become highly salable items that several large companies are looking at in a new way." Large beverage corporations seized the opportunity. Canada Dry Beverage Company marketed "Pure Drinking Water," in 28-ounce bottles, which it had previously produced only for use by the British royal family during visits to North America, to meet the United States's "mounting concern over the nation's ecology, and wide consumer demand for pure water," said the company's president. Schweppes and Coca-Cola also began selling water in quart bottles. Nestlé was the market leader, selling bottles under the name Deer Park spring water. Radio ads for the water stated, "What do you do when you're thirsty? Most people don't go to the faucet. Our water is so filled with chlorine and chemicals that we go to the refrigerator for a bottle of something." Deer Park water, the ad said, is "nature's way to satisfy your thirst." "Bottled water, long the pet of hypochondriacs and travelers," proclaimed *Look* magazine, "is fast becoming the rage of Aquarians."[20]

The rise in green consumption was also evident in a marked increase of sales of outdoor gear. Seattle-based Recreational Equipment Inc. (REI), a leading outdoor clothing and gear company since 1938 that also did a large mail-order business, saw sales increase an astonishing eightfold, from $3.5 million in 1969 to $28 million in 1970.[21] That boost was attributable not only to the growing popularity of outdoor activities but also to outdoor clothing including mountain parkas, rustic sweaters, ponchos, and hiking boots, increasingly entering mainstream fashion. Outdoor clothing and gear was itself part of the zeitgeist in more ways than its association with increasingly fashionable nature and wilderness. Not only was REI organized as a cooperative, but most of the manufacturers of outdoor clothing and gear—like Holubar Mountaineering and Gerry's Mountaineering Equipment, both founded in Colorado in 1946— suggested small cottage industries of innovators, unlike the giant corporations that dominated so many other industries. Yvon Chouinard started Patagonia in 1974 with the company creed, "We're not rulers of the resources. We are just another animal in the food chain. Everything's weighed equally. We need to treat this as an ecosystem. From that, all things fall out."[22] By 1976 top fashion designers picked up on the trend, and clothing based on rugged outdoor gear appeared in Paris and New York fashion shows, hailed by fashionistas as fall's hot look.[23]

For many Americans such accoutrements signified an embrace of the environmental ethos, even if their lives did not always fully conform. For critics they signaled the commodification of leisure and the growing inability of Americans to experience nature without a variety of products that they had been convinced were necessary for the endeavor. Whatever else it might have been, green consumption was an effort by citizens to assert their will. Said journalist Harold Gilliam of the growing popularity of environmentalism and organics, "There's a great ferment going on.... It is rooted deep in the contemporary crisis... the ordinary citizen's growing feeling that his life and environment are increasingly at the mercy of forces over which he has no control. The symbols of these forces are bureaucracy and the bulldozer."[24] Green consumption afforded at least some measure of agency. The consumer activism of environmentalists was most often a loose affiliation of like-minded people who met in the green marketplace, or perhaps worked together in co-ops where members provided a share of the labor to run the business.

But there were also more organized efforts. In New York City, an environmental group called Consumer Action Now (C.A.N.) was formed by Lola Redford, wife of actor Robert Redford, and Ilene Goldman, wife of author and screenwriter William Goldman, who met when their husbands were working on the film *Butch Cassidy and the Sundance Kid*. On Earth Day Goldman's five-year-old daughter came home from nursery school and pleaded with her mom, "Please don't open the window because air's gonna come in and kill me." When Goldman mentioned the incident to Redford, the two decided that the only choices were to move away from the city to cleaner air or to stay and fight. They determined to stay and, with the help of 15 of their friends who each contributed money and formed committees to study various environmental problems, they began publishing an environmental consumer education newspaper (on recycled paper) that soon had 7,000 subscribers. "There are so many people living in large urban areas who do want to help preserve the planet's resources and use those resources wisely... but who become so frustrated when dealing with city governments and large corporations," said Redford. She first became concerned about chemicals when her grandfather, a farmer, died of liver cancer that the family doctor attributed to his use of pesticides.[25]

In Washington, DC, a similar group that called itself Concern, Inc., was headed by Nancy Ignatius, whose husband Paul Ignatius was president of the *Washington Post* and former Secretary of the Navy, and Cynthia Helms, whose husband Richard was head of the CIA. Dedicated to providing consumers with information on shopping for a better environment, the group was best known for its "Eco-Tips" cards that recommended, in shopping-list style, products in a variety of categories that, through research from "outside, authoritative sources," they believed caused the least harm to the environment. The cards began with the statement, "What you choose at the store reflects your concern for the quality of our environment." Beyond specific product recommendations, Concern, Inc., told consumers to never use pesticides like dieldrin, heptachlor, DDT, and lindane. It urged them to purchase products with as little packaging as possible and buy beverages in returnable containers. "What we aim to do," said Cynthia Helms, "is to channel information from the expert to the consumer to the manufacturer, to let him know women prefer to buy the product that is ecologically good." By November 1970, they had mailed out 250,000 Eco-Tips guides.[26]

Much like the consumers' leagues that formed in the late nineteenth century to emphasize "ethical" consumption and help consumers ascertain whether products were produced with care for the treatment and well-being of workers, groups like C.A.N. and Concern, Inc., emphasized ethical consumption and sought to help consumers ascertain whether the products they might purchase were produced with care for the treatment and well-being of the planet. Green consumer groups hoped that their actions would pressure manufacturers into treating the earth better.[27]

Once again women, who, despite the women's movement, often did most of the shopping for their families and thus continually found themselves on the front lines in the struggle for a safe and healthy environment, led the fight and chose to stage the battle at the site where they believed they had the greatest chance for success: consumption. In late 1970 C.A.N. and Concern, Inc. were joined by a book from organic gardener Betty Ann Ottinger entitled *What Every Woman Should Know and Do About Pollution: A Guide to Global Good Housekeeping*. She was the wife of Richard L. Ottinger, a US Representative from New York who once accused the Interior Department and the Federal Power Commission of "sycophantic fearfulness" in their dealings with electric utility companies.[28] "As housewives, we American women are responsible for determining how more than two-thirds of our consumer dollars are spent," she said, before calling for three "rules of environmental preservation": "The first rule is that we must completely change our patterns of consumption and use"; "The second rule is to have a healthy suspicion of each new technological development and each new product"; "The third and final rule is to learn to live harmoniously with other forms of life." Ottinger urged all women to shop, like European women, with their own reusable string bags to avoid using paper bags.[29] Notably, none of her rules involved traditional political engagement but instead focused solely on pursuing change through consumer behavior. In addition to the usual outlets, the book was available through conservation groups like the Sierra Club and Friends of the Earth.[30]

Friends of the Earth also sponsored Frances Moore Lappé's wildly popular *Diet for a Small Planet*, first published in 1971. It is not only how the food that we eat is produced, Lappé emphasized, but what we eat that has significant implications for sustainability and the environment. Lappé made clear that the meat-centered diet of the United States exacted a devastating toll on the environment. "I discovered that half of our harvested acreage went to feed livestock," she said. "It takes 16 pounds of grain and soybeans to produce just 1 pound of beef in the United States today."[31] Further, it took 2,500 gallons of water to produce just one pound of beef, and the pound of steak that provided some 500 food calories ultimately required 20,000 calories of fossil fuels to produce. Corn, the primary feed for livestock, annually used about 40 percent of fertilizers.[32] Lappé's book has sold over three million copies and influenced the way generations of Americans view their relationship to food and the environment.

Selling the Earth

Along with the growing popularity of green consumption was a rising wave of "green" advertising by producers seeking to associate themselves with environmentalism—even if their products sometimes provided no discernible environmental benefit. The rush of companies seeking to convince the public that they were environmentally sensitive was so great that it created something of a new genre for advertising. As a headline on the cover of an issue of the industry journal, *Advertising Age*, proclaimed, "Pollution—It's Today's Bonanza for Advertisers."[33] A study of *BusinessWeek, Newsweek*, and *Time* for the year 1970 found that in those magazines alone there were a total of 289 pages of environmental advertising by 27 different companies.[34]

The majority of the new environmental advertising attempted to boost a company's image by convincing the public that it cared about the environment. Although companies had long sought to tie products to images of nature and authenticity to appeal to consumers, the nature of that appeal changed with Earth Day. One study of advertising throughout the twentieth century found that "companies have begun to portray themselves as nature's caretakers: environmentally friendly, responsible, and caring."[35]

Green advertising often appeared contrived. Today's Girl sold "Ecology Panty Hose" with a knitted ecology symbol on the ankle.[36] L'Air du Temps promoted its perfume—"This public service message is brought to you from Paris, with love"—as a means to "Fight air pollution."[37] *Seventeen* magazine offered readers a 1970–1971 "Earth-Lovers Calendar" for $1.00, including a donation to the National Wildlife Federation. "Be an Earth Lover," the ad admonished, "5 cents out of your dollar proves you meant it!"[38] Mini-Mist instant-dry aerosol shampoo held forth the promise that users could "Live in the city without wearing it." "Pollution's not in style this year," the ad read, "but it happens to be all that's around. And if you think it's rough on you, pity the hair on your head. Thanks to all the buses, and trains, and factories and planes that leave tons of little nasties to float around and settle on your head, your hair starts getting dirty the minute you wash.... Why don't you use your head and give your hair a breather. Spray on Mini-Mist."[39] An ad for Maverick Jeans pictured four girls alongside a pond with a headline that read, "There's a whole new way of seeing. And there's a whole new way of looking, too. Natural."[40]

Capitol Records produced a green image ad with a specially produced album, *Listen in Good Health: Songs of Celebration and Decay*, sent to radio stations for the Earth Day broadcast of Capitol artists including the Steve Miller Band, the Beatles, and Pink Floyd. On the cover of the album was a black-and-white photograph of a person wearing a gas mask and headphones, very grainy so as to appear in a haze of pollution. In the album's liner notes Capitol stated, "We sell music. In recent months we've become increasingly aware of an obstacle. Our market may disappear in ten years or so. And our artist roster. Everyone else. Leaving only the Capitol Tower in a haze. The issue is survival. Ecological collapse is terminal; the earth won't wait long for the proper solution. Nor will it endure many more fruits of technological progress: oil rigs in the oceans; chemical sprays; detergents; internal combustion engines; rhetoric; all that has made life easier, and finally impossible."[41]

Viewing the record's liner notes it is easy to imagine Capitol's public relations department anticipating a cynical response to the album from disc jockeys across the country and attempting to quell such notions with a preemptive appeal. "A number of musicians have something to say about the issue," it continued. "But surely music is no more an answer than public statements of corporate concern. Words, alone, can expand the general feeling of despair of the illusion that something's being done. So as we use this space for a bit of rhetoric, we'll use additional space in the coming months to Attack the problem. Corporate activism. If such a thing's possible, we'll find out.... We're an institution, with all the implicit powers and obvious weaknesses. We join you all in the last good fight. Perhaps, for one last gasp, it will serve to bring us all together; for as long as it lasts. In the meantime, we'll continue to sell music."[42] Three months later Capitol affiliate Apple Records presented record-store owners with "a program designed to let you take full sales advantage of the 'awareness' phenomenon associated with ecology," which consisted of free fruit-and-vegetable "stickums" to give away with the sale of every Beatles record.[43] Clearly, the "last good fight" was on.

Corporations' desperate efforts to portray themselves as environmentalists can be explained by a 1970 survey commissioned by *Reader's Digest* that revealed, "the public primarily blames business for environmental pollution." It found that 72 percent of respondents placed "a great deal" of the responsibility for pollution on private industry, nearly half rated industry's attempts to curb pollution as "poor" or "very poor," and, what certainly got business's attention, 83 percent said that they were willing to give up certain products to help solve pollution problems.[44]

Business moved aggressively to defend itself and "correct" what it insisted was a "misunderstanding" by the public.[45] Both Budweiser and Schlitz brewing companies ran full-page newspaper ads asking readers to please not throw cans and bottles in rivers, lakes, or the countryside, even though bottling companies routinely did all that they could to block "bottle bills" in state legislatures that would mandate cash deposits on all bottles to help assure that they made their way back to the beverage company.[46] A Weyerhaeuser ad, picturing deer standing in front of trees, explained that the company clear-cut forests because animals like "the open, sunlit areas."[47] Most of the major oil companies ran series of environmental ads. Prominent in Texaco's campaign was a television spot that showed a mother and child playing in the surf with a voice-over that assured viewers, "This is our commitment that we will never willfully pollute the beaches of our world." Full-page magazine and newspaper ads for Texaco that pictured a vast stretch of sparkling ocean with a superimposed headline reading, "We swim in it too," made the same promise.[48] In April 1971, 200,000 gallons of diesel oil were spilled in Puget Sound at Texaco's Anacortes refinery; 17.6 miles of beach in and around Padilla Bay were contaminated and some 30,000 black geese threatened.[49] As Earth Day organizer Denis Hayes stated about the wave of green image ads: "There have been a record number of such ads...but the people of Gary and Detroit and Birmingham are still coughing."[50]

Many of the green image ads stressed how much money the companies were spending to combat pollution. In a full-page ad International Paper announced a "$101 Million, Four Year Plan to Combat Pollution."[51] But at the same time International Paper was running another ad, "The Story of the Disposable Environment," which pictured a futuristic world made of disposable paper, including paper diapers, sheets, pillowcases, furniture—"an entire paper world." It was, the company boasted, "the kind of fresh thinking we bring to every problem. Nice to know it's at your disposal, isn't it?"[52] Others advertisers just shamelessly misled. Lumber company Potlatch Forests, Inc., ran an ad in 1970 boasting of its efforts to stop water pollution from a pulp mill in Lewiston, Idaho. "It cost us a bundle but the Clearwater River still runs clear," read a headline accompanying a photograph of a pristine river. It was later discovered that the photo was taken upstream from the plant.[53]

Green image ads sometimes pleaded that if corporations did not always appear environmentally responsible, it was only because they were trying to do what was best for the economy and the American people. Such ads exploited a wedge issue between labor and environmentalists, at the same time furthering environmentalism's elitist reputation, by insisting that environmental improvements would necessarily cost jobs. Bethlehem Steel, in an ad with text surrounding a photograph of a half-dozen young people whose appearances—especially their earnest expressions—marked them as activists, attempted to turn the tables by taunting, "Our Challenge to the college generation. If you really want to do something about the problems you decry, join us." The ad described a scenario where company earnings were low and costs were high, "yet a deep sense of public responsibility urges you to spend many millions on air and water pollution abatement and beautification projects." But, "On the other hand the same investment in new or improved production facilities would produce income and provide jobs. How do you strike a balance?"[54] Environmentalists often did not help themselves and too often appeared to display indifference for workers. Yet research has shown, contrary to industry claims, environmental regulations have little, if any, impact on employment.[55]

In the midst of such advertising, environmentalism often appeared to be less a threat to corporate capitalism than it was a grand marketing opportunity. Through such ads corporations attempted to mediate environmental concerns for their own ends and in the process frame the discourse on the environment.[56] Environmentalism was just one more gimmick to be used to differentiate products in the mind-numbing sea of consumer goods.

Nevertheless, green ads emphasized and further legitimized the issue of the environment to large and varied audiences. Even ads aimed at selling could nevertheless serve to educate on environmental issues. When Friends of the Earth waged a boycott of furs, a series of ads for E. F. Timme & Son trumpeting the environmental attributes of "fake-fur" coats began appearing in the summer of 1970 in *Vogue, Esquire, Life, New York,* and the *New York Times Magazine,* featured the slogan "Fur coats shouldn't be made of fur." One two-page ad played on widely reported news that actress Gina Lollobrigida had bought a tiger-skin coat. It pictured a woman in what looked like a tiger coat with a headline reading, "Does the famous movie actress who recently bought a 10-skin tiger maxi-coat know that there are now only 590 tigers left?" In a full page of text the ad went on to state, "Our Bengal tiger fake is so convincing that we are sending the erring actress the coat shown at the right in the hope it will persuade her to publicly renounce her real one. So one part of our interest in animal conservation is business; we make fake fur and we want to sell a lot more of it. But the other aspect of our passion for conservation is far realer to us than mere dollar profit. Like you, we are guests on this planet. By continuing recklessly to strip it of its wild life, poison its air and water, and in general upset the natural balance of things, we are rapidly wearing out our welcome." The ad concluded apocalyptically, "And even if the penalty for destroying the animals weren't death for man—which it most surely is—we at Timme would hate to live in a world where the only animal skins around were ours." A similar ad ran after news reports of another famous person wearing real fur, which stated, "We're sending the Secretary of the Interior [Walter Hickel] a fake seal coat in the hope he'll stop wearing his real one."[57]

The Scandinavian Mink Association soon expressed alarm at reports of boycotts against certain furs, and furrier Jacques Kaplan urged the industry to take a stand before all furs were considered unfashionable. His company stopped offering coats made from endangered leopard, cheetah, tiger, and snow leopard. Simulated fur fabric first hit the market in 1954, and among its manufacturers were Union Carbide, Monsanto Chemical, DuPont, and American Cyanamid.[58] Rather than synthetics from a collection of the most despised chemical companies, some environmentalists urged those who had to wear fur to instead recycle old furs from secondhand clothing stores.

On the Meaning of Green Consumption

For critics, green advertising and the mainstreaming of the green market meant corporations had successfully seized control of the environmental movement and blunted its potential. Speaking in Paris in 1972, Herbert Marcuse complained, "Coming from the United States, I am a little uneasy discussing the ecological movement, which has already by and large been co-opted [there].... Today, there is hardly an ad which doesn't exhort you to 'save the environment.'"[59]
But in a climate where corporate hegemony had rendered government regulation insufficient and citizens largely powerless in the polity when their interests clashed with those of corporations, consumption proved more liberatory than traditional electoral politics. Emerging from the underground world of green consumption that had been growing since World War II, the expanded alternative green marketplace was the site where most citizens believed they could have the greatest and most meaningful direct influence on the environment. At the same time, earth-friendly goods and services functioned as signifiers of environmental concern that served to strengthen cultural identity in an imagined community. As one environmental writer stated about green consumers:

> They "are not waiting for laws to ban cars in cities or for compulsory controls to be instituted. They do not wait for new standards that will ban certain additives in foods, or will limit the amount of crud that may be shunted into air, water or land.... They are living the best kind of life possible in today's unhealthy surroundings. They are the activists who put theory into practice. They are the Thoreaus of the 1970s, only they don't retreat to a Walden Pond (there's an industrial park next to

the Pond anyway). They make a Walden Pond out of their home, their grounds, and their activities."[60]

Even Marcuse acknowledged that something significant was transpiring. "Obviously, this is a co-optation, but it is also a progressive element because," he correctly observed, "in the course of the co-optation, a certain number of needs and aspirations are beginning to be expressed within the heart of capitalism and change is taking place in people's behavior, experience, and attitudes toward their work. Economic and technical demands are transcended in a movement of revolt which challenges the very mode of production and model of consumption."[61] The ironic postwar dreams of thinkers like conservationist Howard Zahniser and Beat poet Gregory Corso that the Bomb might inspire humans to live more thoughtfully on earth had, over the course of the following 25 years, in some measure come true.

Later Days

Earth Day was never declared an official holiday, but since 1970 it has been observed annually, in some fashion, in most cities and schools across the nation. On the twentieth anniversary of the original teach-in, after the nation had just survived what environmentalists considered the dual disasters of eight years of President Ronald Reagan and the Exxon *Valdez* tanker accident that dumped some 10.8 million gallons of oil into Prince William Sound, Alaska, in 1989, Denis Hayes was summoned by leaders of some of the foremost national environmental organizations to again head a major event: "Earth Day 1990." By then it was an international happening, spread across 140 different countries with events attended by an estimated 200 million people, focused on global issues like greenhouse gases, chlorofluorocarbons, and the expanding hole in the earth's ozone layer.[62]

Earth Day 1990 made little push for political solutions to these environmental concerns, and the celebration lacked the broad-based themes and grassroots, freewheeling atmosphere of the original event. For many of the environmentally minded in the United States the intervening 20 years had confirmed that government could not be counted on to effectively regulate corporations and protect the environment, and that the only realistic recourse for citizens was their own actions as consumers. In Europe, where parliamentary systems and stronger traditions of social welfare permitted Green Parties to build coalitions and gain increasing power, political solutions gained greater traction.[63] But in the United States "there were just a whole lot of things that couldn't be solved by law," concluded Hayes, who had steered Environmental Action, Inc. in the direction of a Washington-based political action and lobbying group after Earth Day in 1970.[64]

After years of observing the mixed record of environmental political action, Hayes and others began placing even greater emphasis on consumer behavior to effect change.[65] "We should encourage environmental shoppers to be mindful of their values when they go shopping," he declared.[66] In an effort to assist those shoppers in determining which products were truly environmentally friendly he even tried, unsuccessfully, to get a Green Seal program up and running that would have given a seal of approval to products that independent research demonstrated were best for the environment.[67]

By 1990 it was clear that the dream of changing the world through green consumption that first emerged in the days after World War II, and that Earth Day had taken mainstream, was institutionalized within American culture and was the primary expression of environmentalism in the lives of most citizens. American consumers, already spending $1.8 billion on natural foods in 1979, spent $3.5 billion in 1988 at some 7,253 natural-food stores, along with growing numbers of supermarkets stocking organics.[68] Marketing surveys in 1990 found that 82 percent of respondents had "changed their purchasing decisions based on concerns about the environment," 76 percent would boycott the manufacturers of polluting products, and 56 percent had refused to buy a product during the preceding year due to environmental concerns.[69] In contrast, only some 46 percent of those surveyed by Gallup reported that they had given money to environmental organizations.[70]

The best-selling environmental books of the era told the story. There was *The Green Lifestyle Handbook: 1001 Ways to Heal the Earth*, which listed which products to buy and which to avoid; *Save Our Planet: 750 Everyday Ways You Can Help Clean Up the Earth*, which provided tips for home, office, and the supermarket; the best-selling *50 Simple Things You Can Do to Save the Earth*; the popular *Heloise: Hints for a Healthy Planet*; *How to Make the World a Better Place: A Guide to Doing Good*, which gave advice on "What you can do today to prevent everything from acid rain to the 'greenhouse effect' while you shop, bathe, travel to work..."; *The Green Consumer*, a buying guide to environmentally friendly products, which promised: "By choosing carefully, you can have a positive impact on the environment without significantly compromising your way of life. That's what being a Green Consumer is all about"; and *Shopping for a Better World: A Quick and Easy Guide to Socially Responsible Supermarket Shopping*. Taking Frances Moore Lappé's Earth Day–era classic, *Diet for a Small Planet*, a step further, David Steinman's *Diet for a Poisoned Planet: How to Choose Safe Foods for You and Your Family* told which foods should be avoided due to high concentrations of toxic chemicals.[71]

The entire emphasis was enormously controversial, with critics arguing that the focus on personal responsibility and shopping obscured the larger issue of corporate power and the actions of companies that posed the real threat to the environment. The message put forth on Earth Day 1990 suggested that corporations, government, and citizens are "all in this together," complained Gary Cohen, executive director of the National Toxics Campaign Fund, with each one as responsible as the other. "It allowed everyone to call themselves environmentalists," he protested, "and encouraged individual consumer solutions to large-scale corporate problems," as if the answer to the environmental crisis was to "just become better consumers."[72] Corporations seized the opportunity to sell both themselves and their products as "environmental" to consumers who sought to bask in the warm glow of environmentalism.[73]

This analysis is certainly not without merit. During Earth Day 1990 dozens of corporations not generally known for their environmental sensibilities, including Domino's Pizza, Union Carbide, DuPont, Westinghouse, and Champion International Paper, clamored to sponsor a variety of events designed to enhance their environmental reputations and credibility. Glynn Young, public-affairs director for Monsanto Chemical Company, observed, "There's a mad scramble for many companies to project an 'I am greener than thou' attitude. The fact of the matter is that Earth Day is the best way to get news coverage."[74] *Time* magazine called Earth Day 1990 a "marketing monster."[75] And investigations also showed that an increasing share of funding for mainstream environmental organizations, like the Sierra Club and Wilderness Society, was coming from corporations like ARCO, British Petroleum, and Waste Management, and that 23 directors and council members for leading mainstream environmental groups came from 19 corporations listed on the National Wildlife Federation's list of the 500 worst industrial polluters.[76] The temptation is simply to declare that it was yet one more example of business blunting the revolutionary potential of a movement by co-opting it and selling it back to citizens in a safe and sanitized version that poses no real threat to the status quo.

However, it appeared most Americans were sophisticated enough to see it for what it was.[77] A Gallup poll found that 73 percent of those surveyed believed the corporations supporting Earth Day 1990 were actually more concerned with good public relations than they were with making the world a safer, cleaner place.[78] Further, the involvement of the ever-growing community of green consumers in daily practices of environmental consumption rendered it continually sensitive to and involved with environmental issues. As a result, it increasingly demanded that corporations make the very type of environmental changes whose scale could render considerable positive environmental impacts. Although corporations surely would not continue to spend money on marketing designed to enhance their environmental reputations—often called "greenwashing"—if their research did not reveal they were reaping benefits, at the same time consumers are not mere dupes. On the day after Earth Day 1990, several hundred demonstrators from various grassroots groups gathered on Wall Street for a day-long protest trying to block the New York Stock Exchange's entrances, holding large banners with messages including, "What's to blame for pollution, racism, and war? Wall Street profits!" and chanting, "Corporate greed has got to go!"[79]

Killing Environmentalism with Kindness

Recent years have seen a growing push to ensure that businesses not only sell environmentally friendly products but that they also operate in environmentally friendly ways. Again, a bevy of books tells the story: *Green to Gold: How Smart Companies Use Environmental Strategy to Innovate, Create Value, and Build Competitive Advantage*; *Natural Capitalism: Creating the Next Industrial Revolution*; *Harvard Business Review on Green Business Strategy*; *The Natural Step For Business: Wealth, Ecology, and the Evolutionary Corporation*; *The Sustainable MBA: The Manager's Guide to Green Business*; *Strategies for the Green Economy: Opportunities and Challenges in the New World of Business*; and *Sustainable Value: How the World's Leading Companies Are Doing Well by Doing Good*, to name just a few. All build on the work of early pioneers in the field like Paul Hawken, whose 1993 book, *The Ecology of Commerce: A Declaration of Sustainability*, set the tone for a turn-of-the-century exploration of how businesses could change their practices to protect the environment while still remaining profitable. It is a growing genre that typically promises companies advice on how to reduce their environmental impact while increasing their profits.[80]

Today nearly all major corporations are involved in some form of green initiative to improve both their environmental practices and public image. Perhaps none of these changes loom larger than the efforts of retail behemoth Wal-Mart to go green. In 2004, troubled by growing middle-class perceptions that its policies damaged employees, communities, and the environment—not to mention declining prices for its stock—Wal-Mart sought the advice of management consultants McKinsey & Company. McKinsey found that 2 percent to 8 percent of Wal-Mart shoppers had stopped shopping at the store due to "negative press they have heard." When McKinsey advised Wal-Mart to "take public leadership on broader societal issues," the company began working with activists to improve its environmental record. Its stores started stocking the type of green products that were formerly found mostly in expensive alternative shops. Because of its purchasing might, it also forced changes on its suppliers, like General Electric and Procter & Gamble, which had to conform to Wal-Mart's new environmental wishes in order to continue to sell their goods in Wal-Mart stores. Shoppers could now find organic foods alongside other foods in Wal-Mart stores, fluorescent light bulbs that used 75 percent less energy than traditional bulbs and lasted longer, reduced packaging on many goods—including prescription drugs with 50 percent less packaging—and concentrated laundry detergent using 50 percent less water and packaging. In 2006 Wal-Mart moved to purchase all its wild-caught seafood from fisheries certified as sustainable. By 2007 one research firm labeled Wal-Mart the nation's largest organic retailer."[81]

Whatever their motivation, their massive scale means that when corporations do take environmental action the effects can be dramatic. For example, when Royal Dutch Shell was pushed to reduce its emission of greenhouse gases at its plants to a level 25 percent below the 1990 levels, it achieved the equivalent of every car owner in New England not turning on the engine for five years. When Boeing switched to energy-efficient lighting it eliminated enough carbon dioxide to equal 500,000 people changing an incandescent bulb to a compact fluorescent.[82]

It is tempting to conclude that the long-hoped-for corporate reforms dreamed about by the likes of William Vogt, Fairfield Osborn, and Aldo Leopold have finally come to pass. Although such initiatives give the appearance that corporations have placed caring for the environment at the center of their raison d'être, the situation is typically far more complicated. As one corporate sustainability executive admitted when discussing the incongruity of highly publicized but selective corporate green initiatives that serve to mask the reality of a company's increasing aggregate environmental impact, "I've succeeded in doing lots of sexy projects yet utterly failed in what I set out to do.... How do you really green your company? It's almost f_____ impossible."[83] Companies often compartmentalize their operations to emphasize environmental aspects of their business, even while they continue to carry on many other practices that evidence little, if any, environmental concern. To paint itself green General Electric, the company that made a 197 mile stretch of the Hudson River in New York an EPA Superfund site by dumping an estimated 1.7 million pounds of polychlorinated biphenyls (PCBs) into its waters, spent the lion's share of its 2007 advertising budget promoting its "Ecomagination" line of products, even though they constituted only about eight percent of the corporation's sales. With their explosion in popularity, natural and organic foods, clothing, and other environmentally focused products became highly profitable, and giant corporations moved to dominate the green marketplace. Stonyfield Farms Organic Yogurt was acquired by French food-products multinational Groupe Danone. Cascadian Farms, begun in Rockport, Washington in 1971 to supply organic food to a hippie collective in Bellingham, was bought by giant food conglomerate General Mills in 2000, joining its line of products that includes Hamburger Helper and Trix cereal. Ben & Jerry's Ice Cream, started in Vermont in 1978 with an alternative business model and lefty politics, was purchased by Anglo-Dutch conglomerate Unilever; it joined Unilever's brands, which include Slimfast and I Can't Believe It's Not Butter! The acquisition led even Vermont's Governor Howard Dean to lament, "It would be a shame if [Ben & Jerry's] were sucked into the corporate homogenization that's taking over the planet."[84]

Corporations give the appearance of environmental care, which diminishes the salience of environmentalism under the impression that citizens have little left to fear. While many companies have been willing to make at least some concessions to soothe society's growing environmental concerns, they have not moved to change their organizational structure or the outsized power they possess in the American polity—two of the original goals of postwar environmentalists that grew during the sixties. On the contrary, easing public suspicions and concerns by giving the appearance of environmentalism may even help corporations to maintain and bolster their cultural and political hegemony. But, in reality, except for actions that might earn companies a good return on investment, green initiatives are often scrapped for investments that are more profitable.[85]

The dream of altering the outsized power of corporate capitalism by means of alternative consumption has in some ways lost touch with the vision of its early proponents, as green consumption has itself become big business. Many small companies with alternative business practices that began in the optimistic wave of green consumerism during the postwar era and following Earth Day in 1970, seeking not only to protect the environment but to redefine business against the prevailing corporate model, have been swallowed up by the very corporate behemoths that motivated them to do business a different way in the first place. On the retail end, although some have managed to remain, many of the alternative "natural" co-ops and small markets that began in the fifties and expanded through the seventies have gone out of business. Some were simply victims of poor management, but many others were bought out, could not compete with corporate giants like Whole Foods, or lost out to conventional supermarkets and Wal-Marts with expanding natural-foods sections.

In the case of Wal-Mart, while its nods to environmentalism may have lured some middle-class shoppers to its stores, they did nothing to change the relatively low wages that the corporation paid its employees, or the way that it denied many of them health insurance. "There is not the ability to change as much in many of those areas as we can change in this area of environmental sustainability," Wal-Mart CEO H. Lee Scott insisted. Scott did not explain how a company with a net profit of $10.3 billion the previous year, earning an astonishing $20,000 per minute around the clock, lacked the ability to pay higher wages or provide health insurance to more of its employees. What was clear is that the money the company planned to invest in environmental initiatives was significantly less than it would have cost to provide either of those benefits for its workers, yet it hoped that its well-publicized green initiative might win it even greater favor from some in the middle class.[86] It was the type of program that old-school conservationists could embrace, but it was a far cry from the broader vision of environmentalists who embraced environmentalism as a means for social and cultural change as well.

While Whole Foods has grown to become, arguably, the preeminent green retailer in the United States (even if Wal-Mart is the largest), its corporate philosophy often appears to have much in common with the most ardent proponents of neoliberal corporate capitalism. At a time when American workers have been steadily losing ground in the United States, Whole Foods has opposed labor unions, and its founder and CEO is an outspoken opponent of universal healthcare.[87]

On the producer side, efforts to act with greater environmental responsibility can be seen in the growing number of acres devoted to organic production, recycled materials used in products and packaging, and production techniques that limit waste while conserving energy. Advertising giant J. Walter Thompson estimated that some 520 new green products, constituting 9 percent of all new goods, were introduced to the marketplace in 1990 alone.[88] By 2003, the organic-food industry itself accounted for some $11 billion and had seen double-digit annual growth for over a decade.[89]

However, in many other respects the dream of transforming corporate culture also seems threatened. Even those companies that sought to avoid corporate homogenization or, with lingering sixties optimism, actually transform mainstream corporate culture often found themselves frustrated in their efforts. White Wave, an organic tofu company founded by Buddhist Steve Demos in Boulder, Colorado in 1978 that expanded exponentially with its successful Silk brand fresh organic soy milk introduced in 1996, teamed with dairy giant Dean Foods, whose brands included Land O' Lakes and Borden, in 1998 to expand production and distribution. It sold out to Dean entirely in 2002, but Demos was kept on as head of White Wave, and he planned to spread its alternative business values to the larger corporate culture of Dean Foods. "That was the entire mission going all the way back to why we all got in business—to influence the way the world works," said Demos. "Not only the way we eat, but the way we derive our livelihoods and exist in our culture. We'll end up with a billion-dollar consumer packaged goods company based on social responsibility!" he optimistically predicted. Instead, less than three years later Dean Foods pushed him and his alternative business values out of the corporation. The mission to change corporate culture was, in the words of Demos, "shot in the head."[90]

As organics have grown into big business, many of the "organic" and "natural" crop and animal practices have become nearly indistinguishable from the factory-farming techniques the movement once sought to combat. Of the 1,533 registered organic growers in 1997, only two were organized as collectives or cooperatives.[91] The Horizon Corporation, acquired by Dean Foods in 2003, controls some 70 percent of the retail organic milk market, ultra-pasteurizing the milk at high temperatures to permit it to be trucked long distances and improve its shelf life, but at the same time destroying its enzymes and many vitamins. The "organic" dairy cattle are confined in dirt feedlots, milked three times daily, and never roam free in a pasture. Most organic produce comes from giant industrial farms, distinguished from neighboring conventional farms only by the fact that no chemicals are sprayed on the crops.[92] "Organic" chickens and hens producing "free-range" eggs spend their days indoors in the same grim warehouses that J. I. Rodale described as "poultry as big business" back in 1945, differing from their conventional counterparts primarily in that their feed contains no hormones or antibiotics. Small doors on either end of the factory are opened after the chickens are five weeks old, theoretically permitting them to go "free range" on narrow strips of grass outside, but by then the outdoors is a foreign environment and they are typically slaughtered at seven weeks.[93] Thus, while the corporatization of natural and organic products has meant, significantly, many more acres of organic farm fields and thus less chemicals in the environment than there would be otherwise, the conduct of "Organic Inc." bears little resemblance to the pastoral ideal and alternative business models embraced by its early champions, even if consumers are still reminded of those notions in the advertising of many "natural" products.

Nowhere is this more evident than with the Department of Agriculture's Organic Standards, which became law in 2001 and which include, thanks to intense corporate lobbying efforts of large food processors who desired a piece of the growing and profitable organic market, a list of additives and synthetics that may be added to processed "organic" foods. In 2002 the list included 77 nonorganic materials. Within a decade the corporate-dominated USDA National Organics Standards Board expanded the list to over 250 nonorganic substances that could be used in "organic" foods. "Organic" TV dinners had arrived. The Board also declared that chickens producing organic eggs need only be given two square feet of living space.[94] The giant food processors that James Rorty and Philip Norman railed against in 1947, when they looked to organics to provide the antidote for the corporate poisoning and malnourishing of American consumers, leveraged their outsized power in the American polity to have their artificial and synthetic processes receive official government certification as "organic." Big business was drawn to organics for the reason that J. I. Rodale foresaw some 60 years earlier when he stated: "A substantial premium will be paid for high quality produces such as those raised by organic methods."[95]

Similarly unsettling for those who hoped green consumption would change the world is evidence that it has instead changed only the wealthy regions of the planet, often at the expense of less fortunate locales. As green consumers have pushed for a better environment many of the United States's environmental problems have simply been outsourced to other countries. It was a trend already disturbingly evident shortly after the first Earth Day, when corporations sought the approval of American consumers by assuring them that they were polluting other countries in order to make air cleaner in the United States. Texaco ran a full-page magazine ad in 1972 that was a photomontage of scenes from a tropical island, including native peoples in traditional dress, breathtaking landscapes, tropical sunsets, and a bikini-clad woman. Above the pictures a headline read, "We're not here for a vacation. We're here to help clean up America's air." Text beneath the picture explained, "The island of Trinidad is a Caribbean paradise to many. But to Texaco it's the place to do an important job. There, as part of our huge refinery, we're building a new plant of advanced design. Its purpose—to remove even more sulfur from fuel oil before it's delivered to American industry... to protect our urban environment. And the people who live in it." The ad said nothing about what it would do for the people and environment of Trinidad.[96]

American industries fled to other countries not only to take advantage of cheaper labor but also to trim costs and complications by polluting more freely. Many built factories, called *maquiladoras*, just across the border in Mexico, an area that fast became one of the most polluted regions in North America. By the early 1990s there were nearly 700 in Tijuana alone. "They have come here from all over, saying they are going to invest, that they are going to help us," said Maurilio Sanchez, a community organizer in Ejido Chilpancingo, just below a big *maquiladora* park on the city's outskirts. "But when it comes to complying with the ecological laws, they say they cannot speak Spanish."[97] In the border region between Brownsville, Texas and the Mexican city of Matamoros babies were born with incomplete brains and other serious neurological defects at an astonishing rate three to four times the Mexican national average.[98]

The situation was so bad that a Federal District Court judge ruled in 1993 that an Environmental Impact Statement should be required before the North American Free Trade Agreement (NAFTA) was considered for Senate approval. President Bill Clinton, however, was determined to get the free-trade agreement put together by his predecessor George H. W. Bush and a group of corporate lobbyists approved, and he successfully appealed the order.[99] During the decade following NAFTA there was a large increase in the number of new factories that opened in Mexico near the border, yet Mexico's spending on enforcement of environmental laws and the number of industrial inspections both fell by 45 percent.[100] That lack of enforcement, according to a study of the impact of a decade of NAFTA on the environment of Mexico, found that "many environmental problems worsened significantly." The environmental costs of expanded industrial development were, according to the Mexican government's own analysis, far greater than the value of economic growth, averaging 10 percent of gross domestic product per annum (compared to an annual rise in economic growth of only 2.6 percent).[101] No country, though, experienced a more dramatic increase in manufacturing by and for United States companies than China. By 2007 pollution there was so bad that there was concern for the health of athletes who would compete in the 2008 Olympics in Beijing.[102]

Although the postwar spirit uniting traditional conservation and the broader environmental concerns of pollution and chemicals, not to mention corporate hegemony, have continued to inform American culture, it has often been a strained union at best. For some, the traditional issues of conservation never really melded into a broader environmental concern over chemicals, corporations, and pollution. And people who endeavor to consume organic foods do not necessarily support broader environmental protection. They may simply be hoping for better health or taste. When *Consumer Reports* did a report on organics in February 2006 entitled "When Buying Organic Pays (and Doesn't)," it focused on which foods provided the best health benefits when purchased organically, and not on the environment.[103] Even so, it was an acknowledgment that a healthier environment provides healthier foods. Recent research has supported the claims of organic pioneers like J. I. Rodale that organic food is more nutritious. A four-year study at Newcastle University funded by the European Union found that organic wheat, tomatoes, potatoes, cabbage, onions, and lettuce had between 20 percent and 40 percent more nutrients than their conventional counterparts. Antioxidant levels in organic milk were between 50 percent and 80 percent higher than in nonorganic milk. As the project coordinator Carlo Leifert summed up the results, "We have shown there are more of certain nutritionally desirable compounds and less of the baddies in organic foods."[104]

Finally, in many ways environmentalism practiced through green consumption is limited to those who possess the economic means to shield themselves and their loved ones from some of the unpleasant realities and dangers that accompany modern life.[105] If green consumption has been revolutionary, because it is consumer-driven it has been a revolution whose benefits have been disproportionately enjoyed by those who are able to afford it. Many earth-friendly products are more expensive, sometimes considerably so, than their less green alternatives. "It's a crime that only the rich and the better educated have access to natural and organic foods," said actress and activist Jane Fonda in 1970. By then, Fonda had been eating organic foods for 15 years.[106] Although many local grassroots groups have formed to confront community environmental problems and issues like environmental justice, as a whole environmentalism still suffers from its association with elitism that has accompanied it since its earliest days in conservation. As Hayes conceded in 1990, "The environmental movement has not diversified. Poor people and people of color are downwind from most toxic incinerators. They are down-gradient from most hazardous waste dumps. They are in the fields when the pesticides are sprayed. They work in factory jobs having the highest exposure to dangerous substances. Yet poor people are not well-represented in our ranks."[107] If green consumption is such an imperfect response to environmental problems, does it serve any meaningful purpose?

Conclusion

"The Clock is Ticking"

Green consumption is sometimes criticized as a movement by the white middle class to secure better consumption for its own at the expense of more difficult, yet potentially far more meaningful, change for all that might be gained through electoral politics and mass political activism on the streets. "After all," say philosophers Joseph Heath and Andrew Potter, "the traditional work of political organizing is extremely demanding and tedious. Politics, in a democracy, necessarily requires bringing enormous numbers of people on board. This creates a lot of unappealing work—licking envelopes, writing letters, lobbying politicians, and the like.... Cultural politics, by contrast, is significantly more fun." In this critique, the left in the United States abandoned the hard work of politics at the end of the sixties, permitting the right to swoop in and take control of a largely abandoned political landscape. Heath and Potter have characterized green consumption as "individualized, and basically apolitical environmentalism" and "a smug and self-indulgent conception of what constitutes meaningful political action."[1] It is a message that resonates with many Americans because it appears to provide an explanation for a phenomenon that has claimed a growing space in society over the past four decades: The reason the United States cannot achieve fundamental economic and political change is because citizens are too caught up in themselves to organize or take to the streets in pursuit of community and genuine change. In essence, it is the fault of individuals.

But viewing the situation through that analytic lens blurs the harsh realities and legacies of a corporate capitalist state that appears so powerful and impenetrable that it renders significant progressive change through traditional political channels highly improbable, if not impossible. For many on the left that was the real lesson of the sixties. Taking to the streets may work to bring about some social change but it will do little, if anything, to alter economic and political power. The corporate capitalist state will still be standing, unmoved, unharmed, and largely unchanged. Is it really a mystery why Americans on the left have instead opted for personal politics, attempting to forge some sort of meaningful existence within the corporate capitalist state? During the Cold War Americans heard about citizens in the Soviet Union who coveted Beatles records and blue jeans. Although it might have been a desperate and limited response, US citizens readily comprehended that type of counterculture consumption as an understandable reaction to an oppressive state that Soviet citizens felt largely powerless to change. Counterculture green consumption might appear desperate and limited, but in the context of its time and place it is nevertheless understandable.

For those who truly believed the notion that political revolution would naturally follow an oppositional counterculture, critiques of green consumption may have a point. But to say that the left abandoned the more difficult work of politics assumes that traditional politics might have turned the tide. In a political system that permits corporations extraordinary power, and in which the political establishment aligns itself with corporate interests, the New Left never stood much of a chance.

Focusing on the failure of mainstream environmentalism and green consumption to fundamentally transform the structures of power in the United States ignores the central reality that this book makes clear. From the earliest days following World War II, in the shadow of the Bomb, those who have advocated green consumption have done so with little real hope that the existing hegemony of corporations and their hold over the government that was supposed to regulate them was going to fundamentally change. The trend that thinkers like William Vogt, Fairfield Osborn, J. I. Rodale, James Rorty, William Longgood, and others spotted in the postwar era of growing corporate power has only intensified, as has its hold on the nation's polity. Following Earth Day 1990, for example, "polluting industries" gave $89 million to congressional campaigns between 1991 and 1996 in order to protect $19 billion in government subsidies.[2] Given that level of return on investment, the symbiotic relationship between corporate capitalism and American politics will not change.

During the sixties the New Left took a brief shot at changing the structural power of the United States, but even most of those passionately committed political activists soon grew disillusioned and instead sought a space within the culture where they could exist, as much as possible, on their own terms—where they could be in the city but not of the city, in the mainstream culture but not of the mainstream culture.[3] Corporate culture dominates American life, even as many in its middle-class foundation appear forever uneasy with it and, as a result, forever uncomfortable within their own skin. As Jonathan Richman sang in "City vs. Country":

> I want to live close to downtown to be near my friends
> I want to be close to them,

> And still be out by the trees and the wind
> Havin' both will be hard to find I'm sure,
> But then ain't that the way of the world,
> I want the city but I want the country too.[4]

Some environmentalists were drawn to the cause because it promised an unpolluted alternative to the mainstream culture they disdained. For them, maintaining and preserving that purity was an essential, almost religious undertaking. Any breaching of purity was abhorrent. For most, however, environmentalism was not an either/or proposition. Rather, it was a site of practical compromises, where people sought to balance their ideals with the realities of their everyday lives. The fact that Americans in the postwar era participated in consumer culture does not mean that all did so without uneasiness and misgivings. The culture of corporate capitalism became amorphous and, short of removing oneself from society like those who took to communes, difficult to avoid. Environmentalism urged a more conscientious consumer culture, one that sought to reconnect citizens to the realities of the processes of production that producers wished to keep hidden beneath the shiny surfaces of the disembodied finished goods that seemed to appear, as if by magic, in the marketplace. Environmentalists dreamed of a more thoughtful United States.

In a society where government insists that agricultural chemicals and food additives, and more recently genetically modified crops and animals, are perfectly safe for humans and the environment, and that nonorganic foods are just as nutritious as organic, every purchase of natural, organic products by citizens is an act of resistance—a statement by those citizens that they have a fundamental distrust in their government's willingness and ability to look out for the well-being of its citizens and environment in the face of corporate power and influence. The continuing growth of mainstream environmentalism expressed in green consumption in the United States since World War II—a phenomenon that has grown to occupy a cultural space so large that it is now difficult to identify a consumer purchase, whether large or small, that does not have a "green" alternative—reflects not only an environmental crisis but a growing crisis in democracy.

Given all the doubts regarding the meaning and significance of mainstream environmentalism and the green consumer culture, it is important to recognize that the movement has never been static. Instead, it often appears more like an elaborate dance between consumers and producers, with each struggling to take the lead (and government playing the role of the chaperone that producers have paid to look the other way). Green consumerism has made "sustainable" part of the popular discourse. And as green consumption has trended toward

"Green, Inc.," it has met its own resistance from green consumer activists. One response has been to reach beyond simple organics to meet the requirements of the more demanding "biodynamics" of Rudolf Steiner that James Rorty and Philip Norman supported some sixty years ago.[5]

In addition, a growing "buy local" countertrend—"community supported agriculture"—has emerged in defiant response. Local farmers markets have become fixtures in many cities and towns. Union Square in New York City, site of the most noted Earth Day gathering in 1970, has since 1976 been the location of a growing "Green Market," one of 44 in the city, where 164 farms ranging in size from four acres to six hundred sell to over 250,000 customers each week. Across the nation growing numbers of citizens belong to local subscription "farm share" clubs, where they buy "shares" of the produce of local farmers and receive a box each week during the growing season. Many chefs, citing the better taste and quality of local foods in addition to their environmental benefits, have been leaders in the local trend and in the process have enhanced the status of their restaurants by prominently featuring local farmers, fishermen, winemakers, and artisanal food producers.[6] In an initiative by the First Lady, in 2009 President Barack Obama and his family announced that they were planting an organic garden in the White House yard to provide produce for family and state meals.[7]

The "local" trend means less transportation and pollution and more consumers who get to know their growers and feel greater assurance about the food they are eating and how it is produced, especially since corporations continue to pressure the Department of Agriculture to weaken what are already, in the estimation of many, inadequate organic standards. It provides support for locally grown produce and, usually, smaller and less industrialized farms. It is a movement that is presently, not unlike Aldo Leopold's characterization of organics in 1949, "something of a cult." However, there are indications that it is poised to become an ever larger and more influential presence in mainstream American culture. A Department of Agriculture survey found that local food economies were a fast-growing part of the economic landscape, particularly on the West Coast and in the Northeast, accounting for some $4.8 billion in sales in 2008. From 1992 to 2007 the number of farms selling produce directly to consumers increased by 58 percent, and sales more than doubled.[8] As community studies scholar Julie Guthman has stated about the transformative power of this trend, "the *reworking of nature* that occurs on such farms, [is] clearly driven by the decommodification of food *and* land, which opens up an economic space where social divisions can be eroded rather than accentuated. This is an alternative agriculture of substance, because it provides an alternative not only to production inputs and methods but to the entire system of industrial farming."[9] But even the movement toward local food economies is hampered by the alliance of corporations and government. USDA policies, in the service of corporate agribusiness, often constitute significant barriers that make expanded local fruit and vegetable production more difficult.[10]

Like organics before it, there are hints that local, too, may soon be corporatized. In a move that may be motivated more by rising diesel fuel costs than environmental concerns, Wal-Mart has moved to purchase at least 9 percent of its fruits and vegetables locally (within 450 miles by its definition) by 2015.[11] Former executives from fast-food giant McDonald's have started a restaurant chain, Lyfe Kitchens, which promises local, organic ingredients in its planned "hundreds" of restaurants to open in the next five years. With the scale of these massive corporate enterprises, and the larger profit margins to be had with local food, it is easy to imagine that it may not be long before local becomes corporate industrial. As *Wired* magazine stated in a profile of Lyfe Kitchens (an acronym for "love your food everyday"): "The former Golden Archers hope to transform the way the world produces organic ingredients, doing for responsibly grown meat and veggies what McDonald's did for factory-farmed beef."[12] The elaborate dance between corporate capitalism and environmentalism continues.

Another "local" green consumer trend gaining momentum in the early twenty-first century is "cohousing," first begun in Denmark and in over 100 intentional communities across the United States. To avoid many of the sources of failure of previous communal living efforts, cohousing usually results after a minimum of two years of preparation when potential residents typically find suitable land and hire both an architect to design houses for each family in the community and a developer to build them. Potential residents take part in a "structured learning process" in an effort to make sure they are suitably minded and motivated for the cohousing life. Like the sixties-era communes that preceded them, cohousing communities vary depending on the whims of their residents, but nearly all have two major goals at the center of their mission: to build and nurture community and practice environmentally sustainable living. Houses are built for energy efficiency, of nontoxic materials, and residents share yards, rides to work and school, food from community organic gardens, and common houses with laundry rooms and meeting areas where meals are often shared. At EcoVillage in Ithaca, New York, built in the mid-1990s as a response to "a world that is inherently flawed," there are two large certified organic gardens worked by the 160 residents who live there and hens that produce a dozen or more eggs a day. "It seems like a better way to live," concluded one observer.[13]

Even sixties SDS and New Left leader Todd Gitlin recently conceded that activism through consumption is not without its merits. "It is in the spirit of this age that activists would rather vote with their dollars, whether for hybrid cars, fair-labor sneakers, or tribal-made goods, than put their bodies on the line," he observed. "They take initiative with their purchases; they seduce, humiliate, and otherwise pressure institutions into change. They promote incentives. They create markets." And "buying green does more than make the buyers feel good," Gitlin acknowledges. "It demonstrates how much better things could be if governments stopped subsidizing the worst forms of production and got serious about promoting the best." Nevertheless, in the end he laments that such efforts are "limited in their effects."[14]

But however limited the effects may be, from the earliest days after the environmental and psychic shock waves of the Bomb to the counterculture days of the sixties and up through the present, the alternative of green consumption has existed as a sanctuary within the corporate capitalist state where citizens no longer trust their government to place their interests before the interests of corporations. Those who criticize environmentalism for failing to revolutionize the structures of American power do so while ignoring the fundamental reality that since its earliest conception green consumption viewed the dominance of corporate power in the American polity as a fait accompli. Indeed, that reality inspired the movement in the first place.

Further, critics ignore the history that many of the citizens who continued to believe that political means could alter the structures of American power were finally disabused of the notion when 12 days after Earth Day, on May 4, 1970, at a demonstration at Kent State University in Ohio, the government showed itself capable of turning its guns on its own people and killing them. For those who failed to get the message, it was repeated 10 days later at Jackson State College in Jackson, Mississippi. In the tumult that followed, many colleges simply closed early that spring. And when students who had dreamed of political change returned to campuses in the fall, often the spirit of political rebellion no longer accompanied them. In December, the San Francisco band Quicksilver Messenger Service released its popular album *What About Me?* The title track assailed corporate capitalism for rendering the planet a dangerous environment: "You poisoned my sweet water / You cut down my green trees / The food you fed my children / Was the cause of their disease. / My world is slowly fallin' down / And the air's not good to breathe. / And those of us who care enough / We have to do something." But what could concerned citizens do when their government was in league with the system that was causing their distress? "And I feel the future trembling, / As the word is passed around. / 'If you stand up for what you do believe, / Be prepared to be shot down.'"[15] Like dogs trained from birth to limit themselves to the borders of their owner's yard for fear of the consequences if they dared disobey, citizens were conscious of the boundaries of their political culture without needing to think. They dared not stray.

If green consumption was limited in its ability to effect change, so too, in the estimation of many, were more traditional forms of politics. In 1971 the Who scored a hit by singing about those limits in lyrics that resonated with a weary generation: "There's nothing in the street / Looks any different to me / And the slogans are replaced, by-the-bye / And the parting on the left / Is now the parting on the right / And the beards have all grown longer overnight."[16] No matter which political party was in power, the feeling went, the real site of power—corporate capitalism—would not budge. As the Who's Pete Townshend famously phrased it, "Meet the new boss, same as the old boss." Struggles for social liberation—which posed little threat to corporate profits and hegemony—might, after predictable and unfortunate lengthy struggle, prove somewhat fruitful. Struggles for environmental and economic liberation—which posed a threat to corporate profits and hegemony—would, after predictable and unfortunate lengthy struggle, prove less than fruitful.

Sons of Bitches (Reprise)

In January 2007, the *Bulletin of Atomic Scientists* moved its doomsday clock forward from seven minutes to five minutes to midnight. The scientists announced that for the first time, and henceforth, in addition to nuclear peril the clock would also reflect the risk of environmental doom. "Global warming poses a dire threat to human civilization that is second only to nuclear weapons," the board of the *Bulletin* stated in its official explanation.[17] Thus, 60 years after their first doomsday clock appeared, the scientists officially acknowledged what many writers and thinkers had argued from the start and a majority of citizens had long since come to believe. As Fairfield Osborn stated back in 1946, "There are two major threats in the world today, either one of which would cause incalculable loss of human life, if not the breakdown of the entire structure of our civilization. The first is the misuse of atomic energy.... The other is the continuing destruction of the natural living resources of this earth."[18]

The board concluded its explanation by quoting Albert Einstein's 1946 observation that "With nuclear weapons, everything has changed, save our way of thinking." They emphasized: "As we stand at the brink of a second nuclear age and at the onset of an era of unprecedented climate change, our way of thinking about the uses and control of technologies must change to prevent unspeakable destruction and future human suffering. The Clock is ticking."[19]

But in truth our way of thinking has, in the nearly seven decades since Einstein uttered his phrase, changed considerably. In an April 2007 poll conducted by the *Washington Post*, ABC News, and Stanford University, 7 out of 10 Americans asked wanted to see more federal action on global warming, with half wanting to see the government do "much more" than it was doing. Americans have changed their thinking, but in a country where the voices of corporations continue to be heard above those of its citizens—General Motors chair Bob Lutz called global warming "a total crock of shit" in 2008—policy and enforcement have failed to adequately reflect the change.[20] Lutz's GM was part of the Global Climate Coalition made up of dozens of leading industries and business associations, including Dow Chemical, the Farm Bureau, the US Chamber of Commerce, and the National Association of Manufacturers. The group concealed its own research in 2005 that concluded: "The scientific basis of the Greenhouse Effect and the potential impact of human emissions of greenhouse gases such as CO_2 on climate is well established and cannot be denied." Instead of acting on those findings, it waged a major public relations campaign for more than a decade refuting evidence that industrial activity could cause global warming—a campaign that stirred enough doubt to justify government inaction.[21]

For many American environmentalists there has been no more reasonable response to the apocalyptic threat of corporate capitalism than to try to find a livable space within a mainstream culture that they feel largely powerless to change, a space where they can exist in a way that is as meaningful and true to their visions and dreams as is practically possible. The real importance of mainstream environmentalism is found not only in its effect upon public policy and regulations but in the way it has changed people's thinking and ways of everyday life. Instead of being blindly led by producers, environmentally minded "green" consumers have played a major role in redefining the culture of the United States by creating, promoting, and solidifying a green market and corresponding consciousness that began exerting its influence upon American culture and life beginning in the postwar era and has continued to grow to this day.

Green consumers are sometimes accused of being lulled into political inaction by the (false) comfort they find in consumption. But many are not blind to the need for significant political and structural change; they simply cannot see how, with the grip of corporations on the American political system, such changes can possibly come about. Even for those who still cling to some hope for significant legislative intervention, green consumption provides a means for personal and cultural liberation during the long, frustrating pursuit of political transformation.

In the end, of course, the personal *is* political. If the crisis in American democracy that grew in the twentieth century as corporate capitalism solidified its hold on the polity, a crisis that has spilled into the twenty-first, is ever to be satisfactorily resolved, environmentalism continues to provide a vision that appears to be the only viable alternative offered up in over half a century. During those decades its influence has continued to grow, suggesting, at least for those still able to muster such optimism, that its revolutionary potential remains intact. Like corporations, environmentalism is global, and green consumption has served to both further environmental goals and maintain the movement's vitality and some measure of salience. The story of environmentalism is still being written.

And for those who seek to transform the structure, and even the politics, of the United States, it remains among the most active and viable means for change.

Ultimately, however, if the vision of environmentalism is ever to fully take hold beyond those who can afford to purchase it, real democracy must somehow be instituted. That process must ultimately include a serious and sustained effort to finally end corporate domination of politics, policy, and policy enforcement—to disembed corporate capitalism from the state. Only when that happens can balance in the American polity finally be restored and the exalted corporation, at long last, be brought back down to earth. The neoliberal corporate capitalist state is not a natural state; it was methodically constructed and maintained. Therein lies hope for the future. We built it, and we can dismantle it to replace it with something that is better for the planet and its inhabitants. In the meantime, whether or not that unlikely change ever comes about, many of those citizens who are able will continue to seek protection for themselves, their loved ones, and the planet in the refuge of green consumer culture. "That the situation is hopeless," Aldo Leopold wrote to his friend William Vogt back in 1946, "should not prevent us from doing our best."[22]

NOTES

Introduction

1. "Whole Foods Market Opens Largest Supermarket in Manhattan," http://media.wholefoodsmarket.com/news/whole-foods-market-opens-largest-supermarket-in-manhattan/ (accessed May 7, 2009).
2. Thomas Frank and Matt Weiland, eds., *Commodify Your Dissent: Salvos from The Baffler* (New York: W. W. Norton & Company, 1997).
3. The influential "quality of life" thesis originated with Samuel P. Hayes, *Beauty, Health and Permanence: Environmental Politics in the United States, 1945–1985* (New York: Cambridge University Press, 1987).
4. On Cold War international liberalism, see G. John Ikenberry, *Liberal Leviathan: The Origins, Crisis, and Transformation of the American World Order* (Princeton: Princeton University Press, 2011).
5. See, for example, Maurice Isserman, *If I Had a Hammer: The Death of the Old Left and the Birth of the New Left* (Champaign: University of Illinois Press, 1993); Robert Korstad and Nelson Lichtenstein, "Opportunities Found and Lost: Labor, Radicals, and the Early Civil Rights Movement," *Journal of American History* 75, no. 3 (December 1988): 786–811; Kathleen A. Weignad, "Vanguard of Women's Liberation: The Old Left and the Continuity of the Women's Movement in the United States, 1945–1970s," (PhD diss., Ohio State University, 1995); Joanne Meyerowitz, ed., *Not June Cleaver: Women and Gender in Postwar America, 1945–1960* (Philadelphia: Temple University Press, 1994); Eric Marcus, *Making Gay History: The Half-Century Fight for Lesbian and Gay Equal Rights* (New York: Harper Paperbacks, 2002).
6. See, for example, Robert Gottlieb, *Forcing the Spring: The Transformation of the American Environmental Movement* (Washington, DC: Island Press, 1993); Mark Hamilton Lytle, *The Gentle Subversive: Rachel Carson, Silent Spring, and the Rise of the Environmental Movement* (New York: Oxford University Press, 2007); Neil M. Maher, *Nature's New Deal: The Civilian Conservation Corps and the Roots of the American Environmental Movement* (New York: Oxford University Press, 2008); Hal K. Rothman, *The Greening of a Nation? Environmentalism in the United States Since 1945* (Orlando, FL: Harcourt Brace & Company, 1998); Linda Lear, *Rachel Carson: Witness for Nature* (New York: Henry Holt & Company, 1997); Samuel P. Hayes, *Beauty, Health and Permanence: Environmental Politics in the United States, 1945–1985* (New York: Cambridge University Press, 1987); also J. R. McNeil, *Something New Under the Sun: An Environmental History of the Twentieth Century World* (New York: W. W. Norton & Company, 2000); Kirkpatrick Sale, *The Green Revolution: The American Environmental Movement, 1962–1992* (New York: Hill and Wang, 1993).
7. For a history of Earth Day see Adam Rome, *The Genius of Earth Day: How a 1970 Teach-In Unexpectedly Created the First Green Generation* (New York: Hill and Wang, 2013).

8. See Ulrich Beck, *Risk Society: Towards a New Modernity* (London: Sage Publications, 1992).
9. Display ad, Standard Oil, *Time*, April 26, 1971, 70–71.
10. Dating the term "environmentalism" is difficult, in part because of its multiple uses. It has long been used to describe the philosophy that human behavior is determined more by environment than by heredity, and geographers have used it to describe the interaction of humans with their environment. Its most popular contemporary use, connoting protection of the natural environment, is more recent, but dates at least to 1966, when journalist John Chamberlain used the terms "environmentalism" and "environmentalist" to describe a person concerned about the health of the planet. See Chamberlain, "These Days..... 'Environmentalist' Ribicoff," *Washington Post*, May 20, 1966.

Chapter 1

1. "Doomsday Clock," *Bulletin of the Atomic Scientists* 3, no. 6 (June 1947): front cover.
2. "10 Minutes to War Is the Latest Time on Doomsday Clock," *New York Times*, March 25, 1969; "MGM Jives Up Birth of Atomic Energy," *Life*, March 17, 1947, 76.
3. Paul Boyer, *Fallout: A Historian Reflects on America's Half-Century Encounter with Nuclear Weapons* (Columbus: Ohio State University Press, 1998), 12; Boyer, *By the Bomb's Early Light: American Thought and Culture at the Dawn of the Atomic Age* (New York: Pantheon, 1985), 182–89.
4. "The Nation: Birth of an Era," *Time*, August 13, 1945, 17.
5. James A. Hijiya, "The Gita of Robert Oppenheimer," *Proceedings of the American Philosophical Society* 1442 (June 2000): 123–24, 130.
6. Kenneth Bainbridge, quoted in Richard Rhodes, *The Making of the Atomic Bomb* (New York: Simon and Schuster, 1986), 675.
7. Harold C. Urey, "I'm a Frightened Man," *Colliers*, January 5, 1946, 18, emphasis in original; Boyer, *Fallout*, 171.
8. Hazel Gaudet Erskine, "The Polls: Atomic Weapons and Nuclear Energy," *The Public Opinion Quarterly* 26, no. 2 (Summer 1963), 156.
9. William Fielding Ogburn, *Social Change with Respect to Culture and Original Nature* (New York: B. W. Heubsch, 1922), especially 200–280.
10. Boyer, *Fallout*, 7, 131.
11. "Bomb Effects: Mission Analyzes Blasts Hiroshima and Nagasaki," *Life*, March 11, 1946, 91–94. See also "What Happened," *Time*, March 4, 1946, 88; "Expert Analyzes Atom Bomb Deaths," *New York Times*, March 12, 1946.
12. John Hersey, *Hiroshima* (New York: Bantam Books, 1959), 59, 67. Originally published in 1946.
13. Boyer, *Fallout*, 66.
14. James Hershberg, *James B. Conant: Harvard to Hiroshima and the Making of the Nuclear Age* (New York: Alfred A. Knopf, 1993), 241–42.
15. For a brief history of apocalyptic visions, see David Seed, "Introduction: Aspects of Apocalypse," *Imagining Apocalypse: Studies in Cultural Crisis*, David Seed, ed. (New York: Palgrave Macmillan, 1999), 1–14.
16. "Alarm on the Rand," *New York Times*, May 19, 1910; "Chicagoans Fear Comet," *New York Times*, April 23, 1910; "Comet's Poisonous Tail," *New York Times*, February 8, 1910; "Queries from the Curious and Answers to Them," *New York Times*, March 27, 1910.
17. David Stradling, *Smokestacks and Progressives: Environmentalists, Engineers, and Air Quality in America, 1881–1951* (Baltimore: The Johns Hopkins University Press, 1999); Richard W. Judd, *Common Lands, Common People: The Origins of Conservation in Northern New England* (Cambridge: Harvard University Press, 1997); John T. Cumbler, *Reasonable Use: The People, the Environment, and the State, New England 1790–1930* (New York: Oxford University Press, 2001); Lawrence M. Lipin, *Workers and the Wild: Conservation, Consumerism, and Labor in Oregon, 1910–30* (Champaign: University of Illinois Press, 2007); Chad Montrie, *A People's History of Environmentalism in the United States* (New York: Continuum, 2011).
18. Anne O'Hare McCormick, "The Promethean Role of the United States," *New York Times*, August 8, 1945, quoted in Boyer, *By the Bomb's Early Light*, xix.

19. Fairfield Osborn, Speech to the Annual Convention of the National Association of Biology Teachers in Conjunction with the American Association for the Advancement of Science, St. Louis, MO, March 30, 1946, 1. Box 1, Speech File, 1946–1949, May. Fairfield Osborn Papers, Manuscript Division, Library of Congress, Washington, DC. Donald Worster has also noted the significance of the atomic bomb in the development of ecological and environmental consciousness in *Nature's Economy: A History of Ecological Ideas*, 2nd ed. (New York: Cambridge University Press, 1994), 343, 359. Worster argues that the Bomb triggered anxieties, especially toward science. I will argue, rather, that most Americans remained enamored with science and technology, and instead did not so much fear science as they did powerful corporations which might behave recklessly and endanger the environment for the sake of profits, and which posed a further threat to democracy.
20. Display ad, *Life*, July 29, 1946, 95.
21. "Editorial: The Atomic Age," *Life*, August 20, 1945, 32; on the significance of *Life*'s image of the mushroom cloud see Boyer, *By the Bomb's Early Light*, 8, 17.
22. Robert W. Potter, "Japan Atom Bombing Condemned In Federal Church Council Report," *New York Times*, March 6, 1946.
23. See Daniel Horowitz, *The Anxieties of Affluence: Critiques of American Consumer Culture, 1939–1979* (Amherst: University of Massachusetts Press, 2004). On earlier cultural anxieties see T. J. Jackson Lears, *No Place of Grace: Antimodernism and the Transformation of American Culture 1880–1920* (New York: Pantheon, 1981).
24. Albert Einstein, in *Einstein on Peace*, Heinz Nathan and Otto Norden, eds. (New York: Simon and Schuster, 1960), 376.
25. Howard Zahniser, "Nature in Print," *Nature Magazine* 38 (October 1945): 394, cited in Mark Harvey, *Wilderness Forever: Howard Zahniser and the Path to the Wilderness Act* (Seattle: University of Washington Press, 2005), 46.
26. Gregory Corso, *Bomb* (San Francisco: City Light Books, 1958).
27. See Boyer, *By the Bomb's Early Light*, 93–106.
28. Siegfried Giedion, *Mechanization Takes Command: A Contribution to Anonymous History* (New York: Oxford University Press, 1948), 715
29. Joni Mitchell, "Woodstock," *Ladies of the Canyon* (1970, Warner Brothers, vinyl recording, B000002KOQ).
30. Fairfield Osborn, Speech at Joint Invitation of Secretary of the Interior and President of Carnegie Institution, Elihu Root Auditorium (Carnegie Institution for Science), Washington, DC, February 8, 1949, 2. Box 1, Speech File, 1946–1949, May. Fairfield Osborn Papers, Manuscript Division, Library of Congress, Washington, DC.
31. Donald Worster, *Nature's Economy: A History of Ecological Ideas* (New York: Cambridge University Press, 1994), 332–33.
32. See Michael G. Barbour, "Ecological Fragmentation in the Fifties," in William Cronon, ed., *Uncommon Ground: Rethinking the Human Place in Nature* (New York: W. W. Norton & Company, 1996), 233–55, especially 234.
33. Worster, *Nature's Economy*, 191–93, 301–4, 350.
34. For more on the topic, see Richard White, *Railroaded: The Transcontinentals and the Making of Modern America* (New York: W. W. Norton & Co., 2012).
35. William Vogt, *Road to Survival* (New York: William Sloane, 1948), 35
36. Vogt, *Road to Survival*, 133.
37. Ibid. 37.
38. Ibid. 36.
39. Ibid. 34–35.
40. Ibid. 17, 264–65, 279.
41. O. W. Willcox, *Nations Can Live At Home* (New York: W. W. Norton & Company, 1935), 204, 206.
42. Willcox, *Nations Can Live At Home*, 223, 235.
43. "Uneasy Peace Seen in Overpopulation," *New York Times*, January 29, 1942, 12.
44. Jesse Steiner, "Dilemma: Twenty Million Surplus Japanese: what can the shrunken and crowded empire do to avert the evils of overpopulation?" *New York Times*, October 7, 1945; "Overpopulation Peril to Peace," *Los Angeles Times*, September 22, 1946.

45. Patrick Ball and John Wilmouth, "The Population Debate in American Popular Magazines," *Population and Development Review* (December 1992): 631–68; "Overpopulation Peril to Peace," *Los Angeles Times*, September 22, 1946. For a history of Malthusianism and environmental thought see Thomas Robertson, "The Malthusian Moment: Global Population Growth and the Birth of American Environmentalism" (New Brunswick: Rutgers University Press, 2012).
46. Vogt, *Road to Survival*, 31.
47. "Paul in a Day's Work" (interview), *Grist*, August 9, 2004, http://www.grist.org/comments/interactivist/2004/08/09/ehrlich/ (accessed April 17, 2007).
48. "William Vogt, Former Director of Planned Parenthood, is Dead," *New York Times*, July 12, 1968, 31; Matthew Connelly, *Fatal Misconception: The Struggle to Control World Population* (Cambridge, MA: Balknap Press, 2008), 129–30.
49. Henry Fairfield Osborn, *Preservation of the Wild Animals of North America* (Washington: Boone and Crockett Club, 1904). The volume is the transcript of a speech Osborn delivered to the Boone and Crockett conservation club on January 23, 1904. As for Osborn's father being a leading eugenicist, the sometimes blurry lines between eugenics and environmentalist concerns about overpopulation have long raised concerns. For critical examinations see Gray Brechin, "Conserving the Race: Natural Aristocracies, Eugenics, and the U.S. Conservation Movement," *Antipode* 28 (Summer 1996): 229–45; Jonathan Spiro, *Defending the Master Race: Conservation, Eugenics, and the Legacy of Madison Grant* (Burlington: University of Vermont Press, 2009); Matthew Connelly, *Fatal Misconception: The Struggle to Control World Population* (Cambridge, MA: Balknap Press, 2008).
50. For evidence of the Osborn family's friendship with John Muir see William Fredrick Bade, *The Life and Letters of John Muir*, vol. 2 (New York: Houghton Mifflin Company, 1924), 266, 298, 312–14, 349, 354, 359, 360, 367, 374, 384–86.
51. John Muir, *My First Summer in the Sierra* (Boston, Houghton Mifflin, 1911), 211.
52. Fairfield Osborn, *Our Plundered Planet* (Boston: Little, Brown and Company, 1948), 49.
53. Osborn, *Our Plundered Planet*, vii (emphasis in original); "Fairfield Osborn, The Zoo's No. 1 Showman, Dies," *New York Times*, September 17, 1969.
54. Osborn, *Our Plundered Planet*, 182–84, 191; Edward K. Muller, ed., *DeVoto's West: History, Conservation, and the Public Good* (Athens, Ohio: Swallow Press, 2005), especially 73–144.
55. Phillip O. Foss, *Politics and Grass* (Seattle: University of Washington Press, 1960). Also, Christopher McGrory Klyza, *Who Controls the Public Lands? Mining, Forestry, and Grazing Policies, 1870–1990* (Chapel Hill: University of North Carolina Press, 1996), 110-16.
56. Osborn, *Our Plundered Planet*, 191.
57. Agnus McDonald, "The Great Rat Race," *The New Republic*, September 6, 1948, 26.
58. Malvina Lindsay, "Improvident Planet," *Washington Post*, May 26, 1948.
59. Vogt, *Road to Survival*, 30.
60. Osborn, *Our Plundered Planet*, 61.
61. Osborn, *Our Plundered Planet*, 158, cited in Russell and Kate Lord, *Forever the Land: A Country Chronicle and Anthology* (New York: Harper & Brothers, 1949), 2.
62. On earlier agricultural chemicals and health concerns, see US Department of Agriculture, *Report of the Secretary of Agriculture—1891* (Washington, DC: Government Printing Office, 1892), 375–76; James Whorton, *Before Silent Spring* (Princeton, NJ: Princeton University Press, 1974); Thomas R. Dunlap, *DDT: Scientists, Citizens, and Public Policy* (Princeton, NJ: Princeton University Press, 1981), 17–55.
63. John H. Perkins, "Reshaping Technology in Wartime: The Effect of Military Goals on Entomological Research and Insect-Control Practices," *Technology and Culture* 19, no. 2 (April 1978): 173, 184.
64. Edmund Russell, *War and Nature: Fighting Humans and Insects with Chemicals from World War I to Silent Spring* (New York: Cambridge University Press, 2001), 154–57.
65. Russell, *War and Nature*, 160–61.
66. Ibid. 161–64.
67. C. H. Curran, "DDT: The Atomic Bomb of the Insect World," *Natural History* (November, 1945): 401, 432.
68. Geoffrey Woodard, Ruth R. Ofner, and Charles Montgomery, "Accumulation of DDT in the Body Fat and its Appearance in the Milk of Dogs," *Science* 102, no. 2642 (August 17, 1945): 177–78.

69. Diane di Prima, "Earth Read Out: Review, *Our Plundered Planet*," *Harbinger* (Toronto), September 2, 1969, 8.
70. Joseph Henry Jackson, "Bookman's Notebook: Are We Informed?" *Los Angeles Times*, March 29, 1949. *Road to Survival* won the prize.
71. Fairfield Osborn letter to William Vogt, October 21, 1947. Box 7, ff 8, Correspondence to Vogt: Fairfield Osborn. William Vogt Papers, CONS76, Conservation Collection, The Denver Public Library.
72. "Conservation Unit Set Up to Warn U.S.," *New York Times*, April 6, 1948. On the threat of totalitarianism, see also Paul B. Sears, "Dust in the Eyes of Science," *The Land* 7, no. 3 (Autumn 1948): 346; and J. A. Hall, "Democracy Can Starve Itself," *The Land* 8, no. 4 (Winter 1949–1950): 447–53.
73. Fairfield Osborn, Speech to the Chamber of Commerce of the State of New York, February 6, 1947, 1–2. Box 2, Speech File 1947–48, July, correspondence and notes relating to 1946–1948. Fairfield Osborn Papers, Manuscript Division, Library of Congress, Washington, DC.
74. "Foundation Formed to Defend Nation's Natural Resources," *Chicago Daily Tribune*, April 11, 1948. Some scholars have argued that because groups like the Conservation Foundation relied on corporate foundations for funding it limited the range of their proposed solutions. See, for example, Robert Gottlieb, *Forcing The Spring: The Transformation of the American Environmental Movement* (Washington, DC: Island Press, 1993), 38–41, and Brian Tokar, *Earth For Sale: Reclaiming Ecology in the Age of Corporate Greenwash* (Boston: South End Press, 1997).
75. "What Hope for Man?" *Town Meeting: Bulletin of America's Town Meeting of the Air*. September 14, 1948. Transcript, 1–23. Subject file, America's Town Meeting of the Air, Sept. 14, 1948. Fairfield Osborn Papers, Manuscript Division, Library of Congress, Washington, DC.
76. Letter to Fairfield Osborn from Robert Allison, producer of CBS television's *People's Platform*, June 1, 1949. Box 2, Speech File, Speeches 1949, Apr.–Oct., correspondence and notes relating to 1948–49. Fairfield Osborn Papers, Manuscript Division, Library of Congress, Washington, DC.
77. Memorandum of New York Zoological Society Office of President (Osborn), January 4, 1950. Box 3, Speech File, Speeches 1950, Jan.–Mar., correspondence and notes relating to 1949–50. Fairfield Osborn Papers, Manuscript Division, Library of Congress, Washington, DC.
78. Kim Phillips-Fein, *Invisible Hands: The Businessmen's Crusade Against the New Deal* (New York: W. W. Norton, 2009), 9–10; Lizabeth Cohen, *Making A New Deal: Industrial Workers in Chicago, 1912–1939* (New York, Cambridge University Press, 1990), especially 251–89; Alan Brinkley, *The End of Reform: New Deal Liberalism in Recession and War* (New York: Knopf, 1995), 3–4.
79. Charles Perrow, *Organizing America: Wealth, Power, and the Origins of Corporate Capitalism* (Princeton, NJ: Princeton University Press, 2002); David F. Noble, *America by Design: Science, Technology, and the Rise of Corporate Capitalism* (New York: Alfred A. Knopf, 1977).
80. Cynthia Lee Henthorn, *From Submarines to Suburbs: Selling a Better America, 1939–1959* (Athens, OH: Ohio University Press, 2006), 74.
81. International Minerals and Chemicals ad, *Business Week* (May 8, 1943): 81. Reproduced in Henthorn, *From Submarines to Suburbs*, 105.
82. James Aulich, *War Posters: Weapons of Mass Communication* (London: Thames & Hudson, 2007), 169–71.
83. Russell, *War and Nature*, 86–87, 146–47; "Insecticide Stronger Than DDT Gets Tests," *Los Angeles Times*, October 26, 1947, A1; Robert Stewart, "The Office of Technical Services: A New Deal Idea in the Cold War," *Knowledge* 15, no. 1 (September 1993): 44–77.
84. On corporations during the Depression, see Frederick Lewis Allen, *Since Yesterday: The 1930s in America, September 3, 1929–September 3, 1939* (New York: Harper & Brothers, 1940), 181, 267–71.
85. "250 Corporations Control 2-3 of U.S.," *The Call*, July 8, 1946, 8; Jesse J. Friedman, "Anti-Monopoly Drive Spurred in Congress," *New York Times*, February 16, 1947, E7; Perrow, *Organizing America*, 204–5; Roland Marchand, *Creating the Corporate Soul: The Rise of Public Relations and Corporate Imagery in American Big Business* (Berkeley: The University of California Press, 1998), 358.

86. See Robert M. Collins, *More: The Politics of Economic Growth in Postwar America* (New York: Oxford University Press, 2000), especially 17–39.
87. Gary Cross, *All Consuming Century: Why Commercialism Won in Modern America* (New York: Columbia University Press, 2000), 88.
88. "Fears for Future of Small Business," *New York Times*, October 16, 1944, 24.
89. Charles Hurd, "Monopoly Called Road to Socialism," *New York Times*, July 21, 1949, 3.
90. Friedman, "Anti-Monopoly Drive Spurred," E7.
91. A. H. Raskin, "Food is Our Crisis, Wallace Asserts," *New York Times*, September 23, 1947, 7.
92. Elizabeth A. Fones-Wolf, *Selling Free Enterprise: The Business Assault on Labor and Liberalism, 1945–1960* (Urbana: University of Illinois Press, 1994), especially 15–57, and 80–81; Henthorn, *From Submarines to Suburbs*; Phillips-Fein, *Invisible Hands*, especially 3–27, 68–86.
93. Philip Mirowski, "Postface: Defining Neoliberalism," in Mirowski and Plehwe, eds., *The Road from Mont Pelerin*, 434–35.
94. Phillips-Fein, *Invisible Hands*, 34–42.
95. Angus Burgin, *The Great Persuasion: Reinventing Free Markets Since the Depression* (Cambridge: Harvard University Press, 2012), 170–74, 180–85; Rob Van Horn, "Reinventing Monopoly and the Role of Corporations: The Roots of Chicago Law and Economics," in Mirowski and Plehwe, eds., *The Road from Mont Pelerin*, especially 218–19, 220; Daniel Steadman Jones, *Masters of the Universe: Hayek, Friedman, and the Birth of Neoliberal Politics* (Princeton: Princeton University Press, 2012), 34. Friedman no longer identified himself as a neoliberal by the late 1950s, and instead saw himself as representing true (radical) liberalism. See Burgin, 175–77.
96. Paul Treanor, "Neoliberalism: Origins, Theory, Definition," http://web.inter.nl.net/users/Paul.Treanor/neoliberalism.html (accessed May 7, 2013); Milton Friedman, *Capitalism and Freedom* (Chicago: University of Chicago Press, 1962), 133.
97. Milton Friedman, "The Social Responsibility of Business is to Increase its Profits," *New York Times Magazine*, September 13, 1970.
98. Philip Mirowski and Rob Van Horn, "The Rise of the Chicago School of Economics and the Birth of Neoliberalism," in Mirowski and Plehwe, eds., *The Road from Mont Pelerin*, 157.
99. Daniel Yergin, *The Prize: The Epic Quest for Oil, Money & Power* (New York: Free Press, 1991), 391–92, 401–2.
100. Paul H. Nitze, "Natural Resources in a World of Conflict," *Department of State Bulletin* 19, no. 490 (November 21, 1948): 625.
101. Karl Polanyi, *The Great Transformation* (Boston: Beacon Press, 1944), 75–80, 138.
102. K. William Kapp, *Social Costs of Private Enterprise* (New York: Schocken Books, 1950), 13–14.
103. Kapp, *Social Costs*, 9.
104. Ibid. 6, 11, 15.
105. Ibid. 264–265.
106. Ibid. 95.
107. Ibid. 12, 287.
108. James A. Swaney and Martin A. Evers, "Social Cost Concepts of K. William Kapp and Karl Polanyi," *Journal of Economic Issues* 23, no. 1 (March 1989): 20; Daniel Immerwahr, "Polanyi in the United States: Peter Drucker, Karl Polanyi, and the Midcentury Critique of Economic Society," *Journal of the History of Ideas* 70, no. 3 (July 2009).
109. Fairfield Osborn, "Modern Economy's Threat to Our Resources," speech to the 37th Annual Meeting of the Chamber of Commerce of the United States, May 4, 1949, 1. Box 1, Speech File, 1946–1949, May. Fairfield Osborn Papers, Manuscript Division, Library of Congress, Washington, DC.
110. On neoliberalism see Kim Phillips-Fein, *Invisible Hands*; Philip Mirowski and Dieter Plehwe, eds., *The Road from Mont Pelerin: The Making of the Neoliberal Thought Collective* (Cambridge: Harvard University Press, 2009).
111. "Sustaining Our Natural Resources," *Business Action* 6, no. 9 (May 13, 1949): 15; Letter from Fairfield Osborn to G. Harris Collingwood, US Chamber of Commerce, undated; Letter from Rosalie E. Sevcik (secretary to Fairfield Osborn) to G. Harris Collingwood, May 19, 1949; Letter from G. Harris Collingwood to Fairfield Osborn, May 18, 1949. Box 7, Subject

File, Chamber of Commerce of the United States, May 4, 1949. Fairfield Osborn Papers, Manuscript Division, Library of Congress, Washington, DC.
112. The Conservation Foundation, *The Conservation Foundation: A Statement of Purpose* (New York: The Conservation Foundation, 1947 [not for publication]), 43–45, Aldo Leopold Papers, box 002, "Organizations, Committees: B-E," folder 005, "Conservation Foundation," University of Wisconsin Archives (Madison, WI) http://digital.library.wisc.edu/1711.dl/AldoLeopold, 241-243. "State, Zoo in Move for Conservation," *New York Times*, May 31, 1949, 18; "Conservation Comes Alive," *New York Times*, June 2, 1949.
113. Harry S. Truman letter to US representative to the Economic and Social Council of the United Nations, September 4, 1946, quoted in Secretariat of the International Union for the Protection of Nature, ed., UNESCO, *Preparatory Documents to the International Conference on the Protection of Nature* (Paris: UNESCO, 1949), 71.
114. On Cold War international liberalism see G. John Ikenberry, *Liberal Leviathan: The Origins, Crisis, and Transformation of the American World Order* (Princeton: Princeton University Press, 2011).
115. *The Proceedings of the United Nations Scientific Conference*, vol. I, x; Gifford Pinchot, *The Fight for Conservation* (New York: Doubleday, 1910), 48.
116. *The Proceedings of the United Nations Scientific Conference*, vol. I, 7. Emphasis mine.
117. "Blueprints Drawn to Effect Point 4," Blueprints Drawn to Effect Point 4," *New York Times* May 6, 1949; James Rorty, "Red-Headed Catalyst: Mrs. Pinchot and the Conference at Lake Success," *The Land* 8, no. 4 (Winter 1949–1950): 470.
118. *The Proceedings of the United Nations Scientific Conference*, vol. I, vii.
119. Ibid. vii, ix–x, xxix–liv; Thomas J. Hamilton, "Resources Parley Will Open Today," *New York Times*, August 17, 1949, 25.
120. John G. Rogers, "Dollar Aid for Development to be Ready Soon, Says Krug," *Washington Post*, August 18, 1949, 1.
121. *The Proceedings of the United Nations Scientific Conference*, vol. I, xvi.
122. Ibid., "Creatable Resources," 161, 163.
123. *The Proceedings of the United Nations Scientific Conference on the Conservation and Utilization of Resources*, vol. VIII (New York: United Nations Department of Economic Affairs, 1951), 3–25.
124. Robert M. Salter, "Techniques for Increasing Agricultural Production," in *The Proceedings of the United Nations Scientific Conference*, vol. I, 85.
125. Mercer H. Parks, "Petroleum Production from Continental Shelves," *The Proceedings of the United Nations Scientific Conference on the Conservation and Utilization of Resources*, vol. V (Lake Success, New York: United Nations Department of Economic Affairs, 1951), 22.
126. A. W. Anderson, "Technological Development in Fisheries with Special Reference to the Factory Ship in the United States," in *The Proceedings of the United Nations Scientific Conference on the Conservation and Utilization of Resources*, vol. VII (Lake Success, New York: United Nations Department of Economic Affairs, 1951), 104–5.
127. "Report on the Conference by the Secretary-General," xvii.
128. "Introductory and Plenary Sessions," *The Proceedings of the United Nations Scientific Conference*, vol. I, 7; George Barrett, "U.N. Calls Parley on Conservation," *New York Times*, March 12, 1949, 5; "Addresses by Secretary Krug and Fairfield Osborn at U.N. Conference on Conservation," *New York Times*, August 18, 1949, p. 14; Fred Mallery Packard, "International Technical Conference on the Protection of Nature," *Journal of Forestry* 47, no. 11 (1 November 1949): 875.
129. *The Proceedings of the United Nations Scientific Conference*, vol. I, xiv–xv. On TVA as model for US international development, see David Ekbladh, *The Great American Mission: Modernization and the Construction of an American World Order* (Princeton, NJ: Princeton University Press, 2009), 11, 37–38, 84–85, 90, 159–61, 165, 169.
130. "Informal Summary of Minutes of Meeting Held at the Request of Dr. Julian Huxley," 4.
131. McCormick, *Reclaiming Paradise*, 34–35.
132. "Informal Summary of Minutes of Meeting Held at the Request of Dr. Julian Huxley," 1–6; UNESCO, *Resolutions Adopted by the General Conference During its Second Session: Mexico, November–December, 1947* (UNESCO, Paris: 1948), 29; UNESCO Secretariat for the

French Government, "Conference for the Establishment of the International Union for the Protection of Nature: Fontainebleau, France, 30 September–7 October 1948," 1, www.iucn.org/dbtw-wpd/edocs/1948-001.pdf (accessed October 11, 2010).

133. "Informal Summary of Minutes of Meeting Held at Request of Dr. Julian Huxley," 2. On Julian Huxley and TVA-style development, see Ekbladh, *The Great American Mission*, 46–48, 84–85, 90.
134. *Preparatory Documents to the International Technical Conference on the Protection of Nature*, 3.
135. Ibid., 3.
136. *Proceedings and Papers—International Technical Conference on the Protection of Nature*, vii; *Preparatory Documents to the International Technical Conference*, 13.
137. Ibid. 31.
138. Jean-Paul Harroy, introduction to *Proceedings and Papers—International Technical Conference on the Protection of Nature*, xi. Harroy's book, *Afrique: Terre Qui Meurt* (Brussels: Marcel Hayez, 1944), detailed how European colonization had devastated Africa's environment and culture.
139. "Talk on Nature Slated," *New York Times*, August 21, 1949; Fred Mallery Packard, "International Technical Conference on the Protection of Nature," *Journal of Forestry* 47, no. 11 (November 1949): 875; *Proceedings and Papers—International Technical Conference on the Protection of Nature*, 1–13, 51.
140. *Proceedings and Papers—International Technical Conference on the Protection of Nature*, 25, 578–80, 875–76.
141. John P. Shea, "Human Relations: An Essential Factor in Resource Protection and Use," in *Proceedings and Papers—International Technical Conference on the Protection of Nature—Lake Success*, 268.
142. Fairfield Osborn, "Opening Address at the First Plenary Session of the International Technical Conference on the Protection of Nature at Lake Success," August 22, 1949, 3, Records of the New York Zoological Society President, Fairfield Osborn, Box 2, Collection 1029, Wildlife Conservation Society Archives.
143. "International Co-operation in the Stimulation of Ecological Research in Various Fields of the Natural Sciences. Special Emphasis to be Given to Planned Enterprises," in *Proceedings and Papers—International Technical Conference on the Protection of Nature*, 67, 69.
144. "International Co-operation in the Stimulation of Ecological Research," 129–43.
145. Douglas E. Wade, "'You Have to Carry the Rope,'" in *Proceedings and Papers—International Technical Conference on the Protection of Nature*, 289.
146. "International Co-operation in the Stimulation of Ecological Research," 67–75.
147. William Vogt, "Words and Maps: Some Observations on Applying T.V.A. Techniques in Latin America," transcript of speech delivered to the Second Congress of General Semantics, printed in *The Land* 7, no. 2 (Summer 1948): 259, 265.
148. Ollie E. Fink, "Let's Teach Water Conservation," in *Proceedings and Papers—International Technical Conference on the Protection of Nature*, 215. Emphasis mine. For an account of Friends of the Land's role as an early promoter of ecology, see Randal Beeman, "Friends of the Land and the Rise of Environmentalism, 1940–1954," *Journal of Agricultural and Environmental Ethics* 8, no. 1 (1995): 1–16.
149. Fink, "Let's Teach Water Conservation," 216.
150. Vernon G. Carter, "Failure and Success in Conservation Education," in *Proceedings and Papers—International Technical Conference on the Protection of Nature*, 197. Emphasis in original.
151. Jean-Paul Harroy, introduction to *Proceedings and Papers—International Technical Conference on the Protection of Nature*, ix.
152. "The Organic World: Spray Likened to Atom Bomb," *Organic Gardening and Farming* 1, no. 7 (January, 1954): 2.
153. Aldo Leopold, *A Sand County Almanac and Sketches Here and There* (New York: Oxford University Press, 1949), 213.
154. Leopold, *A Sand County Almanac*, 214.
155. Ibid. 203.
156. Ibid. viii, 224–25.

157. Aldous Huxley Letter to Fairfield Osborn, January 16, 1948, 2. Box 1, General Correspondence 1924–69, undated. Fairfield Osborn Papers, Manuscript Division, Library of Congress, Washington, DC.
158. Leopold, *A Sand County Almanac*, 225.
159. Ibid. 224.
160. Leopold, "The Ecological Conscience," speech delivered 1947, quoted in Curt Meine, *Aldo Leopold: His Life and Work* (Madison: University of Wisconsin Press, 1988), 499.
161. Leopold, *A Sand County Almanac*, 224.
162. Aldo Leopold to William Vogt, January 25, 1946, "Correspondence to Vogt: Aldo Leopold and Mrs. Leopold," ff 1, box 2, CONS76, Conservation Collection, The Denver Public Library. Emphasis added.
163. William Vogt to Aldo Leopold, January 28, 1946, "Correspondence from Vogt: Aldo Leopold, 1943–1967," ff 12, box 3 CONS76, Conservation Collection, The Denver Public Library.
164. Aldo Leopold to William Vogt, January 25, 1946.
165. Leopold, *A Sand County Almanac*, viii.
166. *Preparatory Documents to the International Technical Conference on the Protection of Nature*, 79–80.
167. Display ad, the National City Bank of New York (Peru Branch), *BusinessWeek*, September 9, 1950, 133; display ad, the National City Bank of New York (India Branches), *BusinessWeek*, October 7, 1950, 12.
168. Fairfield Osborn, Lecture given at the University of Michigan, May 2, 1950, 4. Box 1, Speech File, 1950–52, Apr., Fairfield Osborn Papers, Manuscript Division, Library of Congress, Washington, DC.

Chapter 2

1. Aldo Leopold, *A Sand County Almanac and Sketches Here and There* (New York: Oxford University Press, 1949), 222.
2. US Department of Commerce, *United States Census of Agriculture: 1954, Volume II, Part 1* (Washington, DC: US Government Printing Office, 1956), 8; Paul K. Conkin, *A Revolution Down on the Farm: The Transformation of American Agriculture Since 1929* (Lexington: University Press of Kentucky, 2008), 51–76; Deborah Fitzgerald, *Every Farm a Factory: The Industrial Ideal in American Agriculture* (New Haven: Yale University Press, 2003), 113; John L. Shover, *First Majority—Last Minority: The Transforming of Rural Life in America* (DeKalb, IL: Northern Illinois University Press, 1976), 165–66.
3. John Morton Blum, *V Was For Victory: Politics and American Culture During World War II* (New York: Harcourt Brace Jovanovich, 1976), 141.
4. Grant McConnell, *Private Power and American Democracy* (New York: Alfred A. Knopf, 1966), 231, 235.
5. Aldo Leopold, letter to Fairfield Osborn, April 3, 1947, Aldo Leopold Papers, box 002, Organizations, Committees: B-E, folder 005, p. 272 "Conservation Foundation," University of Wisconsin Archives (Madison, WI) http://digital.library.wisc.edu/1711.dl/AldoLeopold.
6. Display ad, *Organic Gardening* 15, no. 1 (July 1949): inside front cover.
7. Carlton Jackson, *J. I. Rodale: Apostle of Nonconformity* (New York: Pyramid Books, 1974).
8. J. I. (Jerome Irving) Rodale, *Pay Dirt: Farming and Gardening with Composts* (New York: Devin-Adair, 1945). See Rodale, "Part Four," 139–98. Another early proponent of the organic method in Britain was Lord Northbourne. See Lord Northbourne, *Look to the Land* (London: J. M. Dent & Sons, 1940). On the origins of organics, especially in Great Britain, see Philip Conford, *The Origins of the Organic Movement* (Edinburgh: Floris Books, 2001).
9. Barton Blum, "Composting and the Roots of Sustainable Agriculture," *Agricultural History* 66, no. 2 (Spring 1992): 171–88; Natural Food Associates, *Natural Food and Farming Digest: A Selection of Articles from the Monthly Magazine Published by Natural Food Associates, Incorporated* (Atlanta, TX: Natural Food Associates, Inc., 1957), 129.

10. Justus Liebig, *Organic Chemistry in Its Applications to Agriculture and Physiology* (Cambridge, MA: John Owen, 1941); Robert Rodale, "The Organic Gardening Idea Goes Back a Long Way," *Organic Gardening and Farming* 17, no. 1 (January 1970): 29–31.
11. See Vaclav Smil, *Enriching the Earth: Fritz Haber, Carl Bosch and the Transformation of World Food Production* (Cambridge, MA: The MIT Press, 2000); Richard A. Wines, *Fertilizer in America: From Waste Recycling to Resource Exploitation* (Philadelphia: Temple University Press, 1985), 96–98, 114–24, 160; Conkin, *A Revolution Down on the Farm*, 108–11.
12. Conkin, *A Revolution Down on the Farm*, 71–72, 111.
13. Rodale, *Pay Dirt*, 129.
14. J. I. Rodale, *The Organic Front* (Emmaus, PA, 1948), 82.
15. Quote from Sir Albert Howard, cited in Rodale, *Pay Dirt*, 123.
16. Rodale, *Pay Dirt*, 23–24. Emphasis in original.
17. In J. I. Rodale, "Why I Started Organic Gardening," *Organic Gardening and Farming* 14, no. 5 (May 1967): 31.
18. Johan Rockstrom et al., "A Safe Operating System for Humanity," *Nature* 461 (September 2009): 474; J. R. Self and R. M. Waskom, "Nitrates in Drinking Water," October 2008, Colorado State University Extension, http://www.ext.colostate.edu/pubs/crops/00517.html (accessed August 14, 2013); Shover, *First Majority*, 150–51; Environmental Protection Agency, "Nutrient Pollution: The Problem," http://www2.epa.gov/nutrientpollution/problem (accessed August 14, 2013).
19. Rodale, *Pay Dirt*, 11.
20. Jim Hightower, "Hard Tomatoes, Hard Times: Failure of the Land Grant Colleges," *Society* 10, no. 1 (November 1972): 11, 14.
21. Rodale, *Pay Dirt*, 239.
22. Siegfried Giedion, *Mechanization Takes Command: A Contribution to Anonymous History* (New York: Oxford University Press, 1948).
23. Sir Albert Howard, in Rodale, *Pay Dirt*, vii.
24. "Shortage of Fertilizers," *Organic Farming and Gardening* 1, no. 3 (July 1942): cover.
25. J. I. Rodale, "Why Organic Gardening Was Started," *Organic Gardening and Farming* 13, no. 5 (March 1966): 74; J. I. Rodale, "Why I Started Organic Gardening," 34. In 1948 Rodale began publishing *The Organic Farmer* for larger growers, before recombining it with *Organic Gardening* in 1954.
26. Jerome Olds, "Organic Living for Half a Million People," *Organic Gardening and Farming* (March 1970): 40–42. In comparison, in 1950 the Sierra Club's membership totaled about 7,000, and it would not reach 100,000 until 1970. In 1970 the Wilderness Society still attracted only some 54,000 to its ranks. See Kirkpatrick Sale, *The Green Revolution: The American Environmental Movement 1962–1992* (New York: Hill and Wang, 1993), 23; Michael P. Cohen, *The History of the Sierra Club* (San Francisco: Sierra Club Books, 1988), 362.
27. Gurney Norman, "The Organic Gardening Books," *Whole Earth Catalog* (Fall 1970): 38.
28. Rodale, *Pay Dirt*, 179.
29. "Farmers Warned on DDT," *New York Times*, May 25, 1947, 52; Leonard Wickenden, *Make Friends with Your Land: A Chemist Looks at Organiculture* (New York: Devin-Adair, 1949), 77.
30. James J. Delaney, et al., "Investigation of the Use of Chemicals in Food Products," January 3, 1951, Report No. 3254 to the U.S. House of Representatives, 81st Congress, 2nd Session, 10; Thomas R. Dunlap, *DDT: Scientists, Citizens, and Public Policy* (Princeton, NJ: Princeton University Press, 1981), 73–74.
31. See *Botanical Gazette* 107, no. 4 (June 1946); George S. Avery, Jr., "New Weed Killers," *New York Times*, August 12, 1945; "A New Weed Killer, 2,4-D, Developed by DuPont Chemists," *Wall Street Journal*, April 22, 1946; Avery, Jr., "Death to Weeds!" *New York Times*, July 28, 1946; "Chemicals That Kill Crops and Weeds," *New York Times*, August 18, 1946; Special Projects Division, Chemical Warfare Services, "Plant Growth Regulators," *Science* 103, no. 2677 (April 19, 1946): 469–70.
32. "Weed Killer 2,4-D," *Audubon* 48 (1946): 244.
33. Wickenden, *Make Friends with Your Land*, 80.

34. Fairfield Osborn, "Action Must be Taken!" in Department of State, *Proceedings of the Inter-American Conference on Conservation of Renewable Natural Resources* (Washington, DC: Department of State Division of Publications, 1948), 507, 509; William M. Blair, "Conservation Plan Put to Hemisphere," *New York Times*, September 18, 1948. Emphasis mine.
35. Osborn, "Action Must be Taken!" 509.
36. Rodale, *Pay Dirt*, 218–24.
37. Alan I. Marcus, *Cancer from Beef: DES, Federal Food Regulation, and Consumer Confidence* (Baltimore: The Johns Hopkins University Press, 1994), 12–13, 18.
38. Rodale, *Pay Dirt*, 219–22.
39. On Rorty see John Michael Boles, "James Rorty's Social Ecology," *Organization & Environment* 11, no. 2 (June 1998): 155-179, and Inger Stole, *Advertising on Trial: Consumer Activism and Corporate Public Relations in the 1930s* (Chicago: University of Illinois Press, 2006), especially 34–35, 203.
40. James Rorty and Philip N. Norman, *Tomorrow's Food* (New York: Prentice Hall, 1947), 145.
41. Rorty and Norman, *Tomorrow's Food*, 137–48.
42. Ibid. 5.
43. James S. Turner, *The Chemical Feast* (New York: Grossman Publishers, 1970), 83; Rorty and Norman, *Tomorrow's Food*, 40–45.
44. Rorty and Norman, *Tomorrow's Food*, 234.
45. Ibid. 69–81, 121–22.
46. Rorty and Norman, *Tomorrow's Food*, 212–23.
47. Ibid. 37, 192-93..
48. Morris L. Ernst, *The First Freedom* (New York: The MacMillan Company, 1946), xii, 33, 74, 79, 98.
49. "Freedom for What? (An Abstract of the Report of the Commission on Freedom of the Press)," *Nieman Reports* 1, no. 2 (April 1947): 4–6; Louis M. Lyons, "A Free and Responsible Press: A Review of the Press Report," *Nieman Reports* 1, no. 2 (April 1947): 1–2; James T. Farrell, "Quest for Profits Limits Press Freedom," *The Call*, June 18, 1947, 4. The report was commonly referred to as the "Hutchins Report" after the group's leader, University of Chicago Chancellor Robert Hutchins.
50. Robert Rodale, "Who Pays for Agricultural Research?" *Organic Gardening and Farming* 1, no. 1 (January 1954): 16–20. In 1939 industry funded $496,344.43 worth of research. By 1952 the figure was $5,040,545.92.
51. Shover, *First Majority—Last Minority*, 230; Robert Rodale, "Who Pays for Agricultural Research?" 16–20.
52. Robert Rodale, "Who Pays for Agricultural Research?" 17; Shover, *First Majority—Last Minority*, 234; Hightower, "Hard Tomatoes, Hard Times," 10; Rorty and Norman, *Tomorrow's Food*, 205–11;
53. Leopold, *A Sand County Almanac*, 223.
54. Robert Finch, "Introduction," *A Sand County Almanac, and Sketches Here and There* (New York: Oxford University Press, 1987), xxii; Osborn, *Our Plundered Planet*, 199–200.
55. For a discussion of corporations infiltrating the classroom, see Lisa Jacobson, *Raising Consumers: Children and the American Mass Market in the Early Twentieth Century* (New York: Columbia University Press, 2004), 42–46.
56. Rorty and Norman, *Tomorrow's Food*, 122–23.
57. Bess Furman, "Atomic Age Needs in School Assayed," *New York Times*, December 29, 1948.
58. Natural Food Associates, *Natural Food and Farming Digest* (Atlanta, TX: Natural Food Associates, 1957), especially 2, 129.
59. William Longgood, *The Poisons in Your Food* (New York: Simon and Schuster, 1960), 271.
60. William H. Young and Nancy K. Young, *The 1950s* (Westport, CT: Greenwood Press, 2004), 97.
61. Rorty and Norman, *Tomorrow's Food*, 192–93, 212–17. Emphasis mine.
62. Steve Leikin, "The Citizen Producer: The Rise and Fall of Working-Class Cooperatives in the United States," in Ellen Furlough and Carl Strikwerda, eds., *Consumers Against Capitalism? Consumer Cooperation in Europe, North America, and Japan, 1840–1990* (New York: Rowman

and Littlefield, 1999), 6–10; US Department of Agriculture Rural Business–Cooperative Service, "Co-ops 101: An Introduction to Cooperatives" (Cooperative Information Report 55), 2–4.
63. "Chicago Co-op Shows Example to Consumers," *The Call*, March 12, 1947, 4; August Gold, "Co-ops in the Building of Real World Peace," *The Call*, March 5, 1945, 6.
64. John P. Callahan, "30-Year Advance by Cooperatives," *New York Times*, March 18, 1946.
65. Rorty and Norman, *Tomorrow's Food*, 212–18.
66. Ibid. 167, 173.
67. Daniel Zwerdling, "The Uncertain Revival of Food Cooperatives," in John Case and Rosemary C. R. Taylor, eds., *Co-ops, Communes & Collectives: Experiments in Social Change in the 1960s and 1970s* (New York: Pantheon Books, 1979), 94–95.
68. "Big Business Seen Like Politburo," *Washington Post*, October 26, 1954.
69. J. I. Rodale, "Introduction to Organic Farming," *Organic Farming and Gardening* 1, no. 1 (May 1942), 4.
70. Rodale, *Pay Dirt*, 196. Emphasis mine.
71. See Glickman, *Buying Power*, especially 1–18, for a concise and illuminating history of consumer activism in the United States. I am indebted to his comprehensive study and analysis.
72. Political scientists are producing a growing body of work on what they term "political consumerism" as a new form of political engagement. See, for example, Michele Micheletti, *Political Virtue and Shopping: Individuals, Consumerism, and Collective Action* (New York: Palgrave Macmillan, 2003), and Michele Micheletti, Andreas Follesdal, and Dietlind Stolle, eds., *Politics, Products, and Markets: Exploring Political Consumerism Past and Present* (New Brunswick, NJ: Transaction Publishers, 2004).
73. Mary McGrory, "Apostle of Conserving World's Resources Says Education is 1 of 3 Main Factors," *Washington Star*, August 22, 1948, C-3.
74. G. E. Hutchinson, "On Living in the Biosphere," *The Scientific American* 67, no. 6 (December 1948): 397.
75. Celanese Chemicals, display ad, *Business Week*, October 7, 1950, 68. Of course, the formaldehyde used in the bonding resins of particleboard would later be deemed an environmental toxin.
76. "Miscellany: Organic Restaurants," *Organic Gardening* 15, no. 5 (November 1949): 20–21.
77. Mary Umbarger, "Frazer Makes Compost," *The Land* 8, no. 3 (Autumn 1949): 339–42; "Car Maker Enters Fertilizer Field," *New York Times*, February 8, 1949; Donald A. Jones, *The Rototiller in America* (Haverford, PA: Infinity Publishing, 2003), 80; Joseph Egelhof, "Economy Key to Success of Meat Packers," *Chicago Tribune*, December 2, 1951.
78. Joseph W. Frazer, "Foreword," in Wickenden, *Make Friends with Your Land*, v–vii.
79. William Vogt to Joseph W. Frazer, February 9, 1949, "Correspondence from Vogt: Fa to Fz, 1945–1965," ff 5, box 3 CONS76, Conservation Collection, The Denver Public Library.
80. Joseph W. Frazer to William Vogt, February 15, 1949, "Correspondence to Vogt: Fl to Fz," ff 27, box 1, CONS76, Conservation Collection, The Denver Public Library.
81. Ibid.
82. H. V. Goodell, "Organic Supermarket Opens," *Organic Gardening and Farming* 1, no. 11 (November 1954): 9–10.
83. "Home Tests Nutrition Principles of Author," *Los Angeles Times*, December 22, 1951.
84. Adelle Davis, *Let's Have Healthy Children* (New York: Harcourt, Brace and Company, 1951), 259–62.
85. Ansel Adams and Nancy Newhall, *This is the American Earth* (San Francisco: The Sierra Club, 1960), xii. The most famous of these early Sierra Club efforts was the twelve-year fight to stop the Hetch Hetchy dam in Yosemite National Park, before the battle was finally lost in 1913.
86. In making this analysis I am encouraged by the work of Robert D. Johnston in *The Radical Middle Class: Populist Democracy and the Question of Capitalism in Progressive Era Portland, Oregon* (Princeton, NJ: Princeton University Press, 2003).
87. R. I. Thockmorton, "The Organic Farming Myth," *Country Gentleman*, September 1951, 21.
88. Leonard Wickenden, *Gardening with Nature: How to Grow Your Own Vegetables, Fruits, and Flowers by Natural Methods* (New York: Devin-Adair, 1954), 368–74; June Owen, "News of

Food: Food Faddists Endanger Health of Multitudes by Their Fallacies," *New York Times*, June 21, 1954, 18.
89. Judson King, "Our Stake in Conservation," *Machinists Monthly Journal* 60, no. 11 (November 1948): 430. Box 4, ff 9 Manuscripts—Reviews about Vogt: *The Road to Survival*. William Vogt Papers, CONS76, Conservation Collection, The Denver Public Library.
90. Bill Davidson, "Our Poisoned Waters," *Colliers*, October 16, 1948, 20.
91. "Waste Disposal Method Deplored at Hearing," *Los Angeles Times*, October 15, 1947.
92. "Bitter Disputes Mark State AFL Convention," *Los Angeles Times*, September 29, 1948.
93. For an examination of state and local pollution and environmental laws during the postwar era, see Karl Boyd Brooks, *Before Earth Day: The Origins of American Environmental Law, 1945–1970* (Lawrence: University Press of Kansas, 2009).
94. Associated Press, "Federal Agency to Allot Funds for Water Supply Purification," *Christian Science Monitor*, August 12, 1948, 17; Davidson, "Our Poisoned Waters," 21; FedCenter, "Federal Water Pollution Control Act (Clean Water Act) of 1948," http://www.fedcenter.gov/Bookmarks/index.cfm?id=2431&pge_prg_id=0&pge_id=0 (accessed April 11, 2008).
95. "Digest From the Report of the President's Materials Policy Commission," (June 23, 1952), 11; Papers of Harry S. Truman, Official File. Student Research File (B File); Energy Policy 36B (Box 2 of 2), folder 19, no. 3. Harry S. Truman Library & Museum, Independence, MO.
96. "Scores of Cities Threatened with Water Shortage," *Boston Globe*, January 29, 1950.
97. "Smoke Campaign by Industry Urged," *New York Times*, April 17, 1951; "Incentive to Fight Pollution Urged," *New York Times*, April 22, 1951.
98. Bill Davidson, "Our Poisoned Air," *Colliers*, October 23, 1948, 70.
99. See Devra Davis, *When Smoke Ran Like Water: Tales of Environmental Deception and the Battle Against Pollution* (New York: Basic Books, 2002); "Donora, Pennsylvania," *The Atlantic* 226, no. 5 (November 1970): 27–34.
100. "Donora, Pennsylvania," *The Atlantic*, 28.
101. "Denies Smog Zinc Blame," *New York Times*, November 17, 1948.
102. "20 Dead in Smog; Rain Clearing Air as Many Quit Area," *New York Times*, November 1, 1948.
103. Bess Furman, "Government Spurs Poisoned Air Study," *New York Times*, October 14, 1959.
104. "Death Over Donora. Smoky, Lethal Fog Kills 19 People in a Little Pennsylvania Mill Town," *Life*, November 15, 1948, 107–9.
105. "U.S. Official Warns on Air Pollution," *New York Times*, January 6, 1950.
106. David Stradling, *Smokestacks and Progressives: Environmentalists, Engineers, and Air Quality in America, 1881–1951* (Baltimore: The Johns Hopkins University Press, 1999), 45–52; Christopher Bryson, *The Fluoride Deception* (New York: Seven Stories Press, 2004), 135.
107. Scott H. Dewey, *Don't Breathe the Air: Air Pollution and U.S. Environmental Politics, 1945–1970* (College Station, TX: Texas A&M University Press, 2000), 116.
108. "Donora Aftermath," *Business Week*, October 22, 1949, 24.
109. Robert L. Heilbroner, "What Goes Up in the Chimney," *Harper's*, January 1951, 62.
110. Robert Karsh and Virginia Brodine, "Should the Air We Breathe Be Cleaned Up?" *The Edwardsville Intelligencer* (Edwardsville, IL), March 6, 1965, 2; Karsh and Brodine, "What's in the Air?" *Scientist and Citizen* 7, no. 3 (1965), 1–5; Dewey, *Don't Breathe the Air*, 48–59.
111. Gladwin Hill, "Lag on Smog Laid to Industrialists," *New York Times*, November 11, 1949.
112. "Death in Donora Dramatizes Smoke Problem," *Business Week*, November 20, 1948, 21.
113. "Death from Dirty Air in Chicago," *Newsweek*, May 23, 1949, 50.
114. "Foul Smog Over Detroit," *New York Times*, December 30, 1950.
115. "The Smog Battle: Crop Loss Raises Consumers' Price," *Los Angeles Times*, November 17, 1953.
116. James E. Krier and Edmund Ursin, *Pollution & Policy: A Case Essay on California and Federal Experience with Motor Vehicle Air Pollution, 1940–1975* (Berkeley: University of California Press, 1977), 52–56.
117. Sarah S. Elkind, *How Local Politics Shape Federal Policy: Business, Power, and the Environment in Twentieth-Century Los Angeles* (Chapel Hill: The University of North Carolina Press, 2011). On the history of local and state anti-pollution measures see Karl Boyd Brooks, *Before*

Earth Day: The Origins of American Environmental Law, 1945–1970 (Lawrence: University of Kansas Press, 2009), 61–66.
118. "California: Only a Question of Time?" Time, December 12, 1949, 21–22.
119. Gerald Markowitz, Deceit and Denial: The Deadly Politics of Industrial Pollution (Berkeley: University of California Press, 2003), 142–43.
120. Ibid. 145, 154.
121. Quoted in Markowitz, Deceit and Denial, 144–45.
122. "Donora Aftermath," BusinessWeek, 24.
123. "Death over Donora," Life, November 15, 1948, 107.
124. "Donora, Pennsylvania," The Atlantic, 28.
125. Ibid. 32–34.
126. Fairfield Osborn, "Conservation and Democracy," speech at 14th Educational Conference, New York, October 28, 1949, 8–9. Box 1, Speeches and Writings File, 1949, Aug.–Oct. Fairfield Osborn Papers, Manuscript Division, Library of Congress, Washington, DC.
127. Jack Kerouac, On The Road (New York: The Viking Press, 1957), 110.
128. T. K. Quinn, Giant Business: Threat to Democracy. The Autobiography of an Insider (New York: Exposition Press, 1953), 10–11.
129. Quinn, Giant Business, 6.
130. Fairfield Osborn, "Introduction" to Yale Conservation Studies, vol. 1 (New Haven: Yale Conservation Club, 1952), quoted in John B. Oakes, "Conservation: Politics," New York Times, October 5, 1952.

Chapter 3

1. Allan M. Winkler, Life Under a Cloud: American Anxiety About the Atom (New York: Oxford University Press, 1993), 93.
2. "How to End a World: The Truth about the Bomb," Newsweek, October 19, 1953, 34–35.
3. Martha Smith-Norris, "American Cold War Policies and the Enewetakese: Community Displacement, Environmental Degradation, and Indigenous Resistance in the Marshall Islands," Journal of Canadian Historical Association 22, no. 2 (2011): 195–236; National Cancer Institute, Estimated Exposures and Thyroid Doses Received by the American People from Iodine-131 in Fallout Fallowing Nevada Atmospheric Nuclear Bomb Tests (Washington, D.C.: U.S. Department of Health and Human Services, 1997), 2.18.
4. Estimated Exposures and Thyroid Doses, 2.2.
5. Howard Ball, "In the 1950's the Government Said its Atomic Tests in Nevada were Safe. Now,..." New York Times, February 9, 1986; Ball, Justice Downwind: America's Atomic Testing Program in the 1950's (New York: Oxford University Press, 1986), 70.
6. Philip L. Fradkin, Fallout: An American Nuclear Tragedy (Tucson: University of Arizona Press, 1989), 146–65; Winkler, Life Under a Cloud, 93; Howard Ball, "In the 1950's the Government Said its Atomic Tests in Nevada were Safe. Now,..."; Ball, Justice Downwind, 70.
7. William E. Schmidt, "Judge Says U.S. Lied in Fallout Case," New York Times, August 5, 1982. Judge Bruce S. Jenkins found the government guilty of negligence in the deaths of 10 downwinders from cancer in 1984. But an appeals court later overturned the ruling under the grounds that the AEC had wide authority to conduct nuclear tests during the era, and under the Government's discretionary function in decision-making it could not be sued. See Barton C. Hacker, "'Hotter than a Two-Dollar Pistol': Fallout, Sheep, and the Atomic Energy Commission, 1953–1986," in Bruce Hevly and John M. Findlay, eds., The Atomic West (Seattle: University of Washington Press, 1998), 164–65. For a study of the incident and examination of the trial which interrogates the AEC's actions, see Howard Ball, Justice Downwind, and for personal accounts of testing victims and photographs see Carole Gallagher, American Ground Zero: The Secret Nuclear War (Cambridge, MA: The MIT Press, 1993).
8. Iver Peterson, "Woman in Fallout Case Grew Up with Testing," New York Times, May 12, 1984.
9. The Bravo test was the second hydrogen bomb test. The first was a secret test, though news of it leaked to the public within a week, on November 1, 1952 at Eniwetok atoll.

10. "264 Exposed to Atomic Radiation After Nuclear Blast in the Pacific," *New York Times*, March 12, 1954.
11. "2d Hydrogen Blast Proves Mightier Than Any Forecast," *New York Times*, March 18, 1954.
12. Robert A. Divine, *Blowing on the Wind: The Nuclear Test Ban Debate, 1954–1960* (New York: Oxford University Press, 1978), 4–5; "'Brilliant Sunrise' Came," *New York Times*, March 17, 1954.
13. Elizabeth Weideman, "Ashes of Death: First H-Bomb Victims," *The Nation*, October 9, 1954, 309; "Brilliant Sunrise' Came," 9.
14. "Fishermen Burned in Bikini Test Blast," *New York Times*, March 16, 1954; Winkler, *Life Under a Cloud*, 94.
15. Lindesay Parrott, "Japan Buries Fish Exposed to Atom," *New York Times*, March 18, 1954; Lindesay Parrott, "Nuclear Downpour Hit Ship During Test at Bikini—U.S. Inquiry Asked," *New York Times*, March 17, 1954; "Japan Talks of Damages for A-Burned Men," *Los Angeles Times*, March 17, 1954; "Fish Put on Japanese Market Feared Tainted by Atom Ash," *Washington Post*, March 17, 1954.
16. "Japan to Certify Tuna," *New York Times*, March 21, 1954; "Fishermen Burned in Bikini Test Blast"; Parrott, "Nuclear Downpour Hit Ship"; "2d Hydrogen Blast Proves Mightier Than Any Forecast"; "Radiation and Fallout," *The Atomic Café*, DVD, directed by Kevin Rafferty, Jayne Loader, and Pierce Rafferty, 1982 (New York: New Video, 2002).
17. Harry Schwartz, "Long-Deadly Part Found in Atom Ash," *New York Times*, March 26, 1954, 5. Scientists later pegged strontium 90's half-life at 28 years.
18. "A.E.C. Manual Cited," *New York Times*, March 26, 1954.
19. Carolyn Kopp, "The Origins of the American Scientific Debate over Fallout Hazards," *Social Studies of Science* 9, no. 4 (November 1979): 405; "Injury Report Minimized," *New York Times*, March 19, 1954; "Inquiry is Begun in Hydrogen Test," *New York Times*, March 20, 1954.
20. "Japanese Dusted by H-Bomb is Dead," *New York Times*, September 24, 1954.
21. "Jaundice—Not Fallout," *New York Times*, August 23, 1955, 7; William L. Laurence, "Scientist Depicts Bikini Bomb Peril," *New York Times*, April 26, 1955; "Red Influences Blamed," *New York Times*, September 24, 1954; "U.S. Scientist Disputed," *New York Times*, March 26, 1955.
22. See Ralph E. Lapp, *The Voyage of the Lucky Dragon* (New York: Harper & Brothers, 1958).
23. Nate Haseltine, "Japanese Fisherman First H-Blast Victim," *Washington Post*, September 24, 1954; Weideman, "Ashes of Death," 308; Divine, *Blowing on the Wind*, 30.
24. "Unlucky Dragon," *Newsweek*, September 13, 1954, 52–55.
25. "Check and Regrets Sent H-Bomb Widow by U.S.," *Los Angeles Times*, September 25, 1954; Ralph E. Lapp, "The Voyage of the Lucky Dragon," *Reader's Digest*, May 1958, 120.
26. H. David Kirk, "Letters to the Times: Our Attitude on Bomb Tests," *New York Times*, April 2, 1954.
27. Thomas E. Murray, "Texts of Murray's Talk on H-Bomb at Fordham Fete and AEC Statement," *New York Times*, November 18, 1955.
28. Robert K. Plumb, "Fallout of Bomb a Defense Factor," *New York Times*, June 10, 1955, 10; Hanson W. Baldwin, "A Military Atom Problem," *New York Times*, June 14, 1956.
29. Ralph E. Lapp, "Civil Defense Faces New Peril," *Bulletin of the Atomic Scientists* 10, no. 9 (November 1954): 350.
30. Divine, *Blowing on the Wind*, 21.
31. Charles H. Coleman, "Today and Tomorrow: Atomic 'Fall-out' Endangers Feeds," *Organic Gardening and Farming* 1, no. 5 (May 1954): 65–66.
32. Joyce A. Evans, *Celluloid Mushroom Clouds: Hollywood and the Atomic Bomb* (Boulder, CO: Westview Press, 1998), 63–113; Jerome F. Shapiro, *Atomic Bomb Cinema* (New York: Routledge, 2002), 58–59; Paul Boyer, *Fallout: A Historian Reflects on America's Half-Century Encounter with Nuclear Weapons* (Columbus: Ohio State University Press, 1998), 200.
33. See Carolyn Kopp, "The Origins of the American Scientific Debate over Fallout Hazards," 36–57, 403–22; Divine, *Blowing on the Wind*, 36–57; Winkler, *Life Under a Cloud*, 95–96; "Strauss Scouts Atomic Injuries: He Asserts No One was Hurt by Radioactive Fall-Out

from Nevada Tests," *New York Times*, April 4, 1955. William L. Laurence, "Radiation Effect in Country Small: Average Exposure from all Atomic Tests Equivalent to a Chest X-Ray," *New York Times*, April 24, 1955; "Public Peril Seen in Atomic Secrecy: Vital New Medical Data Kept From Physicians, Expert Tells Senate Inquiry," *New York Times*, March 15, 1955; "Scientist Disputes AEC's Blast Data," May 30, 1955, 1, "How Fatal is Fallout?" *Time*, November 22, 1945, 81.

34. A. H. Sturtevant, "Social Implications of the Genetics of Man," *Science*, 120 (September 10, 1954): 6–7. North American Newspaper Alliance, "Geneticist Warns on Radiation Rise," *New York Times*, September 12, 1954; Kopp, "The Origins of the American Scientific Debate," 405.
35. Divine, *Blowing on the Wind*, 105.
36. "How Fatal is Fallout?" 79, 81.
37. Samuel H. Ordway, *Resources and the American Dream* (New York: The Ronald Press, 1953), 51.
38. Ordway, *Resources and the American Dream*, 50–55.
39. Ibid. 30–33, 42, 51, 53.
40. John H. Storer, *The Web of Life: A First Book of Ecology* (New York: The Devin-Adair Company, 1953), 16.
41. William A. Dreyer, "A First Book of Ecology, Review," *Ecology* 35, no. 4 (October 1954), 588.
42. Storer, *The Web of Life*, x.
43. "The Web of Life: A First Book on Ecology Explains Nature's Pattern," *Organic Gardening and Farming* 1, no. 1 (January, 1954): 20–21.
44. Storer, *The Web of Life*, 110.
45. Harrison Brown, *The Challenge of Man's Future* (New York: The Viking Press, 1954), 65; Fritz Leiber, "Our Plundered Earth: The Day of Reckoning," *Chicago Tribune*, April 4, 1954.
46. See E. F. Schumacher, "Buddhist Economics," *Alternative Society* (Welland, ON) January 1970, 16.
47. John Kenneth Galbraith, *American Capitalism: The Concept of Countervailing Power* (New Brunswick: Transaction Publishers, 1993 [originally published 1952]), 109.
48. Paul B. Sears, "The Processes of Environmental Change by Man," in William L. Thomas, Jr., ed., *Man's Role in Changing the Face of the Earth* (Chicago: University of Chicago Press, 1956), 474.
49. Thomas, Jr., "Introductory," *Man's Role*, xxviii–xxx; Lewis Mumford, *The Brown Decades, 1865–1895: A Study of the Arts in America* (New York: Harcourt, Brace and Company, 1931), 77.
50. "Discussion: The Unstable Equilibrium of Man in Nature," in Thomas Jr., *Man's Role*, 1127.
51. E. A. Gutkind, "Our World from the Air: Conflict and Adaptation," in Thomas Jr., *Man's Role*; Thomas Jr., "Introductory," xxxvii.
52. Thomas, *Man's Role*, 1087.
53. Thomas Jr., *Man's Role in Changing the Face of the Earth*, 1118–19.
54. Marston Bates, "Process," in Thomas Jr., *Man's Role*, 1140, and Thomas Jr., *Man's Role*, 1112.
55. Ordway, "Possible Limits," in Thomas Jr., *Man's Role*, 1006.
56. Allen Ginsberg, "Howl," in Ann Charters, ed., *The Portable Beat Reader* (New York: Penguin Books, 1992), 68.
57. Ginsberg, "Howl," 132–33.
58. *Metropolis* (Restored Authorized Edition), dir. Fritz Lang (1927; Kino Video, 2003 DVD). Ginsberg cited *Metropolis* as an inspiration for Part II of *Howl*, the portion focused on "Moloch." See Allen Ginsberg, *Howl: Original Draft Facsimile, Transcript & Variant Versions, Fully Annotated by Author...* Barry Miles, ed. (New York: Harper Perennial Modern Classics, 1986), 139–42.
59. Mumford, "Prospect," in Thomas Jr., *Man's Role*, 1151–52.
60. "A Conference on Using the Sun," *Los Angeles Times*, May 30, 1954; Gladwin Hill, "Scientists Cheer Sun-Power Gains," *New York Times*, November 1, 1955; Waldemar Kaempffert, "Large-Scale Utilization of Solar Energy Is Not Yet a Practical Solution," *New York Times*, November 6, 1955.

61. Daniel M. Berman and John T. O'Connor, *Who Owns the Sun?* (White River Junction, VT: Green River Publishing, 1996), 13–15; Adam Rome, *Bulldozer in the Countryside: Suburban Sprawl and the Rise of American Environmentalism* (New York: Cambridge University Press, 2001), 45–64.
62. William L. Laurence, "Taming Of H-Bomb as Fuel Forecast Within 20 Years," *New York Times*, August 9, 1955. On the future of fusion power see, for example, Leo Hickman, "Fusion Power: Is it Getting any Closer?" *The Guardian*, August 23, 2011.
63. "U.S. Town Relied on Atomic Power," *New York Times*, August 13, 1955, 6.
64. "Private Atom Plants Approved for Chicago and Detroit Areas," *New York Times*, August 9, 1955.
65. Mumford, "Prospect," in Thomas Jr., *Man's Role*, 1147.
66. "Strauss Foresees New Atomic Era," *New York Times*, April 29, 1954, 21; "General Dynamic Posters will Push 'Atoms for Peace' at Show in Geneva," *New York Times*, August 4, 1955.
67. Eric Hodgins, "Power from the Sun," *Fortune*, September 1953, 134, cited in Adam Rome, *Bulldozer in the Countryside: Suburban Sprawl and the Rise of American Environmentalism* (New York: Cambridge University Press, 2001), 52.
68. Robert Griffith, "The Last Hurrah for New Deal Liberalism," in Michael J. Lacey, ed., *The Truman Presidency* (New York: Cambridge University Press, 1989), 86; Richard N. L. Andrews, *Managing the Environment, Managing Ourselves: A History of American Environmental Policy* (New Haven: Yale University Press, 1999), 183–85.
69. Jared Farmer, *Glen Canyon Damned: Inventing Lake Powell and the Canyon Country* (Tucson: The University of Arizona Press, 1999), 23–27.
70. Environmental Protection Agency, Region 8, "EPA Fact Sheet: Rocky Mountain Arsenal," (Denver: EPA, 1992); EPA Superfund, "Rocky Mountain Arsenal," http://www.epa.gov/superfund/accomp/success/rma.htm (accessed May 8, 2012); Mark W. T. Harvey, *A Symbol of Wilderness: Echo Park and the American Conservation Movement* (Seattle: University of Washington Press, 2000), 36.
71. Farmer, *Glen Canyon Damned*, 26–27. The Atomic Energy Commission's "Access Road Program" ran from 1951–1958; For a detailed account of Civilian Conservation Corps activities see Neil M. Maher, *Nature's New Deal: The Civilian Conservation Corps and the Roots of the American Environmental Movement* (New York: Oxford University Press, 2008).
72. Harvey, *A Symbol of Wilderness*, 57; for an excellent account of conservationists' opposition to road building see Paul S. Sutter, *Driven Wild: How the Fight Against Automobiles Launched the Modern Wilderness Movement* (Seattle: University of Washington Press, 2004).
73. Harvey, *A Symbol of Wilderness*, 23–49.
74. Nash, "Exporting and Importing of Nature—Appreciation as a Commodity, 1850–1980," *Perspectives in American History* 3 (1979): 521; Harvey, *A Symbol of Wilderness*, 57–58, 164–67.
75. Maher, *Nature's New Deal*, 5; Harvey, *A Symbol of Wilderness*, 5, 82, 171, 270; John B. Oakes, "Conservation: Fate of Monument," *New York Times*, July 3, 1955.
76. Harvey, *A Symbol of Wilderness*, xix, xxi, 63, 239–41.
77. Harvey, *A Symbol of Wilderness*, 284–85; Farmer, *Glen Canyon Damned*, 143–46.
78. Raymond R. Camp, "Wood, Field and Stream: Public Increasing Pressure on Congress for Preservation of Wildlife," *New York Times*, December 22, 1955, 32; Oakes, "Conservation: A Growing Force," *New York Times*, November 13, 1955, x33; Oakes, "Conservation: Platform Pledges," *New York Times*, September 2, 1956.
79. "Highlights of the Sierra Club's History," http://www.sierraclub.org/history/timeline.asp (accessed May 19, 2007).
80. J. I. Rodale, "What is Behind the Smog?" *Organic Gardening and Farming* 1, no. 1 (January 1954): 30.
81. "Sky to Stay Murky Two Days at Least; Road Mishaps Rise," *New York Times*, November 22, 1955; "3-Day Smog Torments Entire East as Cold 'Lid' Traps Irritants in Air," *New York Times*, November 20, 1953; "Heavy Smog Darkens Day in City, Hides Sun Event Awaited 59 Years," *New York Times*, November 15, 1953; "Rain and Wind Lift City's 6-Day Siege of Smaze and Smog," *New York Times*, November 23, 1953; Kirk Johnson, "You Should Have Seen the Air in '53," *New York Times*, September 29, 2002; Dewey, *Don't Breathe the Air*, 130.

82. "Blight on the Land of Sunshine," *Life*, November 1, 1954, 17–18.
83. Dewey, *Don't Breathe the Air*, 58–59.
84. James E. Krier and Edmund Ursin, *Pollution and Policy: A Case Essay on California and Federal Experience With Motor Vehicle Air Pollution, 1940–1975* (Berkeley: University of California Press, 1977), 90–91.
85. J. I. Rodale, "Are We Breathing Disease?" 51. The six-part series on smog ran from January–June, 1954 in *Organic Gardening and Farming*.
86. "Text of the President's Health Message to Congress," *New York Times*, February 1, 1955.
87. J. Clarence Davies III and Barbara S. Davies, *The Politics of Pollution* (Indianapolis: Pegasus/Bobbs-Merrill, 1975), 27–32.
88. "Letter from Roger Jones (Bureau of the Budget) to President Eisenhower concerning the Federal-aid highway construction program," June 28, 1956. The Eisenhower Presidential Library at http://www.eisenhower.archives.gov/dl/InterstateHighways/InterstateHighwaysdocuments.html (accessed April 17, 2008).
89. Charles Grutzner, "Urban Talks Ask Cut in Auto Size," *New York Times*, September 24, 1957; "Auto-Industry Replies: Air Pollution Work is Cited in Retort to Governors," *New York Times*, September 25, 1957.
90. Dewey, *Don't Breathe the Air*, 60.
91. Bess Furman, "Smog is Termed a Cancer Cause," *New York Times*, November 19, 1958; "Exhaust Fumes: Relation to Lung Cancer is Indicated by Study," *New York Times*, May 27, 1956.
92. Sarah S. Elkind, *How Local Politics Shape Federal Policy: Business, Power, and the Environment in Twentieth-Century Los Angeles* (Chapel Hill: The University of North Carolina Press, 2011). On the history of local and state anti-pollution measures see Karl Boyd Brooks, *Before Earth Day: The Origins of American Environmental Law, 1945–1970* (Lawrence: University of Kansas Press, 2009), 61–66.
93. "Effect of H-Bomb Called Lingering," *New York Times*, June 13, 1955; Anthony Leviero, "Scientists Term Radiation a Peril to Future of Man," *New York Times*, June 13, 1956; "Text of the Digest of Findings and Recommendations on Effects of Radiation," *New York Times*, June 13, 1956; "Radiation and Man's Future," *New York Times*, June 14, 1956; Baldwin, "A Military Atom Problem," 14.
94. "Effect of H-Bomb Called Lingering," 17; Leviero, "Radiation a Peril," 1; "Text of the Digest of Findings and Recommendations on Effects of Radiation," 19; Baldwin, "A Military Atom Problem," 14.
95. Norman Isaac Silber, *Test and Protest: The Influence of Consumers Union* (New York: Holmes & Meier, 1983), 108.
96. Merrill Eisenbud and John H. Harley, "Radioactive Fallout Through September, 1955," *Science* 124, no. 3215 (August 10, 1956), 251–55; "Fall-Out Menace to Milk Minimized by Scientists," *New York Times*, August 10, 1956.
97. Donald Fleming, "The New Conservation Movement," *Perspectives in American History* 6 (1972): 42.
98. John B. Oakes, "Conservation: Platform Pledges," *New York Times*, September 2, 1956.
99. "Stevenson Sees Cover-up on Bomb: Says Administration Kept Secret Contamination of U.S. Milk by Strontium," *New York Times*, November 3, 1956.
100. Harrison E. Salisbury, "Stevenson Calls for World Pact to Curb H-Bomb," *New York Times*, October 16, 1956; "Scientists Dispute President on Bomb," *New York Times*, October 25, 1956; "Atom Experts Urge Bomb Study; Scientists Note Peril," *New York Times*, October 20, 1956; "Grave Peril Seen in Strontium-90," *New York Times*, October 24, 1956.
101. "Knowland Scores Bulganin Letter," *New York Times*, October 22, 1956, 12; Divine, *Blowing on the Wind*, 98–100.
102. Winkler, *Life Under a Cloud*, 101.
103. William G. Cahan, MD, "Letters to the Editor: Effects of Radioactivity," *New York Times*, October 31, 1956.
104. Cahan, "Letters to the Editor: Effects of Radioactivity," 32.
105. "2 New Cancer Agents Reported in Tars from Cigarette Smoke," *New York Times*, April 12, 1959.

106. "Bone Cancer Link to H-Bomb Feared," *New York Times*, April 17, 1957; "Pauling Lists 10,000 as Fallout Victims," *New York Times*, May 1, 1957; "Science Notes: Leukemia Danger in Radiation Cited," *New York Times*, May 19, 1957.
107. James T. Patterson, *The Dread Disease: Cancer and Modern American Culture* (Cambridge, MA: Harvard University Press, 1987), 160.
108. Patterson, *The Dread Disease*, 236.
109. Robert K. Plumb, "Leukemia Deaths Reported on Rise," *New York Times*, May 17, 1959; Ball, "In the 1950's the Government Said its Atomic Tests in Nevada were Safe," SM41. Although often thought to be a childhood cancer, in truth leukemia killed more adults each year than it did children, and that disparity increased between 1930 and 1960.
110. Patterson, *The Dread Disease*, 143.
111. Charles Sellers, "Discovering Environmental Cancer: Wilhelm Hueper, Post-World War II Epidemiology, and the Vanishing Clinician's Eye," *American Journal of Public Health* 87, no. 11 (November 1997): 1825–29; Wilhelm C. Hueper, *Occupational Tumors and Allied Diseases* (Springfield, IL: Charles C. Thomas, 1942).
112. Patterson, *The Dread Disease*, 187, 201–11.
113. Marjorie Ayearst, "Irony of Cancer Crusade," *New York Times*, April 16, 1958.
114. Patterson, *The Dread Disease*, 139.
115. Divine, *Blowing on the Wind*, 116.
116. Pare Lorentz, "The Fight for Survival," *McCall's*, January 1957, 29, 73–74. Cited in Spencer R. Weart, *Nuclear Fear: A History of Images* (Cambridge, MA: Harvard University Press, 1988), 297.
117. Albert Schweitzer, "Excerpts From Message by Schweitzer," *New York Times*, April 24, 1957; George Gallup, *The Gallup Poll: Public Opinion, Volume 2 (1949–1958)* (New York: Random House, 1972). Placing in front of Schweitzer in the poll were, in order, President Eisenhower, Winston Churchill, and Bishop Fulton J. Sheen.
118. Edward L. Dale, Jr., "AEC Aide Says Dr. Schweitzer Errs," *New York Times*, April 26, 1957; Milton S. Katz, *Ban the Bomb: A History of SANE, the Committee for a Sane Nuclear Policy* (New York: Praeger, 1986), 16–17.
119. Divine, *Blowing on the Wind*, 165.
120. Ralph Lapp and Jack Shubert, "Radiation Dangers," *New Republic*, May 20, 1957, 13.
121. Katz, *Ban the Bomb*, 21–23.
122. "New Group to Seek 'SANE' Atom Policy," *New York Times*, November 15, 1957; Katz, *Ban the Bomb*, 24.
123. Katz, *Ban the Bomb*, 24; Divine, *Blowing on the Wind*, 165–67.
124. "Display Ad 44," *New York Times*, November 15, 1957.
125. Katz, *Ban the Bomb*, 28–29; Divine, *Blowing on the Wind*, 168, 195.
126. Katz, *Ban the Bomb*, 29.
127. Divine, *Blowing on the Wind*, 169.
128. "Persistent Fallout," *Time*, February 17, 1958, 63; Murray Illson, "Rises in Strontium Noted in Humans," *New York Times*, February 7, 1958. The report tracked changes in the year ended June 30, 1957.
129. Katz, *Ban the Bomb*, 31.
130. Jack Gould, "Television: The Hazards of Fall-Out," *New York Times*, March 31, 1958.
131. J. I. Rodale, "Organic World: What the Common Man Can Do," *Organic Gardening and Farming* 6, no. 6 (June 1959): 2.
132. J. I. Rodale, "Organic World: What the Common Man Can Do," 2.
133. Divine, *Blowing on the Wind*, 212–38.
134. Divine, *Blowing on the Wind*, 238–39.
135. "8 of 10 Cities Show Rise in Strontium," *New York Times*, January 5, 1959.
136. "A.E.C. is Called Lax on Fall-Out in Food," *New York Times*, March 1, 1959.
137. "Faster Fall-Out is now Indicated," *New York Times*, March 20, 1959.
138. "The Milk All of Us Drink—and Fallout," *Consumer Reports*, March 1959, 102–3.
139. "The Milk All of Us Drink," 103.
140. Ibid. 104.
141. Ibid. 111; Stuart Chase, "How it All Began... By One Who Began It," *Consumer Reports*, May 1961, 258, 260–61; Silber, *Test and Protest*, 112.

142. See Glickman, *Buying Power*, 212–16.
143. "A New Dimension," *Consumer Reports*, May 1961, 278. Rodale's *Organic Gardening and Farming* carried its own six-page article on the "menace" of strontium-90 in May 1959. See M. C. Goldman, "What You Can Do About Strontium-90," *Organic Gardening and Farming* 6, no. 5 (May 1959): 24–29.
144. Worried Mother, "Effect of Fall-Out on Children," *New York Times*, March 28, 1959.
145. Lawrence S. Wittner, "Gender Roles and Nuclear Disarmament Activism, 1954–1965," *Gender and History* 12, no.1 (April 2000): 206–8.
146. Charles Bazerman, "Nuclear Information: One Rhetorical Moment in the Construction of the Information Age," *Written Communication* 18, no. 3 (July 2001): 259–95.
147. "Fallout in Our Milk: A Follow-up Report," *Consumer Reports*, February 1960, 70; "Teeth to Measure Fall-Out," *New York Times*, March 19, 1959, 67; "CU Continues its Radiation Studies," *Consumer Reports*, September 1961, 489; Divine, *Blowing on the Wind*, 268. Louise Reiss published the results of the baby teeth survey in the November 24, 1961 issue of *Science*.
148. Robert K. Plumb, "Fall-Out Iodine is Found in Milk," *New York Times*, June 21, 1959.
149. Steven M. Spencer, "FALLOUT: The Silent Killer," *The Saturday Evening Post*, August 29, 1959, 26–27, 87, 89, 90; Spencer, "FALLOUT: The Silent Killer (How Soon is Too Late)," *The Saturday Evening Post*, September 5, 1959, 25, 84–85.
150. Bazerman, "Nuclear Information," 279. The journal *Information* was renamed *Scientist and Citizen* in 1964.
151. On the significance of children and family in the postwar era, see Elaine Tyler May, *Homeward Bound: American Families in the Cold War Era* (New York: Basic Books, 1988, 1999), 17.

Chapter 4

1. Leopold Trouvelot, "The American Silkworm," *American Naturalist* 1, no. 1 (March 1867): 32–38; William H. Blair, "U.S. Sets Sights on Gypsy Moths," *New York Times*, March 30, 1957. For a complete history see Robert J. Spear, *The Great Gypsy Moth War: The History of the First Campaign in Massachusetts to Eradicate the Gypsy Moth, 1890–1901* (Amherst: University of Massachusetts Press, 2005).
2. Arthur Grahame, "Insecticides and Dead Fish," *Outdoor Life*, August 1957, 17; Blair, "U.S. Sets Sights on Gypsy Moths," 23; John C. Devlin, "Air Spray Attack on Moths Begins," *New York Times*, April 24, 1957; James P. McGaffrey, "Air Spray of DDT Upheld by Court," *New York Times*, June 25, 1958; Grahame, "Will Spraying Boomerang?," *Outdoor Life*, June 1958, 22. For a comprehensive history of DDT see David Kinkela, *DDT and the American Century: Global Health, Environmental Politics, and the Pesticide that Changed the World* (Chapel Hill: University of North Carolina Press, 2011).
3. Leonard Wickenden, "The Fish Died," in Natural Food Associates, *Natural Food and Farming Digest* (Atlanta, TX: Natural Food Associates, 1957), 71–73.
4. "The Moth and Men," *Newsweek*, May 20, 1957, 108; "U.S. Denies Air Spray of Moth Is Menace," *New York Times*, May 10, 1957; Harold M. Schmeck, Jr., "Long Islanders Ask Court to Halt DDT War on Moth as Health Risk," *New York Times*, May 9, 1957.
5. John W. Randolph, "Wood, Field and Stream: Plan for DDT Spraying Upstate to Combat Gypsy Moth Worries Angling Club," *New York Times*, April 21, 1957; Harold M. Schmeck Jr., "Long Islanders Ask Court to Halt DDT War on Moth as Health Risk," *New York Times*, May 9, 1957; "DDT Spraying Called Boondoggle," *New York Times*, May 14, 1957; "Court Test Opens on Aerial Spraying," *New York Times*, May 16, 1957.
6. William Longgood, "Poison Strafes a Farm," *The New York World-Telegram and Sun*, May 28, 1957, in *Natural Food and Farming Digest*, 95–96.
7. Longgood, "Poison Strafes a Farm," 95–96; Thomas Powell, "The People Who Sued the Government," *Organic Gardening and Farming* 6, no. 7 (July 1959): 29.
8. Display ad, *New York Times*, May 21, 1957. 26.
9. Pete Daniel, *Toxic Drift: Pesticides and Health in the Post-World War II South* (Baton Rouge: Louisiana State University Press, 2005), 56–57.

10. Grahame, "Insecticides and Dead Fish," 17, 82.
11. "DDT Spraying Arraigned," *New York Times*, May 24, 1957; "Spraying Goes on Despite Protests," *New York Times*, May 25, 1957.
12. "D.D.T. Fight Renewed," *New York Times*, June 5, 1957; "DDT Fight is Lost in Supreme Court," *New York Times*, March 29, 1960; Randolph, "Wood, Field and Stream: Trout are Jumping, Flies are Hatching, Week-End Looms as Best so Far," *New York Times*, May 24, 1957; "DDT Spray Task Nears End Here," *New York Times*, June 12, 1957; Christopher Sellers, "Body, Place and the State: The Makings of an 'Environmentalist' Imaginary in the Post-World War II U.S." *Radical History Review* 74 (1999): 35.
13. "Scientists Argue Harm of L.I. Spray," *New York Times*, July 7, 1957; "Witness Believes DDT is in City Food," *New York Times*, September 13, 1957.
14. Creighton Peet, "Are We Slowly Committing Suicide?" *American Forest* 64 (May 1958): 16; "DDT Sprays Called a Cancer Menace," *New York Times*, February 14, 1958.
15. "Prison Test Cited in DDT's Defense," *New York Times*, February 25, 1958.
16. "L.I. Residents Lose Appeal on DDT Suit," *New York Times*, October 3, 1959; "DDT Fight is Lost in Supreme Court."
17. Sellers, "Body, Place, and the State," 48; Powell, "The People Who Sued the Government," 26.
18. Cited in Edmund Russell, *War and Nature: Fighting Humans and Insects with Chemicals from World War I to Silent Spring* (New York: Cambridge University Press, 2001), 213.
19. "Organic World: Brainwashing Versus Clean Brains," *Organic Gardening and Farming* 6, no. 12 (December 1959): 2.
20. "Bird Deaths Laid to DDT," *New York Times*, June 3, 1949.
21. Thomas R. Dunlap, *DDT: Scientists, Citizens, and Public Policy* (Princeton: Princeton University Press, 1981), 79–86; Nate Haseltine, "Kennedy Urges Action to Cut Pesticide Perils," *Washington Post*, May 16, 1963.
22. John C. Devlin, "U.S. is Losing its Bald Eagles; Sterility is Suspected, DDT Cited," *New York Times*, September 13, 1958, reprinted in *Audubon* 60 (November/December 1958): 275.
23. "Organic World: How Earthworms Become Deadly," *Organic Gardening and Farming* 6, no.1 (January 1959): 2; John K. Terres, "Conservation: The Menace of DDT," *New York Times*, March 1, 1959; Dunlap, *DDT: Scientists, Citizens, and Public Policy*, 83–86; "Save the American Eagle," *Boston Globe*, September 19, 1958.
24. Robert Rodale, "Our Protectors—The Animals," *Organic Gardening and Farming* 10, no. 10 (October 1963): 16. Emphasis in original.
25. J. I. Rodale, "Nature in Action," *Organic Gardening and Farming* 6, no. 8 (August 1959): 16.
26. John C. Devlin, "U.S. Helping South in Fire Ant Fight," *New York Times*, December 23, 1957; Oscar Keeling Moore, "South Wages War on Imported Fire Ant," *New York Times*, January 19, 1958.
27. "Naturalists Urge Pesticide Research," *New York Times*, January 7, 1958; John W. Randolph, "Wood, Field and Stream: Spraying for Insect Control Held Likely to Continue Despite Latest Protest," *New York Times*, January 5, 1958; "The Greatest Killing Program of All?" *Audubon Magazine* 60 (November 1958): 254–55, 294.
28. Charles S. Elton, *The Ecology of Invasions by Animals and Plants* (London: Chapman and Hall, 1958); Irston R. Barnes, "The Cost of 'Improving' on Nature," *Washington Post*, September 20, 1959.
29. "Pesticides Held Wildlife Hazard," *New York Times*, November 11, 1958. "3 Experts Protest Fire Ant Program," *New York Times*, December 27, 1957; "Society Widens Anti-Spray Fight," *New York Times*, January 2, 1958; "Naturalists Urge Pesticide Research"; Randolph, "Wood, Field and Stream: "Spraying for Insect Control Held Likely to Continue Despite Latest Protest"; "The Greatest Killing Program of All?" 254–55, 294.
30. James W. Hancock, "Letters: Protests Aerial Spraying," *Organic Gardening and Farming* 6, no. 11 (November 1959): 6.
31. Joshua Blu Buhs has argued that corporate responsibility for the spraying programs was more perception than reality, noting, "I have been through thousands of boxes of USDA files in the National Archives, and I found only very little material connecting the chemical industry to the campaign." See Joshua Blu Buhs, *The Fire Ant Wars: Nature, Science,*

and Public Policy in Twentieth Century America (Chicago: University of Chicago Press, 2004), 61.

32. Pete Daniel, "A Rogue Bureaucracy: The USDA Fire Ant Campaign of the Late 1950s," *Agricultural History* 64, no. 2 (Spring 1990): 100.
33. James I. Hambleton and Theodore R. Gardner to Avery S. Hoyt, November 1, 1951, box 159, Correspondence Relating to Bureau Programs and Plans 1930–51, Records of the Bureau of Entomology and Plant Quarantine, Record Group 7, National Archives. Cited in Richard C. Sawyer, "Monopolizing the Insect Trade: Biological Control in the USDA, 1888–1951," *Agricultural History* 64, no. 2 (Spring 1990): 272; Jim Hightower, "Hard Tomatoes, Hard Times: Failure of the Land Grant College Complex," *Society* 10, no.1 (November 1972): 17.
34. Durward L. Allen, "Poison From the Air," *Field & Stream*, February 1959, 49–51. Emphasis in original.
35. Grahame, "Will Spraying Boomerang?" *Outdoor Life*, June 1958, 24. Emphasis in original.
36. Allen, "Poison From the Air," 50–51, 129.
37. Irston R. Barnes, "Returning Travelers Note Bird Shortage," *Washington Post*, March 15, 1959.
38. "U.S. Limits Pesticide," *New York Times*, October 28, 1959, 25; William M. Blair, "Crop-Spray Fight Going to Congress," *New York Times*, January 20, 1960; US Environmental Protection Agency, "Heptachlor Epoxide Fact Sheet," CAS 1024-57-3 (United States. Environmental Protection Agency, Chemical Hazard Identification Branch, Washington, DC, 2012), 1, www.epa.gov/osw/hazard/wastemin/minimize/factshts/hepchl.pdf (accessed August 14, 2012). Rachel Carson later argued that the FDA had known since 1952 that heptachlor, after a short period of contact with the tissues of animals or plants or with the soil, became the much more toxic heptachlor epoxide. See Rachel Carson, *Silent Spring* (Boston: Houghton Mifflin Company, 1962), 170.
39. J. I. Rodale, "Nature in Action," *Organic Gardening and Farming* 6, no. 8 (August, 1959): 15–18.
40. "Cranberry Smash," *Science* 130, no. 3387 (November 27, 1959): 1447; Clarence Dean, "Cranberry Sales Curbed," *New York Times*, November 11, 1959; James J. Nagle, "Cranberry Scare Hits Old U.S. Crop," *New York Times*, November 15, 1959.
41. "Cranberries, With Honor," *New York Times*, November 28, 1947.
42. Milton Viorst, "Farmers Violate Food Act Daily in Using Forbidden Pesticides: How it Happened Facilities Exhausted," *Washington Post*, February 5, 1960; John E. Blodgett, "Pesticides: The Regulation of an Evolving Technology," in *Consumer Health and Product Hazards: Cosmetics and Drugs, Pesticides, Food Additives*, Samuel S. Epstein and Richard D. Grundy, eds. (Cambridge: The MIT Press, 1974), 211.
43. "Those Cranberries," *The New Republic*, November 30, 1959, 3–4; "The Cranberry Boggle," *Time*, November 23, 1959, 25; "The Cranberry Affair," *Newsweek*, November 23, 1959, 35–36; "Some of Cranberry Crop Contaminated by a Weed Killer, U.S. Warns," *New York Times*, November 10, 1959, 1; Nagle, "Cranberry Scare Hits Old U.S. Crop."
44. Bess Furman, "Cranberries Set for Thanksgiving," *New York Times*, November 20, 1959.
45. "Display Ad 182," *Washington Post and Times Herald*, November 19, 1959.
46. "Environmental Health Research," *Science* 206, no. 4425 (December 21, 1979): 1361; "Substitutes Listed for Cranberries," *New York Times*, November 11, 1959.
47. "Tainted Berries Sold in Missouri," *New York Times*, November 26, 1959.
48. "Mercy, Ma! No Cranberries?" *Life*, November 23, 1959, 29–32; "Calls it Irresponsible," *New York Times*, November 11, 1959; "A Lesson from Cranberries," *Consumer Reports*, January 1960, 47–48; "The Cranberry Affair," 35; "The Cranberry Boggle," 25; "Those Cranberries," 3–4; "Protection of Food Supply" ("Letters to the Times"), *New York Times*, December 18, 1959.
49. "Mail on Cranberry Controversy Said to Support Flemming, 7-1," *New York Times*, November 22, 1959. "Mercy, Ma! No Cranberries?" 30.
50. Viorst, "Farmers Violate Food Act Daily in Using Forbidden Pesticides."
51. "Trace of DDT Found in 1958 Tests of Milk in Washington, Other Cities," *Washington Post*, December 22, 1959.
52. Peter B. Bart, "Surging Chemicals Leave a Firm Imprint on 1950's," *New York Times*, January 11, 1960.
53. "P.S. to 'Chemicals in Food,'" *Consumer Reports*, July 1958, 349.

54. Richard D. Lyons, "Ousted F.D.A. Chief Charges 'Pressure' From Drug Industry," *New York Times*, December 31, 1969; Lyons, "Dr. Ley Leaving U.S. Service Today," *New York Times*, December 12, 1969.
55. Leonard Wickenden, *Our Daily Poison: The Effects of DDT, Fluorides, Hormones and Other Chemicals on Modern Man* (New York: Devin-Adair, 1955).
56. Wickenden, *Our Daily Poison*, xiv.
57. Frederick H. Mueller, "The Latest Challenge Confronting American Business," speech at the Economic Club of Detroit, Civic Center, October 19, 1969, 6, in "Business in Politics" folder, Box 3, Ewald Research Files, Fred A. Seaton: Papers, 1946\–1972, Dwight D. Eisenhower Presidential Library.
58. Wickenden, *Our Daily Poison*, 171–73.
59. Display ad, *Organic Gardening and Farming* 6, no. 7 (July 1959): 47. Numbers for display ads are given for the New York Times ads in Proquest database, so I have used them in the hope that it might help other researchers. For other sources, I have no numbers but have borrowed the phrase "display ad" from the NY Times listings in Proquest for the sake of consistency.
60. V. O. Key, *Politics, Parties, and Pressure Groups*, 4th ed. (New York: Crowell, 1958), 83.
61. Fairfield Osborn, Speech at the 67th Annual Convention of the General Federation of Women's Clubs, Detroit, MI, June 3, 1958, 4. Box 1, Speech File, 1952, Sept.–1959. Fairfield Osborn Papers, Manuscript Division, Library of Congress, Washington, DC.
62. T. K. Quinn, *Giant Corporations: Challenge to Freedom* (New York: Exposition Press, 1956), 101. Emphasis in original.
63. See, for example, "These Precious Days," *New Yorker*, December 12, 1959, 194–95; "These Precious Days," *New Yorker*, December 19, 1959, 121–22.
64. For chemicals and Rachel Carson's decision to write *Silent Spring*, see Mark Hamilton Lytle's *The Gentle Subversive: Rachel Carson's Silent Spring and the Rise of the Environmental Movement* (New York: Oxford University Press, 2007), especially 112–54, and William Souder, *On a Farther Shore: The Life and Legacy of Rachel Carson* (New York: Crown, 2012),
65. John A. Osmundsen, "Food-Additive Curb Is in Effect; Doubts Over Its Meaning Linger," *New York Times*, March 6, 1960.
66. John A. Osmundsen, "Food Trade Awaits Impact of U.S. Law on Additives," *New York Times*, February 23, 1959.
67. Ruth E. Brecher, "The Chemicals We Eat," *The Nation*, July 23, 1951, 584.
68. "Some Principles for a Bill to Safeguard Consumers," *Consumer Reports*, February 1958, 106.
69. "Food Chemicals Hit," *New York Times*, December 14, 1950.
70. M. C. Goldman, "The Congressman Who Fights for Safe Food," *Organic Gardening and Farming* 17, no. 5 (May 1970): 67.
71. James J. Delaney, et al., "Investigation of the Use of Chemicals in Food Products," January 3, 1951, Report No. 3254 to the *U.S. House of Representatives, 81st Congress, 2nd Session*, 2-3.
72. "Food Man Depicts Fight on Pesticides," *New York Times*, February 1, 1952; "Testimony of L. G. Cox" in *Chemicals in Food Products*, 82nd Congress, 1st Session (Washington: Government Printing Office, 1953), 594.
73. Louly Baer, "Keeping Foods Pure," *New York Times*, February 9, 1952.
74. Dunlap, *DDT: Scientists, Citizens, and Public Policy*, 73.
75. "Pre-Testing Urged," 31.
76. Dunlap, *DDT, Scientists, Citizens, and Public Policy*, 64–65.
77. M. C. Goldman, "Poison by the Plateful," *Organic Gardening and Farming* 1, no. 3 (March 1954): 47.
78. William L. Laurence, "Scientists Rate Food Additives," *New York Times*, September 18, 1956; E. W. Kentworthy, "U.S. Seeks to Curb Food Chemicals," *New York Times*, March 3, 1957.
79. Arnaldo Cortesi, "Cancer is Traced to Food Additives," *New York Times*, August 21, 1956.
80. W. C. Hueper, "The Potential Role of Non-Nutritive Food Additives and Contaminants as Environmental Carcinogens," in "Report of Symposium on Potential Cancer Hazards from Chemical Additives and Contaminants to Foodstuffs," *ACTA UNIO Internationales Contra Cancrum* 13 (1957): 220; Christopher Sellers, "Discovering Environmental Cancer: William Hueper, Post-World War II Epidemiology, and the Vanishing Clinician's Eye," *American Journal of Public Health* 87, no. 11 (November 1997): 1827; James Patterson,

The Dread Disease: Cancer and American Culture (Cambridge: Harvard University Press, 1987), 187–90.
81. Thomas Powell, "New Poisons Imperil Our Meat," *Organic Gardening and Farming* 6, no. 3 (March 1959): 103; W. C. Hueper, "The Potential Role of Non-Nutritive Food Additives and Contaminants as Environmental Carcinogens," 220; Cortesi, "Cancer is Traced to Food Additives," 31; John Lear, "Food and Cancer," *Saturday Review of Literature* 39 (October 6, 1956): 57–62; Laurence, "Scientists Rate Food Additives."
82. Alan I. Marcus, *Cancer from Beef: DES, Federal Food Regulation, and Consumer Confidence* (Baltimore: The Johns Hopkins University Press, 1994), 40.
83. David A. Kessler, "Implementing the Anticancer Clauses of the Food, Drug and Cosmetic Act," *The University of Chicago Law Review* 44, no. 4 (Summer 1977): 822, n. 31; Nicholas Wade, "Delaney Anti-Cancer Clause: Scientists Debate on Article of Faith," *Science* 177, no. 4049 (August 1972): 588, 591.
84. Lyons, "Congressman Says Actress's Speech Helped Bar Cyclamates," *New York Times*, October 22, 1969.
85. Wade, "Delaney Anti-Cancer Clause," 588–89.
86. "You Ought to Know About:" *Consumer Reports*, April 1953, 140.
87. Peter B. Bart, "Pesticide Scare Worries Makers," *New York Times*, November 22, 1959.
88. "United States to Pay Indemnity for Cranberry Loss," *Science* 131, no. 3406 (April 8, 1960): 1033–34.
89. "U.S. Ends Testing of 188 Food Items," *New York Times*, November 25, 1958; John A. Osmundsen, "New Law Likely to Improve Foods," *New York Times*, February 24, 1959; "Some Principles for a Bill to Safeguard Consumers," *Consumer Reports*, February 1958, 107.
90. "Locking the Barn Door First," *Science* 129, no. 3343 (January 23, 1959): 177; "Numerous 'Small' Adulterations Make Big Holes in Food and Drug Control," *Consumer Bulletin* 43 (June 1960): 10–11; William F. Longgood, *The Poisons in Your Food* (New York: Simon and Schuster, 1960), 235–36.
91. Cited in Longgood, *The Poisons in Your Food*, 238–39. Emphasis in original.
92. Bess Furman, "Poultry Treated by Drug Barred," *New York Times*, December 11, 1959; "Food Man Depicts Fight on Pesticides."
93. Powell, "New Poisons Imperil Our Meat," 100.
94. Marcus, *Cancer from Beef*, 1–2, 15, 22.
95. Marcus, *Cancer from Beef*, 1, 20–25; Longgood, *The Poisons in Your* Food, 132.
96. Drew Pearson, "The Washington Merry-Go-Round: Cancer Laid to Cattle Feed Drug," *Washington Post*, November 18, 1959. Marcus, *Cancer from Beef*, 1.
97. Wade, "Delaney Anti-Cancer Clause," 589.
98. R. M. Melampy, John Gurland, and J. M. Rakes, "Estrogen Excretion by Cows after Oral Administration of Diethylstilbestrol," *Journal of Animal Science* 18, no. 1 (February 1959): 178–86; S. Biswas, C.A. Sapiro, et al., "Current Knowledge on the Environmental Fate, Potential Impact, and Management of Growth-Promoting Steroids Used in the US Beef Cattle Industry," *Journal of Soil and Water Conservation* 68, no. 4 (July/August 2013): 325–336.
99. Marcus, *Cancer from Beef*, 1, 20–23, 54–55, 59, 113. Although DES was banned, other synthetic steroids have taken its place. In the year 2000, 96 percent of cattle in feedlots received some type of growth-promoting steroid. See Biswas, Sapiro, et al., 325.

Chapter 5

1. Vance Packard, *The Waste Makers* (New York: David McKay Company, 1960), 233.
2. Packard, *The Waste Makers*, 6, 196.
3. John Kenneth Galbraith, *The Affluent Society* (New York: Mentor Books, 1958), 272.
4. Galbraith, "How Much Should a Country Consume?" in Henry Jarrett, ed., *Perspectives on Conservation: Essays on America's Natural Resources* (Baltimore: The Johns Hopkins Press, 1958), 92.
5. Galbraith, "How Much Should a Country Consume?" 95, 98.
6. Ibid. 96.

7. Ibid. 99.
8. Ibid. 94.
9. Ibid. 95, 97.
10. Philip M. Hauser, "The Crucial Value Problems," in Jarrett, ed., *Perspectives on Conservation*, 105.
11. Colin Campbell, *The Romantic Ethic and the Spirit of Modern Consumerism* (Oxford: Blackwell, 1987).
12. For the paradox of consumption and idealism, see Campbell, *The Romantic Ethic*, especially 204–216.
13. Arlene Dahl, "A Road to Beauty: Organic Foods," *Chicago Daily Tribune*, July 17, 1959; Bob Thomas, "Stars Go for Organic Food Fad; Make the Aware Inn Prosperous," *The Milwaukee Journal*, April 24, 1959; Akasha Richmond, *Hollywood Dish* (New York: Penguin Books, 2006), 135; Art Buchwald, "The Hollywood Health Faddists," *Los Angeles Times*, December 25, 1959; "Display Ad 37," *Los Angeles Times*, May 13, 1955.
14. Richard D. Lyons, "Congressman Says Actress's Speech Helped Bar Cyclamates," *New York Times*, October 22, 1969.
15. William Longgood, *The Poisons in Your Food* (New York: Simon and Schuster, 1960), 1, 3.
16. Longgood, *The Poisons in Your Food*, 129.
17. "Display Ad 35," *New York Times*, April 13, 1960, 35.
18. Longgood, *The Poisons in Your Food*, 246–47.
19. J. O. Moffett, "Grasshopper Spraying and Honey Bees," *American Bee Journal* 98, no. 441 (1958): 115; L. D. Andersen and E. L. Atkins, Jr., "Pesticide Usage in Relation to Beekeeping," *Annual Review of Entomology* 13 (January 1968): 213–38; "Organic World: Grasshopper Spray Controversy," *Organic Gardening and Farming* 6, no. 3 (March 1959), 3. J. O. Moffett later returned to his academic life in entomology at Oklahoma State University.
20. Longgood, *The Poisons in Your Food*, 259; Nate Haseltine, "Heart Disease Experiments Hint That Not All Fats Clog Arteries," *Washington Post*, September 13, 1957, D4; Graham Berry, "Heart Disease Linked to Hydrogenated Fats," *Los Angeles Times*, May 1, 1958, B3.
21. Ibid. 248.
22. Cited in Roland Marchand, *Creating the Corporate Soul: The Rise of Public Relations and Corporate Imagery in American Big Business* (Berkeley: The University of California Press, 1998), 357. Emphasis in original.
23. Thomas Jundt, "Keep America Beautiful," in Shepard Krech III, J. R. McNeill, and Carolyn Merchant, eds., *Encyclopedia of World Environmental History* (New York: Routledge, 2003); Inger L. Stole, *Advertising on Trial: Consumer Activism and Corporate Public Relations in the 1930s* (Urbana: University of Illinois Press, 2005), 185–87; Ad Council, "Pollution: Keep American Beautiful," http://www.adcouncil.org/default.aspx?id=132 (accessed October 17, 2006).
24. William J. Darby, book review of *The Poisons in Your Food* by William Longgood, *Science* 131, no. 3405 (April 1960): 979.
25. "Panel Discussion of Additives and Residues in Human Food," *The American Journal of Clinical Nutrition* 9 (May–June 1961): 299.
26. John A. Osmundsen, "Chemicals for Dinner," *New York Times*, May 1, 1960.
27. Longgood, *The Poisons in Your Food*, 271.
28. Ibid. 271–72.
29. Franklin Bicknell, *Chemicals in Your Food and in Farm Produce: Their Harmful Effects* (New York: Emerson Books, 1960), 1.
30. Bicknell, *Chemicals in Your Food*, 44–45, 60, 88. Research had demonstrated that DDT collected in the body fat of mammals, and concentrated in mother's milk, as early as 1945 in research on dogs reported in Geoffrey Woodard, Ruth R. Ofner, and Charles Montgomery, "Accumulation of DDT in the Body Fat and its Appearance in the Milk of Dogs," *Science*, New Series, 102, no. 2642 (August 17, 1945): 177–78.
31. Bicknell, *Chemicals in Your Food*, 71–78, 135.
32. World Health Organization, "WHO Global Strategy for Containment of Anti-Microbial Resistance," (2001) http://www.who.int/drugresistance/en/ (accessed April 11, 2008).
33. Bicknell, *Chemicals in Your Food*, 7–8.

34. Norma H. Goodhue, "U.S. Official Blasts 'Food Quacks,'" *Los Angeles Times*, August 27, 1959.
35. Longgood, *The Poisons in Your Food*, 129; Dick Kidson, "Farmers Market Today," *Los Angeles Times*, September 7, 1960.
36. "Display Ad 21," *New York Times*, February 19, 1960, 19; Robert Rodale, "1963—A Year for Action," *Organic Gardening and Farming* 10, no. 9 (September 1963): 16.
37. Louise Hughston, "Crusading Zeal Abounds in Health Food Sales," *Washington Post*, September 27, 1959.
38. Robert Rodale, "1963—A Year for Action," 16. Rodale reported that the Chicago cooperative had been in operation for "several" years.
39. "Display Ad 175," *New York Times*, July 13, 1958, SM49; Margalit Fox, "Paul K. Keene, 94, Organic Farming Pioneer," *New York Times*, May 18, 2005; "Display Ad 142," *Los Angeles Times*, November 10, 1957, 16.
40. Longgood, *The Poisons in Your Food*, 269–71.
41. "Our History," Arrowhead Mills, http://www.arrowheadmills.com/content/our-history (accessed February 6, 2012).
42. "Display Ad" *Organic Gardening and Farming* 8, no. 8 (August 1961): 83.
43. "Display Ad," *Organic Gardening and Farming* 10, no. 7 (July 1963): 42.
44. "Display Ad 248," *New York Times*, May 11, 1958, SM73.
45. "Organic Camp Sites: A National Listing," *Organic Gardening and Farming* 6, no. 6 (June 1959): 43–48.
46. "Display Ad," *Organic Gardening and Farming* 8, no. 7 (July 1961): 9.
47. René Dubos, *Torch of Life: Continuity in Living Experience* (New York: Trident Press, 1962), 79–80. Dubos coined the phrase when an advisor to the United Nations Conference on Human Environment in 1972. See Ruth A. Eblen and William A. Eblen, eds., *The Encyclopedia of the Environment* (Boston: Houghton Mifflin Company, 1994), 702.
48. Dubos, *Torch of Life*, 118, 124.
49. Ibid. 137.
50. Ansel Adams and Nancy Newhall, *This Is the American Earth* (San Francisco: The Sierra Club, 1960), iv.
51. Adams and Newhall, *This Is the American Earth*, 1–47.
52. Adams and Newhall, *This Is the American Earth*, 60, 62, 74.
53. "Highlights of the Sierra Club's History," http://www.sierraclub.org/history/timeline.asp (accessed May 19, 2007).
54. John F. Kennedy, "We Must Climb to the Hilltop," *Life*, August 22, 1960, 75; Richard M. Nixon, "Our Resolve is Running Strong," *Life*, August 29, 1960, 85–94.
55. John F. Kennedy, "Campaign Remarks, Redding, Calif., September 8, 1960," John F. Kennedy Presidential Library and Museum, http://www.jfklibrary.org/Research/Ready-Reference/JFK-Speeches/Remarks-of-Senator-John-F-Kennedy-Redding-California-September-8-1960.aspx (accessed September 26, 2012).
56. John F. Kennedy, "Remarks at the Hanford, Washington Electric Generating Plant," September 26, 1963, in John Woolley and Gerhard Peters, *The American Presidency Project* [online]. Santa Barbara, CA: University of California (hosted), Gerhard Peters (database), http://www.presidency.ucsb.edu/ws/?pid=9436 (accessed April 2, 2007). The first reactors at Hanford were part of the Manhattan Project to build the Bomb. It presently holds the distinction of being the country's most contaminated nuclear site. See Shannon Dininny, "U.S. to Assess the Harm from Hanford," *Seattle Post-Intelligencer*, April 3, 2007.
57. Robert A. Divine, *Blowing on the Wind: The Nuclear Test Ban Debate, 1954–1960* (New York: Oxford University Press, 1978), 291; Milton S. Katz, *Ban the Bomb: A History of SANE, the Committee for a Sane Nuclear Policy* (New York: Praeger, 1986), 41.
58. Murray Schumach, "'Thinking' Actors in Vogue on Coast," *New York Times*, May 5, 1960, 41; Katz, *Ban the Bomb*, 42–43.
59. The one-year moratorium on testing ended in November 1959, but was extended for another two months in the hope of reaching an agreement.
60. "Senator Demands Group 'Purge' Reds," *New York Times*, May 26, 1960.

61. Barbara Deming, "The Ordeal of SANE," *The Nation*, March 11, 1961: 200–205; "SANE—and Others," *Time*, April 27, 1962, 22; "Unhelpful Fringes," *Life*, May 12, 1961, 32; Katz, *Ban the Bomb*, 45–64.
62. "Strontium-90 in the Total Diet," *Consumer Reports*, June 1960, 289–92.
63. "20 Dead in Smog; Rain Clearing Air as Many Quit Area," *New York Times*, November 1, 1948; "Pollution Curbs Asked," *New York Times*, June 26, 1960; Robert J. Brulle, *Agency, Democracy, and Nature: The U.S. Environmental Movement from a Critical Theory Perspective* (Cambridge, MA: The MIT Press, 2000), 141.
64. James T. Patterson, *Grand Expectations: The United States, 1945–1974* (New York: Oxford University Press, 1996), 497; Allan M. Winkler, *Life Under a Cloud: American Anxiety About the Atom*, (New York: Oxford University Press, 1993), 126–27.
65. Marjorie Hunter, "12 States Record Rise in Fallout," *New York Times*, September 19, 1961.
66. "Fall-out Increases 400 Times," *New York Times*, October 12, 1961.
67. Marjorie Hunter, "A Radiation Rise in Milk Detected," *New York Times*, October 13, 1961; John W. Finney, "Congress Told New Soviet A-Tests Could Bring Milk Hazard," *New York Times*, June 8, 1962.
68. "Fall-Out Held Cancer Peril to Future Generations," *New York Times*, October 18, 1961.
69. "Soviet Bomb's Victims of Future Get Obituary," *New York Times*, October 25, 1961.
70. "Excess of Leukemia Detected in Fallout Zones, Doctor Says," *New York Times*, September 18, 1982; Howard Ball, "In the 1950's the Government Said its Atomic Tests in Nevada were Safe. Now,..." *New York Times*, February 9, 1986.
71. "Display Ad 161," *New York Times*, October 29, 1961, E5.
72. John W. Finney, "Test Denounced," *New York Times*, October 31, 1961; Katz, *Ban the Bomb*, 68–69.
73. Paul Boyer, *Fallout: A Historian Reflects on America's Half-Century Encounter with Nuclear Weapons* (Columbus: Ohio State University Press, 1998), 122–25; "SANE—and Others," 22–23; Foster Hailey, "White House Vigil Reflects Peace Drive on Campuses," *New York Times*, November 24, 1961; Todd Gitlin, *The Sixties: Years of Hope, Days of Rage* (New York: Bantam, 1987), 87–94.
74. Amy Swerdlow, *Women Strike for Peace* (Chicago: The University of Chicago Press, 1993), 15–26.
75. Swerdlow, *Women Strike for Peace*, 17, 46.
76. Ibid. 1, 17–19.
77. "2d A-Test 'Strike' Staged by Women," *New York Times*, December 2, 1961; Swerdlow, *Women Strike for Peace*, 83.
78. Swerdlow, *Women Strike for Peace*, 83.
79. "Food and Nutrition: Advice on a Healthful Diet and Avoiding the Wrong Foods and Harmful Chemical Additives," *Consumer Bulletin* 36 (1961–1962), 175–76.
80. Ibid.
81. Robert Rodale, "Now the Chemical People are Zealots," *Organic Gardening and Farming* 8, no. 11 (November 1961): 17–20.
82. Harold Aaron, "How Safe are the Chemicals in Our Food?" *Consumer Reports*, January 1958, 46.
83. See, for example Annelise Orleck, "We Are That Mythical Thing Called the Public: Militant Housewives during the Great Depression," *Feminist Studies* 19, no. 1 (Spring 1993): 147–72; Dana Frank, *Purchasing Power: Consumer Organizing, Gender, and the Seattle Labor Movement, 1919–1929* (New York: Cambridge University Press, 1994), especially 108–38; or Orleck, *Common Sense and a Little Fire: Women and Working-Class Politics in the United States, 1900–1965* (Chapel Hill: The University of North Carolina Press, 1995).
84. Philip Benjamin, "Steep Drop in Milk Consumption Stirs Government and Dairymen," *New York Times*, February 18, 1962.
85. Tom Wicker, "President Hails American Cow: Again Pleads for Drinking Milk," *New York Times*, January 25, 1962.
86. Swerdlow, *Women Strike for Peace*, 83–84; Katz, *Ban the Bomb*, 71.

87. "Text of Kennedy's Conservation Message Asking an Expanded 8-Year Program," *New York Times*, March 2, 1962; Felix Belair, Jr., "Billion is Sought for Conservation," *New York Times*, March 2, 1962.
88. Joseph A. Loftus, "Udall Urges Aid on Conservation," *New York Times*, May 25, 1962, 30; Loftus, "Kennedy Accents Use of Resources," *New York Times*, May 26, 1962.
89. Landon Y. Jones, *Great Expectations: America and the Baby Boom Generation* (New York: Coward, McCann & Geoghegan, 1980), 48.
90. Katz, *Ban the Bomb*, 75; "SANE—and Others," 22.
91. Katz, *Ban the Bomb*, 72–75. In 1963, Spock became co-chair of SANE.
92. Benjamin Spock, "Display Ad 122," *New York Times*, April 16, 1962, 30. Emphasis in original.
93. Phyllis Ehrlich, "Young React To the Fear Of Radiation," *New York Times*, November 6, 1961.
94. Robert K. Plumb, "Deformed Babies Traced to a Drug," *New York Times*, April 12, 1962; "Thalidomide and Strontium," *The Nation*, August 11, 1962, 42–43; "Sleeping Pill Nightmare," *Time*, February 23, 1962, 86; "10,000 Malformed Babies," *Time*, September 7, 1962, 49; "Drug that Left a Trail of Heartbreak," *Life*, August 10, 1962, 24–36; "Tragedy From a Pill Bottle," *Newsweek*, August 13, 1962, 52–54. See Arthur Daemmrich, "A Tale of Two Experts: Thalidomide and Political Engagement in the United States and West Germany," *Social History of Medicine* 15, no. 1 (2002): 137–39; "Doctor's Actions Bars Birth Defects," *New York Times*, July 16, 1962.
95. *The Day the Earth Caught Fire*, written by Wolf Mankowitz and Val Guest, directed by Val Guest (2012, Lionsgate, DVD. Original release 1961, US debut 1962); "'The Day the Earth Caught Fire' Opens," *New York Times*, March 16, 1962.
96. Malvina Reynolds, "What Have They Done to the Rain?" *Ear to the Ground* (2000, Smithsonian Folkways, CD, B00004SU9Z).
97. Bob Dylan, "A Hard Rain's A-Gonna Fall," *The Freewheelin' Bob Dylan* (1963, Columbia, vinyl recording, PC8686).
98. "Bob Dylan Sings His Compositions," *New York Times*, April 13, 1963. Dylan has denied that "hard rain" refers to fallout.
99. Allen Ginsberg in *No Direction Home*, directed by Martin Scorsese (Hollywood, CA: Paramount, 2005, DVD).
100. John W. Finney, "Iodine Fall-Out Still High in Milk," *New York Times*, June 15, 1962, William Laurence, "Fall-Out Concern," *New York Times*, June 24, 1962; Divine, *Blowing on the Wind*, 316.
101. Murray Bookchin, *Our Synthetic Environment*, rev. ed. (New York: Harper Colophon Books, 1974), 175.
102. Bookchin, *Our Synthetic Environment*, xxxiv.
103. Ibid. 62-88, 210.
104. Ibid. 223.
105. Bookchin, *Our Synthetic Environment*, 239–40; "Dangerous Environment of Man," *Consumer Bulletin* 45 (August 1962): 23.
106. Bookchin, *Our Synthetic Environment*, 242–45.
107. "The Dangerous Environment of Man," *Consumer Bulletin* 45, no. 8 (August 1962): 24.
108. "Display Ad 153," *New York Times*, July 5, 1962, 40.
109. "Milk Plan Fights Iodine 131 Danger," *New York Times*, August 19, 1962.
110. Eric Bentley and Frank Rich, *Thirty Years of Treason* (New York: Nation Books, 2002), 951, cited in Swerdlow, *Women Strike for Peace*, 97–98.
111. Swerdlow, *Women Strike for Peace*, 111.
112. Ibid. 117.
113. John W. Finney, "U.S. Report on 12-Month Fallout Shows High Iodine 131 Levels Only in Alaska and Utah," *New York Times*, November 15, 1962; Finney, "A.E.C. Retreats on Utah Fallout," *New York Times*, October 2, 1963.
114. "Eskimos in Peril in Fallout Taint," *New York Times*, January 12, 1963.
115. Morris Kaplan, "Geneticist Asks Storage of Sperm to Circumvent Radiation Perils," *New York Times*, April 27, 1963.

116. Max Frankel, "Impact on the Cold War: It Will Continue, but Both Sides in the Struggle Have Learned Lessons for the Future From Cuban Crisis," *New York Times*, November 4, 1962; "West Acts Anew for Ban on Tests," *New York Times*, November 3, 1962.
117. Swerdlow, *Women Strike for Peace*, 81.
118. Winkler, *Life Under a Cloud*, 182.
119. Stewart Alsop, "Neither Will I Again Smite Every Thing Living," *Saturday Evening Post*, June 17, 1967, 16; cited in Boyer, *Fallout*, 355.
120. Douglas Coupland, *Life after God* (New York: Pocket Books, 1994), 101.
121. Gitlin, *The Sixties*, 22–23.
122. Robert Rodale, "1963—A Year for Action," 15.
123. About half of *Silent Spring* appeared in a series in the *New Yorker* in June 1962. For a detailed study of Carson's use of the fallout as a metaphor in *Silent Spring*, see Ralph H. Lutts, "Chemical Fallout: Rachel Carson's *Silent Spring*, Radioactive Fallout, and the Environmental Movement," *Environmental Review* 9, no. 3 (1985): 210–25; for its comparison with *Uncle Tom's Cabin* see, for example, Walter Sullivan, "Books of the Times," *New York Times*, September 27, 1962.
124. Rachel Carson, *Silent Spring* (Boston: Houghton Mifflin, 1962), 6.
125. "Rachel Carson Dies of Cancer; 'Silent Spring' Author was 56," *New York Times*, April 15, 1964.
126. Carson, *Silent Spring*, 13.
127. Ibid. 174.
128. Ibid. 183.
129. Fairfield Osborn, untitled speech, February 1962, 1–2. Box 2, speech file, 1960–66 and untitled. Fairfield Osborn Papers, Manuscript Division, Library of Congress, Washington, DC.
130. Linda Lear, *Rachel Carson: Witness for Nature* (New York: Henry Holt & Company, 1997), 374–75.
131. "Rachel Carson's Warning," *New York Times*, July 2, 1962. Paul Herman Muller, inventor of DDT, received the Nobel Prize in 1948.
132. Frank Graham, Jr., *Since Silent Spring* (Greenwich, CT: Fawcett Publications, 1970), 59–60, 63–76. See also Lear, *Rachel Carson*, 428–48.
133. "President's Scientific Panel Warns against Pesticide Use," [excerpts] *Organic Gardening and Farming* 10, no. 7 (July 1963): 43–44.
134. William L. Laurence, "Pesticide Danger: Report Points Up Need for Greater Knowledge of Chemical Effects," *New York Times*, May 19, 1963.
135. Fairfield Osborn, *Our Plundered Planet* (Boston: Little, Brown and Company, 1948), 61. DDT's ban was official at the end of 1972.

Chapter 6

1. Martin V. Melosi, "Johnson and Environmental Policy," in *The Johnson Years, Volume Two: Vietnam, the Environment, and Science* (Lawrence: University Press of Kansas, 1987), 118–19.
2. Aldous Huxley, *The Politics of Ecology: The Question of Survival* (New York: Center for the Study of Democratic Institutions, 1963), 1–7.
3. Lyndon B. Johnson, "Great Society Speech," May 22, 1964 http://www.teachingamericanhistory.org/library/index.asp?document=92 (accessed January 28, 2007). See Adam Rome, "Give Earth a Chance: The Environmental Movement and the Sixties," *The Journal of American History*, September 2003, http://www.historycooperative.org/journals/jah/90.2/rome.html (January 28, 2007).
4. Lyndon B. Johnson, "Remarks on Conservation at a Breakfast in Portland Saluting the Northwest-Southwest Power Transmission Intertie," in John Woolley and Gerhard Peters, *The American Presidency Project* [online]. Santa Barbara, CA: University of California (hosted), Gerhard Peters (database), http://www.presidency.ucsb.edu/ws/?pid=26507 (accessed April 2, 2007).
5. Johnson, "Remarks on Conservation."
6. Melosi, "Johnson and Environmental Policy," 119–23.

7. Mark Harvey, *Wilderness Forever: Howard Zahniser and the Path to the Wilderness Act* (Seattle: University of Washington Press, 2005), 238.
8. Raymond F. Dasmann, *The Last Horizon* (New York: The Macmillan Company, 1963), 230, 232.
9. Arthur Koestler, *The Lotus and the Robot* (New York: Harper Collins, 1960).
10. Dasmann, *The Last Horizon*, 229.
11. Ibid. 229–30.
12. Ibid. 232.
13. Hyman Rickover, "Energy Resources and Our Future," (speech, Annual Scientific Assembly of the Minnesota State Medical Association, St. Paul, MN, May 14, 1957), http://www.archive.org/details/rickover0557 (accessed June 10, 2010).
14. Dasmann, *The Last Horizon*, 5–6. Emphasis mine.
15. On white masculinity and wilderness see Tracy Marafiote, "Gender, Race, and Nature: A Cultural History of the Wilderness Society and the Wilderness Act of 1964" (PhD diss., University of Utah, 2006), especially 63–73, 86–88, 210–11, 218–21.
16. "Wilderness Bill is Facing Defeat," *New York Times*, September 16, 1962, 56; Stewart Udall, *The Quiet Crisis* (New York: Holt, Rinehart & Winston, 1963).
17. Robert Gottlieb, *Forcing the Spring*, 43–44; Hal K. Rothman, *The Greening of a Nation: Environmentalism in the United States Since 1945* (New York: Harcourt Brace College Publishers, 1998), 48–55; Kirkpatrick Sale, *The Green Revolution: The American Environmental Movement 1962–1992* (New York: Hill and Wang, 1993), 14–16. The first area reclassified as wilderness in 1968 was San Rafael Wilderness in Los Padres National Forest in California.
18. Among the Endangered Species Act provisions were $15 million per year to buy habitat for listed species, and a direction to federal land agencies to preserve endangered species' habitat on those lands "insofar as is practicable and consistent with their primary purpose."
19. Walter Sullivan, "DDT Detected in Aquatic Life in Both the Atlantic and Pacific," *New York Times*, November 15, 1963.
20. "Scientists Discover Why Fish Caught Here Taste Peculiar," *New York Times*, January 24, 1964.
21. "Omaha Promises to End Pollution," *New York Times*, July 26, 1964.
22. David Anderson, "Poisons Kill Fish in the Mississippi," *New York Times*, March 22, 1964.
23. Cited in Anderson, "Poisons Kill Fish in the Mississippi," 79.
24. John W. Finney, "U.S. Agency Warned Year Ago that Pesticides Could Kill Fish," *New York Times*, April 7, 1964.
25. Donald Janson, "Pesticides Fatal to Gulf Shrimp," *New York Times*, March 26, 1964.
26. Oscar Godbout, "The Death of 70,000 Trout in Oregon is Traced to Use of Pesticide," *New York Times*, September 19, 1963.
27. "Use of Pesticides Backed by Maker," *New York Times*, April 11, 1964.
28. Robert C. Toth, "Pesticide Makers Score U.S. Report," *New York Times*, June 26, 1963.
29. Robert Rodale, "1963—A Year for Action," *Organic Gardening and Farming* 10, no. 9 (September 1963): 16.
30. Lyndon B. Johnson: "Presidential Policy Paper No. 3: Conservation of Natural Resources," November 1, 1964. Online by Gerhard Peters and John T. Woolley, *The American Presidency Project*, http://www.presidency.ucsb.edu/ws/?pid=26705 (accessed March 13, 2007).
31. Lyndon B. Johnson, "Special Message to the Congress on Conservation and the Restoration of Natural Beauty," February 8, 1965, in *Public Papers of the Presidents of the United States: Lyndon B. Johnson, 1965* (Washington, DC: Government Printing Office, 1966), vol. 1, entry 54, 155–65, http://www.lbjlib.utexas.edu/johnson/archives.hom/speeches.hom/650208.asp (accessed March 13, 2007).
32. Johnson, "Special Message to the Congress on Conservation."
33. Ibid.
34. Nan Robertson, "89th Congress Enacted Laws that Benefited the Consumer," *New York Times*, October 24, 1966, 34.
35. "Pollution Agency Shift Stirs Hassle," *Washington Post*, July 5, 1968, A22; "Hansler Heads New Agency," *New York Times*, January 27, 1969.

36. Public Health Service, *History, Mission, and Organization of the Public Health Service* (Washington, DC: Government Printing Office, 1976), 3.
37. National Research Council, *Ensuring Safe Food: From Production to Consumption* (Washington, DC: National Academy Press, 1998), 144.
38. The White House, *Restoring the Quality of Our Environment: Report of the Environmental Pollution Panel, President's Science Advisory Committee* (Washington, DC: US Government Printing Office, 1965), 112–31; Gladwin Hill, "Government Plans National Parley as Part of Stepped-Up Campaign Against Air Pollution," *New York Times*, September 29, 1966.
39. Lyndon B. Johnson, in *Restoring the Quality of Our Environment*, iii.
40. Spencer Weart, *The Discovery of Global Warming* (Cambridge: Harvard University Press, 2008), especially 20–38.
41. *Restoring the Quality of Our Environment*, 9, 126. Actual atmospheric carbon dioxide increased from 317.94 ppm in January 1962 to 369.14 ppm in January 2000; about 16.1 percent.
42. *Restoring the Quality of Our Environment*, 16–38.
43. William H. Blair, "President Asks Federal Power to End Pollution," *New York Times*, February 9, 1965.
44. "Highlights of the Sierra Club's History," http://www.sierraclub.org/history/timeline.asp (accessed June 3, 2007).
45. Riley E. Dunlap, "Trends in Public Opinion Toward Environmental Issues: 1965–1990," in Dunlap and Angela G. Mertig, *American Environmentalism: The U.S. Environmental Movement, 1970–1990* (New York: Taylor & Francis, 1992), 93.
46. Melosi, "Lyndon Johnson and Environmental Policy," 134–41; "Battle for Cleaner Air," *New York Times*, January 8, 1968; Clayton Knowles, "Great Society: What it Was, Where it Is," *New York Times*, December 9, 1968, 1; Gladwin Hill, "Government Plans Parley as Part of Stepped-Up Campaign Against Air Pollution," *New York Times*, September 29, 1966.
47. Melosi, "Lyndon Johnson and Environmental Policy," 139–40.
48. Clayton Knowles, "Great Society: What it Was, Where it Is," *New York Times*, December 9, 1968; Gladwin Hill, "Government Plans Parley as Part of Stepped-Up Campaign Against Air Pollution," *New York Times*, September 29, 1966.
49. Melosi, "Lyndon Johnson and Environmental Policy," 119–20.
50. Melosi, "Lyndon Johnson and Environmental Policy," 135; "Battle for Cleaner Air," 38; John E. Fallon, "Deficiencies in the Air Quality Act of 1967," *Law and Contemporary Problems* 33, no. 2 (Spring 1968): 277–281, 292.
51. George R. Stewart, *Not So Rich as You Think* (New York: Signet, 1967), 7–10.
52. Robert Martin and Lloyd Symington, "A Guide to the Air Quality Act of 1967," *Law and Contemporary Problems* 33, no. 2 (Spring 1968): 273–274.
53. *Restoring the Quality of Our Environment*, 19.
54. Jamie Lincoln Kitman, "The Secret History of Lead," *Nation* 270, no. 11 (March 20, 2000): 14, 16; David Rosner and Gerald Markowitz, "A 'Gift of God'?: The Public Health Controversy over Leaded Gasoline during the 1920s," *American Journal of Public Health* 75, no. 4 (April 1985): 344–51.
55. Kitman, "The Secret History of Lead," 18–19, 25.
56. Rosner and Markowitz, "A 'Gift of God'?" 345–47.
57. Walter Sullivan, "Lead Pollution of Air 'Alarming,'" *New York Times*, September 8, 1965; George Getze, "Caltech Scientist Tells of Lead Poison Damage," *Los Angeles Times*, September 12, 1965.
58. Eric Wentworth, "Lead-in-Air Issue Grows Sensitive," *Washington Post*, January 1, 1966; Howard Simons, "Lead in Gasoline Seen as Threat to Health," *Washington Post*, September 12, 1965; Michael Weisskopf, "U.S. Backs Off Plans to Cut Lead Pollution of Air, Water," *Washington Post*, December 24, 1987; "Leaded Gas Issue to Get a Rehearing," *Washington Post*, March 19, 1975; US Environmental Protection Agency, "EPA Takes Final Step in Phaseout of Leaded Gasoline," January 29, 1996 (Press Release) http://www.epa.gov/history/topics/lead/02.htm (accessed April 20, 2009).
59. For a study detailing this shift see Jeffrey M. Berry, *The New Liberalism: The Rising Power of Citizen Groups* (Washington, DC: Brookings Institution Press, 1999).

60. Memo, Ben Wattenberg to Douglas Cater, February 4, 1967, "Talking points for Monday speech to AFL-CIO Policy Committee," Collection: Ex WE9, WHCF, Box 28, folder WE9, 1/1/67–2/28/67, LBJ Library.
61. Richard J. Barber, *The American Corporation: Its Power, Its Money, Its Politics* (New York: E. P. Dutton & Company, 1970), 185–86; Herbert E. Alexander, *Financing the 1964 Election* (Princeton, NJ: Citizens' Research Foundation, 1966), 9.
62. Barber, *The American Corporation*, 199–200; George A. Gonzalez, *Corporate Power and the Environment* (New York: Rowman & Littlefield, 2001), 16; Alexander, *Financing the 1964 Election*, 94.
63. "The Polluters Score Again," *New York Times*, October 25, 1968.
64. Pantagruel, "Earth Revolt," reprinted and edited in *News from Nowhere* (DeKalb, IL) February, 1970.
65. Mancur Olson, *The Logic of Collective Action: Public Goods and the Theory of Groups* (Cambridge, MA: Harvard University Press, 1965), especially 143–48. Quote page 144.
66. Grant McConnell, *Private Power & American Democracy* (New York: Alfred A. Knopf, 1966), 255.
67. Robert Dallek, *Flawed Giant: Lyndon Johnson and His Times 1961–1973* (New York: Oxford University Press, 1998), 229–30.
68. Ada Louise Huxtable, "The Crisis of the Environment," *New York Times*, December 29, 1969.
69. Ralph Nader, "The Profits in Pollution," *The Progressive* 34 (April 1970): 19–22, reprinted in Carroll W. Pursell, ed., *From Conservation to Ecology: The Development of Environmental Concern* (New York: Thomas Y. Crowell Company, 1973), 116–19.
70. "Auto Safety: New Study Criticizes Manufacturers and Universities," *Science* 150, no. 3700 (November 26, 1965), 1136.
71. John C. Devlin, "Use of Resources Called Wasteful," *New York Times*, March 20, 1966.
72. "Cousins Will Head New Panel to Study City's Air Pollution," *New York Times*, January 13, 1966.
73. Odom Fanning, *Man and His Environment: Citizen Action* (New York: Harper & Row, 1975), 138.
74. Harold M. Schmeck, Jr., "Pesticides Found in Unborn Babies," *New York Times*, January 30, 1966.
75. William V. Shannon, "The Struggle for Grand Canyon," *New York Times*, April 25, 1966, 30; Shannon, "The Battle of the Canyon is Joined," *New York Times*, July 31, 1966.
76. "Club Backs Right to Tax Exemption," *New York Times*, June 13, 1966; "I.R.S. and the Grand Canyon," *New York Times*, June 17, 1966.
77. McCandlish Phillips, "Con Ed's Project on Hudson Fought," *New York Times*, July 26, 1964; Philips, "Foes of Storm King Plant Assail Con Ed at Federal Hearing Here," *New York Times*, November 16, 1966; David Bird, "Con Ed Shifting Site of Plant on Hudson," *New York Times*, September 28, 1967.
78. Walter H. Waggoner, "100 Rally at Doomed Pond in Rain," *New York Times*, May 8, 1967; "Kentucky Governor Meets Both Sides in Dam Dispute," *New York Times*, November 23, 1967; "Wilderness in Danger," *New York Times*, May 14, 1968; William H. Blair, "New Hell's Canyon Group Fights Snake River Dam," *New York Times*, May 19, 1968; Devlin, "Use of Resources Called Wasteful."
79. Homer Bigart, "Great Swamp Endangered by Pollution from Town Dump," *New York Times*, November 18, 1968.
80. William H. Blair, "Conservationists Fight Disney Resort Plan," *New York Times*, March 13, 1967; Gladwin Hill, "Sierra Club's Suit: For More Than Nature's Sake," *New York Times*, June 9, 1969; Arnold Hano, "The Battle of Mineral King," *New York Times*, August 17, 1969.
81. "Conservationists Win Oregon Fight," *New York Times*, September 5, 1967.
82. "Sierra Club Scores Company for Starting to Cut Redwoods," *New York Times*, December 17, 1967; "Sierra Club Backs Deal on Redwoods," *New York Times*, October 31, 1967.
83. Lawrence E. Davis, "Redwood Plans Hit by Industry," *New York Times*, March 13, 1966.
84. Maurice Carroll, "Sierra Club Irks Lawyer for F.P.C.," *New York Times*, December 9, 1966.
85. John Kenneth Galbraith, *The New Industrial Order* (Boston: Houghton Mifflin Company, 1967).

86. Barber, *The American Corporation*, 136–37.
87. Ibid. 105.
88. See, for example, "Stop the Military-Industrial Complex," *Helix* (Seattle), July 10, 1969, 18.
89. Tony Wagner, "Ecology of Revolution," *Win* 5, no. 14 (August 1969): 7; Max Crawford, "Despite Hayes—Stanford Struggle Moving Left," *Peninsula Observer* (Palo Alto), through May 5, 1969, 10; Lawrence E. Davies, "Students Occupy Stanford Electronics Laboratory," *New York Times*, April 11, 1969.
90. "Operation Wasteland," *Time*, May 25, 1970, 73; Santa Barbara Women Strike for Peace, "Ecology and Justice for All: The Disembowelment of Vietnam's Environment," *Northwest Passage*, April 6, 1970, 5; Marilyn B. Young, "Bombing Civilians from the Twentieth to the Twenty-first Centuries," in Yuki Tanaka and Marilyn B. Young, *Bombing Civilians: A Twentieth-Century History* (New York: The New Press, 2010), 157.
91. "Operation Wasteland," 70–73; Robert E. Cook, William Haseltine, and Arthur W. Galston, "What Have We Done to Vietnam?" *The New Republic*, January 10, 1970, 18–21; Santa Barbara Women Strike for Peace, "Ecology and Justice for All," 4; Robert M. Smith, "U.S. Curbs Use of Weed Killer That Produces Rat Deformities," *New York Times*, October 30, 1969; John Deedy, "The Deflowering Process," *Commonweal* 90 (May 30, 1969): 306. The popular Smoky Bear advertising slogan was: "Only you can prevent forest fires."
92. "Operation Wasteland," 73; "Ravaging Vietnam," *The Nation*, April 21, 1969, 484–85; Deedy, "The Deflowering Process," 306.
93. Wilfred Burchett, "Deadly Chemicals Poison Vietnam," *Guardian*, December 6, 1969, 20.
94. Santa Barbara Women Strike for Peace, "Ecology and Justice for All," 4–5.
95. "Defoliant Linked to Cancer, Birth Defects," *GI Press Service*, November 13, 1969, 165; Smith, "U.S. Curbs Use of Weed Killer."
96. Robert Reinhold, "Scientists Call for a Ban on 2 Vietnam Defoliants," *New York Times*, December 31, 1969.
97. Robert E. Cook, William Haseltine, and Arthur W. Galston, "Deliberate Destruction of the Environment: What Have We Done to Vietnam?" *New Republic* 163 (January 10, 1970): 18–21, cited in *Earth Times* 1, no. 1 (April 1970): 8. For more on Agent Orange and Vietnam see David Zierler, *The Invention of Ecocide: Agent Orange, Vietnam, and the Scientists Who Changed the Way We Think About the Environment* (Athens: University of Georgia Press, 2011).
98. Paul Delaney, "Detergents Held Pollution Factor," *New York Times*, December 15, 1969; Melissa Queen, "Detergent Dilemma: Whiter than White, Greener than Green," *Northwest Passage*, April 6, 1970, 8.
99. Jane E. Brody, "Biologist Says Nitrate Fertilizer Could Be Hazard in Some Food," *New York Times*, December 28, 1967.
100. "The Cities: The Price of Optimism," *Time*, August 1, 1969, 41.
101. Gladwin Hill, "Secrecy in Government: Suppressed Reports Seen as Evidence that Cause of Conservation is Gaining," *New York Times*, October 13, 1969.
102. Fred P. Graham, "U.S. Settles Suit on Smog Devices," *New York Times*, September 12, 1969; Gladwin Hill, "Air Pollution Grows Despite Rising Public Alarm," *New York Times*, October 19, 1969. The "Big Four" were General Motors, Ford, Chrysler, and American Motors.
103. Fairfield Osborn, *The Limits of the Earth* (New York: Little, Brown and Company, 1953); William Vogt, *People!* (New York: Hillman/MacFadden, 1961).
104. Stewart Udall, "Foreword," in *The Population Challenge: What It Means to America* (Washington, DC: US Government Printing Office, 1966), 3.
105. Task Force on Environmental Health and Related Problems, "A Strategy for a Livable Environment," (Washington, DC: US Government Printing Office, 1967), 16.
106. Paul Ehrlich, *The Population Bomb* (New York: Sierra Club/Ballantine Books, 1971), vi. For an account of the origins and significance of the population control movement, see Matthew Connelly, *Fatal Misconception: The Struggle to Control World Population* (Cambridge, MA: Belknap Press of Harvard University Press, 2008).
107. Ehrlich, *The Population Bomb*, 128–29; "Television," *New York Times*, August 13, 1970.
108. "Population Control: Imperialist Style," *Off Our Backs* 1, no. 3 (April 11, 1970): 10.

109. The Lake Winnebago Mud Fish, "Mother Earth Notes: ZPG + (U.S.) = $," *Fox Valley Kaleidoscope* (Oshkosh, WI), April 13–27, 1970, 8.
110. Connelly, *Fatal Misconception*, 117.
111. Matthew Connelly, author talk at Brown University Department of History, Providence, RI, on April 24, 2008.
112. Constance Holden, "Ehrlich versus Commoner: An Environmental Fallout," *Science* 177, no. 4045 (July 21, 1972): 245–47.
113. Robert Olney Easton, *Black Tide: The Santa Barbara Oil Spill and its Consequences* (New York: Delacorte Presss, 1972), 6–10, 66–70; Gladwin Hill, "Slick Off California Coast Revives Oil Deal Disputes," *New York Times*, February 2, 1969.
114. Easton, *Black Tide*, 95–96; Hill, "Slick Off California Coast."
115. Ross MacDonald and Robert Easton, "Santa Barbarans Cite an 11th Commandment: 'Thou Shalt Not Abuse the Earth,'" *New York Times*, October 12, 1969.
116. MacDonald and Easton, "Santa Barbarans Cite an 11th Commandment."
117. Gladwin Hill, "Hole in Pollution Law," *New York Times*, June 2, 1969.
118. MacDonald and Easton, "Santa Barbarans Cite an 11th Commandment."
119. *County of Santa Barbara, et al. v. J. Walter Hickel et al.* (426 F.2d 164), http://cases.justia.com/us-court-of-appeals/F2/426/164/71167/ (accessed February 12, 2009); Easton, *Black Tide*, 77; MacDonald and Easton, "Santa Barbarans Cite an 11th Commandment."
120. Jack Gould, "TV: Man and His Future," *New York Times*, March 18, 1969.
121. Robert Cameron Mitchell, "From Elite Quarrel to Mass Movement," *Society* 18, no. 5 (July/August 1981): 77; Victor Cohn, "Public Fights A-Power," *Washington Post*, October 19, 1969; Students for a Democratic Society, "Port Huron Statement," 1962 http://coursesa.matrix.msu.edu/~hst306/documents/huron.html (accessed October 23, 2008).
122. Cohn, "Public Fights A-Power,"; "Minnesota Utility Fights Nuclear Plant Standards," *Wall Street Journal*, August 27, 1969.
123. Elizabeth Heger Boyle, "Political Frames and Legal Activity: The Case of Nuclear Power in Four Countries," *Law & Society Review* 32, no. 1 (1998): 153.
124. "The Cities: The Price of Optimism," 41.
125. Gary Hirshberg, "Organic Love Story," underside of Stonyfield Yogurt container lid, April 2011.
126. Jeff Cox, "The Go-to Court to Protect the Environment," *Organic Gardening and Farming* 17, no. 9 (September, 1970): 78–81.
127. Alan Steinbach, "Poison in the Air," *Guardian*, July 5, 1969, 7.
128. Michael McCloskey, telephone interview with the author from Portland, OR on July 11, 2003.
129. Lawrence E. Davies, "Sierra Club, Marking 75th Year, Maps Expansion," *New York Times*, December 9, 1967; "Sierra Club Gains in Fight on Taxes," *New York Times*, August 7, 1966.
130. Michael P. Cohen, *The History of the Sierra Club, 1892–1970* (San Francisco: Sierra Club Books, 1988), 443; Michael McCloskey, telephone interview with the author from Portland, OR on July 11, 2003.
131. Zager and Evans, *2525 (Exordium & Terminus)*, RCA Victor LSP-4214, 1969, vinyl LP.

Chapter 7

1. Floyd Allen, "The Santa Barbara Plan," *Organic Gardening and Farming* (January 1971): 68–70.
2. Miller, *The 60s Communes*, xvii–xx.
3. Jeanie Darlington, "Grow Your Own," *Good Times* 3, no. 13 (February, 1970): 20.
4. Miller, *The 60s Communes*, 139–41, 157–58.
5. Martin Jezer, "Longhair Manifest Destiny," *WIN* 5, no. 4 (March, 1970), 14.
6. Gorkin, "Mecca on the Mesa," *Good Times* (San Francisco), June 4, 1969, 11; Miller, *The 60s Communes*, 43–46, 92–143.
7. Jeffrey Jacob, *New Pioneers: The Back-to-the-Land Movement and the Search for a Sustainable Future* (University Park, PA: Pennsylvania State University Press, 1997), 3.
8. Canned Heat, "Going Up the Country," *Living the Blues* (1968, Liberty LST-27200).

9. See, for example, David Owen, *Green Metropolis: Why Living Smaller, Living Closer and Driving Less Are the Keys to Sustainability* (New York: Riverhead Books, 2009).
10. James Rado and Gerome Ragni, *Hair—The American Tribal Love Rock Musical*, 1968 Original Broadway Cast (1990, RCA Victor Broadway, CD B000002W1S).
11. Theodore Roszak, "Youth and the Great Refusal," *The Nation*, March 25, 1968, 400–407; "The Future as Community," *The Nation*, April 15, 1968, 502; and *The Making of a Counter Culture* (New York: Anchor Books, 1968), 8.
12. Roszak, *The Making of a Counter Culture*, 49.
13. Charles A. Reich, *The Greening of America* (New York: Bantam Books, 1971 [first published 1970]): 2–3, 6.
14. Charles Curtis, "Another Customer Turns Shopkeeper," *New York Times*, November 16, 1967.
15. Dirick Van Sickle, *The Ecological Citizen: Good Earthkeeping in America* (New York: Harper & Row, 1971), 77.
16. Warren J. Belasco, *Appetite for Change: How the Counterculture Took on the Food Industry* (Ithaca, NY: Cornell University Press, 1989), 96–98; Jeff Cox, "The 'Nowhere' Store That's Going Places," *Organic Gardening and Farming* 17, no. 8 (August 1970): 57–58.
17. Display ad, "Natural Foods Store," 414 Soquel Avenue, Santa Cruz, CA; Display ad, "Pacific Grain and Grocery," 817 Pacific Avenue, Santa Cruz, *Free Spaghetti Dinner*, October 31, 1969, 10, 12.
18. Display ad, *Philadelphia Free Press*, December 1, 1969, 15.
19. Windcatcher, "There's No Reason Why We Can't Exchange Our Goods and Smoke Our Money," *Good Times*, July 17, 1969, 7, cited in Belasco, 88.
20. Belasco, *Appetite for Change*, 88–89.
21. "Statement from Co-op," *Madison Kaleidoscope*, March 18, 1970, 6, http://www.mifflincoop.com/index.html (accessed June 6, 2007); Barry Adams, "Mifflin Street Co-op: Its Time is Over," *Madison Commons*, http://www.madisoncommons.org/article.php?storyid=737 (accessed June 6, 2007). The Mifflin Street Co-op closed in 2006.
22. Daniel Zwerdling, "The Uncertain Revival of Food Cooperatives," in John Case and Rosemary C. R. Taylor, eds., *Co-ops, Communes & Collectives: Experiments in Social Change in the 1960s and 1970s* (New York: Pantheon Books, 1979), 92.
23. Wallace Stegner, "Conservation Equals Survival," *American Heritage* 21, no. 1 (December 1969): 15.
24. Gurney Norman, "The Organic Gardening Books," *Whole Earth Catalog* (Fall 1970): 38.
25. Andrew Kirk, *Counterculture Green: The Whole Earth Catalog and American Environmentalism* (Lawrence: University of Kansas Press, 2007), 31–32.
26. Display ad, *Good Times* (San Francisco), April 23, 1969, 10.
27. William Bryant, "The Re-Vision of Planet Earth: Space Flight and Environmentalism in Postmodern America," *American Studies* 36 (Fall 1995): 61. See also Denis Cosgrove, "Contested Global Visions: One-World, Whole-Earth, and the Apollo Space Photographs," *Annals of the Association of American Geographers* 84, no. 2 (June 1994): 270–94.
28. "Tipis," and "9100A Calculator," *Whole Earth Catalog* (Winter 1968): 20, 36–37 http://findarticles.com/p/articles/mi_m0GER/is_1998_Winter/ai_53489459/pg_36 (accessed May 30, 2007).
29. Stewart Brand, "We Are as Gods," *Whole Earth Catalog* (Fall 1968): 3.
30. "The War on Fur Coats Grows," *New York Times*, November 20, 1969, 52.
31. Doug Rossinow, *The Politics of Authenticity: Liberalism, Christianity, and the New Left in America* (New York: Columbia University Press, 1998), 263.
32. Melody Kilian, "Why Hippies Need Politics," *Peninsula Observer* (Palo Alto, CA), through May 19, 1969.
33. See Keith M. Woodhouse, "The Politics of Ecology: Environmentalism and Liberalism in the 1960s," *Journal for the Study of Radicalism* 2, no. 2 (2009): 53–84.
34. Gitlin, *The Sixties*, 354–55; Art Goldberg, "The Battle of Berkeley," *Guardian*, June 7, 1969, 3, 8.

35. David Burner, *Making Peace with the 60s* (Princeton, NJ: Princeton University Press, 1996), 163–64; Gitlin, *The Sixties*, 356–57; Winthrop Griffith, "People's Park—270' x 450' of Confrontation," *New York Times*, June 29, 1969.
36. Keith Lampe, "Earth Read-out: People's Park Ecology," *Madison Kaleidoscope*, June 20–July 3, 1969, 3; Lampe, "Earth Read-Out," *The Fifth Estate* (Detroit), June 12–25, 1969, 10.
37. Gary Snyder, "Smokey The Bear Sutra," *The Rag* (Austin, TX), June 12, 1969, 20; or *The Fifth Estate* (Detroit), June 12–25, 1969, 3; Gitlin, *The Sixties*, 360.
38. "Smokey Drops Out," *WIN*, reprinted in *Other Sources* (New York City), August 15–30, 1969, 2.
39. Gitlin, *The Sixties*, 361.
40. See Gitlin, *The Sixties*, 419, 422, 424–25.
41. Hunter S. Thompson, "The 'Hashbury' is the Capital of the Hippies," *New York Times*, May 14, 1967.
42. Gitlin, "Snyder's Book a Green Arsenal," *Peninsula Observer* (Palo Alto, CA), through July 14, 1969, 16. Emphasis in original.
43. Front cover, *Good Times* (San Francisco), September 18, 1969, 1.
44. Ned Groth, "Smogmen Sneak into City," *Peninsula Observer* (Palo Alto, CA), through September 22, 1969, 4.
45. Richard J. Barber, *The American Corporation: Its Power, Its Money, Its Politics* (New York: E. P. Dutton & Company, 1970), 20–21.
46. Charles R. Ross, "The Federal Government as an Inadvertent Advocate of Environmental Degradation," in Harold W. Helfrich, Jr., ed., *The Environmental Crisis: Man's Struggle to Live with Himself* (New Haven: Yale University Press, 1970), 174.
47. Barber, *The American Corporation*, 73–74, 253, 254, 256.
48. Ibid. 250–51, 271–72.
49. Steven V. Roberts, "Bombings on Rise Over the Nation," *New York Times*, March 13, 1970.
50. "Text of Terrorist Letter," *New York Times*, March 13, 1970.
51. Homer Bigart, "Many Buildings Evacuated Here in Bomb Scares," *New York Times*, March 13, 1970.
52. "Ecology Action Is," *WIN* 5, no. 14 (August 1969), 31; Steven V. Roberts, "The Better Earth: A Report on Ecology Action," *New York Times*, March 29, 1970.
53. Roberts, "The Better Earth," 53–54; Keith Lampe, "Earth Read Out," *The Fifth Estate* (Detroit), June 12–25, 1969, 10.
54. Roberts, "The Better Earth," 54.
55. Ned Groth, "Polluters Hanged at Fair," *Peninsula Observer* (Palo Alto, CA), May 5, 1969, 9; Guy Mendes, "Gurney Norman, A Conversation," Kentucky Educational Television, November 28, 2001 http://www.ket.org/livingbywords/authors/norman_interview1.htm (accessed February 3, 2009).
56. Edward E. C. Clebsch, "The Campus Teach-In on the Environmental Crisis—1970," *The Living Wilderness* 34, no. 109 (Spring 1970): 10.
57. Tony Wagner, "Ecology of Revolution," *WIN* 5, no. 14 (August 1969), 8.
58. Ned Groth, "Smogmen Sneak into City," *Peninsula Observer* (Palo Alto, CA), through September 22, 1969, 4.
59. Ronald Eber, correspondence with author, April 30, 2004.
60. Donna Schor, "Around Town," *Washington Life Magazine*, September 2003, http://www.washingtonlife.com/issues/2003-09/aroundtown/index.html (accessed August 7, 2007); Pete McCloskey, "Earth Day '04: Thinking & Acting Globally," Panel Discussion, The Commonwealth Club of California, April 22, 2004, http://www.commonwealthclub.org/archive/04/04-04earthdaypanel-speech.html (accessed August 7, 2007). This is contrary to the legend of Earth Day's origin, told by Senator Gaylord Nelson, that he first thought of the idea for Earth Day while flying in a plane after speaking in California and reading an article on Vietnam teach-ins in *Ramparts*. See, for example, "Honor the Earth: Reading Ramparts, Senator Gaylord Nelson Got the Idea for a Mass Teach-In on the Environment," *Mother Jones*, April/May 1990, 12–13; Philip Shabecoff, *A Fierce Green Fire: The American Environmental Movement* (Washington, DC: Island Press, 2003), 106–7.
61. Bill Christofferson, *The Man From Clear Lake: Earth Day Founder Senator Gaylord Nelson* (Madison, WI: The University of Wisconsin Press), 302–3.

62. M. C. Goldman, "The Organic Revolution Goes to College," *Organic Gardening and Farming* (January 1970): 56–57.
63. Robert Gottlieb, *Forcing the Spring: The Transformation of the American Environmental Movement* (Washington, DC: Island Press, 1993), 106.
64. Christofferson, *The Man From Clear Lake*, 146.
65. Adam Rome, *The Genius of Earth Day: How a 1970 Teach-In Unexpectedly Made the First Green Generation* (New York: Hill and Wang, 2013), 65–66.
66. McCloskey, "Earth Day '04."
67. "Earth Day Broom Sweeps in on Business," *BusinessWeek*, April 18, 1970, 22–24; Nelson, interview with author, tape recording, Wilderness Society, Washington, DC, July 1, 2003; Rome, *The Genius of Earth Day*, 68.
68. Denis Hayes, Telephone interview with author, March 21, 2006; Nelson, interview with author, July 1, 2003.
69. Hayes, Telephone interview with author, March 21, 2006.
70. Margaret Crimmins, "DAR Assails Anti-Pollution Movement," *Washington Post*, April 23, 1970.
71. Barry Weisberg, "April 22: A One Day Teach-in is Like an All Day Sucker," *Liberation* 15, no. 2 (April 1970), 38.
72. Joseph Kraft, "Environmental Teach-In Stirs Pros—Cons," *Washington Post*, March 12, 1970; Gladwin Hill, "Pollution Parley Opens in Michigan," *New York Times*, March 13, 1970.
73. Kraft, "Environmental Teach-In Stirs Pros—Cons"; Gladwin Hill, "Michigan Teach-In Offers Four Days of Soul-Searching About the Environment," *New York Times*, March 16, 1970.
74. Charlotte Robinson, "'Indian Power' Disrupts Ecology Talks," *Milwaukee Sentinel*, April 1, 1970, included in *Akwesasne Notes*, June 1970, 38.
75. "Editorial," *Ramparts* 8, no. 11 (May 1970): 3–4.
76. "Manifesto Ecology Action East: The Power to Destroy—The Power to Create," *Root & Branch*, June 1970, 13. Murray Bookchin claims authorship of the "Manifesto." See Murray Bookchin, *Which Way for the Ecology Movement?* (San Francisco: AK Press, 1994), 15.
77. "How Students See the Pollution Issue," *BusinessWeek*, February 7, 1970, 86–88.
78. Hayes, Telephone interview with author, March 21, 2006.
79. "Display ad 1065," *New York Times*, January 18, 1970, E5.
80. Adam Rome has noted, "The activism of women was crucial in making the environment an issue in communities across the nation" during the Sixties. See Adam Rome, "Give Earth A Chance: The Environmental Movement and the Sixties," *The Journal of American History* 90, no. 2 (September 2003): 534–41.
81. Hayes, Telephone interview with author, March 21, 2006.
82. "Editorial: Sisters," *Off Our Backs* (Washington, DC), April 11, 1970, 2. On research detailing the presence of DDT in milk, see Ruth M. Heifetz and Sharon S. Taylor, "Mother's Milk or Mother's Poison? Pesticides in Breast Milk," *Journal of Pesticide Reform* 9, no. 3 (Fall 1989): 15–17.
83. Stanley M. Brown, "Environmentalists Use Commando Tactics in Miami Area," *Washington Post*, December 10, 1970; Georgia Straight, "The Eco-Guerrillas Are Coming," *Harry* (Baltimore), April 24–May 7, 1971, 9. See Edward Abbey, *The Monkey Wrench Gang* (Philadelphia, J. B. Lippincott Company, 1975).
84. Georgia Straight, "The Eco-Guerrillas are Coming," *Harry* (Baltimore), April 24–May 7, 1971, 9.
85. Douglas Martin, "James Phillips, 70, Environmentalist Who Was Called the Fox," *New York Times*, October 22, 2001; "The Kane County Pimpernel," *Time* 96, no. 14 (October 5, 1970), http://www.time.com/time/magazine/article/0,9171,904353,00.html (accessed May 20, 2011).
86. "Another Spaceship Low On Water, Oxygen And Other Life Support Systems" (editorial cartoon), *The Lincoln Star*, April 23, 1970, 4. "Earth Day and Space Day," *New York Times*, April 19, 1970. Archibald MacLeish first called the earth a "tiny raft in an enormous, empty night." Joseph Kraft, "The Proper Place for Space Exploration," *Providence Journal*, April 23, 1970, 22.
87. "A Giant Step—Or a Springtime Skip?" *Newsweek*, May 4, 1970, 26.

88. Charles A. Hayes, "A Time to Live," in *Earth Day—The Beginning* (New York: Bantam Books, 1970), 154–55.
89. Richard Harwood, "Earth Day Stirs Nation; Millions Observe Earth Day in U.S.," *Washington Post*, April 23, 1970.
90. Barbara Reid, "Roots of Crisis," in *Earth Day—The Beginning*, 145.
91. George Wiley, "Ecology and the Poor," in *Earth Day—The Beginning*, 213.
92. Kraft, "Environmental Teach-In Stirs Pros—Cons"; Hill, "Michigan Teach-In," 31.
93. Hayes, Telephone interview with author, March 21, 2006.
94. Ibid.
95. Stephen Cotton, "Earth Day Got a Good Press," *Washington Post*, April 18, 1971; Hayes, Telephone interview with author, March 21, 2006.
96. Fred Ferretti, "Broadcasters Give Earth Day Special Attention," *New York Times*, April 22, 1970; Paul Jones, "Join Big Teach-In!—It's Earth Day," *Atlanta Constitution*, April 22, 1970; Diana Loercher, "TV Alerts Nation to Pollution," *Christian Science Monitor*, April 22, 1970.
97. Quoted in Stanley I. Kutler, *The Wars of Watergate: The Last Crisis of Richard Nixon* (New York: W. W. Norton, 1992), as cited in Byron W. Daynes and Glen Sussman, *White House Politics and the Environment: Franklin D. Roosevelt to George W. Bush* (College Station: Texas A&M University Press, 2010), 71.
98. Gaylord Nelson, interview with author, July 1, 2003.
99. For an account of environmental policies and legislation during the Nixon Administration, see J. Brooks Flippen, *Nixon and the Environment* (Albuquerque: University of New Mexico Press, 2000).
100. Michael McCloskey, Telephone interview with author on July 11, 2003, from Portland, OR.
101. "Congress Gets Bill to Ban Auto Engine," *Organic Gardening and Farming* (October 1970): 2.
102. Jacqueline Vaughn Switzer, *Green Backlash: The History and Politics of Environmental Opposition in the U.S.* (Boulder, CO: Lynne Rienner Publishers, 1997), 140–44.
103. Andrew Rowell, *Global Subversion of the Environmental Movement* (New York: Routledge, 1996), 84–89; Sharon Beder, "Ecological Double Agents," *Australian Science* 19, no. 1 (February 1998): 19–22.
104. Rowell, *Global Subversion of the Environmental Movement*, 7–8.
105. Rowell, *Global Subversion of the Environmental Movement*, 8; James Patterson, *Restless Giant: The United States from Watergate to Bush v. Gore* (New York: Oxford University Press, 2005), 176; Vaughn Switzer, *Green Backlash*, 164–65; Angus Phillips, "Environmentalists United Against Watt," *Washington Post*, August 30, 1981.
106. On the growth and influence of citizen groups, see Jeffrey M. Berry, *The New Liberalism: The Rising Power of Citizens Groups* (Washington, DC: Brookings Institution Press, 1999).
107. Michael McCloskey, Telephone interview with author on July 11, 2003.
108. J. Brooks Flippen, *Nixon and the Environment* (Albuquerque: University of New Mexico Press, 2000), 192.
109. Quoted in Tom Wicker, *One of Us: Richard Nixon and the American Dream* (New York: Random House, 1991), 556, as cited in Daynes and Sussman, *White House Politics*, 77.
110. Hayes, Telephone interview with author, March 21, 2006.
111. Matthew Alan Cahn, *Environmental Deceptions: The Tension Between Liberalism and Environmental Policymaking in the United States* (Albany: State University of New York Press, 1995), 50–62; Congressional Research Service, "Clean Air Act: A Summary of the Act and its Major Requirements," CRS Report for Congress, January 6, 2011, http://www.fas.org/sgp/crs/misc/RL30853.pdf (accessed April 6, 2012).
112. Harvey Black, "Imperfect Protection: NEPA at 35 Years," *Environmental Health Perspectives* 112, no. 5 (April 2004): A293–A295; Robert H. Nelson, review of Matthew J. Lindstrom and Zachary A. Smith, "The National Environmental Policy Act: Judicial Misconstruction, Legislative Indifference, and Executive Neglect," *Perspectives on Politics* 1, no. 1 (March 2003): 191–92; Sam Love, "The Failures of an Act that Once Sparked Hope," *Environmental Action* (January 9, 1971): 4–5.
113. James S. Bowman, "The Environmental Movement: An Assessment of Ecological Politics," *Boston College Environmental Affairs Law Review* 5, no. 4 (January 1976): 654, n. 31.
114. Matthew J. Lindstrom and Zachary A. Smith, *The National Environmental Policy Act: Judicial Misconstruction, Legislative Indifference, & Executive Neglect* (College Station: Texas A&M

University Press, 2001); John H. Cushman, Jr., "E.P.A. and States Found to be Lax on Pollution Law," *New York Times*, June 7, 1998, 1. Also Joel Mintz, *Enforcement of the EPA* (Austin: University of Texas Press, 1995).
115. Michael E. Kraft, "Congressional Attitudes Toward the Environment: Attention and Issue-Orientation in Ecological Politics" (diss., Yale University, 1973), 387–88; Bowman, "The Environmental Movement," 654.
116. Cahn, *Environmental*, especially 1–2, 28, and 120.
117. Bill Mauk, Telephone interview with author, August 24, 2007.
118. Ralph Miliband, *The State in Capitalist Society* (New York: Basic Books, 1969).
119. Michael E. Kraft, "Environmental Policy and Politics in the United States: Toward Sustainability?" in Uday Desai, ed., *Environmental Politics and Policy in Industrialized Countries* (Cambridge, MA: The MIT Press, 2002), 58.
120. US Environmental Protection Agency, "Fish Consumption Advisories," http://fishadvisory-online.epa.gov/Advisories.aspx (accessed February 22, 2010).
121. Augustine Kong et al., "Rate of De Novo Mutations and the Importance of Father's Age to Disease Risk," *Nature* 488, no. 7412 (August 23, 2012): 471–75.
122. Morris Kaplan, "Geneticist Asks Storage of Sperm to Circumvent Radiation Perils," *New York Times*, April 27, 1963; Benedict Carey, "Father's Age is Linked to Risk of Autism and Schizophrenia," *New York Times*, August 24, 2012.

Chapter 8

1. Kenneth E. F. Watt, "Whole Earth," *Earth Day—The Beginning* (New York: Bantam Books, 1970), 24.
2. Leroy F. Aarons, "'O.K., So What Can I do About It? I'm Just a Person....'" *Washington Post*, April 23, 1970: "Earth Day Utilized by Firms for Vowing To Be Cleaner, or Telling of Steps Taken," *Wall Street Journal*, April 23, 1970.
3. Richard Harwood, "Earth Day Stirs Nation; Millions Observe Earth Day in U.S.," *Washington Post*, April 23, 1970.
4. Roderick A. Cameron, "Demonstrate," in *Earth Day—The Beginning*, 173–74, 177.
5. Harwood, "Earth Day Stirs Nation," A20.
6. Display ad, *Time*, February 10, 1975, 79; Kathleen Adams and Lina Lofaro, "The Fate of the Earth Shoe," *Time*, May 1, 1995, 32; Angela Taylor, "Shoes That Make You Waddle Like a Duck—And They Sell," *New York Times*, February 25, 1974.
7. Adams and Lofaro, "The Fate of the Earth Shoe," 32.
8. David A. Lingwood, "Environmental Education Through Information-Seeking: The Case of an 'Environmental Teach-In,'" *Environment and Behavior* 3, no. 3 (September 1971): especially 258–59.
9. Lingwood, "Environmental Education Through Information-Seeking," 258.
10. Jerome Olds, "Where to Buy Organic Foods and Products," *Organic Gardening and Farming* (May 1970): 64; "'Ordinary Housewives' Flocking to Health Food Stores? There Must be a Reason—Maybe It's DDT," *Organic Gardening and Farming* (March 1970): 47.
11. M. C. Goldman, "Southern California—Food-Shopper's Paradise!" *Organic Gardening and Farming* (November 1970): 38–45.
12. M. C. Goldman, "Organic Food Symposium Makes History," *Organic Gardening and Farming* (August 1970): 43.
13. "The Action's at the Boston Area Ecology Action Center," *Organic Gardening and Farming* (August 1970): 64–65.
14. Hy Sirota, "The Chain Store That Dared," *Organic Gardening and Farming* (August 1970): 66–67; "Supermarket Chain Goes Eco-Logical," *Organic Gardening and Farming* (January 1971): 2–3.
15. "Ecological Drive Aids Store Sales," *New York Times*, April 12, 1971.
16. M.C. Goldman, "More Organic Foods for Wise Shoppers," *Organic Gardening and Farming* (March 1970): 79.
17. James F. Carberry, "Our Daily Bread: Food Faddism Spurts as Young, Old People Shift to Organic Diets," *Wall Street Journal*, January 21, 1971.

18. M. C. Goldman, "More Farms for Organic Food," *Organic Gardening and Farming* (December 1970): 69.
19. "The Mother Earth News...It Tells You How," *The Mother Earth News*, January 1970, 65; "Remember Ecology?" *The Mother Earth News*, May 1970, 2.
20. John Ravett, "Fears of Pollution Create Demand for Bottled, Pure Water," *Advertising Age* 41, no. 39 (September 28, 1970): 1, 123; John J. O'Connor, "Pure Water Joins List of New Products Introduced in September," *Advertising Age* 41, no. 40 (October 5, 1970): 42; "Schweppes Push Attacks Tap Water," *Advertising Age* 41, no. 49 (December 7, 1970): 76; Elizabeth Alston, "The Good Taste of Fresh Waters," *Look*, July 14, 1970, 46–47.
21. Harriet King, "The Outdoor Industry Settles Down," *New York Times*, November 27, 1977.
22. For a history of outdoor and mountaineering gear, see Bruce B. Johnson "The History of Gear," http://www.oregonphotos.com/Backpacking-Revolution1.html (accessed August 18, 2007); on Patagonia, see Adam S. Weinberg, "Distinguishing Among Green Businesses: Growth, Green, and Anomie," *Society & Natural Resources* 11, no. 3 (April/May 1998): 244.
23. Bernadine Morris, "High Marks for Dior, as Fall Collections Get Under Way," *New York Times*, July 27, 1976; Patricia Peterson, Anne-Marie Schiro, "Rugged Individualists: Fashion Pathfinders Have Fun with Some Practical Ideas from the Great Outdoors," *New York Times*, August 29, 1976.
24. Jerome Olds, "Organic Living for Half a Million People," *Organic Gardening and Farming* (March 1970): 40–42.
25. Judy Klemesrud, "Deciding to 'Stay and Fight' Pollution," *New York Times*, March 11, 1971; Marian Burros, "Environmental Emotions," *Washington Post*, June 13, 1976; "The Plowboy Interview: Lola Redford and Ilene Goldman of C.A.N.," *Mother Earth News*, July/August 1972, http://www.motherearthnews.com/Nature-and-Environment/1972-07-01/The-Plowboy-Interview-Redford-Goldman.aspx (accessed August 19, 2007).
26. Elizabeth Shelton, "'Eco-Tips' From Concern Inc.," *Washington Post*, November 17, 1970; Jeanette Smyth, "Concern, Inc.: Eco-Tips No. 2," *Washington Post*, February 27, 1971; "Concern, Inc.: An Ecology Crusade Waged in Supermarket," *New York Times*, July 10, 1970.
27. On consumers leagues, see Lawrence Glickman, *Buying Power: A History of Consumer Activism in America* (Chicago: University of Chicago Press, 2009), 155–62.
28. William G. Cushing, "Utilities Warned on Environmental Issues," *Washington Post*, January 20, 1970.
29. Betty Ann Ottinger, *What Every Woman Should Know and Do about Pollution: A Guide to Good Global Housekeeping* (New York: EP Press: 1970), 11, 72; Angela Taylor, "To Betty Ottinger, Ecology is a Fighting Word," *New York Times*, December 20, 1970.
30. Taylor, "To Betty Ottinger," 56.
31. Frances Moore Lappe, *Diet for a Small Planet* (20th Anniversary Edition) (New York: Ballantine Books, 1991), 9.
32. Lappe, *Diet for a Small Planet*, 10.
33. Nancy Giges, "Pollution—It's Today's Bonanza for Advertisers," *Advertising Age* 41, no. 16 (April 20, 1970), 1.
34. "Council Calls Most Environment Ads Exercise in 'Self-Aggrandizement,'" *Advertising Age* 15, no. 46 (November 15, 1971): 60.
35. Michael Howlett and Rebecca Raglon, "Constructing the Environmental Spectacle: Green Advertisements and the Greening of Corporate Image, 1910–1990," *Environmental History Review* 16, no. 4 (Winter 1992): 53–55. On the history of imaging products as "natural," see Miles Orvell, *The Real Thing: Imitation and Authenticity in American Culture, 1880–1914* (Chapel Hill: University of North Carolina Press, 1989).
36. Display ad, *Seventeen*, April 1971, 57.
37. Display ad, *Seventeen*, August 1970, 154.
38. Display ad, *Seventeen*, August 1970, 283.
39. Display ad, *Seventeen*, November 1970, 99.
40. Display ad, *Seventeen*, August 1970, 95.
41. Various artists, *Listen in Good Health: Songs of Celebration and Decay, April 1970* (1970, Capitol Records Promotional Record, vinyl recording SPRO 5003).

42. Various artists, *Listen in Good Health,* April 1970.
43. Display ad, *Billboard,* July 18, 1970, 67.
44. National Family Opinion, Inc., Environment Study Conducted for *Reader's Digest,* May, 1970, in *Reader's Digest* Prospectus for Advertising Supplement, "What Are We Doing About Our Environment?" (September 1971). Cited in Charles E. Ludlam, "Abatement of Corporate Image Environmental Advertising," *Ecology Law Review* 4, no. 2 (1974): 250; "Corporate Advertising and the Environment," *Economic Priorities Report* 2, no. 3 (September–October 1971): 3.
45. Robin T. Peterson, "The Marketing-Ecology Interface," *Marquette Business Review* (Fall 1971): 168, cited in William R. Brown and Richard E. Crable, "Industry, Mass Magazines, and the Ecology Issue," *The Quarterly Journal of Speech* 59, no. 3 (October 1973): 260.
46. Budweiser display ad, *Daily Nebraskan,* April 22, 1970, 7; Schlitz display ad, *Daily Nebraskan,* May 11, 1970.
47. Display ad, *Time,* October 2, 1972, 21.
48. "New Texaco Corporate Campaign Talks About Pollution Control," *Benton & Bowles News* 4, no. 1 (January 1971): 7, D'Arcy Masius Benton & Bowles Archive, Corporate Publications Series, 1938–1985, House Organs: Box B & B 15, folder B & B News, 1971–1981, John W. Hartman Center for Sales, Advertising, and Marketing History, Rare Book, Manuscript, and Special Collections Library, Duke University; display ad, appeared in consumer magazines in 1971, D'Arcy Masius Benton & Bowles Archive, Advertisements Series, 1932–1984, 1987, Texaco, 1967–1980, Box 123, John W. Hartman Center for Sales, Advertising, and Marketing History, Rare Book, Manuscript, and Special Collections Library, Duke University.
49. *Seattle Times,* April 27, 1971, cited in "Corporate Advertising and the Environment," 33.
50. Denis Hayes, "Environmental Teach-in," *Living Wilderness* 34, no. 109 (Spring 1970): 13.
51. Display ad, *Harper's,* August 1970, 13.
52. Anthony Wolff, "Caveat Lector," *American Heritage,* October 1970, 106–7.
53. Raymond A. Joseph, "Critics Say Misleading Environmental Ads Inflate Corporate Efforts Against Pollution," *Wall Street Journal,* November 5, 1971.
54. Display ad, *Time,* January 4, 1971, 6.
55. Richard D. Morgenstern, William A. Pizer, and Jhih-Shyang Shih, "Jobs versus the Environment: An Industry-level Perspective," Resources for the Future (December 1998, revised June 2000), http://www.globalurban.org/Jobs_vs_the_Environment.pdf (accessed August 14, 2012); Jia Lynn Yang, "Does Federal Regulation Really Kill Jobs? Economists Say Overall Effect Minimal," *Washington Post,* November 13, 2011.
56. Julia B. Corbett, *Communicating Nature: How We Create and Understand Environmental Messages* (Washington, DC: Island Press, 2006), 306–7.
57. "Timme Ads for Fake Furs Point Finger at Lollobrigida Tiger Skins, Hickel Seal Coat," *Advertising Age* 41, no. 9 (March 2, 1970): 8. The tiger-skin ad can be found, among other places, in *Vogue,* July 1970, 14–15.
58. "Saga Mink Market Plan, 1970–71," 10–12, J. Walter Thompson Company. Review Board Records, Meeting Series 1950–1974, Saga Mink Minutes, 1970. John W. Hartman Center for Sales, Advertising, and Marketing History, Rare Book, Manuscript, and Special Collections Library, Duke University.
59. Herbert Marcuse, "Ecology and Revolution," *Liberation* 17, no. 6 (September 1972): 10.
60. Jerome Olds, "In 1970, the Topics Are All Organic," *Organic Gardening and Farming* (January 1970): 34.
61. Marcuse, "Ecology and Revolution," 11–12.
62. See, for example, Michael E. Kraft and Norman J. Vig, "Environmental Policy in the Reagan Presidency," *Political Science Quarterly* 99, no. 3 (Autumn, 1984): especially 426–39; Wolfgang Saxon, "On Earth Day, Plans to Make a Point," *New York Times,* April 21, 1990.
63. See, for example, Miranda A. Schreurs, *Environmental Politics in Japan, Germany, and the United States* (New York: Cambridge University Press, 2003).
64. Denis Hayes, telephone interview with author, March 21, 2006.

65. One of the most noted political actions taken by Environmental Action, Inc. shortly after Earth Day in 1970 (and biannually after), was the "Dirty Dozen" campaign that targeted the reelections of 12 members of Congress who were judged to have "legislatively contributed to the problems that confront us today." Of the 12 targeted in 1970, 7 lost their reelection bids. See "The Dirty Dozen," *Environmental Action*, June 24, 1972, 13–15.
66. Hayes, "In the Name of Earth Day," 31.
67. Laurie Freeman and Christy Fisher, "Popeye Lends Muscle to 'GH' Green Seal," *Advertising Age* (June 25, 1990): 58; Hayes, telephone interview with author, March 21, 2006. Hayes found that an independent agency seeking to assure the environmental credentials of a product, and charging corporations for the service to fund the necessary research, could be easily undermined by other independent agencies that charged corporations a considerably lower fee, did no research to measure a product's environmental impact, yet nevertheless provided the product with some sort of seal of supposed environmental quality that would fool many consumers into believing a product was environmentally friendly even when it was not, while requiring the corporation to take no measures to improve its environmental practices.
68. Jack Steinberg, "What's New in the Natural Foods Business? Capitalizing on a New Crop of Customers," *New York Times*, July 16, 1989.
69. Judann Dagnoli, "Green Marketing; Green Buys Taking Root," *Advertising Age* (September 3, 1990): 27; Susan Hayward, "The Environmental Opportunity," *Marketing Research* 1, no. 4 (December 1989): 67.
70. N. Zeman and L. Howard, "Earth Day: Who Cares?" *Newsweek*, April 16, 1990, 6.
71. Beth Levine, "Earth Day Anniversary Celebrated with Bumper Crop of Books," *Publisher's Weekly* 237, no. 11 (March 16, 1990): 41–43; Jeffery Hollender, *How to Make the World a Better Place: A Guide to Doing Good* (New York: Quill, 1990), 11; John Elkington, Julia Hailes, and Joel Makower, *The Green Consumer* (New York: Penguin Books, 1990), 5; David Steinman, *Diet for a Poisoned Planet: How to Choose Safe Foods for You and Your Family* (New York: Ballantine Books, 1990).
72. Gary Cohen, "It's Too Easy Being Green: Earth Day 1990," *Social Policy* 21, no. 1 (Summer 1990): 20–33.
73. See, for example, Toby Smith, *The Myth of Green Marketing: Tending Our Goats at the Edge of Apocalypse* (Toronto: University of Toronto Press, 1998).
74. Adam Shell, "Earth Day Spawns Corporate 'Feeding Frenzy,'" *Public Relations Journal* 46, no. 2 (February 1990): 9.
75. Eugene Linden, "Earth Day; Will the Ballyhoo Go Bust?" *Time*, April 23, 1990, 86.
76. Brian Tokar, *Earth For Sale: Reclaiming Ecology in the Age of Corporate Greenwash* (Boston: South End Press, 1999), 19–21.
77. Sharon Begley and Mary Hager, "The Selling of Earth Day," *Newsweek*, March 26, 1990, 60.
78. Zeman and Howard, "Earth Day: Who Cares?" 6.
79. Donatella Lorch, "Protesters on the Environment Tie Up Wall Street," *New York Times*, April 24, 1990.
80. Daniel C. Etsy and Andrew S. Winston, *Green to Gold: How Smart Companies Use Environmental Strategy to Innovate, Create Value, and Build Competitive Advantage* (New Haven: Yale University Press, 2006); L. Hunter Loving, Amory Loving, and Paul Hawken, *Natural Capitalism: Creating the Next Industrial Revolution* (Boston: Little, Brown and Company, 1999); Harvard Business School Press, *Harvard Business Review on Green Business Strategy* (Cambridge: Harvard Business School Press, 2007); Brian Nattrass and Mary Altomare, *The Natural Step for Business: Wealth, Ecology and the Evolutionary Corporation* (Gabriola Island, BC: New Society Publishers, 1999); Giselle Weybrecht, *The Sustainable MBA: The Manager's Guide to Green Business* (Hoboken: Wiley, 2009); Joel Makower, *Strategies for the Green Economy: Opportunities and Challenges in the New World of Business* (New York: McGraw-Hill, 2008); Gil Friend, *The Truth About Green Business* (Saddle River, NJ: FT Press, 2009); Christopher Lazio, *Sustainable Value: How the World's Leading Companies Are Doing Well by Doing Good* (Palo Alto: Stanford Business Books, 2008); Paul Hawken, *The Ecology of Commerce: A Declaration of Sustainability* (New York: HarperCollins, 1993).
81. Amy Joyce and Ben White, "Wal-Mart Pushes to Soften its Image," *Washington Post*, October 29, 2005; Stephanie Rosenbloom and Michael Barbaro, "Green-Light Specials, Now at

Wal-Mart," *New York Times*, January 25, 2009; Jared Diamond, "Will Big Business Save the Earth?" *New York Times*, December 6, 2009; Miguel Bustillo and David Kesmodel, "'Local' Grows on Wal-Mart," *Wall Street Journal*, August 1, 2011; Edward Humes, *Force of Nature: The Unlikely Story of Wal-Mart's Green Revolution* (New York: Harper Business, 2011).

82. Sharon Begley, "The Battle for Planet Earth," *Newsweek*, April 24, 2000, 50.
83. Ben Elgin, "Little Green Lies," *BusinessWeek*, October 29, 2007, 046.
84. Andrew C. Revkin, "Dredging of Pollutants Begins in Hudson," *New York Times*, May 15, 2009; David Goodman, "Culture Change: Does the Selling of Stonyfield Farm Yogurt Signal the End of Socially Responsible Businesses—Or a New Beginning?" *Mother Jones*, January/February 2003, 52–57; Michael Pollan, "Naturally: How Organic Became a Marketing Niche and a Multibillion-Dollar Industry," *New York Times Magazine*, May 13, 2001; Elgin, "Little Green Lies," 046
85. Elgin, "Little Green Lies," 046.
86. Michael Barbaro and Felicity Barringer, "Wal-Mart to Seek Savings in Energy," *New York Times*, October 25, 2005; Hubert R. Herring, "Wal-Mart's Profits: Nearly $20,000 (Per Minute, That Is)," *New York Times*, February 27, 2005.
87. John Mackey, "The Whole Foods Alternative to ObamaCare," *Wall Street Journal*, August 11, 2009; Alec MacGillis, "Executives Lay Out Compromise to 'Card Check' Labor Bill," *Washington Post*, March 22, 2009.
88. Gary Levin, "Consumers Turning Green: JWT Survey," *Advertising Age* (November 12, 1990): 74.
89. See, for example, Samuel Fromartz, *Organic Inc.: Natural Foods and How They Grew* (New York: Harcourt, Inc., 2006), and Michael Pollan, *The Omnivore's Dilemma: A Natural History of Four Meals* (New York: Penguin Press, 2006), especially 134–84.
90. Fromartz, *Organic Inc.*, 145–87. Demos quote, 184.
91. Julie Guthman, *Agrarian Dreams: The Paradox of Organic Farming in California* (Berkeley: University of California Press, 2004), 45.
92. Pollan, "Naturally: How Organic Became a Marketing Niche," 31–32.
93. Pollan, *The Omnivore's Dilemma*, 169–73.
94. Stephanie Strom, "Has 'Organic' Been Oversized?" *New York Times*, July 7, 2012; Pollan, "Naturally: How Organic Became a Market Niche," 32–36.
95. J. I. Rodale, "Introduction to Organic Farming," *Organic Farming and Gardening* 1, no. 1 (May 1942): 4.
96. Display ad, Magazines, 1972, D'Arcy Masius Benton & Bowles Archive, Advertisements Series, 1932–1984, 1987, Texaco, 1967–1980, Box 123, John W. Hartman Center for Sales, Advertising, and Marketing History, Rare Book, Manuscript, and Special Collections Library, Duke University.
97. Tim Golden, "A History of Pollution in Mexico Casts Cloud Over Trade Accord," *New York Times*, August 16, 1993.
98. Robert Suro, "Rash of Brain Defects in Newborns Disturbs Border City in Texas," *New York Times*, May 31, 1992.
99. Keith Bradsher, "Court Ruling Lets Trade Agreement Move to Congress," *New York Times*, September 25, 1993; John R. MacArthur, *The Selling of Free Trade: NAFTA, Washington, and the Subversion of American Democracy* (New York: Hill & Wang, 2000).
100. Kevin Gallagher, *Free Trade and the Environment: Mexico, NAFTA, and Beyond* (Palo Alto, CA: Stanford University Press, 2004), 79, 89.
101. Gallagher, *Free Trade and the Environment*, 2–3, 82–83.
102. Juliet Macur, "Beijing Air Raises Questions for Olympics," *New York Times*, August 26, 2007.
103. "When Buying Organic Pays (and Doesn't)," *Consumer Reports* 71, no. 2 (February 2006): 12–17.
104. Ian Herbert, "It's Not Just a Fad—Organic Food Is Better for You, Say Scientists," *The Independent*, April 3, 2007.
105. Elaine Tyler May, "Gimme Shelter: Do-It-Yourself Defense and the Politics of Fear," in John W. Cook, Lawrence Glickman, and Michael O'Malley, *The Cultural Turn in U.S. History: Past, Present, and Future* (Chicago: University of Chicago Press, 2008), 217–38.

106. Jean Hewitt, "Organic Food Fanciers Go to Great Lengths for the Real Thing," *New York Times*, September 7, 1970.
107. Hayes, "In the Name of Earth Day," *Environmental Action* 21, no. 5 (March/April 1990): 14.

Conclusion

1. Joseph Heath and Andrew Potter, *The Rebel Sell: Why the Culture Can't be Jammed* (Toronto: Harper Perennial, 2004), 62, 288, 308.
2. Brad Knickerbocker, "Why 'Green' is No Longer Radical," *Christian Science Monitor*, April 21, 1997.
3. See, for example, Todd Gitlin, *The Sixties: Years of Hope, Days of Rage* (New York: Bantam, 1987), 420–27.
4. Jonathan Richman, "City vs. Country," *You Must Ask the Heart* (1995, Rounder, CD).
5. Julie Guthman, *Agrarian Dreams: The Paradox of Organic Farming in California* (Berkeley: University of California Press, 2004), 170.
6. Jerry Shriver, "Portland's Palate Takes an Artisanal Turn," *USA Today*, January 5, 2007; Thomas A. Lyson, *Civic Agriculture: Reconnecting Farm, Food, and Community* (Medford, MA: Tufts University Press, 2004).
7. Andrew Martin, "Is a Food Revolution Now in Season?" *New York Times*, March 21, 2009.
8. Sarah A. Low and Stephen Vogel, *Direct and Intermediated Marketing of Local Food in the United States* (Washington, DC: United States Department of Agriculture, 2011), 2–6.
9. Guthman, *Agrarian Dreams*, 185. Emphasis in original.
10. Jack Hedin, "My Forbidden Fruits (and Vegetables)," *New York Times*, March 1, 2008. For a farmer's view on government policies hindering small farms and local food, see Joel Salatin, *Everything I Want To Do Is Illegal: War Stories From the Local Food Front* (Swoope, VA: Polyface Press, 2007).
11. Miguel Bustillo and David Kesmodel, "'Local' Grows on Wal-Mart," *Wall Street Journal*, August 1, 2011.
12. Frederick Kaufman, "Former McDonald's Honchos Take on Sustainable Cuisine," *Wired*, August 2012, http://www.wired.com/business/2012/07/ff_lyfekitchens (accessed September 18, 2012).
13. Charles McChesney, "As More Search for Community, Ithaca's EcoVillage Gets Ready to Expand," *The Post-Standard* (Syracuse, NY), January 25, 2009, http://www.syracuse.com/news/index.ssf/2009/01/as_more_search_for_community_i.html (accessed February 9, 2009); Adrian Sainz, "Cohousing Offers Green Living, Sense of Belonging," *The Mercury News* (San Jose, CA), February 6, 2009, http://www.mercurynews.com/business/ci_11644373?nclick_check=1 (accessed February 9, 2009).
14. Todd Gitlin, "The Kids Are Alright," *Plenty*, December/January, 2007, 71–72.
15. Quicksilver Messenger Service, *What About Me?* (1970, Capitol, vinyl recording, SMAS-630).
16. Pete Townshend, *Who's Next*, The Who (1971, Decca, vinyl recording, DL 79182).
17. The Board of *Bulletin of Atomic Scientists*, "Board Statement," *Bulletin of Atomic Scientists* (*The Bulletin Online*), January 17, 2007, http://www.thebulletin.org/minutes-to-midnight/board-statements.html (accessed September 17, 2007).
18. Quoted in Curt Meine, *Aldo Leopold: His Life and Work* (Madison: University of Wisconsin Press, 1988), 479.
19. The Board of *Bulletin of Atomic Scientists*, "Board Statement."
20. Juliet Eilperin and Jon Cohen, "Growing Number of Americans See Warming as Leading Threat," *Washington Post*, April 20, 2007; Glenn Hunter, "GM's Lutz on Hybrids, Global Warming and Cars as Art," *D Magazine*, January 30, 2008, http://frontburner.dmagazine.com/2008/01/30/gms-lutz-on-hybrids-global-warming-and-cars-as-art/ (accessed November 28, 2008).
21. Andrew C. Revkin, "On Climate Issue, Industry Ignored Its Scientists," *New York Times*, April 24, 2009.
22. Aldo Leopold to William Vogt, January 25, 1946, "Correspondence to Vogt: Aldo Leopold and Mrs. Leopold," ff 1, box 2, CONS76, Conservation Collection, The Denver Public Library.

INDEX

2,4,5-T (herbicide), 179–180
2,4-D (herbicide), 53–54, 179–180
Abbey, Edward, 87
Abrams, Henry, 140
Adams, Ansel, 137
Advertising Council, 29–30, 66, 133
The Affluent Society (Galbraith), 128
Agent Orange, 54, 178–180
An Agricultural Testament (Howard), 49
agriculture. *See also* organic farming: animal treatment and, 55; antibiotics use in, 134; chemical and pesticide use in, 49–57, 65–66, 110–114, 116–118, 134, 187, 216, 222, 242; corporate agribusiness and, 48–51, 53–57, 65–66, 107, 109, 117, 160, 236, 242–243; factory farming and, 55, 236; radioactive contamination of, 78, 90, 93, 96–97
"A Hard Rain's a-Gonna Fall" (Dylan), 148
Air Pollution Control Act (1955), 89, 158
Air Quality Act (1967), 168–169
Air Quality Advisory Board, 168–169
Albert, Stew, 198
Aliamus, Joan, 112
Allen, David, 205
Allen, Steve, 139
The Amazing Colossal Man, 78
Amchem Corporation, 111
American Civil Liberties Union, 185
American Cyanamid Corporation, 71, 111, 120, 228
American Farm Bureau Federation, 49, 109, 247
American Federation of Teachers, 197, 202
American Feed Manufacturers Association, 122
American Heritage Foundation, 29
American Liberty League, 30
American Petroleum Institute, 170
American Steel and Wire Company, 68
aminotriazole, 111, 120
Anderson, Clinton P., 97

Annand, P. N., 53
antibiotics in agriculture, 134
Anti-Pollution Fair (Palo Alto, California, 1969), 202
Antipollution Task Force (New York), 174–175
Apollo 13, 208–209
Apple Records, 225
Applied Electronics Laboratory (Stanford University), 178
"Aquarius" (song from the musical *Hair*), 191
Arant, F.S., 107
Arco (Idaho), 85
Arizona, hydroelectric proposals in, 175–176
Arness, James, 130
Arrowhead Mills, 136
A Sand County Almanac (Leopold), 43, 45
Atlantic Richfield Corporation (ARCO), 210, 231
atomic bomb: cultural anxiety regarding, 11–15, 20–21, 24–25, 34, 46, 72, 74, 76–78, 81–82, 98, 101, 112, 127, 140–141, 147, 153; cultural hopes regarding, 16–17, 72, 229; "doomsday clock" and, 11, 152, 246; economic development and, 86; environmentalism and, 2–3, 6–7, 13–17, 25–26, 34, 42, 72, 74, 76–78, 90, 93–94, 98, 127, 137, 142–144, 148, 153, 157; fallout from testing of, 2–3, 11, 74–79, 85, 89–90, 92–94, 96–98, 137, 139, 141–142, 148, 151, 157; Hiroshima atomic blast (1945), 9, 11, 13, 15; Manhattan Project and, 11–13; science fiction films and, 78; test ban proposals and, 91–93, 96, 139–140, 142–145, 147, 149, 151–152, 157–158, 175; testing of, 12–14, 40, 74–76, 93, 95–97, 140–143; thermonuclear (hydrogen) variety of, 74–78; World War II and, 11–12
atomic energy, 85–86, 185–186
Atomic Energy Act (1954), 86
Atomic Energy Commission (AEC), 75, 77–79, 90, 93, 97, 99, 186

Audubon Society, 87, 106–108, 136, 162
Automobile Manufacturers Association, Inc., 122, 181
Aware Inn (Hollywood, Calif.), 130

back-to-the-land movement, 190
Bainbridge, Kenneth, 12
Baker, John H., 108
bald eagles, 105–106
Barber, Richard, 172, 177, 200
Bare, Louly, 117
The Beast From 20,000 Fathoms, 78
Beaverkill–Willowemoc Rod & Gun Club, 104
Beech-Nut, 116–117
Ben & Jerry's Ice Cream, 234
Benson, Ezra, 112
Berkeley (California), 196–198, 201–202
Berle, Adolf A., 29
Berlin Crisis (1961), 141, 153
Bernbach, William, 146–147
Bethlehem Steel, 227
Bhabha, Homi J., 85
Bhagavad-Gita, 12
Bicknell, Franklin, 134–135
big business. *See* corporate capitalism
Bikini Atoll atomic bomb tests (1946), 13, 75
biodynamic agriculture (Steiner), 56, 104, 243
birth control pill, 181
Black Action Movement, 205
Blahnik, Manolo, 219
The Blob, 78
Bloomfield, J. J., 69
Boeing, 233
Bolin, Bert, 167
"Bomb" (Corso), 17, 72
the bomb. *See* atomic bomb
Bookchin, Murray, 149–150
Bosch, Carl, 50
Boston Area Ecology Action Center, 220
bottled water market, 221
Boulding, Kenneth, 82–83
boycotts, 195–196, 202, 227–228
Bradley, David, 13
Brand, Stewart, 194–195, 202
"Brand New Start" (Weller), 125
Bridge Canyon dam proposal, 175–176
British Petroleum, 231
Bronx Zoo conservation exhibit (1949), 33–34
Brooks, Paul, 155
Brower, David, 195
Brown, Harrison, 81
The Brown Decades (Mumford), 81
Brownsville (Texas), 237
Buckeye Cotton Company, 59
Budweiser, 226
Bulganin, Nikolai A., 91

Bulletin of Concerned Atomic Scientists, 11, 139, 152, 246
Burroughs, Wise, 121
Bush, George H.W., 237
Business Council, Johnson Administration and, 172
Butrico, Frank, 75
Buttons, Red, 130

Cahan, William C., 91–92
Cahn, Matthew, 215
Cameron, Roderick, 217–218
Canada Dry Beverage Company, 221
cancer: DDT and pesticides' link to, 104–105, 110–111, 118; diethylstilbestrol (DES) and, 122–123; fallout radiation and, 91–93, 99, 141; food additives' link to, 118–119; Food and Drug Administration and, 115
Canned Heat, 190–191
Capitol Records, 225
Carney, Thomas P., 122
Carson, Rachel: on corporate capitalism, 154–155; ecological perspective of, 154; on Food and Drug Administration (FDA), 155; *Silent Spring* and, 2, 15, 115, 153–157
Cascadian Farms, 233–234
Caston, Arthur W., 179
Cato Institute, 212
Cave, Don, 176
The Challenge of Man's Future (Brown), 81
Chamber of Commerce: US, 30, 33, 36, 66, 247; New York, 25; Pittsburgh, 37
Champion International Paper, 231
Chatham Township (New Jersey), 176
Chekhov, Anton, 1
Chemicals in Your Food and in Farm Produce (Bicknell), 134
Chicago (Illinois): ecotage in, 208; organic movement in, 136, 220; pollution in, 70
"Chicago School," 30–31
China, 238
chlordane, 156
Chouinard, Yvon, 221
Christensen, Sherman, 75
Citibank, 46
"City v. Country" (Jonathan Richman), 241–242
Civilian Conservation Corps, 86, 146
civil rights movement, 205
Clarkson, M.R., 107
Clean Air Act, 158, 168–169, 212, 214
Clean Waters Restoration Act (1966), 168
Clearwater River, 226
Cleveland (Ohio), pollution in, 181, 186–187
climate change: denial of, 212, 246–247; warnings regarding, 166–167, 209, 246
Clinton, Bill, 237
Cohen, Gary, 231

cohousing, 244
Cold War: atomic bombs and, 11, 14, 74, 78–79, 93, 95–96, 139, 147, 153; corporate capitalism and, 161; cultural anxiety during, 14, 16, 34, 72, 78, 94–96, 140, 147–148, 153
Colorado River Basin Project, 175
Columbia River, 175, 204
commercial feedlots, 122
Commission on Freedom of the Press, 1947 report by, 58
Committee for 10,000 Babies, 94
Committee for Environmental Information, 175
Commoner, Barry, 99, 183
communes, 189–191, 201
Community Environmental Council, 189
community-supported agriculture, 243
Conant, James B., 13
Concern, Inc., 222–223
Connelly, Matthew, 183
Connor, John, 172
Conrad, Paul, 209
conservation: aesthetic approach to, 45–46, 64, 87, 128, 137, 165, 176, 187; Bronx Zoo exhibit (1949) on, 33–34; environmental movement and, 2, 14, 18, 23, 25, 33–34, 45–46, 66, 73, 87–88, 90, 128, 137, 146, 187, 198, 215, 238; hydroelectric dam projects and, 175–176; International Technical Conference on the Protection of Nature (ITCPN) and, 38–42; Johnson's "new" approach to, 159–160, 165, 175, 189; Kennedy and, 138, 146; National Historic Preservation Act (1966) and, 168; Nelson's support for, 204; nineteenth-century notions of, 2, 14; Pinchot's definition of, 35; Sierra Club and, 25, 64, 87, 137, 187, 212; Wilderness Act and, 162–163
Conservation Foundation, 25, 33–34, 108
"A Conservationist's Lament" (Boulding), 82
Consolidated Edison, 176
Consumer Action Now (CAN), 222–223
consumer behavior: boycotts and, 195–196, 202, 227–228; Earth Day (1970) and, 5, 135, 219–220, 224, 234; environmentalism and, 1, 3–7, 48, 61–62, 65, 73, 79–80, 123, 129–130, 133–135, 139, 143–145, 150, 165, 189, 193–195, 201–203, 206, 217–225, 227–235, 238, 240–242, 244–245, 247; Galbraith on, 128–129, 160; government policy regarding, 28, 166; green consumption and, 3–7, 48, 62, 129–130, 133–136, 189, 193–195, 201–203, 217–224, 228–235, 238, 240–242, 244–245, 247; marketing's impact on, 127–129; organic products and, 4, 6, 61–65, 114, 130, 135–136, 164–165, 192–193, 203, 219–222, 230, 233, 235–236, 242–243; political agency and, 4, 6–7, 62, 218, 222, 228, 244–245, 247; post–World War II boom and, 44, 128–129; women's role in, 223

Consumer Bulletin, 144
consumer movement, 174
Consumer Protection and Environmental Health Service (CPEHS), 166
Consumer Reports, 194; on strontium-90 contamination of milk, 97–98, 140
Consumers Union, 98–99, 112
Coolidge, Calvin, 66
cooperative movement, 60–61
Coors, Joseph, 213
corn, 122, 224
corporate capitalism: agribusiness and, 48–51, 53–57, 65–66, 107, 109, 117, 160, 236, 242–243; Carson on, 154–155; cultural anxiety regarding, 16, 27–29, 46, 72–73, 83–84, 127, 131, 179–180, 195, 199, 216, 245; cultural homogenization and, 160–161; education system and, 59; environmentalism's concerns regarding, 2–4, 6–7, 19–23, 26, 32–35, 38–39, 41–46, 50–52, 62–64, 66–67, 73, 79–85, 87–88, 94, 100, 105, 119–120, 127–128, 150, 154–155, 157, 159, 161, 163, 166, 173–174, 176–177, 180–185, 190, 193–195, 197–199, 201–202, 205–207, 210, 214–215, 217, 219, 234–236, 244; free market emphasis of, 30–31; globalization and, 199–200, 237–238; government subsidization of, 19, 22, 49–50, 72, 86, 89, 164, 177, 241; Great Depression and, 27; growth of, 3, 16, 25, 27, 30–31, 44, 61, 72–73, 81, 83, 172, 199–200, 234, 240–242; lobbying and, 29–30, 57, 72, 113, 117–122, 132, 135, 169–170, 172–173, 201, 212, 216, 218, 226, 241, 248; media control and, 57–58; neoliberalism and, 30–31, 248; physical attacks against institutions of, 200–201, 207–208; political donations and, 171, 173–174, 213, 241, 248; pollution and, 20, 32, 62, 68–72, 85; public land use and, 22–23; public relations and marketing for, 27, 30, 56, 59, 66, 71, 107, 117, 128, 132–133, 155, 170, 181, 212–213, 225–227, 231–233, 237, 247; scientific research and, 58–59, 109, 119–120, 131–132, 177; *Silent Spring* and, 156; sustainability emphasis in, 232–233; think-tank funding and, 212–213; threats to democracy from, 25, 29, 72–73, 81, 114–115, 151, 172, 177, 192, 217–218; World War II and, 27–28
Corso, Gregory, 17, 72, 229
Cory, Catherine, 94
Coupland, Douglas, 153
Cousins, Norman, 94–95, 140, 174–175
Cowan, Rachel, 182–183
Cox, L.G., 116–117
cranberry contamination warnings (1959), 110–115, 139
Crown Zellerbach, 204
Cuban Missile Crisis (1962), 151–153

"The Cultural Revolution to End War" (Sullivan), 9
Curran, C. H., 25
Cuyahoga River, 186–187

dairy industry, 90, 145
Darby, William J., 133
Darling, Fraser, 39
Darlington, Jeanie, 190
Dasmann, Raymond, 160–162
Daughters of the American Revolution, 205
Davis, Adelle, 64
The Day the Earth Caught Fire (film), 147–148
DDT: cancer and, 104–105; commercial development of, 24–25, 86; comparison to atomic blasts and, 154–155; Congressional investigation of, 115–118; creation of, 23; delousing applications for, 23; Dutch elm disease eradication campaigns and, 106; environmental impact of, 15, 23–24, 53, 102–106, 115–116, 134, 163–164; fire ant eradication program (1957) and, 107; food supply contamination and, 103, 105, 113, 116–117, 164, 207; gypsy moth eradication campaign (1957) and, 102–106, 110, 187; legal cases regarding, 105, 110; political mobilization against use of, 102–106, 108, 187, 202; restrictions regarding use of, 24, 157; scientific warnings regarding, 24–25, 52–53, 102–105, 118, 175; *Silent Spring* and, 15, 115, 154–155
DDT Producers Industry Advisory Committee, 24
"DDT: The Atomic Bomb of the Insect World" (Curran), 25
Dean, Howard, 234
Dean Foods, 235–236
Deer Park spring water, 221
Defense Department, 86, 97
Delaney, James J., 115–118, 130–131
Delaney Clause, 115–116, 119–120
Delaware River, 67
Democratic Party. *See also* Johnson, Lyndon B.; Kennedy, John F.: corporate political donors and, 171; environmental appeals by, 170–171
Demos, Steve, 235
Department of Agriculture: chemical and pesticide spraying campaigns by, 101–105, 107, 109–110; chemical industry and, 109; corporate agribusiness and, 53, 243–244; Organic Standards (2001) in, 236, 243
Des Moines (Iowa), iodine 131 levels in, 141, 149
Detroit (Michigan), pollution in, 70, 181
DeVoto, Bernard, 22
Dewey, Scott, 69
Diamond Shamrock Company, 179

dieldrin, 107–110, 164
Diet for a Poisoned Planet (Steinman), 230
Diet for a Small Planet (Lappé), 223–224, 230
diethylstilbestrol (DES), 55, 121–123
Diggers (anarchist community), 193
Dodd, Thomas J., 140
Dodds, Sir Charles, 55
Donora (Pennsylvania): air pollution deaths in, 68–72, 88; plant closures in, 71–72
"doomsday clock," 11, 152, 246
Douglas, William O., 105
Dow Chemical, 59, 179, 247
Dresden fire bombings (1945), 17
Dubos, René, 136–137
DuBridge, Lee A., 179, 184
DuPont Corporation, 92, 118, 170, 231
Dust Bowl, 14, 19
Dutch elm disease, 106
Dutton, Fred, 203–204
Dylan, Bob, 148

Earth Day (1970): anti-poverty and social justice themes in, 209; *Apollo 13* and, 208–209; Congressional support for, 204; continuing annual celebrations of, 229; consumer behavior and, 5, 135, 219–220, 224, 234; criticism of, 205–206; criticisms of corporate capitalism and, 210; decentralized nature of, 210; environmental legislation and, 5, 211–213, 217; Kent State killings and, 245; media coverage and, 210–211, 218, 231; New York City and, 210, 218; planning of, 4, 203–207; precursors to, 202–203; Sierra Club and, 212; success of, 4, 11, 157, 209, 211–212, 218, 230; teach-in and education efforts on, 5, 218–219; Vietnam War and, 209
Earth Day (1990), 229, 231–232
Earth Shoe, 218–219
Eber, Ronald, 203
Echo Park (Colorado) dam proposal controversy, 87
Eco-Commando Force 70, 207–208
ecology: academic discipline of, 18; chemical and pesticide threats to, 53–54, 101–103, 105, 109, 122, 154, 179; environmentalism and, 2–3, 17–18, 23, 25–26, 34, 51–52, 66, 80–81, 203; hydroelectric projects' threats to, 175; International Technical Conference on the Protection of Nature (ITCPN) and, 38, 40, 42; invasive species' threat to, 108; Osborn on, 21; popularization of the term, 18
Ecology Action, 201–202, 206, 217–218, 220
The Ecology of Commerce: A Declaration of Sustainability (Hawken), 232
The Ecology of Invasions by Insects and Plants (Elton), 108
ecotage, 207–208

EcoVillage (Ithaca, NY), 244
Ecuador, 182–183
Edsall, John T., 180
"The Effects of Atomic Weapons" (U.S. Atomic Energy Commission), 77
E. F. Timme & Son, 227–228
Egler, Frank, 83
Ehrlich, Paul, 21, 181–183
Einstein, Albert, 16, 40, 246
Eisenhower, Dwight: on air pollution, 89; atomic bomb test bans and, 96; cranberry contamination warnings (1959) and, 112; financial contributors to, 122; military-industrial complex and, 29, 178; presidential election of 1956 and, 90–91
Eli Lilly and Company, 121–122
Elugelab Island, thermonuclear bomb testing at, 74
Endangered Species Preservation Act (1966), 163, 169
Environmental Action, Inc., 205–207, 210, 215
Environmental Defense Fund, 187
environmental impact statements, 215, 237
environmentalism: alternative and public transportation emphasis in, 202–203; alternative energy and, 84–85, 190; as an advertising theme, 63, 224–228, 231; atomic bomb and, 2–3, 6–7, 13–17, 25–26, 34, 42, 72, 74, 76–78, 90, 93–94, 98, 127, 137, 142–144, 148, 153, 157; atomic energy and, 185–186; biodiversity and, 160–161; chemical and pesticide concerns within, 2–3, 23–25, 50–51, 53–54, 64–66, 101–114, 116–117, 123, 131, 144, 149, 151, 155–157, 163–164, 175, 179–180, 187, 222–223; civil rights movement and, 205; communes and, 189–191, 201; conservation and, 2, 14, 18, 23, 25, 33–34, 45–46, 66, 73, 87–88, 90, 128, 137, 146, 187, 198, 215, 238; consumer behavior and, 1, 3–7, 48, 61–62, 65, 73, 79–80, 123, 129–130, 133–135, 139, 143–145, 150, 165, 189, 193–195, 201–203, 206, 217–225, 227–235, 238, 240–242, 244–245, 247; corporate capitalism and, 2–4, 6–7, 19–23, 26, 32–35, 38–39, 41–46, 50–52, 62–64, 66–67, 73, 79–85, 87–88, 94, 100, 105, 119–120, 127–128, 150, 154–155, 157, 159, 161, 163, 166, 173–174, 176–177, 180–185, 190, 193–195, 197–199, 201–202, 205–207, 210, 214–215, 217, 219, 234–236, 244; counterculture and, 5–6, 189–198, 201, 241–242; decentralization emphasis in, 150–151, 190; ecology and, 2–3, 17–18, 23, 25–26, 34, 51–52, 66, 80–81, 203; ecotage and, 207–208; efforts to discredit, 66, 156, 176–177, 205, 213; electoral politics and, 5, 7, 62, 88, 90, 114, 138–139, 171, 205, 215, 240–241, 247–248; endangered species and, 21, 106, 163, 227; feminism and, 207; greenhouse gas emissions and, 229, 233; impact on employment from, 226–227; lack of socioeconomic diversity within, 6, 238–239; legislation and policy regarding, 3–4, 7, 73, 158–159, 167–169, 173–174, 211–216, 229–230; mainstreaming of, 7, 115, 154, 167, 175, 180, 219, 230, 242; media coverage of, 26, 184–185; New Left and, 196; oil spills and, 183–185, 229; origins of, 1–4, 6, 18–19, 35, 44, 47; pollution and, 2–3, 80, 82, 89, 127, 137, 151, 158–159, 166–167, 186–187, 202; population growth and control issues in, 2, 20–21, 181–183, 218; Progressive Era and, 64; radical potential of, 65, 247; recycling and reuse emphasis in, 202, 223, 226; *Silent Spring* and, 2; sustainable development emphasis in, 79–80, 82; teach-ins and, 197, 202–204, 206, 218–219; technology and, 82–85; wilderness preservation and, 86–88, 161–162; women's involvement in, 98–100, 142–146, 207, 223
Environmental Pollution Panel (1965), 166
Environmental Protection Agency (EPA), 211, 214
Environmental Quality Council, 211
environmental-review process (NEPA), 214–215
Environmental Teach-in, Inc., 204–205
Erewhon (Boston food store), 193
Eriksson, Erik, 167
Ernst, Morris L., 58
Eweson, Eric, 63
Ewing, Oscar R., 69
Exploratory Project for Economic Alternatives, 194
Exxon Valdez oil spill (1989), 229

Fabre, Edwin, 205
fallout and radiation. *See also under* atomic bomb: cancer risks and, 91–93, 99, 141; impact on food supplies and, 90–91, 93, 97–99, 131, 139, 142–145; scientific warnings regarding, 78–79, 90–91, 99; strontium-90 and, 76–77, 90, 96, 140–141, 143, 145, 147, 154, 175
"Fallout: The Silent Killer" (*Saturday Evening Post* series), 99
Far Fetched Foods (San Francisco store), 193
Federal Aid Highway Act (1956), 89
Federal Council of the Churches of Christ, 15–16
Federal Food, Drug, and Cosmetic Act, 115, 130–131
Federal Insecticide, Fungicide, and Rodenticide Act (1947), 53
Federal Power Commission, 176, 223
Federal Water Pollution Control Administration, 184

Fellowship of Reconciliation, 142
Fenton, Faith, 116
Field & Stream coverage of chemical pesticides, 109–110
Fink, Ollie, 41–42
fire ant eradication campaign (1957), 101, 107, 109–110
fish deaths from chemical poisoning, 164
Fisher, Hugo, 174
Flemming, Arthur S., 111–113, 121
Fonda, Jane, 238
Food Additives Amendment (1958), 115
Food and Drug Administration (FDA): Bicknell on, 135; birth control pill, 181; Carson on, 155; corporate lobbying and, 57, 113, 120, 135; cranberry warnings (1959) and, 110–113; diethylstilbestrol (DES) regulation and, 121–122; food additives regulation and, 115–116, 119–121, 155; resource limitations of, 113; restrictions on pesticide use and, 110; on women in the workforce and "convenience foods," 144–145
"Food Facts *vs.* Food Fallacies" (FDA pamphlet), 135
Ford Motor Company, 214
Foss, Phillip O., 22
"The Fouling of the American Environment" (*Saturday Review* series), 174
Foundation of Economic Education, 29–30
"Fox" (Chicago-based eco-guerilla), 208
Frank, Thomas, 1
Frazer, Joseph W., 63–64
Frazer Products, 63
Fredonia (Arizona), 141
Free Stores (San Francisco), 193
Freud, Sigmund, 26
Fried, Hanes, 104
Friedman, Milton, 30–31, 33
Friends of the Earth, 195, 213, 227
Fromm, Erich, 94–95
Fundamentals of Ecology (Odum), 80

Galbraith, John Kenneth, 81, 128–129, 160, 177, 191
Gandy's Restaurant (Buffalo), 63
Gardening with Nature (Wickenden), 65
Gardner, John, 169, 182
Garrett, Paul, 132
Gelbart, Larry, 130
General Electric, 186, 210, 232–233
General Mills, 233–234
General Motors (GM), 169–170, 246–247
General Telephone and Electronics, 200
Germany, chemical production in, 50
Gerry's Mountaineering Equipment, 221
Giant Business: Threat to Democracy (Quinn), 72–73

Giant Corporations: Challenge to Freedom (Quinn), 114–115
Giedion, Siegfried, 17, 52
Gilliam, Harold, 222
Ginsberg, Allen, 83–84, 148
Gitlin, Todd: anti-nuclear protests and, 142; on consumer activism, 244–245; on cultural fears of the atomic bomb, 153; on People's Park, 198
Glen Canyon (Arizona), 87
Glickman, Lawrence, 62
Global Climate Coalition, 212, 247
globalization of corporate capitalism, 199–200, 237–238
global warming. *See* climate change
Globe Hill Farms (New York), 136
Godwin, Margaret, 185
"Going Up the Country" (Canned Heat), 190–191
Goldman, Ilene, 222
Goldmark, Peter, 142
GOO (Get Oil Out), 184
Graham, David, 68
Grand Canyon (Arizona), 175–176
Great Britain, 95, 152
Great Society programs, 159
Great Swamp (New Jersey), 176
The Great Transformation (Polanyi), 32
green consumption. *See also under* consumer behavior: criticism of, 133, 228, 240, 247; mainstream appeal of, 228; upscale nature of, 5–6, 61–62, 150, 238
greenhouse gas emissions, 229, 233. *See also* climate change
The Greening of America (Reich), 192
Green Parties (Europe), 229
Greenpeace, 213
Groth, Ned, 199
Groupe Danone, 233
Gulf Oil Company, 31
Guthman, Julie, 243
gypsy moth outbreak and eradication campaign (1957), 101–106, 110, 187

Haber, Fritz, 50
Haeckel, Ernst, 18
Hair (musical), 191
Hancock, James, 108
Hargraves, Malcolm M., 104–105
Harroy, Jean-Paul, 39, 42
Haseltine, Leonard F., 64
Haskins, Harold, 185
Hauser, Philip M., 129
Hawken, Paul, 232
Hayek, Friedrich, 30
Hayes, Charlie, 209
Hayes, Denis: biography of, 204–205; on corporate capitalism, 210, 226; Earth Day and,

204–205, 207, 210; on electoral politics and policy, 214, 229–230; Environmental Action and, 206–207; on lack of socioeconomic diversity in environmentalism, 239; Stanford University Vietnam War protests (1969) and, 178
Hayes, Wayland J., 105
Health Food International (California organic market), 220
Heath, Joseph, 240
Helms, Cynthia, 222–223
heptachlor, 107–110, 115, 156, 164
Herbst, Gary, 206
Heritage Foundation, 212
Hersey, John, 13, 95
Hetch Hetchy dam (Yosemite Valley), 21, 87
Hickel, Walter, 185, 228
The Hidden Persuaders (Packard), 16, 127, 155
Highway Beautification Act (1965), 168
Hinds, Roger, 103
Hines, Don Carlos, 121
Hinshaw, Carl, 77
hippies, 196
Hiroshima (Hersey), 13
Hiroshima atomic blast (1945), 9, 11, 13, 15–16
Hirshberg, Gary, 187
Holifield, Craig, 186
Holubar Mountaineering, 221
Horizon Corporation, 236
hormone treatment for meats, 121–122, 131
Houghton Mifflin, 156
House Un-American Activities Committee (HUAC): Consumers Union and, 98; Hollywood and, 139; Women Strike for Peace (WSP) and, 151–152
Howard, Sir Albert, 49–52
Howl (Ginsburg), 83–84
Hudson River, 176, 233
Hueper, Wilhelm C., 92, 118
Humphrey, Cliff, 201–202
Humphrey, Mary, 201, 217
Hutchinson, George E., 63
Huxley, Aldous, 43, 158
Huxley, Julian, 38
Huxtable, Ada Louise, 173
hydroelectric dam projects, 87, 175–176

I. G. Farben, 27
Ignatius, Nancy, 222
"Insecticides and Dead Fish" (*Outdoor Life* article), 104
Inter-American Conference on Conservation of Renewable Natural Resources (1948), 54
Interior Department, 87, 170, 182, 184–185, 223
International Conference on Solar Energy, 84
International Conference on the Peaceful Uses of Atomic Energy, 85

International Industrial Conference (San Francisco, 1969), 203
International Minerals and Chemicals Corporation, 27
International Planned Parenthood, 182
International Technical Conference on the Protection of Nature (ITCPN): conservation and, 38–42; ecology and, 38, 40, 42; endangered species and, 40; environmentalism and, 35, 38–40
International Union for the Protection of Nature (IUPN), 38–39, 45
"In the Year 2525" (Zager and Evans), 188
invasive species, 108
iodine 131, 99, 141, 149, 151–152
Izaak Walton League, 87, 140

Jackson State College killings (1970), 245
Jacobs, Ellie and Raymond, 218–219
Japan: impact of atomic bomb blasts in, 13; *Lucky Dragon* incident and, 76–77; Malthusian predictions regarding, 20
Jezer, Martin, 190
Johnson, Lady Bird, 160, 165, 168
Johnson, Lyndon B.: auto industry and, 181; corporate supporters of, 171–172; environmental policies of, 158–160, 165–175, 180–181; Great Society programs and, 159; "new" conservation approach of, 159–160, 165, 175, 180, 189; on pollution, 165–168; Vietnam War and, 171, 178; Wildness Act and, 160
J. R. Geigy (chemical company), 23
The Jungle (Sinclair), 57
Justice Department, 67–68, 181

Kalso, Anne, 218–219
Kansas City (Missouri), 112
Kaplan, Jacques, 228
Kapp, K. William, 32–33
Keene, Paul, 136
Keep America Beautiful (KAB), 132–133
Keith, Frank R., 115
Kennedy, John F.: on atomic testing, 145; Berlin Crisis (1961) and, 141; conservation and environmental policies of, 138, 146, 156; cranberry contamination warnings (1959) and, 112; on milk and the dairy industry, 145; Wilderness Act and, 160
Kent State University killings (1970), 245
Kerouac, Jack, 72
Key, V.O., 114
Khrushchev, Nikita, 162
Kidson, Dick, 135
Kilian, Melody, 196
King, Judson, 66
Kitchen Debate (Nixon and Khrushchev), 162

Kleinfold, Vincent A., 130
Koestler, Arthur, 161
Kraus, Ezra J., 53
Krug, Julius A., 35, 37
Kuboyama, Aikichi, 77
Kushi, Michio, 193
Kuwait, 31

Lake Erie, 180–181
Lake Ontario, 180
Lake Powell (Arizona), 87
Lake Tahoe (California), 203
Land Conservation Fund, 146
"land ethic" (Leopold), 43–45, 48, 59, 114, 184
Lane, John, 176
Lang, Fritz, 84
Lapp, Ralph, 78
Lappé, Frances Moore, 223–224, 230
Larimer County (Colorado), 132
The Last Horizon (Dasmann), 160
Lawes, John Bennet, 49–50
lead fuel additives, 169–170
League of Women Voters, 88
Lehman, Arnold J., 120
Leifert, Carlo, 238
Leopold, Aldo: on conservation, 42–44; on consumer behavior, 73; on corporate capitalism, 42–43, 45, 127; ecological perspective of, 43–44; on education, 59; "land ethic" and, 43–45, 48, 59, 114, 184; on nutrition, 50; organic movement and, 48–49, 243; Vogt's correspondence with, 44–45, 248; Wilderness Society and, 43
Leslie Salt, 202
Let's Have Healthy Children (Davis), 64
leukemia, 92, 141
LeVander, Harold, 186
Levitt, Alice, 192
Levitt, William J., 192
Lewis, Edward B., 92, 99
Ley, Herbert, 113
Libby, Willard F., 93–94
Liebig, Justus von, 49
Life After God (Coupland), 153
Lillie, Harry, 40
Lincoln, Murray, 61
Lindsay, Malvina, 22
Listen in Good Health (album), 225
livestock industry, 22
lobbying. *See under* corporate capitalism
local foods movement, 243–244
Lollobrigida, Gina, 227
Longgood, William: on corporate control of government policy, 132, 134–135, 139, 241; on corporate control of scientific research, 131–132; critics of, 133; on DDT, 103; on green consumption, 134; on synthetic chemicals in food, 131

Long Island (New York), DDT use and gypsy moth eradication campaign in, 102–104, 187
Lorentz, Pare, 93
Lorenz, Fred W., 55
Los Angeles (California): organic movement in, 130, 135, 220; pollution in, 67, 70–71, 88
Louisiana, mass fish deaths in, 164
Luce, Henry, 58
Lucky Dragon (Japanese fishing boat), 76–77
Lutz, Bob, 246–247
Lyfe Kitchens (restaurant chain), 244
Lyons, Louis M., 58

Make Friends With Your Land (Wickenden), 54
The Making of a Counter Culture (Roszak), 191–192
Malthus, Thomas, 20
Man and Nature; or Physical Geography as Modified by Human Behavior (Marsh), 81
Manhattan Project, 11–13
"Man's Role in Changing the Face of the Earth" (1955 conference), 81–83, 195
Manufacturing Chemists' Association (MCA), 71, 117
maquiladora factories (Mexico), 237
Marble Gorge dam proposal, 175–176
Marcuse, Herbert, 228–229
Marine Mammal Protection Act, 211
Marsh, George Perkins, 81–82
Marshall Islands, atomic bomb tests in, 74–76
Massachusetts, gypsy moth outbreak in, 101–102
Matamoros (Mexico), 237
Materials Policy Commission, 46
Mauk, Bill, 215–216
Maverick Jeans, 225
MBF Products, Inc., 136
McArthur, Rudger, 75
McCabe, Louis, 70
McCloskey, Jr., Paul (Pete) N., 204
McCloskey, Michael, 187, 211–212, 214
McConnell, Grant, 173
McCormick, Anne O'Hare, 15
McDonald's, 244
McHugh, Harry, 164
McKeon, Daniel, 103
McKinsey & Company, 232
meat, hormone treatment and, 121–122, 131
Merchants and Manufacturers Association, 70
Meselson, Matthew S., 179
Metropolis (Lang), 84
Mexico, 237–238
Miami (Florida), 207–208
Mifflin Street Community Co-op (Madison, Wisconsin food store), 193–194
Miliband, Ralph, 216
milk supply: DDT contamination and, 103, 105, 113, 207; strontium-90 contamination and, 90, 97–100, 140, 142–146, 151–152

Miller, Timothy, 190
Mineral King Valley (California), 176
Minneapolis (Minnesota), 141, 149, 186
Minnesota: atomic energy and, 186; strontium-90 levels in, 97
Mintener, Bradshaw, 122
Mirowski, Philip, 31
Mississippi River, pollution in, 164, 186
Missouri River, 163
Mitchell, J. Murray, 209
Mitchell, Joni, 18
Mobil Oil, 200
Modern Natural Foods (Washington, DC), 135–136
Moffet, Joseph, 132
Monsanto Chemical, 179, 228, 231
Morse, Wayne, 29
Mother Earth News (magazine), 220
Mountaineering and Conservation Club (San Fernando State College), 203
Mountain States Legal Foundation, 213
Mueller, Frederick, 114
Muir, John, 21
Muller, Hermann J., 152, 216
Mumford, Lewis, 81, 84–85, 95
Murphy, Robert Cushman, 102–104
Murray, James E., 29
Murray, Thomas E., 77
Murrow, Edward R., 96
Muscle Shoals (Alabama), 50
Muskie, Edmund, 211, 217
Myroup, Wayne, 220
My Weekly Reader (newspaper for schoolchildren), DDT article in, 105–106

Nader, Ralph, 134, 173–174, 218
Nagasaki atomic blast (1945), 11, 16
Nash, Roderick, 184
National Academy of Sciences report on atomic fallout (1956), 89–90
National Agricultural Chemicals Association, 117
National Ambient Air Quality Standards (NAAQS), 214
National Association of Manufacturers (NAM), 30, 66, 247
National City Bank of New York (Citibank), 46
National Committee for a Sane Nuclear Policy (SANE): accusations of communism against, 140; on corporate capitalism, 94; Dodd's targeting of, 140; establishment of, 94; iodine 131 as a mobilizing issue for, 151–152; public relations and advocacy work by, 94–96; Spock and, 146–147; strontium-90 as a mobilizing issue for, 94; student movement criticism of, 142; test ban campaigns by, 139–140, 142, 147, 152; Women Strike for Peace's criticism of, 143
National Environmental Education Act, 211

National Environmental Policy Act (NEPA), 211, 214–215
National Fertilizer Development Center, 50
National Food Associates, 59–60
National Historic Preservation Act (1966), 168
National Legal Center for the Public Interest, 213
National Organics Standards Board, 236
National Register of Historic Places, 168
National Trails System Act (1968), 168
National Wetlands Coalition, 213
National Wild and Scenic Rivers Act (1968), 165, 168
Native Americans, 205–206
Natural Food and Farming Digest, 60
Nature Food Centers (Massachusetts), 136
Nelson, Gaylord: Clean Air Act automobile proposal and, 212; Earth Day and, 5, 203–204, 206, 211, 217; environmental record of, 204, 211; National Environmental Education Act and, 211; Vietnam War and, 205
neoliberalism, 30–31, 33
Nestlé, 221
Nevada Test Site, 74–75, 141
New Deal: agricultural and land policy in, 22, 49–50; corporate capitalism's resistance to, 30, 129; Democratic Party and, 170
The New Industrial State (Galbraith), 177
New Jersey, 176
New Left: anti-nuclear issues in, 142; environmentalism and, 196, 198, 207; grassroots politics and, 195; revolutionary goals of, 196, 241
New Orleans (Louisiana), 164
New York City: bombings in, 200; Earth Day in, 210, 218; environmental activism in, 222, 232; organic movement in, 135, 243; pollution in, 88; strontium-90 levels in, 97
New York Zoological Society, 108
Night, Granville, 42
Ninth Amendment, 187
nitrogen, 49–51
Nitze, Paul, 31–32
Nixon, Richard: *Apollo 13* and, 208; auto industry and, 181, 214; cranberry contamination warnings (1959) and, 112; environmental policy and, 211, 214–216; Environmental Protection Agency (EPA) and, 211, 214; "Kitchen Debate" with Khrushchev (1959) and, 162; presidential election of 1960 and, 138; Vietnam War and, 179
No Place to Hide (Bradley), 13
Norman, Gurney, 194, 202
Norman, N. Philip: on agribusiness, 56–57, 236; on chemical agriculture, 56; on cooperatives, 60–61, 150; on corporate influence in educational system, 59; on corporate lobbying, 57, 139; on corporate support for scientific research, 59

North American Free Trade Agreement (NAFTA), 237–238
Northeastern United States, gypsy moth outbreak in, 101–102
Northeast Governors Conference (1957), 89
Northern States Power Company, 186
Not So Rich as You Think (Stewart), 169
nuclear power. *See* atomic energy
Nutrition Foundation, 66

Oak Ridge nuclear laboratory (Tennessee), 91
Obama, Barack, 243
O'Brien, Larry, 173
Ocean Spray Cranberries Incorporated, 111
Odum, Eugene, 80
Office of Technical Services, 27
Off Our Backs (underground women's newspaper), 207
Ogburn, William F., 12–13
oil industry, 31–32
Olson, Mancur, 172
Omaha (Nebraska), meat-packing industry in, 163–164
On the Road (Kerouac), 72
Operation Ranch Hand, 178
Oppenheimer, Armand, 113
Oppenheimer, J. Robert, 12
Ordway, Samuel, 79–80, 83, 128
Oregon, 164, 176
organic farming. *See also* organic movement: communes and, 190; community-supported agriculture and, 243; corporatization of, 236; DDT's threat to, 103–105; ecological perspective in, 52, 54; Osborn on, 54; post-World War II expansion in, 48–49, 64; promotion and advertising of, 59–60, 63, 116, 131, 150, 192, 220, 223–224; urban community gardens and, 189
Organic Farming and Gardening (journal), 49, 52
Organic Gardening and Farming (journal), 52, 88, 105–106, 194
organic movement: celebrities and, 130; community-supported agriculture and, 243; consumer cooperatives and, 60–61, 194, 222; consumer demand for organic products and, 4, 6, 61–65, 114, 130, 135–136, 164–165, 192–193, 203, 219–222, 230, 233, 235–236, 242–243; critique of mainstream society in, 56–57, 65–66, 130, 193–194, 242; efforts to discredit, 65–66, 133, 135, 144; local foods movement and, 243–244; media coverage and, 220; nutrition emphasis in, 56, 64, 238
Organic Standards (Department of Agriculture), 236, 243
Organic-ville (Los Angeles natural food store), 64, 130, 220

Osborn, Fairfield: on atomic energy, 15, 246; on atomic power, 21; on benefits of science, 72; Chamber of Commerce and, 33; on chemical agriculture, 54; on commercial use of public lands, 22; on conservation, 46, 73, 155; Conservation Foundation and, 25, 33–34, 79, 108; on corporate capitalism, 22, 25, 33, 114, 241; on DDT, 23, 157; ecological worldview of, 18, 21, 23, 25–26, 54, 154–155, 246; on electoral politics, 114; ITCPN conference and, 40; media presence of, 26; on organic farming, 54; on population control, 182; Vogt's correspondence with, 25; on World War II, 21
Osborn, Henry, 21
Osmundsen, John, 133
Ottinger, Betty Ann, 223
Ottinger, Richard L., 223
Our Daily Poison (Wickenden), 113–114
Our Plundered Planet (Osborn), 21, 25, 182
Our Synthetic Environment (Bookchin), 149
outdoor clothing and gear market, 221
Outdoor Life coverage of chemical pesticides, 109

Packard, Vance, 127–129, 155
Padilla Bay (Washington), 226
Paley, William S., 46
Palmer (Alaska), 152
Palo Alto (California), 202
Parowan (Utah), 141
Partial Test Ban Treaty (1962), 152, 157–158, 175
Parties, Politics, and Interest Groups (Key), 114
Pasadena (California), 71, 88
Patagonia clothing company, 221
Patterson, Clair C., 170
Pauling, Linus, 92, 140, 152
Pay Dirt (J.I. Rodale), 49, 52, 61, 63
People Against Pollution, 202
People's Park (Berkeley, California), 196–198
Permanente Cement, 202
Peru, 46
Philadelphia (Pennsylvania), pollution in, 88
Phillips, James F. ("Fox"), 208
phosphorous, 49–50
Pickett, Clarence, 94–95
Picton, Lionel James, 131
Pinchot, Gifford, 35, 43
Pius XII (pope), 78
Plains Indians, 201
The Poisons in Your Food (Longgood), 131
Polanyi, Karl, 32–33
pollution: of the air, 2–3, 14, 51, 68–71, 85, 88–89, 136, 158–159, 165–170, 173–174, 181, 202, 214, 216, 222; automobiles and, 70, 88–89, 136, 168–170, 173–174, 181, 202, 214; corporate advertising regarding,

226, 237; health consequences from, 69, 89, 92, 158, 169–170, 216; laws and enforcement regarding, 67–68, 70–72, 158, 167–169, 172–174, 212, 214, 216; lead fuel additives and, 169–170; pre-twentieth century levels of, 14; of water, 2–3, 14, 20, 32, 51, 63, 67–68, 80, 85, 104, 159, 163–168, 172, 180–181, 183–187, 216, 221, 226, 233; World War II and, 67
polychlorinated biphenyls (PCBs), 233
The Population Bomb (Ehrlich), 21, 182
The Population Challenge: What It Means to America (Interior Department report), 182
population growth and control issues, 2, 20–21, 181–183, 218
Port Huron Statement, 185–186
Posner, Blanche, 152
Potlatch Forests, Inc., 226
Potter, Andrew, 240
Proctor & Gamble, 233
Proxmire, William, 112
Puget Sound (Washington), 226
Pure Food and Drug Act (1906), 57

Quaker Oats, 122
Quicksilver Messenger Service, 245
The Quiet Crisis (Udall), 160
Quinn, T.K., 72–73, 114–115

radiation. *See* fallout and radiation
Radio City Health Shop (New York), 135
Ralston Purina, 122
Ramparts magazine, 206
Reagan, Ronald, 184, 197, 213, 229
Recreational Equipment Inc. (REI), 221
Redford, Lola, 222
Redwoods National Park proposal, 176
Reich, Charles A., 192
Reid, Barbara, 210
Republican Party, corporate political donors and, 171
Republic Steel Corporation, 181
Resources and the American Dream (Ordway), 79
Resources for the Future Forum, 46, 128
Restoring the Quality of Our Environment (Johnson Administration report), 166–167, 169
Revolutionary Force 9, 200–201
Reynolds, Malvina, 148
Richman, Jonathan, 241–242
Rickover, Hyman, 161–162
Road to Serfdom (Hayek), 30
Road to Survival (Vogt), 19, 21, 25, 44, 63, 182
Rockefeller, Laurance, 165
Rocky Mountain Arsenal (Colorado), 86
Rodale, J.I.: on the atomic bomb, 96; on automobiles and pollution, 88; on chemical agriculture, 50–53, 56, 105, 107, 114, 116; on consumer behavior, 73; on corporate capitalism, 241; on DDT, 52–53; on diethylstilbestrol (DES), 121, 123; ecological perspective of, 51; on factory farming and farm animal treatment, 55, 236; organic movement and, 49, 52, 61, 116, 133, 144, 238; on strontium-90, 96
Rodale, Robert: on chemical agriculture, 144; on DDT, 106; organic farming advocacy and, 144; *Organic Gardening and Farming* journal and, 194; on organic products, 164–165; on *Silent Spring*, 154
Rongaus, William, 68–69, 71
Roosevelt, Archibald, 104
Roosevelt, Eleanor, 95, 140
Roosevelt, Franklin D., 49, 146
Rorty, James: on agribusiness, 56–57, 236; on chemical agriculture, 56, 114; consumer movement and, 56; on cooperatives, 60–61, 150; on corporate influence in educational system, 59; on corporate lobbying, 57, 139, 241; on corporate support for scientific research, 59; on consumer behavior, 73
Roscoe (New York), 104
Ross, Charles, 199
Roszak, Theodore, 191–192
Royal Dutch Shell, 31, 233
Russell, Edmund, 24

"Sagebrush Rebellion," 213
Saint George (Utah), 75
Saint George, Katherine, 104
Saint Louis (Missouri) Committee for Nuclear Information, 99–100, 175
Salter, Robert M., 36–37
Salt Lake City (Utah), 152
Sanchez, Maurilio, 237
Sanders, Jacqueline, 75
SANE. *See* National Committee for a Sane Nuclear Policy (SANE)
San Fernando State College, 203
San Francisco (California): bombings in, 200; environmental protests in, 202–203; organic movement in, 193; pollution in, 67, 88
Santa Barbara (California) oil spill (1969), 183–185, 189
Saturday Evening Post, 99, 144
Saudi Arabia, 31
Scandinavian Mink Association, 228
Schlink, F. J., 116
Schlitz, 226
Schumacher, E.F., 150
Schweitzer, Albert, 93, 153
Science Advisory Committee, 156–157, 166
Scott, Douglas, 205
Scott, H. Lee, 234
Sealund, Jerry, 193

Sears, Paul, 81
Seattle (Washington), bombings in, 200
Sequoia National Park, 176
Shea, John P., 40
Shell Chemical Company, 107, 164
Sherman Antitrust Act, 181
Shuman, Charles, 112
Siegel, Dan, 197
Sierra Club: Arizona hydroelectric dam proposals and, 176; conservation emphasis of, 25, 64, 87, 137, 187, 212; corporate funding for, 231; Earth Day and, 212; Echo Park dam proposal and, 87–88; expanding membership of, 137, 167, 187, 213; shift toward broader environmentalism by, 137, 187; Wilderness Act and, 162
Silent Spring (Carson): corporations' efforts to discredit, 156; environmental movement and, 2, 153–155, 157; *New York Times* editorial on, 155–156; origins of, 115
Sinclair, Thomas J., 59
Sinclair, Upton, 57
Small Is Beautiful (Schumacher), 150
Smith, Gary, 185
Smith, William, 118–119
Smokey Bear, 197–199
"Smokey Bear Sutra" (Snyder), 197
Snyder, Gary, 197–198
The Social Costs of Private Enterprise (Kapp), 32
solar energy, 84–85
Solid Waste Disposal Act (1965), 167–168
Soviet Union: atomic bomb test bans and, 96, 152; atomic bomb testing by, 14, 40, 74, 93, 95–96, 141–143, 147; countercultural consumption in, 241; Cuban Missile Crisis (1962) and, 151; UNSCCUR and, 36
Special Senate Committee to Study Small Business Problems, 29
Spock, Benjamin, 104, 146–147
Spock, Marjorie, 104
Standard Oil, 6, 170
Stanford Research Institute, 84, 203
Stanford University, 1969 protests at, 178
State Department, United Nations and, 37–38
The State in Capitalist Society (Miliband), 216
Stegner, Wallace, 194
Steiner, Rudolf, 56, 104, 243
Steinman, David, 230
Stevenson, Adlai, 90–91
Stevenson, Natalie, 195–196
Stewart, George R., 169
stilbestrol. *See* diethylstilbestrol (DES)
Stonyfield Farms Organic Yogurt, 233
Storer, John, 80
Storm King Mountain (New York), 176
Strauss, Lewis, 79

strontium-90: atomic bomb fallout and, 76–77, 90, 96, 140–141, 143, 145, 147, 154, 175; cancer risks and, 91–92; food contamination from, 78, 90, 96–97, 140; increasing international levels of, 95–96; *Lucky Dragon* fishing boat incident and, 76–77; milk supply contamination and, 90, 97–100, 140, 142–146, 151–152; political mobilization regarding, 94, 99, 175; presidential campaign of 1956 and, 90–91; scientific warnings regarding, 90–92, 97; wildlife contamination and, 152
Student Peace Union (University of Minnesota), 142
Students for Democratic Society (SDS): anti-nuclear protest and, 142; on atomic energy, 185–186; breakup of, 198, 200
Students for Peace and Disarmament (University of Wisconsin), 142
Sturtevant, A. H., 78
Sullivan, Harry Stack, 9
Surnise Farm (Chicago food store), 220
Swanson, Gloria, 130–131
Symposium of the International Union Against Cancer (1956), 118

Tansley, Arthur George, 18
Task Force on Environmental Health and Related Problems, 182
Taylor Chemical, 59
Taylor Grazing Act (1934), 22
"Techniques for Increasing Agricultural Production" (Department of Agricultural report), 36–37
"The Technologist's Reply" (Boulding), 83
Tennessee Valley Authority (TVA), 37, 40, 50
Terry, Luther L., 163
test ban proposals regarding atomic weapons, 91–93, 96, 139–140, 142–145, 147, 149, 151–152, 157–158, 175
Test Ban Treaty. *See* Partial Test Ban Treaty (1962)
tetraethyl lead (TEL), 170
Texaco, 226, 237
thalidomide, 147
Theberge, Leonard, 213
"These Precious Days" (New Yorker series), 115
This Is the American Earth (Sierra Club), 137
Thomas, Frank, 112
Thomas, Norman, 94
Thomas Jr., William L., 81–82
Thompson, Hunter S., 198
Three Young Americans in Search of Survival (ABC television program), 185
Throckmorton, R. I., 65
Tibet, 161
timber industry, 22

Tocsin (Harvard-Radcliffe student group), 142
Tokyo fire bombings (1945), 17
Tomorrow's Food: The Coming Revolution in Nutrition (Norman and Rorty), 56
Tonopah Bombing and Gunnery Range (Nevada), 74
The Torch of Life (Dubos), 136–137
Townshend, Pete, 246
transfats, 132
Trinidad, 232
Trouvelot, Leopold, 101
Truman, Harry, 34, 36, 46, 111
Tsutsui, Isao, 76
Tsuzuki, Masao, 77

Udall, Morris, 175–176
Udall, Stewart, 146, 160, 165, 175–176
Uncle Vanya (Chekhov), 1
UNESCO (United Nations Educational, Scientific and Cultural Organization): International Technical Conference on the Protection of Nature (ITCPN) and, 38–41; UNSCCUR and, 35, 38–41
Unilever, 234
Union Carbide, 228, 231
Union Oil Company, 183–184, 202
Uniroyal, 179
United Fruit Company, 183
United Nations: atomic energy and, 85; Educational, Scientific and Cultural Organization (UNESCO), 35, 38–41; Scientific Conference on the Conservation and Utilization of Resources (UNSCCUR), 34–41, 54; U.S. State Department and, 37–38
United States Steel Corporation, 68–69, 71–72, 208
United States Supreme Court, 105, 186
University of California, Berkeley. *See* People's Park (Berkeley)
University of Wisconsin, teach-ins at, 202–203
Unsafe at Any Speed (Nader), 134, 174
UNSCCUR (United Nations Scientific Conference on the Conservation and Utilization of Resources): corporate capitalism emphasis at, 36–37; ecology and, 34, 36; on population growth, 36; on resource use, 35–36, 38–39; on technological solutions, 36–37, 39; UNESCO and, 35, 38–41; United States and, 36, 41
Uphoff, Norman, 142
uranium mining, 86
Urey, Harold C., 12
U.S. Agency for International Development (USAID), 182–183
U.S. Forest Service, 22, 37, 197–198
U.S. Public Health Service, 24, 52, 71, 97, 99, 152

Van Horn, Rob, 31
Velsicol Chemical Corporation, 107, 110, 156
Vietnam War: defoliant use and environmental devastation in, 54, 178–180, 205; Earth Day (1970) and, 209; government misinformation and, 213; Johnson Administration and, 171; opposition to and protests against, 178, 200, 203, 205; teach-ins and, 197
Viorst, Milton, 113
Vogt, William: on atomic weapons, 20; on consumer behavior, 62; on corporate capitalism, 19, 45, 241; correspondence with Frazer and, 63; on DDT, 23; on erosion, 19; International Technical Conference on the Protection of Nature (ITCPN) and, 38, 41; Leopold's correspondence with, 44–45, 248; Osborn's correspondence with, 25; on population control, 20–21, 182; on railroads, 19; on resource use, 62; on water issues, 20

Wade, Douglas, 40
Wagner, Tony, 203
Wald, George, 178
Walden Pond, 229
Wallace, George J., 106
Wallace, Henry A., 29, 60
Waller, Wilhelmine, 108
Wal-Mart, 232–235, 244
Walnut Acres Farm (Pennsylvania), 136
Walt Disney Corporation, 176
War Production Board, 24
Warren, Shields, 13
Washington (District of Columbia): environmental activism in, 222–223; organic movement in, 135–136
Waste Management, 231
Water Pollution Control Act (1948), 67, 89
Water Quality Act (1965), 168
Watt, James, 213
Watt, Kenneth, 217
Wattenberg, Ben, 171
Waubanaseum, Sandra, 206
Weather Underground, 200
The Web of Life: A First Book of Ecology (Storer), 80
Weigand v. Hickel, 185
Weisberg, Barry, 205
Weller, Paul, 125
Welsh's Natural Foods (Laguna Beach, California), 136
Wenner-Gren Foundation, 81
Westinghouse, 186, 231
Weyl, A. E., 104
"What About Me?" (Quicksilver Messenger Service), 245
What Every Woman Should Know and Do About Pollution (Betty Ann Ottinger), 223

"What Have They Done to Rain?" (Reynolds), 148
"What Have We Done to Vietnam?" (investigative report), 180
White House Conference on Natural Beauty (1965), 165
White Wave (natural food company), 235
The Who, 245–246
Whole Earth Catalogue, 194–195, 202
Whole Foods, 1, 5–6, 234–235
Wickenden, Leonard: on chemical agriculture and pesticides, 53–54, 113–114; on organic movement, 65–66
Wiesner, Jerome, 152, 157
wilderness, cultural myths regarding, 161–162
Wilderness Act, 138, 160, 162–163, 168
Wilderness Society, 16, 25, 43, 87, 162, 213, 231
Wildlife Management Institute, 109
Wildwood Nature Camp (Massachusetts), 136
Wiley, George, 210
Williams, James, 205
Wilson, Dagmar, 143
Wilson, Edward O., 108
Wisconsin Student Indian Movement (WSIM), 205–206

women's involvement in environmental issues, 98–100, 142–146, 207, 223
Women Strike for Peace (WSP), 142–146, 149, 151–152
"Won't Get Fooled Again" (The Who), 245–246
"Woodstock" (Joni Mitchell), 18
Working Men's Protective Union, 60
World Bank, 183
World War II: atomic bomb and, 11–12; chemical production during, 50, 67; environmentalism and, 6; pollution and, 67–68; population issues and, 20; scale of destruction during, 17
Worster, Donald, 18

Yannacone, Victor, 187
Yellowstone National Park, 104
Yellowstone River, 104
Yosemite Valley (California), 87
Young, Glynn, 231
Youth Conservation Corps, 146

Zager and Evans (music group), 188
Zahniser, Howard, 16–17, 160, 162, 229
Zavon, Mitchell R., 164
Zero Population Growth, 182